TravelWise

SPANISH

Carlos Segoviano

BARRON'S

All inquiries should be addressed to:
Barron's Educational Series, Inc.
250 Wireless Boulevard
Hauppauge, NY 11788
http://www.barronseduc.com

Library of Congress Catalog Card No. 97-47437

International Standard Book No. 0-7641-7100-3 (package)
0-7641-0376-8 (book)

Library of Congress Cataloging-in-Publication Data
Segoviano, Carlos.
[Reisewörterbuch Spanisch. English & Spanish]
Travelwise Spanish / Carlos Segoviano ; translated by Ana Simo.
p.   cm.
Text in English and Spanish.
ISBN 0-7641-0376-8 (pbk.). — ISBN 0-7641-7100-3 (bk. / cassette)
1. Spanish language—Conversation and phrase books—English.
I. Title.
PC4121.S4413   1998
468.3'421—DC21   97-47437
CIP

PRINTED IN HONG KONG
9 8 7 6 5 4 3 2 1

Contents

Preface

The *Barron's TravelWise Spanish Travel Phrasebook* is a guide to both comprehension and conversation in Spanish. By using it you will not only acquire a series of useful words and phrases, but, more importantly, you will learn how to understand and be understood.

The most commonly heard expressions are provided for everyday situations you will encounter during your travels. These are structured as dialogues, so that you not only learn what to say, but will also understand the corresponding responses.

The *Barron's TravelWise Spanish Travel Phrasebook* is divided into eleven topical units, which accompany you through every phase of your travel: your arrival, checking into a hotel, at the beach, and even a meeting with business associates.

With the help of phrases and word lists, as well as the additional glossary provided at the end of the book, you can readily adapt the sample sentences to your own individual, real-life situations.

The following Pronunciation Guide and the Short Grammar toward the back of the book will help familiarize you with the sounds and constructions of the Spanish language, while pictures and useful tips provided throughout the book will help you better appreciate the special cultural features and natural scenic attractions of Spain.

Pronunciation

• **a, e,** or **o** ("strong" vowels) combined with **i, y,** or **u** ("weak" vowels) form a diphthong (one syllable), with the accent always on the strong vowel: fu**e**go ['fweh-goh] *fire;* h**o**y ['oh-ee] *today.* Two weak vowels can also form a diphthong, with the accent always falling on the second vowel: Lu**i**s [loo-'ees] fu**i**mos ['fwee-mohs]

b,v	[b]	Both pronounced the same in Spanish; at the beginning of words and after written **m** and **n,** sounds like English **b;** otherwise, it's softer.	buen vino nuevo ['bwehn 'vee-noh noo-'eh-voh]; brazo ['brah-soh]; sombra ['sohm-brah]; envío [ehn-'vee-oh]; habla ['ah-blah]; servir [sehr-'veer]; abuela [ah-'bweh-lah]
c	[k] [T]	Before **a, o, u,** or consonants, sounds like English **k,** before **e, i,** sounds close to English **th** (Spain) or English **s** in *same (Am).*	creo ['kreh-oh]; casa ['kah-sah]; cura ['koo-rah]; acción [ahk-see-'ohn]; cenicero [seh-nee-'seh-roh]; gracias ['grah-see·ahs]
ch	[tt]	Like English **ch** in *church.*	muchacho [moo-'chah-choh]
d,t	[d,t]	At the beginning of words, sounds like English **d;** elsewhere, softer (closer to English **th** in *this;* often omitted in **-ado** endings and when it's the last letter of a word.	día ['dee-ah]; dama ['dah-mah]; sidra ['see-drah]; sentado [sehn-'tah-doh]; verdad [vehr-'dahd]; caridad [kah-ree-'dahd]
g	[g]	At the beginning of words and after **n,** sounds like English **g** in *get;* elsewhere, softer before **a, o, u,** and consonants.	guardia ['gwahr-dee·ah]; gorra ['goh-rrah]; tengo ['tehn-goh agua ['ah-gwah]; acelga [ah-'sehl-gah]

	[x]	Before **e, i,** sounds like Spanish **j** (see below).	gitano [hee-'tah-noh]; gente ['hehn-teh]
gue, gui	[g]	The **u** is silent, except when marked by an umlaut; in either case, the **g** sounds like the English **g.**	seguir [seh-'geer]; guitarra [gee-'tah-rrah]
h		Always silent.	hora ['oh-rah]
j	[x]	Sounds like the **ch** of the Scottish *loch* or the German *Achtung* or *Bach.*	jardín [hahr-'deen]; naranja [nah-'rahn-hah]
ll,y	[l]	Like English **y** in *yes.*	yo llevo [yoh 'yeh-voh]; guerrilla [geh-'rree-yah]
ñ	[ny]	Somewhat similar to the English **ni** in *onion,* but harsher.	niño ['nee-nyoh]
que, qui	[k]	The **q** sounds like the English **k;** it's always followed by a silent **u.**	porque ['pohr-keh]; quiero [kee-'eh-roh]
rr r	[rr] [rr]	This strongly rolled sound doesn't exist in English; at the beginning of words and after **l, n, s,** pronounced like **rr;** otherwise, a single roll, but still stronger than any English **r;** softer or even silent at the end of words.	perro ['peh-rroh]; rosa ['roh-sah]; sonrisa [sohn-'ree-sah]; enriquecer [ehn-ree-keh-'sehr]; muerte ['mwehr-teh]; madre ['mah-dreh]; caro ['kah-roh]; dolor [doh-'lohr]; amor [ah-'mohr]
s	[s]	Before **b, d, g, l, m, n,** sounds like the English **s** in *rose;* otherwise, it's like the softer **s** in *same.*	desde ['dehs-deh]; sesgo ['sehs-goh]; asma ['ahs-mah]; casa ['kah-sah]; sala ['sah-lah]

| z | [T] | Like the English **th** in *thin* (Spain, except Andalusia); like the English **s** in *same* (Andalusia, most of *Am*). | Zaragoza [sah-rah-'goh-sah] Spain: [thah-rah-'goh-thah] jerez [heh-'rehs] Spain: [heh-'rehths] |

Accents

- If the word ends in a vowel, or in *n* or *s*, the accent falls on the **penultimate syllable:** mésa, Carmen.

  Exceptions to this rule have a written acute accent over the stressed vowel: café [kah-'feh], después [deh-'spwehs].

- If the word ends in a consonant other than *n* or *s*, the **last syllable** is stressed: cantár, doctór.

  Again, exceptions are indicated by a written acute accent: fácil ['fah-seel], huésped ['weh-spehd].

- Words with **three or more syllables** have an acute accent written on the **antepenultimate** syllable: música, médico, artístico ['moo-see-kah, 'meh-dee-koh, ahr-'tee-stee-koh]

- Interrogative and exclamatory pronouns have a written accent: quién, cómo, qué bonito [kee-'ehn, 'koh-moh, keh boh-'nee-toh]

- **Some single-syllable words also have written accents:** mí, tú, él, sí, sé, más [mee, too, ehl, see, seh, mahs]

- **í** and **ú**—with written acute accents—indicate two separate syllables (no diphthong): día, púa, país ['dee-ah, 'poo-ah, pah-'ees]

- Nouns ending in **a** are generally feminine [la, las], and those ending in **o** masculine [el, los]. However, gender agreement is still enforced for words that don't conform to this pattern: **cura** ['koo-rah] (priest) is masculine; therefore, it is **el cura** [ehl 'koo-rah] while **la cura** [lah 'koo-rah] is a cure.

Spanish Abbreviations

a.C.	antes de Cristo	B.C., before Christ
afmo.	afectísimo	yours truly
Av.	Avenida	avenue
C.	centígrado	Celsius
c.	calle	street
CE	Comunidad Económica Europea	EEC (European Economic Community)
Cía.	compañía	company
CV	caballos de vapor/ de fuerza	metric hp (horsepower)
D.	Don	Mr.
Dª	Doña	Mrs.
d.C.	después de Cristo	A.D., after Christ
dcha.	derecha	right
D.m.	Dios mediante	God willing
EE. UU.	Estados Unidos	U.S. (United States)
etc.	etcétera	etc., et cetera
gral.	general	general
id.	idem	idem, ditto
incl.	inclusive	including
izda.	izquierda	left
km/h	kilómetros por hora	kilometers per hour
Lle.	llegada	arrival
N.B.	nota bene	nota bene
ONU	Organización de las Naciones Unidas	U.N. (United Nations)
OTAN	Organización del Tratado del Atlántico Norte	NATO (North Atlantic Treaty Organization)
p., pág.	página	page

P.D.	posdata	P.S., postscript
p.ej.	por ejemplo	i.e., for example
Pl.	Plaza	Square
pral.	principal	head, chief, principal
Pta.	peseta	peseta
q.e.p.d.	que en paz descanse	R.I.P., rest in peace
R.A.C.E.	Real Automóvil Club de España	Royal Automobile Club of Spain
RENFE	Red Nacional de los Ferrocarriles Españoles	Spanish National Railway System
R.I.P.	requiescat in pace	R.I.P., rest in peace
S.A.	Sociedad Anónima	Corporation (Corp.), Incorporated (Inc.)
Sal.	salida	departure
S.Juan	San Juan	San Juan (Puerto Rico)
S.L.	sociedad (de responsabilidad) limitada	Ltd. (Limited)
sr., Sr.	señor	Mr., Sir
sra., Sra.	señora	Mrs., Madam
Sras.	señoras	ladies
Sres.	señores	gentlemen
srta., Srta.	señorita	Miss
TAV	Tren de Alta Velocidad	HVT, high velocity train
TVE	Televisión Española	Spanish television
V°o B°	visto bueno	approved, passed
Vd., Ud.	usted	you (polite or formal)
Vda.	viuda	widow
Vds., Uds.	ustedes	you (plural)

Glossary

adj	adjective	adjetivo
adv	adverb	adverbio
Am	Latin American usage	latinoamericanismo
anat	anatomy	anatomía
arch	architecture	arquitectura
Arg	Argentina	Argentina
comm	commercial	comercial
conj	conjunction	conjunción
cul	culinary	culinario
el	electricity	electricidad
f	feminine, female	femenino
fam	colloquial	familiar, coloquial
fest	festival	festividad
fig	figuratively	sentido figurado
fin	financial	financiero
inter	interjection	interjección
lang	language	lenguaje
m	masculine, male	masculino
mech	mechanical	mecánico
med	medical	médico
naut	nautical	náutico
neut	neuter	neutro
n	noun	nombre
pers prn	personal pronoun	pronombre personal
pl	plural	plural
pop	common usage	popular
poss prn	possessive pronoun	pronombre posesivo
prp	preposition	preposición
ptp	past participle	participio pasado
rel	religious	religioso
sing	singular	singular
tel	telephone, telegraph	teléfono, telégrafo
v	verb	verbo

The Spanish Alphabet

A	a	[ah]	M	m	['eh-meh]
B	b	[beh]	N	n	['eh-neh]
C	c	[seh (Spain: theh)]	O	o	[oh]
CH	ch	[cheh]	P	p	[peh]
D	d	[deh]	Q	q	[koo]
E	e	[eh]	R	r	['eh-reh]
F	f	['eh-feh]	S	s	['eh-seh]
G	g	[heh]	T	t	[teh]
H	h	['ah-cheh]	U	u	[oo]
I	i	[ee]	V	v	[veh 'chee-kah]
J	j	['hoh-tah]	W	w	['doh-bleh veh]
K	k	[kah]	X	x	['eh-kees]
L	l	['eh-leh]	Y	y	[ee-gree-'eh-gah]
LL	ll	['eh-yeh]	Z	z	['seh-tah (Spain: 'theh-tah)]

1 The Essentials
Lo más importante

Frequently Used Expressions
Expresiones de todos los días

Yes.	Sí. [see]
No.	No. [noh]
Please.	Por favor. [pohr fah-'vohr]
You're welcome.	De nada. [deh 'nah-dah]
Thanks.	Gracias. ['grah-see-ahs]
What are you saying?	¡Cómo dice/dices? ['koh-moh 'dee-seh, 'dee-sehs]
Of course.	Desde luego. ['dehs-deh loo-'eh-goh]
Agreed!/All right!	¡De acuerdo! [deh ah-'kwehr-doh]
OK!	¡De acuerdo! [deh ah-'kwehr-doh]
Fine!/Good!	¡Está bien! [eh-'stah 'bee-ehn]
Excuse me.	¡Perdón! [pehr-'dohn]
Just a minute, please.	Un momento, por favor. [oon moh-'mehn-toh, pohr fah-'vohr]
Enough!	¡Basta (ya)! ['bah-stah (yah)]
Help!	¡Ayuda!, ¡Socorro! [ah-'yoo-dah, soh-'koh-rroh]
Who?	¿Quién? [kee-'ehn]
What?	¿Qué? [keh]
Which?	¿Cuál? [kwahl]
Who ...to?/To whom?	¿A quién? [ah kee-'ehn]
Where?	¿Dónde? ['dohn-deh]
Where is...?/Where are…?	¿Dónde está/están…? ['dohn-deh eh-'stah, eh-'stahn]
Where from?	¿De dónde? [deh 'dohn-deh]
Where to?	¿Adónde? [ah-'dohn-deh]
Why?	¿Por qué? [pohr keh]
What for?	¿Para qué? ['pah-rah keh]
How?	¿Cómo? ['koh-moh]
How much?	¿Cuánto? ['kwahn-toh]
How many?	¿Cuántos? ['kwahn-tohs]

How long?	¿Cuánto tiempo? ['kwahn-toh tee-'ehm-poh]
When?/At what time?	¿Cuándo? ¿A qué hora? ['kwahn-doh, ah keh 'oh-rah]
I'd like…	Quisiera…, Me gustaría… [kee-see-'eh-rah, meh goo-stah-'ree-ah]
Is there…?/Are there?	¿Hay…? ['ah-ee]

Numbers/Measures/Weights
Números/Medidas/Pesos

zero	cero ['seh-roh]
one	un, uno [oon, 'oo-noh]
two	dos [dohs]
three	tres [trehs]
four	cuatro ['kwah-troh]
five	cinco ['seen-koh]
six	seis ['seh-ees]
seven	siete [see-'eh-teh]
eight	ocho ['oh-choh]
nine	nueve [noo-'eh-veh]
ten	diez [dee-'ehs]
11	once ['ohn-seh]
12	doce ['doh-seh]
13	trece ['treh-seh]
14	catorce [kah-'tohr-seh]
15	quince ['keen-seh]
16	dieciséis [deh-ehs-ee-'seh-ees]
17	diecisiete [dee-ehs-ee-see-'eh-teh]
18	dieciocho [dee-ehs-ee-'oh-choh]
19	diecinueve [dee-ehs-ee-noo-'eh-veh]
20	veinte ['veh-een-teh]
21	veintiuno, -a, veintiún [veh-een-teh-ee'oo-noh, -ah, veh-een-teh-ee-'oon]
22	veintidós [veh-een-teh-ee-'dohs]

23	veintitrés [veh-een-teh-ee-'trehs]
24	veinticuatro [veh-een-teh-ee-'kwah-troh]
25	veinticinco [veh-een-teh-ee-'seen-koh]
26	veintiséis [veh-een-teh-ee-'seh·ees]
27	veintisiete [veh-een-teh-ee-see-'eh-teh]
28	veintiocho [veh-een-teh-ee-'oh-choh]
29	veintinueve [veh-een-teh-ee-noo-'eh-veh]
30	treinta ['treh-een-tah]
31	treinta y uno, -a, treinta y un ['treh·een-tah ee 'oo-noh, -ah, 'treh·een-tah ee oon]
32	treinta y dos ['treh·een-tah ee dohs]
40	cuarenta [kwah-'rehn-tah]
50	cincuenta [seen-'kwehn-tah]
60	sesenta [seh-'sehn-tah]
70	setenta [seh-'tehn-tah]
80	ochenta [oh-'chehn-tah]
90	noventa [noh-'vehn-tah]
100	cien ['see-ehn]
101	ciento uno [see-'ehn-toh 'oo-noh]
200	doscientos, -as [dohs-see-'ehn-tohs, -'ahs]
300	trescientos, -as [trehs-see-'ehn-tohs, -ahs]
1,000	mil [meel]
2,000	dos mil [dohs meel]
3,000	tres mil [trehs meel]
10,000	diez mil [dee-'ehs meel]
100,000	cien mil ['see-ehn meel]
1,000,000	un millón [oon mee-'yohn]
first	primero, primer [pree-'meh-roh, pree-'mehr]

second	segundo [seh-'goon-doh]
third	tercero, tercer [tehr-'seh-roh, tehr-'sehr]
fourth	cuarto ['kwahr-toh]
fifth	quinto ['keen-toh]
sixth	sexto ['sehks-toh]
seventh	séptimo [sehp-tee-moh]
eighth	octavo [ohk-'tah-voh]
ninth	noveno [noh-'veh-noh]
tenth	décimo ['deh-see-moh]
1/2	medio ['meh-dee-oh]
1/3	un tercio [oon 'tehr-see-oh]
1/4	un cuarto [oon 'kwahr-toh]
3/4	tres cuartos [trehs 'kwahr-tohs]
3.5%	tres y medio por ciento [trehs ee 'meh-dee-oh pohr see-'ehn-toh]
27°C	veintisiete grados (sobre cero) [veh-een-teh-see-'eh-teh 'grah-dohs ('soh-breh 'seh-roh)]
–5°C	cinco grados bajo cero ['sehn-koh 'grah-dohs 'bah-hoh 'seh-roh]
1998	mil novecientos noventa y ocho [meel noh-veh-see-'ehn-tohs noh-'vehn-tah ee 'oh-choh]
millimeter	milímetro [mee-'lee-meh-troh]
centimeter	centímetro [sehn-'tee-meh-troh]
meter	metro ['meh-troh]
kilometer	kilómetro [kee-'loh-meh-troh]
mile	milla ['mee-yah]
square meter	metro cuadrado ['meh-troh kwah-'drah-doh]
square kilometer	kilómetro cuadrado [kee-'loh-meh-troh kwah-'drah-doh]
area	área ['ah-reh-ah]
hectare	hectárea [ehk-'tah-reh-ah]
liter	litro ['lee-troh]

gram	gramo ['grah-moh]
kilogram	kilo, kilogramo ['kee-loh, kee-loh-'grah-moh]
dozen	docena [doh-'seh-nah]

Expressions of Time

Fecha y hora

Telling Time	**La hora**
What time is it?	¿Qué hora es? [keh 'oh-rah ehs]
Can you tell me what time it is?	¿(Puede decirme) Qué hora es, por favor? ['pweh-deh deh-'seer-meh, keh 'oh-rah ehs, pohr fah-'vohr]
What time is it, please?	¿Qué hora es, por favor? [keh 'oh-rah ehs pohr fah-'vohr]
It's (exactly/about) …	Son (exactamente/aproximadamente)… [sohn (ehk-sahk-tah-'mehn-teh/ah-prohk-see-mah-dah-'mehn-teh)]
three o'clock.	las tres. [lahs trehs]
five after three.	las tres y cinco. [lahs trehs ee 'seen-koh]
ten after three.	las tres y diez. [lahs trehs ee dee-'ehs]
three fifteen.	las tres y cuarto. [lahs trehs ee 'kwahr-toh]
three thirty.	las tres y media. [lahs trehs ee 'meh-dee-ah]
a quarter to four.	las cuatro menos cuarto. [lahs 'kwah-troh 'meh-nohs 'kwahr-toh]
five minutes to four.	las cuatro menos cinco. [lahs 'kwah-troh 'meh-nohs 'seen-koh]
It's one o'clock.	Es la una. [ehs lah 'oo-nah]
It's twelve noon/midnight.	Son las doce del mediodía/de medianoche. [sohn lahs 'doh-seh dehl meh-dee-oh-'dee-ah/deh meh-dee-ah-'noh-cheh]
Is that clock right?	¿Anda/Va bien ese reloj? ['ahn-dah/vah 'bee-ehn 'eh-seh reh-'loh]

It's fast/slow.	Va adelantado/atrasado. [vah ah-deh-lahn-'tah-doh/ah-trah-'sah-doh]
It's late/early.	Es tarde/temprano. [ehs 'tahr-deh/tehm-'prah-noh]
At what time?/When?	¿A qué hora?/¿Cuándo? [ah keh 'oh-rah/'kwahn-doh]
At one o'clock.	A la una. [ah lah 'oo-nah]
At two o'clock.	A las dos. [ah lahs dohs]
Around four o'clock.	Alrededor de las cuatro. [ahl-reh-deh-'dohr deh lahs 'kwah-troh]
In an hour.	Dentro de una hora. ['dehn-troh deh 'oo-nah 'oh-rah]
In two hours.	Dentro de dos horas. ['dehn-troh deh dohs 'oh-rahs]
Not before 9 A.M.	No antes de las nueve de la mañana. [noh 'ahn-tehs deh lahs noo-'eh-veh deh lah mah-'nyah-nah]
After 8 P.M.	Después de las ocho de la noche. [deh-'spwehs deh lahs 'oh-choh deh lah 'noh-cheh]
Between three and four.	Entre las tres y las cuatro. ['ehn-treh lahs trehs ee lahs 'kwah-troh]
How long?	¿Cuánto tiempo? ['kwahn-toh tee-'ehm-poh]
(For) two hours.	(Durante) dos horas. [(doo-'rahn-teh) dohs 'oh-rahs]
From ten to eleven.	Desde las diez hasta las once. ['dehs-deh lahs dee-'ehs 'ah-stah lahs 'ohn-seh]
Until five o'clock.	Hasta las cinco. ['ah-stah lahs 'seen-koh]
Since when?	¿Desde cuándo? ['dehs-deh 'kwahn-doh]
Since 8 A.M.	Desde las ocho de la mañana. [dehs-deh lahs 'oh-choh deh lah mah-'nyah-nah]
For half an hour.	Desde hace media hora. [dehs-deh 'ah-seh 'meh-dee-ah 'oh-rah]

For a week.

Desde hace una semana. [dehs-deh 'ah-seh 'oo-nah seh-'mah-nah]

Other Expressions of Time

Otras indicaciones de tiempo

in the afternoon/evening	por la tarde [pohr lah 'tahr-deh]
every half hour	cada media hora ['kah-dah 'meh-dee·ah 'oh-rah]
every two days	cada dos días ['kah-dah dohs 'dee-ahs]
on Sunday/on the weekend	el domingo/el fin de semana [ehl doh-'meen-goh/ehl feen deh seh-'mah-nah]
soon	pronto ['prohn-toh]
this week	esta semana ['eh-stah seh-'mah-nah]
around noon	alrededor del mediodía [ahl-reh-deh-'dohr dehl meh-dee-oh-'dee-ah]
yesterday	ayer [ah-'yehr]
today	hoy ['oh-ee]
this morning/evening	esta mañana/tarde ['eh-stah mah-'nyah-nah/'tahr-deh]
in fifteen days/two weeks	dentro de quince días/dos semanas ['dehn-troh deh 'keen-seh 'dee-ahs/dohs seh-'mah-nahs]
in a week	en una semana [ehn 'oo-nah seh-'mah-nah]
every day, each day	todos los días, cada día ['toh-dohs lohs 'dee-ahs, 'kah-dah 'dee-ah]
now	ahora [ah-'oh-rah]
recently	hace poco (*Am* recién) ['ah-seh 'poh-koh (reh-see-'ehn)]
last Monday	el lunes pasado [ehl 'loo-nehs pah-'sah-doh]
sometimes	a veces, algunas veces [ah-'veh-sehs, ahl-'goo-nahs 'veh-sehs]
at noon	a mediodía [ah meh-dee-oh-'dee-ah]

morning	mañana [mah-'nyah-nah]
tomorrow morning/ afternoon	mañana por la mañana/tarde [mah-'nyah-nah pohr lah mah-'nyah-nah/'tahr-deh]
in the morning	por la mañana [pohr lah mah-'nyah-nah]
in the afternoon/evening	por la tarde [pohr lah 'tahr-deh]
next year	el año que viene [ehl 'ah-nyoh keh vee-'eh-neh]
at night	por la noche [pohr lah 'noh-cheh]
every hour	cada hora ['kah-dah 'oh-rah]
daily, every day	a diario, todos los días [ah dee-'ah-ree-oh, 'toh-dohs lohs 'dee-ahs]
during the day	durante el día [doo-'rahn-teh ehl 'dee-ah]
the day after tomorrow	pasado mañana [pah-'sah-doh mah-'nyah-nah]
at the same time	a esta hora [ah 'eh-stah 'oh-rah]
from time to time, occasionally	de vez en cuando [deh vehs ehn 'kwahn-doh]
ten minutes ago	hace diez minutos ['ah-seh dee-'ehs mee-'noo-tohs]
the day before yesterday	anteayer [ahn-teh-ah-'yehr]
in the morning	por la mañana [pohr lah mah-'nyah-nah]

Days of the Week   Los días de le semana

Monday	el lunes [ehl 'loo-nehs]
Tuesday	el martes [ehl 'mahr-tehs]
Wednesday	el miércoles [ehl mee-'ehr-koh-lehs]
Thursday	el jueves [ehl 'hweh-vehs]
Friday	el viernes [ehl vee-'ehr-nehs]
Saturday	el sábado [ehl 'sah-bah-doh]
Sunday	el domingo [ehl doh-'meen-goh]

Months of the Year	Los meses del año
January	enero [eh-'neh-roh]
February	febrero [feh-'breh-roh]
March	marzo ['mahr-soh]
April	abril [ah-'breel]
May	mayo ['mah-yoh]
June	junio ['hoo-nee-oh]
July	julio ['hoo-lee-oh]
August	agosto [ah-'goh-stoh]
September	septiembre [sehp-tee-'ehm-breh]
October	octubre [ohk-'too-breh]
November	noviembre [noh-vee-'ehm-breh]
December	diciembre [dee-see-'ehm-breh]

Seasons	Las estaciones del año
spring	primavera [pree-mah-'veh-rah]
summer	verano [veh-'rah-noh]
fall/autumn	otoño [oh-'toh-nyoh]
winter	invierno [een-vee-'ehr-noh]

Holidays	Los días de fiesta/festivos
New Year's Day	Año Nuevo ['ah-nyoh 'noo-'eh-voh]
Day of the Three Kings, Epiphany	los Reyes Magos, Epifanía [lohs 'reh-yehs 'mah-gohs, eh-pee-fah-'nee-ah]
Mardi Gras	el Carnaval [ehl kahr-nah-'vahl]
Ash Wednesday	el miércoles de ceniza [ehl mee-'ehr-koh-lehs deh seh-'nee-sah]
St. Joseph (March 19)	San José [sahn hoh-'seh]
Maundy Thursday	el Jueves Santo [ehl 'hweh-vehs 'sahn-toh]
Good Friday	el Viernes Santo [ehl vee-'ehr-nehs 'sahn-toh]

Easter	Pascua (de Resurrección) ['pah-skwah (deh reh-soo-rehk-see-'ohn)]
Easter Monday	el Lunes de Pascua [ehl 'loo-nehs de 'pah-skwah]
May Day (May 1st)	el Día del trabajo [ehl 'dee-ah dehl trah-'bah-hoh]
Ascension Day	La Ascensión [lah ah-sehn-see-'ohn)]
Pentecost	Pentecostés [pehn-teh-koh-'stehs]
Corpus Christi	el Corpus (Christi) [ehl 'kohr-poos ('kree-stee)]
St. John (June 24)	San Juan [sahn wahn]
Assumption of Mary (August 15)	La Asunción [lah ah-soon-see-'ohn]
Columbus Day (October 12)	el Día de la Hispanidad [ehl 'dee-ah deh lah ee-spah-nee-'dahd]
All Saints' Day (November 1)	Todos los Santos ['toh-dohs lohs 'sahn-tohs]
All Souls' Day (November 2)	el Día de los Difuntos [ehl 'dee-ah deh lohs dee-'foon-tohs]
The Immaculate Conception (December 8)	la Inmaculada (*Am* el día de la Virgen) [lah een-mah-koo-'lah-dah (ehl 'dee-ah deh lah 'veer-hehn]
Christmas Eve	Nochebuena [noh-cheh-'bweh-nah]
Christmas	Navidad [nah-vee-'dahd]
New Year's Eve	Año Viejo; fiesta de fin de año/de esperar el año/de vísperas del Año Nuevo ['ah-nyoh vee-'eh-hoh; fee-'eh-stah deh feen deh 'ah-nyoh/deh eh-spreh-'rahr ehl 'ah-nyoh/deh 'vee-speh-rahs dehl 'ah-nyoh noo-'eh-voh]

The Date   La fecha

What day is today?/ What's the date?	¿Qué día/fecha es hoy?/¿A cuántos estamos? [keh 'dee-ah/'feh-chah ehs 'oh-ee/ah 'kwahn-tohs eh-'stah-mohs]

Today is May 1 st.	Hoy es el primero de mayo. ['oh-ee ehs ehl pree-'meh-roh deh 'mah-yoh]

> *In Spanish, the first day of the month is always said to be primero (first), instead of uno (one), even when it is written with a number; "1 de mayo" reads "primero de mayo." All other days of the month are expressed as cardinal numbers; "2 de mayo" reads "dos de mayo," etc.*

Weather
El tiempo atmosférico

What's the weather going to be like today?	¿Qué tiempo tendremos hoy? [keh tee-'ehm-poh tehn-'dreh-mohs 'oh-ee]
It's going to be... good/fair. rainy. changeable.	Va a hacer… [vah ah ah-'sehr...] buen tiempo. [bwehn tee-'ehm-poh] mal tiempo. [mahl tee-'ehm-poh] tiempo inestable. [tee-'ehm-poh een-eh-'stah-bleh]
It's going to stay fair/rainy.	Seguirá el buen/mal tiempo. [seh-gee-'rah ehl bwehn/mahl tee-'ehm-poh]
It's going to get warmer/colder.	Va a hacer más calor/más frío. [vah ah ah-'sehr mahs kah-'lohr/mahs 'free-oh]
It's going to rain/snow.	Va a llover/nevar. [vah ah yoh-'vehr/neh-'vahr]
It's cold/hot/muggy.	Hace frío/calor/bochorno (*Am* humedad). ['ah-seh 'free-oh/kah-'lohr/boh-'chohr-noh (oo-meh-d'ahd)]
There's a storm coming.	Va a haber una tormenta/tempestad. [vah ah ah-'behr 'oo-nah tohr-'mehn-tah/tehm-peh-'stahd]
It's foggy.	Hay niebla. ['ah-ee nee-'eh-blah]
It's windy.	Hace (*Am* Corre) viento. ['ah-seh ('koh-rreh) vee-'ehn-toh]

It's sunny.
Hace/Hay sol. ['ah-seh/'ah-ee sohl]

The sky is clear/cloudy.
El cielo está despejado/nublado. [ehl see-'eh-loh eh-'stah deh-speh-'hah-doh/noo-'blah-doh]

What's the temperature today?
¿Qué temperatura hace hoy? [keh tehm-peh-rah-'too-rah 'ah-seh 'oh-ee]

It's twenty degrees (Celsius).
Hace veinte grados (centígrados). ['ah-seh 'veh·een-teh 'grah-dohs (sehn-'tee-grah-dohs)]

What are the roads like in …?
¿Qué tal están las carreteras en…? [keh tahl eh-'stahn lahs kah-rreh-'teh-rahs ehn]

The roads are slippery/icy.
Las carreteras están resbaladizas. [lahs kah-rreh-'teh-rahs eh-'stahn rehs-bah-lah-'dee-sahs]

The visibility is only 20 meters/less than 50 meters.
La visibilidad es de 20 metros/menos de 50 metros. [lah vee-see-bee-lee-'dahd ehs deh 'veh-een-teh 'meh-trohs/'meh-nohs deh seen-'kwehn-tah 'meh-trohs]

You need snow chains.
Es necesario el uso de cadenas. [ehs neh-seh-'sah-ree-oh ehl 'oo-soh deh kah-'deh-nahs]

Word List: Weather

air	el aire [ehl 'ah·ee-reh]
atmospheric pressure	la presión atmosférica [lah preh-see-'ohn aht-mohs-'feh-ree-kah]
barometer	barómetro [bah-'roh-meh-troh]
clear	despejado [dehs-peh-'hah-doh]
climate	el clima [ehl 'klee-mah]
cloud	la nube [lah 'noo-beh]
cloudy	nublado [noo-'blah-doh]
cold	frío ['free-oh]
cool and wet	fresco y húmedo ['freh-skoh ee 'oo-meh-doh]
dawn	el alba [ehl 'ahl-bah]
dead calm	calma chicha ['kahl-mah 'chee-chah]

Pyrenees

downpour/torrential rain	el chaparrón/la lluvia torrencial [ehl chah-pah-'rrohn/lah 'yoo-vee-ah toh-rrehn-see-'ahl]
drizzle	llovizna [yoh-'vees-nah]
drought	sequía [seh-'kee-ah]
dusk	crepúsculo [kreh-'poo-skoo-loh]
flood	la inundación [lah een-oon-dah-see-'ohn]
fog	niebla [nee-'eh-blah]
frost	helada [eh-'lah-dah]
gust of wind	ráfaga, racha ['rah-fah-gah, 'rah-chah]
hail, hailstone	granizo [grah-'nee-soh]
hazy	brumoso [broo-'moh-soh]
heat	el calor [ehl kah-'lohr]
heat wave	ola de calor ['oh-lah deh kah-'lohr]
high-pressure area (anticyclone)	el área de alta presión (el anticiclón) [ehl 'ah-reh-ah deh 'ahl-tah preh-see-'ohn (ehl ahn-tee-see-'klohn)]
high tide	marea alta [mah-'reh-ah 'ahl-tah]
hot	cálido, caluroso ['kah-lee-doh, kah-loo-'roh-soh]
humid	húmedo ['oo-meh-doh]
ice	hielo ['yeh-loh]
icy road	la superficie helada [lah soo-pehr-'fee-see·eh eh-'lah-dah]

lightning	rayo ['rah-yoh]
low-pressure area (depression, cyclone)	el área de baja presión (la depresión, el ciclón) [ehl 'ah-reh-ah deh 'bah-hah preh-see-'ohn (lah deh-preh-see-'ohn, ehl see-'klohn)]
low tide	marea baja [mah-'reh-ah 'bah-hah]
muggy/humid	bochornoso (*Am* húmedo) [boh-chohr-'noh-soh ('oo-meh-doh)]
powder (snow)	la nieve polvo [lah nee-'eh-veh 'pohl-voh]
precipitation	las precipitaciones [lahs preh-see-pee-tah-see-'oh-nehs]
rain	lluvia ['yoo-vee·ah]
rainy	lluvioso [yoo-vee-'oh-soh]
shower	chubasco [choo-'bah-skoh]
snow	la nieve [lah nee-'eh-veh]
snowstorm	tormenta de nieve [tohr-'mehn-tah deh nee-'eh-veh]
sun	el sol [ehl sohl]
sunny	soleado [soh-leh-'ah-doh]
sunrise	salida del sol [sah-'lee-dah dehl sohl]
sunset	puesta del sol ['pweh-stah dehl sohl]
starry	estrellado [eh-streh-'yah-doh]
temperature	temperatura [tehm-peh-rah-'too-rah]
thaw	deshielo [dehs-'yeh-loh]
thunder	trueno [troo-'eh-noh]
variable	inestable [een-eh-'stah-bleh]
warm	caliente, cálido [kah-lee-'ehn-teh, 'kah-lee-doh]
weather forecast	la predicción del tiempo [lah preh-deek-see-'ohn dehl tee-'ehm-poh]
weather report	el boletín meteorológico [ehl boh-leh-'teen meh-teh-oh-roh-'loh-hee-koh]
wind	viento [vee-'ehn-toh]
wind force	fuerza del viento ['fwehr-sah dehl vee-'ehn-toh]

Word List: Colors

beige	beige, beis ['beh·eesh, 'beh-ees]
black	negro ['neh-groh]
blue	azul [ah-'sool]

brown	marrón, carmelita, pardo [mah-'rrohn, kahr-meh-'lee-tah, 'pahr-doh]
chestnut brown	castaño [kah-'stah-nyoh]
colored	de colores [deh koh-'loh-rehs]
dark	oscuro [oh-'skoo-roh]
gold, golden	dorado [doh-'rah-doh]
gray	gris [grees]
green	verde ['vehr-deh]
light	claro ['klah-roh]
multicolored	de varios colores [deh 'vah-ree-ohs koh-'loh-rehs]
orange	naranja [nah-'rahn-hah]
pink	rosa ['roh-sah]
plain	de un solo color [deh oon 'soh-loh koh-'lohr]
purple, mauve	lila, malva ['lee-lah, 'mahl-vah]
purple, violet	morado, violeta [moh-'rah-doh, vee-oh-'leh-tah]
red	rojo ['roh-hoh]
silver	plateado [plah-teh-'ah-doh]
turquoise	turquesa [toor-'keh-sah]
white	blanco ['blahn-koh]
yellow	amarillo [ah-mah-'ree-yoh]

2 Making Contact
Cómo entrar en contacto

Saying Hello/Introductions/Getting Acquainted
Saludos/Presentación/Relaciones

Good morning!	¡Buenos días! ['bweh-nohs 'dee-ahs]
Good afternoon!	¡Buenas tardes! ['bweh-nahs 'tahr-dehs]
Good evening/night!	¡Buenas tardes!/¡Buenas noches! ['bweh-nahs 'tahr-dehs/'bweh-nahs 'noh-chehs]

"Buenos días" is used in the morning (before 12 noon). "Buenas tardes" is used in the afternoon and early evening. "Buenas noches" is used after dark (later in the evening and at night), especially when leaving.

Hello!/Hi/How are you?	¡Hola! ¿Qué tal? ['oh-lah keh tahl]
What's your name?	¿Cómo se llama usted, por favor? ['koh-moh seh 'yah-mah oo-'stehd, pohr fah-'vohr]
	¿Cómo te llamas? ['koh-moh teh 'yah-mahs]
My name's …	Me llamo… [meh 'yah-moh]
I'd like to introduce you to.../This is...	Le/Te presento… [leh/teh preh-'sehn-toh]
Mrs. X.	a la señora X. [ah lah seh-'nyoh-rah]
Miss X.	a la señorita X. [ah lah seh-nyoh-'ree-tah]
Mr. X.	al señor X. [ahl seh-'nyohr]
my husband.	a mi marido. [ah mee mah-'ree-doh]
my wife.	a mi esposa/mujer. [ah mee eh-'spoh-sah/moo-'hehr]
my son.	a mi hijo. [ah mee 'ee-hoh]
my daughter.	a mi hija. [ah mee 'ee-hah]
my brother/sister.	a mi hermano/a mi hermana. [ah mee ehr-'mah-noh/ah mee ehr-'mah-nah]
my friend (male/female).	a mi amigo/a mi amiga. [ah mee ah-'mee-goh/ah mee ah-'mee-gah]
my colleague.	a mi colega. [ah mee koh-'leh-gah]

*"Don," "Doña" before the first name indicates respect.
An acquaintance is "un conocido"; the boyfriend or girl-
friend is "el novio," "la novia."*

How are you?	¿Qué tal está usted? [keh tahl eh-'stah oo-'stehd]
	¿Qué tal estás? ¿Qué tal? [keh tahl eh-'stahs, keh tahl]
Fine, thank you. And you?	Bien, gracias. ¿Y usted/tú? ['bee-ehn 'grah-see-ahs, ee oo-'stehd/too]
Where are you from?	¿De dónde es usted/eres? [deh 'dohn-deh ehs oo-'stehd/'eh-rehs]
I'm from...	Soy de... ['soh-ee deh]
Have you been here long?	¿Lleva usted/Llevas ya mucho tiempo aquí? ['yeh-vah oo-'stehd/'yeh-vahs yah 'moo-choh tee-'ehm-poh ah-'kee]
I've been here since...	Estoy aquí desde... [eh-'stoh-ee ah-'kee 'dehs-deh]
How long are you staying?	¿Cuánto tiempo se queda/te quedas? ['kwahn-toh tee-'ehm-poh seh 'keh-dah/teh 'keh-dahs]

Is this your first time here?	¿Es la primera vez que está usted/estás aquí? [ehs lah pree-'meh-rah vehs keh eh-'stah oo-'stehd/eh-'stahs ah-'kee]
Are you by yourself?	¿Está usted/Estás solo/sola? [eh-'stah oo-'stehd/eh-'stahs 'soh-loh/'soh-lah]
No, I'm traveling with my family/friends.	No, estoy aquí de paso con mi familia/mis amigos. [noh, eh-'stoh-ee ah-'kee deh 'pah-soh kohn mee fah-'mee-lee-ah/mees ah-'mee-gohs]
Are you staying at the Astoria Hotel/at the camping, too?	¿Está usted/Estás también en el hotel Astoria/en el cámping…? [eh-'stah oo-'stehd/eh-'stahs tahm-bee-'ehn ehn ehl 'oh-tehl ah-'stoh-ree-ah/ehn ehl 'kahm-peen]

Traveling Alone/Making a Date
Solo y de paso/Citas

Are you waiting for someone?	¿Espera usted/Esperas a alguien? [eh-'speh-rah oo-'stehd/eh-'speh-rahs ah 'ahl-gee-ehn]
Do you have any plans for tomorrow?	¿Tiene usted/Tienes algún plan para mañana? [tee-'eh-neh ahl-'goon plahn 'pah-rah mah-'nyah-nah]
Do you want to go together?	¿Vamos juntos? ['vah-mohs 'hoon-tohs]
Would you like to go out in the evening?	¿Salimos juntos esta tarde? [sah-'lee-mohs 'hoon-tohs 'eh-stah 'tahr-deh]
Would you like to have lunch/dinner with me?	¿Me gustaría invitarle/invitarla/invitarte a comer? [meh goo-stah-'ree-ah een-vee-'tahr-leh/een-vee-'tahr-lah/een-vee-'tahr-teh ah koh-'mehr]
When do we meet?	¿A qué hora nos encontramos? [ah keh 'oh-rah nohs ehn-kohn-'trah-mohs]

Is it OK if I pick you up?	¿Puedo ir a recogerla/recogerle (*Am* buscarla/buscarle)/ recogerte (*Am* buscarte)? ['pweh-doh eer ah reh-koh-'hehr-lah/reh-koh-'hehr-leh (boo-'skahr-lah/ boo-'skahr-leh)/reh-koh-'hehr-teh (boo-'skahr-teh)]
What time do you want me to come by?	¿A qué hora quiere/s que venga? [ah keh 'oh-rah kee-'eh-reh/rehs keh 'vehn-gah]
I'll see you at 9 P.M....	Le/La espero a las nueve... [leh/lah eh-'speh-roh ah lahs noo-'eh-veh]
in front of the movie house.	delante del cine. [deh-'lahn-teh dehl 'see-neh]
at the...square.	en la plaza. [ehn lah 'plah-sah]
at the cafe.	en el café. [ehn ehl kah-'feh]
Are you married?	¿Está usted casado/casada? [eh-'stah oo-'stehd kah-'sah-doh/kah-'sah-dah]
Do you have a boyfriend/ girlfriend?	¿Tienes novio/novia? [tee-'eh-nehs 'noh-vee-oh/'noh-vee-ah]
Can I take you home?	¿Puedo acompañarla/acompañar-le/acompañarte a casa? ['pweh-doh ah-kohm-pah-'nyahr-lah/ ah-kohm-pah-'nyahr-leh/ah-kohm-pah-'nyahr-teh ah 'kah-sah]
I'll go with you to...	Yo la/le/te acompaño a... [yoh lah/leh/teh ah-kohm-'pah-nyoh ah]
I'd love to see you again.	Me agradaría volver a verle/ verla/verte. [meh ah-grah-dah-'ree-ah vohl-'vehr ah 'vehr-leh/'vehr-lah/'vehr-teh]
I hope to see you again.	Espero volver a verle/verla/ verte. [eh-'speh-roh vohl-'vehr ah 'vehr-leh/'vehr-lah/'vehr-teh]
Thanks for the lovely evening.	Muchas gracias por esta velada tan agradable. ['moo-chahs 'grah-see-ahs pohr 'eh-stah veh-'lah-dah tahn ah-grah-'dah-bleh]

Please leave me alone.	¡Por favor, déjeme en paz! [pohr fah-'vohr, 'deh-heh-meh ehn pahs]
Go away!/Get lost (now)!	¡Lárgate (ya)! ['lahr-gah-teh (yah)]
Enough!	¡Ya basta! [yah 'bah-stah]

A Visit
Una visita

Excuse me, does Mr./Mrs./Miss X live here?	Perdón, ¿vive aquí el señor/la señora/la señorita X? [pehr-'dohn, 'vee-veh ah-'kee ehl seh-'nyohr/lah seh-'nyoh-rah/lah seh-nyoh-'ree-tah eks]
No, he/she moved.	No, se ha mudado de casa. [noh, seh ah moo-'dah-doh deh 'kah-sah]
Do you know where he's/she's living now?	¿Sabe usted dónde vive ahora? ['sah-bee oo-'stehd 'dohn-deh 'vee-veh ah-'oh-rah]
Can I speak to Mr./Mrs./Miss X, please?	¿Puedo hablar con el señor/la señora/la señorita X? ['pweh-doh ah-'blahr kohn ehl seh-'nyohr/lah seh-'nyoh-rah/lah seh-nyoh-'ree-tah eks]
When will he/she be home?	¿Cuándo estará en casa? ['kwahn-doh eh-stah-'rah ehn 'kah-sah]
Can I leave a message?	¿Puedo dejar un recado? ['pweh-doh deh-'hahr oon reh-'kah-doh]
I'll come back later.	Volveré más tarde. [vohl-veh-'reh mahs 'tahr-deh]
Come in.	Pase, pase./Pasa, pasa. ['pah-seh, 'pah-seh/'pah-sah, 'pah-sah]
Please sit down.	¿Quiere sentarse?/¿Quieres sentarte? [kee-'eh-reh sehn-'tahr-seh/kee-'eh-rehs sehn-'tahr-teh]
Paul says hello/sends you his regards.	Muchos saludos de Paul. ['moo-chohs sah-'loo-dohs deh pahl]

Would you like something to drink?	¿Quiere/Quieres tomar algo? [kee-'eh-reh/kee-'eh-rehs toh-'mahr 'ahl-goh]
Cheers!	¡Salud! [sah-'lood]

Other toasts are "¡Salud, amor y dinero!" (health, love, and money!), "¡Felicidades!" (best wishes! congratulations!), "¡Feliz cumpleaños!" (Happy Birthday!), "Feliz Navidad!" (Merry Christmas!) and "Feliz Año Nuevo!" (Happy New Year!)

Would you like to stay for lunch/dinner?	¿No puede/puedes quedarse/quedarte a comer (*Am* almorzar)/cenar? [noh 'pweh-deh/'pweh-dehs keh-'dahr-seh/keh-'dahr-teh ah koh-'mehr (ahl-mohr-'sahr)/seh-'nahr]
Thank you. I'd love to stay, if it's not too much trouble.	Muchas gracias. Me quedo con mucho gusto si no les molesto. ['moo-chahs 'grah-see-ahs. meh 'keh-doh kohn 'moo-choh 'goo-stoh see noh lehs moh-'leh-stoh]
I'm sorry, but I have to go.	Lo siento, pero tengo que marcharme. [loh see-'ehn-toh, 'peh-roh 'tehn-goh keh mahr-'chahr-meh]

Saying Good-bye
Despedida

Good-bye!	¡Hasta la vista!/¡Adiós! ['ah-stah lah 'vee-stah/ah-dee-'ohs]
See you soon!	¡Hasta pronto! ['ah-stah 'prohn-toh]
See you later!	¡Hasta luego! ['ah-stah 'lweh-goh]
See you tomorrow!	¡Hasta mañana! ['ah-stah mah-'nyah-nah]
Good night!	¡Buenas noches! ['bweh-nahs 'noh-chehs]
Take care!	¡Que le/te vaya bien! [keh leh/teh 'vah-yah 'bee-ehn]

Have fun!	¡Que se divierta!/¡Que te diviertas! [keh seh dee-vee-'ehr-tah/keh teh dee-vee-'ehr-tahs]
Have a good trip.	¡Buen viaje! [bwehn vee-'ah-heh]
I'll be in touch.	Yo daré noticias de mi vida. [yoh dah-'reh noh-'tee-see-ahs deh mee 'vee-dah]
Give my regards to...	Muchos saludos a...de mi parte. ['moo-chohs sah-'loo-dohs ah...deh mee 'pahr-teh]

Asking a Favor/Expressing Thanks
Cómo pedir un favor y dar las gracias

Yes, please.	Sí, por favor. [see, pohr fah-'vohr]
No, thanks.	No, muchas gracias. [noh, 'moo-chahs 'grah-see-ahs]
Can I ask you a favor?	¿Puedo pedirle un favor? ['pweh-doh peh-'deer-leh oon fah-'vohr]
May I?	¿Permite? [pehr-'mee-teh]
Can you help me, please?	¿Puede usted ayudarme, por favor? ['pweh-deh oo-'stehd ah-yoo-'dahr-meh, pohr fah-'vohr]
Thanks.	Gracias. ['grah-see-ahs]
Thank you very much.	Muchas gracias. ['moo-chahs 'grah-see-ahs]
My pleasure.	Gracias, con mucho gusto. ['grah-see-ahs, kohn 'moo-choh 'goo-stoh]

"Favor" can mean please ("por favor") or a favor ("haga/haz el favor de …"). "You're welcome" is "de nada" or "no hay de qué."

Thanks. Same to you!	Gracias, igualmente. ['grah-see-ahs, ee-gwahl-'mehn-teh]

That's very nice of you, thank you.	Gracias, es muy amable de su parte. ['grah-see-ahs, ehs 'moo-ee ah-'mah-bleh]
Thanks a lot for your help/interest.	Muchas gracias por su ayuda/interés. ['moo-chahs 'grah-see-ahs pohr soo ah-'yoo-dah/een-teh-'rehs]
You're welcome.	De nada./No hay de qué. [deh 'nah-dah/noh 'ah-ee deh keh]

Apologies/Regrets
Cómo pedir excusas o lamentar algo

I'm sorry!	¡Perdón! [pehr-'dohn]
I'd like to apologize.	Tengo que pedir excusas. ['tehn-goh keh peh-'deer ehk-'skoo-sahs]
I'm very sorry.	Lo siento/lamento mucho. [loh see-'ehn-toh 'moo-choh/lah-'mehn-toh 'moo-choh]
I didn't mean to say that/it that way.	No quería decir eso. [noh keh-'ree-ah deh-'seer 'eh-soh]
What a pity!	¡Qué pena/lástima! [keh 'peh-nah/'lah-stee-mah]
I'm sorry, but that's not possible.	Lo siento, pero no es posible. [loh see-'ehn-toh, 'peh-roh noh ehs poh-'see-bleh]
Maybe some other time.	Otra vez, quizás. ['oh-trah vehs kee-'sahs]

Congratulations/Best Wishes
Felicitación

Congratulations!	¡Felicidades! ¡Enhorabuena! [feh-lee-see-'dah-dehs, ehn-oh-rah-'bweh-nah]

"Enhorabuena" also implies wishing the best of luck. "Felicidades" also implies wishing happiness.

All the best!	¡Que le/te vaya bien! [keh leh/teh 'vah-yah 'bee-ehn]
Happy birthday!	Muchas felicidades en el día de su/tu cumpleaños/santo. ['moo-chahs feh-lee-see-'dah-dehs ehn ehl 'dee-ah deh soo/too koom-pleh-'ah-nyohs/'sahn-toh]
I wish you every success.	¡Mucho éxito! ['moo-choh 'ehk-see-toh]
Good luck!	¡Mucha suerte! ['moo-chah 'swehr-teh] ¡Buena suerte! ['bweh-nah 'swehr-teh]
Get well!/Feel better!	¡Que se mejore!/¡Que te mejores! [keh seh meh-'hoh-reh/keh teh meh-'hoh-rehs]
Happy holidays!	¡Felices fiestas! [feh-'lee-sehs fee-'eh-stahs]

Language Difficulties
Dificultades de comprensión

Pardon?	¿Cómo dice/dices? ['koh-moh 'dee-seh/'dee-sehs]
I don't understand. Could you repeat that, please?	No le/la/te entiendo. ¿Puede/Puedes repetir, por favor? [noh leh/lah/teh ehn-tee-'ehn-doh. 'pweh-deh/pweh-dehs reh-peh-'teer, pohr fah-'vohr]
Could you slow down a bit/speak louder, please?	Por favor, hable/habla un poco más despacio/alto. [pohr fah-'vohr, 'ah-bleh/'ah-blah oon 'poh-koh mahs deh-'spah-see-oh/'ahl-toh]
I understand.	Entiendo./He entendido. [ehn-tee-'ehn-doh/eh ehn-tehn-'dee-doh]
Do you speak...	¿Habla usted/Hablas... ['ah-blah oo-'stehd/'ah-blahs]
English? German?	inglés? [een-'glehs] alemán? [ah-leh-'mahn]

French?	francés? [frahn-'sehs]
Spanish?	español? [eh-spah-'nyohl]
I just speak a little...	Hablo sólo un poco de... ['ah-bloh 'soh-loh oon 'poh-koh deh]
How do you say . . . in Spanish?	¿Cómo se dice... en español? ['koh-moh seh 'dee-seh ehn eh-spah-'nyohl]
What does that mean?	¿Qué significa/quiere decir eso? [keh seeg-nee-'fee-kah/kee-'eh-reh deh-'seer 'eh-soh]
How do you pronounce this word?	¿Cómo se pronuncia esta palabra? ['koh-moh seh proh-'noon-see-ah 'eh-stah pah-'lah-brah]
Write it down for me, please.	Escríbamelo/Escríbemelo, por favor. [eh-'skree-bah-meh-loh/eh-'skree-beh-meh-'loh, pohr fah-'vohr]
Spell it, please.	Deletree/Deletrea, por favor. [deh-leh-'treh-eh/deh-leh-'treh-ah, pohr fah-'vohr]

Expressing Opinions
Opiniones

I (don't) like it.	(No) me gusta. [(noh) meh 'goo-stah]
I prefer...	Prefiero... [preh-fee-'eh-roh]
I'd really like...	Lo mejor sería... [loh meh-'hohr seh-'ree-ah]
That would be nice/I'd like that.	Me alegraría/gustaría. [meh ah-leh-grah-'ree-ah/goo-stah-'ree-ah]
With pleasure.	Con (mucho) gusto. [kohn ('moo-choh) 'goo-stoh]
Great!	¡Fantástico! [fahn-'tah-stee-koh]
I don't feel like it.	No tengo ganas. [noh 'tehn-goh 'gah-nahs]
I don't want to.	No quiero. [noh kee-'eh-roh]
Absolutely not!	¡Nada de eso! ['nah-dah deh 'eh-soh]

No way!/That's out of the question.	De ninguna manera. [deh neen-'goo-nah mah-'neh-rah]
I don't know yet.	No sé todavía. [noh seh toh-dah-'vee-ah]
Maybe/perhaps.	Quizás. [kee-'sahs]
Probably.	Probablemente. [proh-bah-bleh-'mehn-teh]

Personal Information
Datos personales

Age
Edad

How old are you?	¿Qué edad tiene usted/tienes? [keh eh-'dahd tee-'eh-neh oo-'stehd/tee-'eh-nehs]
I'm thirty-nine.	Tengo treinta y nueve años. ['tehn-goh 'treh·een-tah ee noo-'eh-veh 'ah-nyohs]
When is your birthday?	¿Cuándo es su/tu cumpleaños? ['kwahn-doh ehs soo/too koom-pleh-'ah-nyohs]
I was born on April 12, 1958.	Nací el doce de abril de mil novecientos cincuenta y ocho. [nah-'see ehl 'doh-seh deh ah-'breel deh meel noh-veh-see-'ehn-tohs seen-'kwehn-tah ee 'oh-choh]

Professions/Education/Training
Profesión/Estudio/Formación profesional

What do you do for a living?	¿Qué profesión tiene usted/tienes? [keh proh-feh-see-'ohn tee-'eh-neh oo-'stehd/tee-'eh-nehs]
I work in a factory.	Soy obrero/obrera. ['soh-ee oh-'breh-roh/oh-'breh-rah]
I work in an office.	Soy empleado/empleada. ['soh-ee ehm-pleh-'ah-doh/ehm-pleh-'ah-dah]

I'm a civil servant.	Soy funcionario/funcionaria. ['soh-ee foonk-see-oh-'nah-ree-oh]
I do freelance work.	Ejerzo una profesión libre. [eh-'hehr-soh 'oo-nah proh-feh-see-'ohn 'lee-breh]
I'm retired.	Estoy jubilado/jubilada. [eh-'stoh-ee hoo-bee-'lah-doh/hoo-bee-'lah-dah]
I'm unemployed.	Estoy parado (*Am* desempleado). [eh-'stoh-ee pah-'rah-doh (dehs-ehm-pleh-'ah-doh)]
I work for…	Trabajo en… [trah-'bah-hoh ehn]
I'm still going to school.	Todavía voy al colegio. [toh-dah-'vee-ah 'voh-ee ahl koh-'leh-hee-oh]
I'm in high school.	Voy al Instituto. ['voh-ee ahl een-stee-'too-toh]
I'm a student.	Soy estudiante. ['soh-ee eh-stoo-dee-'ahn-teh]
Where/What do you study?	¿Dónde/Qué estudia usted/estudias? ['dohn-deh/keh eh-'stoo-dee-ah oo-'stehd/eh-'stoo-dee-ahs]
I study…in Chicago	Estudio…en Chicago [eh-'stoo-dee-oh ehn Chee-'kah-goh]
What are your hobbies?	¿Cuáles son sus/tus aficiones particulares? ['kwah-lehs sohn soos/toos ah-fee-see-'oh-nehs pahr-tee-koo-'lah-rehs]

Word List: Professions/Education/Training

accountant	el/la contable (Am contador/contadora) [ehl/lah kohn-'tah-bleh (ehl kohn-tah-'dohr/kohn-tah-'doh-rah)]
actor/actress	actor/actriz [ahk-'tohr/ahk-'trees]
apprentice	aprendiz/aprendiza [ah-prehn-'dees/ah-prehn-'dee-sah]
archeology	arqueología [ahr-keh-oh-loh-'hee-ah]
art academy	academia de arte [ah-kah-'deh-mee-ah deh 'ahr-teh]
art history	historia del arte [ee-'stoh-ree-ah dehl 'ahr-teh]

architect	arquitecto/arquitecta [ahr-kee-'tehk-toh/ahr-kee-'tehk-tah]
architecture	arquitectura [ahr-kee-tehk-'too-rah]
artist	el/la artista [ehl/lah ahr-'tee-stah]
auditor	auditor/auditora, revisor/revisora de cuentas [ow-dee-'tohr/ow-dee-'toh-rah, reh-vee-'sohr/reh-vee-'soh-rah deh 'kwehn-tahs]
baker	panadero/panadera [pah-nah-'deh-roh/pah-nah-'deh-rah]
biologist	biólogo/bióloga [bee-'oh-loh-goh/bee-'oh-loh-'gah]
biology	biología [bee-oh-loh-'hee-ah]
blue-collar worker	obrero/obrera [oh-'breh-roh, oh-'breh-rah]
bookstore clerk	librero/librera [lee-'breh-roh/lee-'breh-rah]
business management	economía/gestión/administración de empresa [eh-koh-noh-'mee-ah/heh-stee-'ohn/ahd-mee-nee-strah-see-'ohn deh ehm-'preh-sah]
business school	escuela de comercio [eh-'skweh-lah deh koh-'mehr-see-oh]
butcher	carnicero/carnicera [kahr-nee-'seh-roh/kahr-nee-'seh-rah]
car mechanic	mecánico de coches [meh-'kah-nee-koh deh 'koh-chehs]
caretaker	el/la conserje, encargado/encargada [ehl/lah kohn-'sehr-heh, ehn-kahr-'gah-doh/ehn-kahr-'gah-dah]
carpenter	carpintero/carpintera [kahr-peen-'teh-roh/kahr-peen-'teh-rah]
cashier	cajero/cajera [kah-'heh-roh/kah-'heh-rah]
chemical engineer	químico/química ['kee-mee-koh/'kee-mee-kah]
chemistry	química ['kee-mee-kah]
civil servant	funcionario/funcionaria del Estado [foonk-see-oh-'nah-ree-oh/foonk-see-oh-'nah-ree-ah dehl eh-'stah-doh]
clerk	empleado/empleada [ehm-pleh-'ah-doh/ehm-pleh-'ah-dah]
college, university	la universidad [lah oo-nee-vehr-see-'dahd]

computer program analyst/programmer	el/la analista programador/programadora [ehl/lah ah-nah-'lee-stah/proh-grah-mah-'dohr/proh-grah-mah-'doh-rah]
computer science	informática [een-fohr-'mah-tee-kah]
cook	cocinero/cocinera [koh-see-'neh-roh/koh-see-'neh-rah]
craftsman/-woman	artesano/artesana [ahr-teh-'sah-noh/ahr-teh-'sah-nah]
data entry clerk	el/la perforista, entrador/entradora de datos [ehl/lah pehr-foh-'ree-stah, ehn-trah-'dohr/ehn-trah-'doh-rah deh 'dah-tohs]
decorator	decorador/decoradora [deh-koh-rah-'dohr/deh-koh-rah-'doh-rah]
dental technician	protésico/protésica dental, mecánico/mecánica dentista [proh-'teh-see-koh/proh-'teh-see-kah dehn-'tahl, meh-'kah-nee-koh/meh-'kah-nee-kah dehn-'tee-stah]
dentist	el/la dentista [ehl/lah dehn-'tee-stah]
designer	diseñador/diseñadora [dee-seh-nyah-'dohr/dee-seh-nyah-'doh-rah]
director	director/directora [dee-rehk-'tohr/dee-rehk-'toh-rah]
doctor (MD)	médico/médica ['meh-dee-koh/'meh-dee-kah]
doctor's assistant	ayudante técnico sanitario (ATS) [ah-yoo-'dahn-teh 'tehk-nee-koh sah-nee-'tah-ree-oh]
draftsman	el/la delineante [ehl/lah deh-lee-neh-'ahn-teh]
driver	el conductor, el chófer (*Am* el chofer) [ehl kohn-dook-'tohr, ehl 'choh-fehr (ehl choh-'fehr)]
driving instructor	profesor/profesora de auto-escuela [proh-feh-'sohr/proh-feh-'soh-rah deh ow-toh-eh-'skweh-lah]
economist	el/la economista [ehl/lah eh-koh-noh-'mee-stah]
editor	redactor/redactora [reh-dahk-'tohr/reh-dahk-'toh-rah]
(education) classes	las clases [lahs 'klah-sehs]
electrician	el/la electricista [ehl/lah eh-lehk-tree-'see-stah]

elementary/primary/ grade school	escuela elemental/primaria [eh-'skweh-lah eh-leh-mehn-'tahl/ pree-'mah-ree-ah]
engineer	ingeniero/ingeniera [een-heh-nee-'eh-roh/een-heh-nee-'eh-rah]
English literature	filología/literatura inglesa, anglística [fee-loh-loh-'hee-ah/lee-teh-rah-'too-rah een-'gleh-sah, ahn-'glee-stee-kah]
farmer	agricultor/agricultora [ah-gree-kool-'tohr/ah-gree-kool-'toh-rah]
fisherman (male/female)	pescador/pescadora [peh-skah-'dohr/peh-skah-'doh-rah]
fitter (mechanic)	el montador, el ajustador [ehl mohn-tah-'dohr, ehl ah-hoo-stah-'dohr]
flight attendant	el/la auxiliar de vuelo/la azafata (*Am* aeromoza) [ehl/lah owk-see-lee-'ahr deh 'vweh-loh/lah ah-sah-'fah-tah (ah-eh-roh-'moh-sah]
florist	el/la florista [ehl/lah floh-'ree-stah]
gardener	jardinero/jardinera [hahr-dee-'neh-roh/hahr-dee-'neh-rah]
geography	geografía [heh-oh-grah-'fee-ah]
geology	geología [heh-oh-loh-'hee-ah]
geriatric nurse	gerocultor/gerocultora [heh-roh-kool-'tohr, heh-roh-kool-'toh-rah]
glass installation and repair working	vidriero/vidriera [vee-dree-'eh-roh/vee-dree-'eh-rah]
hairdresser	peluquero/peluquera [peh-loo-'keh-roh, peh-loo-'keh-rah]
healer	curandero/curandera naturista [koo-rahn-'deh-roh/koo-rahn-'deh-rah nah-too-'ree-stah]
high school	instituto de enseñanza media/segunda enseñanza [een-stee-'too-toh deh ehn-seh-'nyahn-sah 'meh-dee-ah/seh-'goon-dah ehn-seh-'nyahn-sah]
history	historia [ee-'stoh-ree-ah]
house husband	amo de casa ['ah-moh deh 'kah-sah]
housewife	(el) ama de casa [(ehl) 'ah-mah deh 'kah-sah]
innkeeper	hostelero/hostelera [oh-steh-'leh-roh/oh-steh-'leh-rah]
institute	instituto [een-stee-'too-toh]

interpreter	el/la intérprete [ehl/lah een-'tehr-preh-teh]
jeweler	joyero [hoh-'yeh-roh]
journalist	el/la periodista [ehl/lah peh-ree-oh-'dee-stah]
judge	juez/jueza [hoo-'ehs/hoo-'eh-sah]
junior high school	escuela primaria superior/secundaria básica [eh-'skweh-lah pree-'mah-ree-ah soo-peh-ree-'ohr/seh-koon-'dah-ree-ah 'bah-see-kah]
laboratory assistant	el/la ayudante de laboratorio [ehl/lah ah-yoo-'dahn-teh deh lah-boh-rah-'toh-ree-oh]
landlord/landlady	propietario/propietaria, dueño/dueña, casero/casera [proh-pee-eh-'tah-ree-oh/proh-pee-eh-'tah-ree-ah, 'dweh-nyoh, 'dweh-nyah, kah-'seh-roh, kah-'seh-rah]
law	derecho [deh-'reh-choh]
lawyer/attorney	abogado/abogada [ah-boh-'gah-doh/ah-boh-'gah-dah]
librarian	bibliotecario/bibliotecaria [bee-blee-oh-teh-'kah-ree-oh]
locksmith	cerrajero/cerrajera [seh-rrah-'heh-roh/seh-rrah-'heh-rah]
mailman/-woman	cartero/cartera [kahr-'teh-roh/kahr-'teh-rah]
management expert	el/la economista de empresa, técnico/técnica de gestión de empresas, de administración de empresas [ehl/lah eh-koh-noh-'mee-stah deh ehm-'preh-sah, 'tehk-nee-koh/'tehk-nee-kah deh geh-stee-'ohn deh ehm-'preh-sahs, deh ahd-mee-nee-strah-see-'ohn deh ehm-'preh-sahs]
manager	el/la gerente [ehl/lah heh-'rehn-teh]
mason, bricklayer	el albañil [ehl ahl-bah-'nyeel]
masseur/masseuse	el/la masajista [ehl/lah mah-sah-'hee-stah]
mathematics	las matemáticas [lahs mah-teh-'mah-tee-kahs]
mechanic	mecánico/mecánica [meh-'kah-nee-koh/meh-'kah-nee-kah]

mechanical engineering	ingeniería mecánica [een-heh-nee-eh-'ree-ah meh-'kah-nee-kah]
medicine	medicina [meh-dee-'see-nah]
merchant	el/la comerciante [ehl/lah koh-mehr-see-'ahn-teh]
meteorologist	meteorólogo/meteoróloga [meh-teh-oh-'roh-loh-goh, meh-teh-oh-'roh-loh-gah]
midwife	comadrona [koh-mah-'droh-nah]
model	el/la maniquí, el/la modelo [ehl/lah mah-nee-'kee, ehl/lah moh-'deh-loh]
music	música ['moo-see-kah]
musician	músico/música ['moo-see-koh/'moo-see-kah]
notary (almost an attorney in some countries)	notario/notaria [noh-'tah-ree-oh/noh-'tah-ree-ah]
nurse	enfermero, enfermera [ehn-fehr-'meh-roh, ehn-fehr-'meh-rah]
office manager, speaker or person presenting a paper at a conference	encargado/encargada de despacho, el/la ponente [ehn-kahr-'gah-doh/ehn-kahr-'gah-dah deh dehs-'pah-choh, ehl/lah poh-'nehn-teh]
optician	óptico/óptica ['ohp-tee-koh, 'ohp-tee-kah]
painter	el pintor [ehl peen-'tohr]
parish priest, priest, pastor	párroco; el cura, pastor/pastora ['pah-rroh-koh; ehl 'koo-rah pah-'stohr/pah-'stoh-rah]
park ranger	el/la guarda forestal, el/la agente forestal [ehl/lah 'gwahr-dah foh-reh-'stahl, ehl/lah ah-'hehn-teh foh-reh-'stahl]
pastry chef	pastelero/pastelera [pah-steh-'leh-roh/pah-steh-'leh-rah]
pharmacist	farmacéutico/farmacéutica [fahr-mah-'seh-oo-tee-koh, fahr-mah-'seh-oo-tee-kah]
pharmacy	farmacia [fahr-'mah-see-ah]
philosophy	filosofía [fee-loh-soh-'fee-ah]
physical therapist	el/la fisioterapeuta [ehl/lah fee-see-oh-teh-rah-peh-'oo-tah]
physicist	físico/física ['fee-see-koh/'fee-see-kah]

physics	física ['fee-see-kah]
photographer	fotógrafo/fotógrafa [foh-'toh-grah-foh, foh-'toh-grah-fah]
pilot	el/la piloto [ehl/lah pee-'loh-toh]
political science	politología, ciencias políticas [poh-lee-toh-loh-'hee-ah, see-'ehn-see-ahs poh-'lee-tee-kahs]
police officer	el/la policía [ehl/lah poh-lee-'see-ah]
porter, janitor, doorman, caretaker	portero/portera [pohr-'teh-roh/pohr-'teh-rah]
postal worker	empleado/empleada de correos [ehm-pleh-'ah-doh/ehm-pleh-'ah-dah deh koh-'rreh-ohs]
pre-school/kindergarten	maestro/maestra de párvulos [mah-'eh-stroh/mah-'eh-strah deh 'pahr-voo-lohs]
professor	profesor/profesora [proh-feh-'sohr/proh-feh-'soh-rah]
psychologist	psicólogo/psicóloga [see-'koh-loh-goh/see-'koh-loh-gah]
psychology	psicología [see-koh-loh-'hee-ah]
plumber	fontanero/fontanera (*Am* plomero/plomera) [fohn-tah-'neh-roh/fohn-tah-'neh-rah (ploh-'meh-roh/ploh-'meh-rah)]
teacher	maestro/maestra [mah-'eh-stroh/mah-'eh-strah]
railway worker	ferroviario [feh-rroh-vee-'ah-ree-oh]
real estate agent	el/la agente de la propiedad immobiliaria [ehl/lah ah-'hehn-teh deh lah proh-pee-eh-'dahd ee-moh-bee-lee-'ah-ree-ah]
representative	el/la representante [ehl/lah reh-preh-sehn-'tahn-teh]
restorer	restaurador/restauradora [reh-stah-oo-rah-'dohr/reh-stah-oo-rah-'doh-rah]
retiree	el/la rentista, jubilado/jubilada [ehl/lah rehn-'tee-stah, hoo-bee-'lah-doh/hoo-bee-'lah-dah]
Romance languages	filología románica [fee-loh-loh-'hee-ah roh-'mah-nee-kah]
roofer	tejador/tejadora [teh-hah-'dohr/teh-hah-'doh-rah]

sailor	marino [mah-'ree-noh]
salesman/-woman	vendedor/vendedora [vehn-deh-'dohr/vehn-deh-'doh-rah]
school	escuela [eh-'skweh-lah]
scientist	científico/científica [see-ehn-'tee-fee-koh/see-ehn-'tee-fee-kah]
secretary	secretario/secretaria [seh-kreh-'tah-ree-oh/seh-kreh-'tah-ree-ah]
shoemaker	zapatero/zapatera [sah-pah-'teh-roh/sah-pah-'teh-rah]
skilled worker	obrero/obrera, especializado/especializada [oh-'breh-roh/oh-'breh-rah, eh-speh-see-ah-lee-'sah-doh/eh-speh-see-ah-lee-'sah-dah]
Slavic studies	eslavística [eh-slah-'vee-stee-kah]
social worker	el/la asistente social [ehl/lah ah-see-'stehn-teh soh-see-'ahl]
sociology	sociología [soh-see-oh-loh-'hee-ah]
student	el/la estudiante, alumno/alumna, colegial/colegiala [ehl/lah eh-stoo-dee-'ahn-teh, ah-'loom-noh/ah-'loom-nah, koh-leh-hee-'ahl, koh-leh-hee-'ah-lah]
studies	estudio [eh-'stoo-dee-oh]
subject	asignatura, materia [ah-seeg-nah-'too-rah, mah-'teh-ree-ah]
tailor/dressmaker, seamstress	sastre/modista ['sah-streh/moh-'dee-stah]
tax consultant	asesor/asesora fiscal [ah-seh-'sohr/ah-seh-'soh-rah fee-'skahl]
taxi driver	el/la taxista [ehl/lah tahk-'see-stah]
teacher (high school, college)/professor	profesor/profesora, docente, maestro/maestra [proh-feh-'sohr/ proh-feh-'soh-rah, ehl/lah doh-'sehn-teh, mah-'eh-stroh/mah-'eh-strah]
technical high school/college	escuela superior técnica [eh-'skweh-lah soo-peh-ree-'ohr 'tehk-nee-kah]
technician	técnico/técnica ['tehk-nee-koh/'tehk-nee-kah]
theology	teología [teh-oh-loh-'hee-ah]

tourist guide	el/la guía turístico/turística [ehl/lah 'gee-ah too-'ree-stee-koh/ too-'ree-stee-kah]
therapist	el/la terapeuta [ehl/lah teh-rah-peh-'oo-tah]
tool fitter	ajustador/ajustadora de herramientas [ah-hoo-stah-'dohr/ah-hoo-stah-'doh-rah deh eh-rrah-mee-'ehn-tahs]
translator	traductor/traductora [trah-dook-'tohr/trah-dook-'toh-rah]
university	la universidad [lah oo-nee-vehr-see-'dahd]
veterinary	veterinario/veterinaria [veh-teh-ree-'nah-ree-oh, veh-teh-ree-'nah-ree-ah]
vocational school	escuela profesional [eh-'skweh-lah proh-feh-see-oh-'nahl]
waiter/waitress	camarero/camarera [kah-mah-'reh-roh/kah-mah-'reh-rah]
watchmaker	relojero/relojera [reh-loh-'heh-roh/reh-loh-'heh-rah]
word processor	el/la perforista, procesador/procesadora de textos [ehl/lah pehr-foh-'ree-stah, proh-seh-sah-'dohr/proh-seh-sah-'doh-rah deh 'tehks-tohs]
writer	escritor/escritora [eh-skree-'tohr/eh-skree-'toh-rah]

3 On the Go
En camino

Giving Directions

Indicaciones de lugar

left	a la izquierda [ah lah ees-kee-'ehr-dah]
right	a la derecha [ah lah deh-'reh-chah]
straight ahead	todo seguido/derecho ['toh-doh seh-'gee-doh/deh-'reh-choh]
in front of	delante de [deh-'lahn-teh deh]
in back of/behind	detrás de [deh-'trahs deh]
after	después de [dehs-'pwehs deh]
next to	junto a ['hoon-toh ah]
across from	frente a, enfrente de ['frehn-teh ah, ehn-'frehn-teh deh]
here	aquí [ah-'kee]
there	ahí, allí [ah-'ee, ah-'yee]
near	cerca ['sehr-kah]
far	lejos ['leh-hohs]
street	la calle [lah 'kah-yeh]
intersection, crossing, junction	el cruce [ehl 'kroo-seh]
curve	curva ['koor-vah]

Car/Motorcycle/Bicycle

El coche/La moto(cicleta)/La bicicleta

Information	**Información**
Excuse me, how can I get to…?	Perdón, ¿cómo se va a…? [perh-'dohn, 'koh-moh seh vah ah]
Can you show me the place/the way/that on the map, please?	¿Me puede mostrar el lugar/el trayecto/eso en el mapa? [meh 'pweh-deh moh-'strahr ehl loo-'gahr/ehl trah-'yehk-toh ehn ehl 'mah-pah]

Monument

Scenic
View

Hotel,
Restaurant
"Parador"

Drinking
Water

State-run
Hotel or
"Parador"

Lane for
Slow-moving
Traffic

Camping

Stop

I. Parking
prohibited
on the right
side of the
the street
on odd-
numbered
days

National
Highway
No. 110
Km. No. 287

No Honking

II. Parking
prohibited
on the left
side of the
the street
on even-
numbered
days.

How far is it? | ¿A qué distancia está? [ah keh dee-'stahn-see·ah eh-'stah]

Excuse me, is this the road to…? | Perdón, señora/señorita/señor, ¿es ésta la carretera de…? [pehr-'dohn, seh-'nyoh-rah/seh-nyoh-'ree-tah/seh-'nyohr, ehs 'eh-stah lah kah-rrreh-'teh-rah deh]

How do I get to the…expressway? | ¿Cómo se va a la autopista de…? ['koh-moh seh vah ah lah ow-toh-'pee-stah deh]

Straight ahead until you get to... Then... | Todo seguido (*Am* derecho) hasta… Luego… ['toh-doh seh-'gee-doh (deh-'reh-choh) 'ah-stah 'lweh-goh]

at the light | en el semáforo [ehn ehl seh-'mah-foh-roh]

at the first corner | en la primera esquina [ehn lah pree-'meh-rah eh-'skee-nah]

turn left/right. | tuerza (*Am* doble) a la izquierda/derecha. ['twehr-sah ('doh-bleh) ah lah ees-kee-'ehr-dah/deh-'reh-chah]

Follow the signs. | Siga los letreros. ['see-gah lohs leh-'treh-rohs]

Is there a road with less traffic to…? | ¿Hay también una carretera con poco tráfico a…? ['ah·ee tahm-bee-'ehn 'oo-nah kah-rrreh-'teh-rah kohn 'poh-koh 'trah-fee-koh ah]

You're on the wrong road. Go back to... | Se ha equivocado de camino. Tiene que volver hasta… [seh ah eh-kee-voh-'kah-doh deh kah-'mee-noh. Tee-'eh-neh keh vohl-'vehr 'ah-stah]

At the Service Station

En la estación de servicio/gasolinera

Where's the nearest service/gas station, please? | ¿Dónde está la estación de servicio más cercana, por favor? ['dohn-deh eh-'stah lah eh-stah-see-'ohn deh sehr-'vee-see·oh mahs sehr-'kah-nah, pohr fah-'vohr]

...liters of...
regular.

super.
diesel.

...unleaded/leaded.

...litros de... ['lee-trohs deh]
gasolina normal. [gah-soh-'lee-nah nohr-'mahl]
súper. ['soo-pehr]
diesel. [dee-eh-'sehl]

sin plomo/con plomo. [seen 'ploh-moh/kohn 'ploh-moh]

Fill it up, please.

Lleno, por favor. ['yeh-noh, pohr fah-'vohr]

Please check...

the oil.

the tire pressure.

¿Quiere comprobar... [kee-'eh-reh kohm-proh-'bahr]
el nivel del aceite? [ehl nee-'vehl dehl ah-'seh·ee-teh]
la presión de las ruedas? [lah preh-see-'ohn deh lahs roo-'eh-dahs]

Please check the radiator water, please.

Controle también el agua del radiador, por favor. [kohn-'troh-leh tahm-bee-'ehn ehl 'ah-gwah dehl rah-dee-ah-'dohr, pohr fah-'vohr]

Can you change the oil, please?

¿Puede cambiarme el aceite? ['pweh-deh kahm-bee-'ahr-meh ehl ah-'seh·ee-teh]

Can you wash the car?

¿Puede usted lavarme el coche? ['pweh-deh oo-'stehd lah-'vahr-meh ehl 'koh-cheh]

I need a road map of the area, please.

Quisiera un mapa de esta zona. [kee-see-'eh-rah oon 'mah-pah deh 'eh-stah 'zoh-nah]

Where's the bathroom, please?

¿Dónde están los servicios, por favor? ['dohn-deh eh-'stahn lohs sehr-'vee-see·ohs, pohr fah-'vohr]

Parking

Is there a parking lot near here?

Aparcamiento

Perdón, señora/señor, ¿hay algún sitio para aparcar por aquí cerca? [pehr-'dohn, seh-'nyoh-rah,/seh-'nyohr, 'ah·ee ahl-'goon 'see-tee-oh 'pah-rah ah-pahr-'kahr pohr ah-'kee 'sehr-kah]

Can I park here?	¿Puedo dejar el coche aquí? ['pweh-doh deh-'hahr ehl 'koh-cheh ah-'kee]
Could you give me some change for the parking meter?	¿Podría usted cambiarme… pesetas para el parquímetro? [poh-'dree-ah oo-'stehd kahm-bee-'ahr-meh peh-'seh-tahs 'pah-rah ehl pahr-'kee-meh-troh]
Is there a parking attendant?	¿Es un estacionamiento vigilado? [ehs oon eh-stah-see·oh-nah-mee-'ehn-toh vee-hee-'lah-doh]
I'm sorry, we're full.	Lo siento, está todo completo. [loh see-'ehn-toh, eh-'stah 'toh-doh kohm-'pleh-toh]
How long can I park here?	¿Cuánto tiempo se puede aparcar aquí? ['kwahn-toh tee-'ehm-poh seh 'pweh-deh ah-pahr-'kahr ah-'kee]
How much is it to park for …	¿Cuál es el precio del aparcamiento por [kwahl ehs ehl 'preh-see·oh dehl ah-pahr-kah-mee-'ehn-toh pohr]
an hour? a day? a night?	una hora? ['oo-nah 'oh-rah] un día? [oon 'dee-ah] una noche? ['oo-nah 'noh-cheh]
Is the parking lot open all night?	¿Está abierto el aparcamiento toda la noche? [eh-'stah ah-bee-'ehr-toh ehl ah-pahr-kah-mee-'ehn-toh 'toh-dah lah 'noh-cheh]

Car Trouble

Una avería

My car broke down./ I have a flat tire.	Tengo una avería/una rueda pinchada. ['tehn-goh 'oo-nah ah-veh-'ree-ah/'oo-nah roo-'eh-dah peen-'chah-dah]
My car/motorcycle registration number is...	La matrícula de mi coche/moto es… [lah mah-'tree-koo-lah deh mee 'koh-cheh/'moh-toh ehs]

Could you send a mechanic/a tow truck?	¿Pueden ustedes enviarme un mecánico/un coche-grúa? ['pweh-dehn oo-'steh-dehs ehn-vee-'ahr-me oon meh-'kah-nee-koh/oon 'koh-cheh-'groo-ah]
Could I borrow some gas, please?	¿Podría usted darme un poco de gasolina, por favor? [poh-'dree-ah oo-'stehd 'dahr-meh oon 'poh-koh deh gah-soh-'lee-nah, pohr fah-'vohr]
Could you help me change the tire, please?	¿Podría usted ayudarme a cambiar la rueda? [poh-'dree-ah oo-'stehd ah-yoo-'dahr-meh ah kahm-bee-'ahr lah roo-'eh-dah]
Could you tow me/take me to the nearest garage/service station?	¿Puede usted remolcarme/llevarme hasta el taller más próximo/la estación de servicio más próxima? ['pweh-deh oo-'stehd reh-mohl-'kahr-meh/yeh-'vahr-meh 'ah-stah ehl tah-'yehr mahs 'prohk-see-moh/lah eh-stah-see-'ohn deh sehr-'vee-see·oh mahs 'prohk-see-mah]

At the Auto Repair Shop / En el taller de reparaciones

Is there a garage near here?	Perdón, señor/señora/señorita, ¿hay algún taller por aquí cerca? [pehr-'dohn, seh-'nyoh-rah/seh-nyoh-'ree-tah/seh-'nyohr, 'ah·ee ahl-'goon tah-'yehr pohr ah-'kee 'sehr-kah]
Can you come with me/tow me?	¿Puede usted venir conmigo/remolcarme? ['pweh-deh oo-'stehd veh-'neer kohn-'mee-goh/reh-mohl-'kahr-meh]
My car won't start.	Mi coche no arranca. [mee 'koh-cheh noh ah-'rrahn-kah]
Do you know what the problem is?	¿Sabe usted a qué se debe? ['sah-beh oo-'stehd ah keh seh 'deh-beh]

There's something wrong with the motor.

El motor no funciona bien. [ehl moh-'tohr noh foonk-see-'oh-nah 'bee·ehn]

The brakes are not working well.

Los frenos no funcionan bien. [lohs 'freh-nohs noh foonk-see-'oh-nahn 'bee·ehn]

  …are damaged

  …están estropeado/s. [eh-'stahn eh-stroh-peh-'ah-dohs]

The car's leaking oil.

El coche pierde aceite. [ehl 'koh-cheh pee-'ehr-deh ah-'seh·ee-teh]

Could you take a look?

¿Puede usted mirar, por favor? ['pweh-deh oo-'stehd mee-'rahr, pohr fah-'vohr]

Change the spark plugs, please.

Cambie las bujías, por favor. ['kahm-bee-eh lahs boo-'hee-ahs, pohr fah-'vohr]

Do you have the parts for this model?

¿Tienen ustedes piezas de recambio (especiales) para este coche? [tee-'eh-nehn oo-'steh-dehs pee-'eh-sahs deh reh-'kahm-bee·oh (eh-speh-see-'ah-lehs) 'pah-rah 'eh-steh 'koh-cheh]

Just fix what's absolutely necessary, please.

Haga sólo las reparaciones estrictamente necesarias. ['ah-gah 'soh-loh lahs reh-pah-rah-see-'oh-nehs eh-streek-tah-'mehn-teh neh-seh-'sah-ree·ahs]

When will the car/ motorcycle be ready?

¿Cuándo estará arreglado el coche/arreglada la moto? ['kwahn-doh eh-stah-'rah ah-rreh-'glah-doh ehl 'koh-cheh/ah-rreh-'glah-dah lah 'moh-toh]

How much is it going to be?

¿Cuánto costará? ['kwahn-toh koh-stah-'rah]

A Traffic Accident

Un accidente de carretera

There's been an accident.

Ha habido un accidente. [ah ah-'bee-doh oon ahk-see-'dehn-teh]

Please call…

Llame enseguida… ['yah-meh ehn seh-'gee-dah]

an ambulance.

una ambulancia. ['oo-nah ahm-boo-'lahn-see-ah]

the police.

a la policía. [ah lah poh-lee-'see-ah]

the fire department.

a los bomberos. [ah lohs bohm-'beh-rohs]

Can you take care of the injured?

¿Puede usted ocuparse de los heridos? ['pweh-deh oo-'stehd oh-koo-'pahr-seh deh lohs eh-'ree-dohs]

Do you have a first aid kit?

¿Tiene usted botiquín de urgencia? [tee-'eh-neh oo-'stehd boh-tee-'keen deh oor-'hehn-see-ah]

It was my/your fault.

Ha sido por mi culpa/por su culpa. [ah 'see-doh pohr mee 'kool-pah/pohr soo 'kool-pah]

You…
ignored the right of way.

Usted… [oo-'stehd]
no ha respetado la preferencia. [noh ah reh-speh-'tah-doh lah preh-feh-'rehn-see·ah]

Weekdays from 9 A.M. to 8 P.M.
Parking Time Limited.
Parking Disc Required

Danger
of Fire

Except
Buses

cut in on the turn.

ha cortado la curva. [ah kohr-'tah-doh lah 'koor-vah]

did not signal when you changed lanes.

ha cambiado de carril sin poner el indicador de dirección. [ah kahm-bee-'ah-doh deh kah-'rreel seen poh-'nehr ehl een-dee-kah-'dohr deh dee-rehk-see-'ohn]

You…
were going too fast.

Usted… [oo-'stehd]
iba demasiado deprisa. ['ee-bah deh-mah-see-'ah-doh deh 'pree-sah]

were tailgating me.

iba demasiado cerca. ['ee-bah deh-mah-see-'ah-doh 'sehr-kah]

ran a red light.

ha pasado con el semáforo rojo. [ah pah-'sah-doh kohn ehl seh-'mah-foh-roh 'roh-hoh]

I was doing…kilometers an hour.

Yo iba a…kilómetros por hora. [yoh 'ee-bah ah kee-'loh-meh-trohs pohr 'oh-rah]

Should we call the police or should we settle this among ourselves?

¿Llamamos a la policía o lo arreglamos entre nosotros? [yah-'mah-mohs ah lah poh-lee-'see-ah oh loh ah-rreh-'glah-mohs 'ehn-treh noh-'soh-trohs]

My insurance company will take care of the damage.

Mi seguro se encargará de los daños. [mee seh-'goo-roh seh ehn-kahr-gah-'rah deh lohs 'dah-nyohs]

Here's my address and my insurance number.

Aquí tiene mi dirección y el número de la póliza del seguro. [ah-'kee tee-'eh-neh mee dee-rehk-see-'ohn y ehl 'noo-meh-roh deh lah 'poh-lee-sah dehl seh-'goo-roh]

Could I have your name and address/the name and address of your insurance comany?

¿Puede usted darme su nombre y dirección/el nombre y dirección de su compañía de seguros? ['pweh-deh oo-'stehd 'dahr-meh soo 'nohm-breh ee dee-rehk-see-'ohn/ehl 'nohm-breh y dee-rehk-see-'ohn deh soo kohm-pah-'nyee-ah deh seh-'goo-rohs]

Are you willing to be a witness?

¿Estaría usted dispuesto/dispuesta a declarar como testigo? [eh-stah-'ree-ah dees-'pweh-stoh/dees-'pweh-stah ah deh-klah-'rahr 'koh-moh teh-'stee-goh]

Thank you very much for your help.

Muchas gracias por su ayuda. ['moo-chahs 'grah-see·ahs pohr soo ah-'yoo-dah]

Car/Motorcycle/Bicycle Rental

Alquiler de automóviles/motos/ bicicletas

I'd like to rent for…days/ weeks…

Quisiera alquilar por…días/una semana… [kee-see-'eh-rah ahl-kee-'lahr pohr 'dee-ahs/'oo-nah seh-'mah-nah]

a car (four-wheel-drive vehicle).

un coche (todo terreno). [oon 'koh-cheh ('toh-doh teh-'rreh-noh)]

a motorcycle/motor-assisted bicycle/light motorcycle with kickstarter/scooter.

una moto/un ciclomotor/un velomotor/un scooter. ['oo-nah 'moh-toh/oon see-kloh-moh-'tohr/ oon veh-loh-moh-'tohr/oon skoo-'tehr]

a bicycle.

una bicicleta. ['oo-nah bee-see-'kleh-tah]

What is the daily/ weekly rate?	¿Qué tarifa se paga por un día/por una semana? [keh tah-'ree-fah seh 'pah-gah pohr oon 'dee-ah/pohr 'oo-nah seh-'mah-nah]
How much do you charge per kilometer?	¿Cuánto se paga por cada kilómetro de recorrido? ['kwahn-toh seh 'pah-gah pohr 'kah-dah kee-'loh-meh-troh deh reh-koh-'rree-doh]
How much is the deposit?	¿A cuánto asciende la fianza? [ah 'kwahn-toh ah-see-'ehn-deh lah fee-'ahn-sah]
I'll take the...	Me llevo el.../la... [meh 'yeh-voh ehl/lah]
Does the vehicle have comprehensive insurance?	¿Está el vehículo asegurado a todo riesgo? [eh-'stah ehl veh-'ee-koo-loh ah-seh-goo-'rah-doh ah 'toh-doh ree-'ehs-goh]
Would you like supple-mentary insurance?	¿Desea usted un seguro comple-mentario? [deh-'seh-ah oo-'stehd oon seh-'goo-roh kohm-pleh-mehn-'tah-ree-oh]
Can I see your driver's license?	¿Puedo ver su carnet de con-ducir? ['pweh-doh vehr soo kahr-'neht deh kohn-doo-'seer]
Can I have the car right now?	¿Puedo llevarme ahora mismo el coche? ['pweh-doh yeh-'vahr-meh ah-'oh-rah 'mees-moh ehl 'koh-cheh]
Is it possible to drop off the car/motorcycle at...?	¿Es posible entregar el coche/la moto en...? [ehs poh-'see-bleh ehn-treh-'gahr ehl 'koh-cheh/lah 'moh-toh ehn]

Signs and Information

accidente en cadena	Multiple Car Accident
aduana	Customs
alta tensión	High Voltage
aparcamiento, estaciona-miento (*Am* playa de estacionamiento, parqueo)	Parking Lot

atención	Attention
bajada peligrosa	Dangerous Descent
calzada en mal estado	Bumpy Road
callejón sin salida	Dead End
cambio de pista	Lane Change
cerrado al tráfico	Closed to Traffic
circulación doble	Two-Way Traffic
circunvalación	Traffic Circle
conducir por la derecha	Drive on the Right
congestión del tráfico, embotellamiento	Traffic Jam
cruce	Crossing
curva peligrosa	Dangerous Curve
choque	Crash
dejar libre la salida	Keep Clear of Exit
desembocadura de una calle/carretera	Road/Highway Junction
desviación	Detour
dirección única	One Way
disco de estacionamiento limitado	Limited Parking Sign
disminuir la marcha	Slow Down, Reduce Speed
escuela	School
estacionamiento limitado	Limited Parking
estrechamiento de la calzada	Road Narrows
fin de la prohibición de estaciona	End No Parking Zone
garaje-aparcamiento (*Am* garaje)	Garage
gravilla	Gravel
hospital	Hospital
limitación de peso	Weight Limit
límite de velocidad	Speed Limit
niños	Children
obras	Road Work
paso a nivel sin barrera	Railroad Crossing (No Gates)
paso de peatones/de cebra	Pedestrian Crossing
paso subterráneo	Underground Crossing

peligro	Danger
pista de bicicletas	Bicycle Lane
precaución	Caution
principiante	Beginner
prohibido adelantar	No Passing
prohibido aparcar	No Parking
prohibido detenerse	No Stopping
prohibido el tráfico (*Am* tránsito)	No Vehicles Allowed
prohibido girar a la derecha	No Right Turn
prohibida la entrada	Do Not Enter
prohibido virar	No Turns
puente	Bridge
respetar la precedencia	Yield
salida	Exit
salida de la autopista	Highway Exit
semáforo	Traffic Light
tomar la fila de la izquierda	Merge Left
tráfico (*Am* tránsito) giratorio	Traffic Circle
trayecto resbaladizo	Slippery Road
túnel	Tunnel
zona de peatones	Pedestrian Area

Word List: Car/Motorcycle/Bicycle

to accelerate, to speed, to step on the gas	acelerar [ah-seh-leh-'rahr]
air filter	filtro de aire ['feel-troh deh 'ah·ee-reh]
air pump	bomba de aire ['bohm-bah deh 'ah·ee-reh]
alarm system	el sistema de alarma [ehl see-'steh-mah deh ah-'lahr-mah]
antifreeze	el anticongelante [ehl ahn-tee-kohn-heh-'lahn-teh]
automatic shift	cambio automático ['kahm-bee·oh ow-toh-'mah-tee-koh)]
axle	el eje [ehl 'eh-heh]

back axle	el eje trasero [ehl 'eh-heh trah-'seh-roh]
backpedal brake (bicycle)	freno de contrapedal ['freh-noh deh kohn-trah-peh-'dahl]
ball bearing	rodamiento a bolas [roh-dah-mee-'ehn-toh ah 'boh-lahs]
bell	el timbre [ehl 'teem-breh]
bicycle, bike	bicicleta [bee-see-'kleh-tah]
bicycle frame	cuadro/armazón cuadricular de la bicicleta ['kwah-droh/ahr-mah-'sohn kwah-dree-koo-'lahr deh lah bee-see-'kleh-tah]
bicycle seat/saddle	sillín (de bicicleta) [see-'yeen (deh bee-see-'kleh-tah)]
bicycle stand	el soporte para bicicletas [ehl soh-'pohr-teh 'pah-rah bee-see-'kleh-tahs]
bicycle tire	rueda/neumático de bicicleta [roo-'eh-dah/neh-oo-'mah-tee-koh deh bee-see-'kleh-tah]
bicycle tool bag	bolsa/cartera de herramientas (de bicicleta) ['bohl-sah/kahr-'teh-rah deh eh-rrah-mee-'ehn-tahs (deh bee-see-'kleh-tah)]
bike lane	pista para bicicletas ['pee-stah 'pah-rah bee-see-'kleh-tahs]
to blind	deslumbrar (*Am* encandilar) [dehs-loom-'brahr (ehn-kahn-dee-'lahr)]
blinker, turn signal	el intermitente [ehl een-tehr-mee-'tehn-teh]
body	carrocería [kah-rroh-seh-'ree-ah]
body (*car*)	casco, carrocería ['kah-skoh, kah-rroh-seh-'ree-ah]
brake	freno ['freh-noh]
to brake	frenar [freh-'nahr]
brake fluid	líquido de freno ['lee-kee-doh deh 'freh-noh]
brake lights	las luces de frenado [lahs 'loo-sehs deh freh-'nah-doh]
brake pedal	pedal de freno [peh-'dahl deh 'freh-noh]
breakdown	avería [ah-veh-'ree-ah]
broken	roto ['roh-toh]

bumper	el parachoques (*Am* el paragolpes) [ehl pah-rah-'choh-kehs (ehl pah-rah-'gohl-pehs]
cable	el cable [ehl 'kah-bleh]
car alarm	(dispositivo de) alarma [(dee-spoh-see-'tee-voh deh) ah-'lahr-mah]
carburetor	el carburador [ehl kahr-boo-rah-'dohr]
car motor fan	el ventilador (del coche) [ehl vehn-tee-lah-'dohr (dehl 'koh-cheh)]
car papers	documentos [doh-koo-'mehn-tohs]
car wash	lavado del coche [lah-'vah-doh dehl 'koh-cheh]
chain	cadena [kah-'deh-nah]
clutch	el embrague, palanca de embrague [ehl ehm-'brah-geh, pah-'lahn-kah deh ehm-'brah-geh]
comprehensive risk insurance	seguro a todo riesgo [seh-'goo-roh ah 'toh-doh ree-'ehs-goh]
crossing light	la luz de cruce [lah loos deh 'kroo-seh]
cycle hub	cubo (de bicicleta), buje ['koo-boh (deh bee-see-'kleh-tah), 'boo-heh]
cylinder	cilindro [see-'leen-droh]
cylinder head	culata, tapa del cilindro [koo-'lah-tah, 'tah-pah dehl see-'leen-droh]
danger sign	la señal de situación de peligro, triángulo de peligro [lah seh-'nyahl deh see-too-ah-see-'ohn deh peh-'lee-groh, tree-'ahn-goo-loh deh peh-'lee-groh]
destination sign, route sign	el indicador de camino [ehl een-dee-kah-'dohr deh kah-'mee-noh]
to dim the headlights	bajar las luces [bah-'hahr lahs 'loo-sehs]
detour	la desviación [lah dehs-vee-ah-see-'ohn]
distributor	el distribuidor, el delco [ehl dee-stree-boo-ee-'dohr, ehl 'dehl-koh]
driver's license	permiso/el carnet de conducir [pehr-'mee-soh/ehl kahr-'neht deh kohn-doo-'seer]
dynamo	la dínamo [lah 'dee-nah-moh]

emergency road service	servicio de ayuda al auto-movilista [sehr-'vee-see-oh deh ah-'yoo-dah ahl ow-toh-moh-vee-'lee-stah]
emergency telephone	el poste de socorro [ehl 'poh-steh deh soh-'koh-rroh]
exhaust pipe	tubo (*Am* caño) de escape ['too-boh ('kah-nyoh) deh eh-'skah-peh]
failure, fault, breakdown	avería, defecto [ah-veh-'ree-ah, deh-'fehk-toh]
fan belt, V-belt	correa trapezoidal (*Am* correa en V) [koh-'rreh-ah trah-peh-soh-ee-'dahl (koh-'rreh-ah ehn V)]
fender	el guardabarros (*Am* el guardafangos) [ehl gwahr-dah-'bah-rrohs (ehl gwahr-dah-'fahn-gohs)]
flat	pinchazo, el reventón [peen-'chah-soh, ehl reh-vehn-'tohn]
fine, ticket	multa ['mool-tah]
first gear	primera (marcha) [pree-'meh-rah ('mahr-chah)]
flashing signal	el avisador luminoso [ehl ah-vee-sah-'dohr loo-mee-'noh-soh]
foot brake	freno de pie ['freh-noh deh 'pee-eh]
four-lane	de cuatro pistas [deh 'kwah-troh 'pee-stahs]
four-wheel drive	la tracción a las cuatro ruedas [lah trahk-see-'ohn ah lahs 'kwah-troh roo-'eh-dahs]
freeway, thruway	autopista [ow-toh-'pee-stah]
freeway tolls	el peaje [ehl peh-'ah-heh]
front axle	el eje delantero [ehl 'eh-heh deh-lahn-'teh-roh]
front wheel	rueda delantera [roo-'eh-dah deh-lahn-'teh-rah]
front-wheel drive	la tracción delantera [lah trahk-see-'ohn deh-lahn-'teh-rah]
fuel injector	bomba de inyección ['bohm-bah deh een-yehk-see-'ohn]
fuse	el fusible [ehl foo-'see-bleh]
gas	gasolina [gah-soh-'lee-nah]
gasket	junta ['hoon-tah]

gas pedal, accelerator	el pedal del gas [ehl peh-'dahl dehl gahs]
gas pump	bomba de gasolina ['bohm-bah deh gah-soh-'lee-nah]
gas station, service station	gasolinera, la estación de servicio [gah-soh-lee-'neh-rah, lah eh-stah-see-'ohn deh sehr-'vee-see·oh]
gas tank	el tanque (*m*), depósito, el bidón (*Am* el tanque) de gasolina [ehl 'tahn-keh, deh-'poh-see-toh, ehl bee-'dohn (ehl 'tahn-keh) deh gah-soh-'lee-nah]
gear	marcha, la velocidad ['mahr-chah, lah veh-loh-see-'dahd]
gearbox	caja de cambio ['kah-hah deh 'kahm-bee·oh]
gears	cambio de marchas ['kahm-bee·oh deh 'mahr-chahs]
gearshift	palanca de cambio [pah-'lahn-kah deh 'kahm-bee·oh]
hand brake	freno de mano, palanca de freno ['freh-noh deh 'mah-noh, [pah-'lahn-kah deh 'freh-noh]
handlebar	el manillar [ehl mah-nee-'yahr]
headlamp	faro ['fah-roh]
headlights	las luces delanteras [lahs 'loo-sehs deh-lahn-'teh-rahs]
heating	la calefacción [lah kah-leh-fahk-see-'ohn]
highway	carretera [kah-rreh-'teh-rah]
to hitchhike	hacer autostop [ah-'sehr ow-toh-'stohp]
hitchhiker	el/la autostopista [ehl/lah ow-toh-'pee-stah]
hood	el capó, capota [ehl kah-'poh, kah-'poh-tah]
horn	bocina, el claxon [boh-'see-nah, ehl klahk-'sohn]
horsepower (HP)	caballos de fuerza (CV) [kah-'bah-yohs deh 'fwehr-sah (CV)]
ignition	encendido (*Am* la ignición) [ehn-sehn-'dee-doh (lah eeg-nee-see-'ohn)]

ignition failure	encendido defectuoso [ehn-sehn-'dee-doh deh-fehk-too-'oh-soh]
ignition key	la llave de encendido [lah 'yah-veh deh ehn-sehn-'dee-doh]
ignition lock	cerradura de contacto [seh-rrah-'doo-rah deh kohn-'tahk-toh]
inner tube	cámara (de aire) ['kah-mah-rah (deh 'ah-ee-reh)]
insurance card	carta/tarjeta del seguro ['kahr-tah/tahr-'heh-tah dehl seh-'goo-roh]
jack	gato, el alzacoches ['gah-toh, ehl ahl-sah-'koh-chehs]
jump cable	el cable de ayuda para el arranque [ehl 'kah-bleh deh ah-'yoo-dah 'pah-rah ehl ah-'rrahn-keh]
to knock (*motor*)	golpetear [gohl-peh-teh-'ahr]
lane	pista [pee-stah]
lever	palanca [pah-'lahn-kah]
license plate	placa de matrícula [('plah-kah deh) mah-'tree-koo-lah]
light motorcycle with kickstarter	el velomotor [ehl veh-loh-moh-'tohr]
limited risk insurance	seguro contra riesgos parciales [seh-'goo-roh 'kohn-trah ree-'ehs-gohs pahr-see-'ah-lehs]
money belt	riñonera [ree-nyoh-'neh-rah]
motor	el motor [ehl moh-'tohr]
motor-assisted bicycle	el ciclomotor [ehl see-kloh-moh-'tohr]
motorcycle	la moto(cicleta) [lah 'moh-toh (see-'kleh-tah)]
mountain bike	bicicleta todoterreno [bee-see-'kleh-tah toh-doh-teh-'rreh-noh]
mudguard	el guardabarros (*Am* el guardafangos) [ehl gwahr-dah-'bah-rrohs (ehl gwahr-dah-'fahn-gohs)]
neutral	punto muerto ['poon-toh 'mwehr-toh]
nozzle	tobera [toh-'beh-rah]
nut, wheel nut (bicycle)	tuerca ['twehr-kah]
octane	número de octanos, el octanaje ['noo-meh-roh deh ohk-'tah-nohs, ehl ohk-tah-'nah-heh]
oil	el aceite [ehl ah-'seh·ee-teh]
to oil, to lubricate	engrasar [ehn-grah-'sahr]

oil change	cambio de aceite ['kahm-bee·oh deh ah-'seh·ee·teh]
oil stick	varilla indicadora del nivel de aceite [vah-'ree-yah een-dee-kah-'doh-rah dehl nee-'vehl deh ah-'seh·ee·teh]
outer case, cover	cubierta [koo-bee-'ehr-tah]
outer tire	cubierta (de neumático) [koo-bee-'ehr-tah (deh neh-oo-'mah-tee-koh)]
parking light	la luz de población/esta-cionamiento [lah loos deh poh-blah-see-'ohn/eh-stah-see·oh-nah-mee-'ehn-toh]
parking meter	parquímetro [pahr-'kee-meh-troh]
parking sign	disco de estacionamiento ['dee-skoh deh eh-stah-see·oh-nah-mee-'ehn-toh]
pedal	el pedal [ehl peh-'dahl]
pedal bearing	el cojinete de pedal [ehl koh-hee-'neh-teh deh peh-'dahl]
per thousand	por mil [pohr meel]
piston	el pistón (m) [ehl pee-'stohn]
porter	mozo ['moh-soh]
puncture repair kit	los parches y el pegamento [lohs 'pahr-chehs ee ehl peh-gah-'mehn-toh]
racing bike	bicicleta de carreras [bee-see-'kleh-tah deh kah-'rreh-rahs]
radar speed check	el control de radar [ehl kohn-'trohl deh rah-'dahr]
radiator	el radiador [ehl rah-dee-ah-'dohr]
radiator water	(el) agua del radiador [(ehl) 'ah-gwah dehl rah-dee-ah-'dohr]
raincoat	capa de agua, impermeable ['kah-pah deh 'ah-gwah, eem-pehr-meh-'ah-bleh]
rear wheel	rueda trasera [roo-'eh-dah trah-'seh-rah]
rearview mirror	el (espejo) retrovisor [ehl (eh-'speh-hoh) reh-troh-vee-'sohr]
rear-wheel drive	la tracción trasera [lah trahk-see-'ohn trah-'seh-rah]
reflector	el reflector [ehl reh-flehk-'tohr]
to release the clutch	desembragar [dehs-ehm-brah-'gahr]

rest area	el albergue de carretera [ehl ahl-'behr-geh deh kah-rreh-'teh-rah]
reverse	marcha atrás ['mahr-chah ah-'trahs]
rim	llanta [yahn-'tah]
road light	la luz de carretera [lah loos deh kah-rreh-'teh-rah]
road work	(las) obras [lahs 'oh-brahs]
saddle	el sillín [ehl see-'yeen]
safety belt	el cinturón de seguridad [ehl seen-too-'rohn deh seh-goo-ree-'dahd]
sandpaper	lija ['lee-hah]
scooter	el escúter, el scooter [ehl eh-'skoo-tehr, ehl skoo-'tehr]
screw	tornillo [tohr-'nee-yoh]
screwdriver	el destornillador [ehl dehs-tohr-nee-yah-'dohr]
screw wrench	la llave de tuercas [lah 'yah-veh deh 'twehr-kahs]
shock absorber	el amortiguador [ehl ah-mohr-tee-gwah-'dohr]
short circuit	cortocircuito [kohr-toh-seer-'koo·ee-toh]
sliding roof	techo corredizo ['teh-choh koh-rreh-'dee-soh]
snow tires	neumáticos de invierno [neh-oo-'mah-tee-kohs deh een-vee-'ehr-noh]
socket wrench	la llave de tubo [lah 'yah-veh deh 'too-boh]
spare parts	piezas de recambio [pee-'eh-sahs deh reh-'kahm-bee·oh]
spare tire	rueda de repuesto [roo-'eh-dah deh reh-'pweh-stoh]
spark plug	bujía [boo-'hee-ah]
speedometer	el cuentakilómetros, velocímetro [ehl kwehn-tah-kee-'loh-meh-trohs, veh-loh-'see-meh-troh]
spoke	rayo ['rah-yoh]
starting motor	el motor de arranque [ehl moh-'tohr deh ah-'rrahn-keh]
state highway	autovía [ow-toh-'vee-ah]
steering wheel	el volante [ehl voh-'lahn-teh]
taillights	las luces traseras [lahs 'loo-sehs trah-'seh-rahs]

three-speed/ten-speed bike	bicicleta de tres/diez marchas [bee-see-'kleh-tah deh trehs/dee-'ez 'mahr-chahs]
tire	rueda, neumático (*Am* llanta) [roo-'eh-dah, 'neh-oo-'mah-tee-koh, 'yahn-tah]
toll	el peaje (*m*) [ehl peh-'ah-heh]
tools	herramientas [eh-rrah-mee-'ehn-tahs]
to tow	remolcar [reh-mohl-'kahr]
towing cable	el cable de remolque [ehl 'kah-bleh deh reh-'mohl-keh]
towing service	servicio de remolque [sehr-'vee-see·oh deh reh-'mohl-keh]
towtruck	grúa, el coche-grúa ['groo-ah, ehl 'koh-cheh 'groo-ah]
traffic jam	atasco, embotellamiento [ah-'tah-skoh, ehm-boh-teh-yah-mee-'ehn-toh]
traffic lights	semáforo, disco [seh-'mah-foh-roh, 'dee-skoh]
trailer	el remolque [ehl reh-'mohl-keh]
truck	el camión [ehl kah-mee-'ohn]
trunk	el portamaletas (*Am* el baúl) [ehl pohr-tah-mah-'leh-tahs (ehl bah-'ool)]
to turn	torcer [tohr-'sehr]
valve	válvula ['vahl-voo-lah]
wheel	rueda [roo-'eh-dah]
windshield	el parabrisas [ehl pah-rah-'bree-sahs]
windshield wiper	el limpiaparabrisas [ehl leem-pee·ah-pah-rah-'bree-sahs]
workshop	el taller [ehl tah-'yehr]

Airplane
Avión

At the Travel Agency/ At the Airport	**En la agencia de viajes/ En el aeropuerto**

Where's the...check-in counter/counter?

¿Dónde está la facturación/ el mostrador de la compañía...? ['dohn-deh eh-'stah lah fahk-too-rah-see-'ohn/ehl moh-strah-'dohr deh lah kohm-pah-'nyee-ah]

When's the next flight to...?

¿A qué hora sale el próximo avión para...? [ah keh 'oh-rah 'sah-leh ehl 'prohk-see-moh ah-vee-'ohn 'pah-rah]

I'd like to make a one way/ round-trip reservation to...

Quisiera reservar un vuelo de de ida/de ida y vuelta a... [kee-see-'eh-rah reh-sehr-'vahr oon 'vweh-loh deh 'ee-dah/deh 'ee-dah ee 'vwehl-tah ah]

Are there still seats available?

¿Hay todavía plazas libres? ['ah·ee toh-dah-'vee-ah 'plah-sahs 'lee-brehs]

Are there charter flights, too?

¿Hay también vuelos chárter? ['ah·ee tahm-bee-'ehn 'vweh-lohs 'chahr-tehr]

How much is the economy/ first class fare?

¿Cuánto cuesta el vuelo en clase turista/en primera clase? ['kwahn-toh 'kweh-stah ehl 'vweh-loh ehn 'klah-se too-'ree-stah/ehn pree-'meh-rah 'klah-seh]

How much baggage can I take with me?

¿A cuántos kilos de equipaje da derecho el billete (*Am* el boleto)? [ah 'kwahn-tohs 'kee-lohs deh eh-kee-'pah-heh dah deh-'reh-choh ehl bee-'yeh-teh (ehl boh-'leh-toh)]

How much is the excess baggage per kilogram?	¿Cuánto se paga por cada kilo de exceso de peso? ['kwahn-toh seh 'pah-gah pohr 'kah-dah 'kee-loh deh ehk-'seh-soh deh 'peh-soh]
I'd like to cancel/change the flight.	Quisiera anular este vuelo/cambiar el vuelo. [kee-see-'eh-rah ah-noo-'lahr 'eh-steh 'vweh-loh/kahm-bee-'ahr ehl 'vweh-loh]
When do I have to be at the airport?	¿A qué hora tengo que estar en el aeropuerto? [ah keh 'oh-rah 'tehn-goh keh eh-'stahr ehn ehl ah·eh-roh-'pwehr-toh]
Where's the information office/the waiting room?	¿Dónde está la oficina de información/la sala de espera? ['dohn-deh eh-'stah lah oh-fee-'see-nah deh een-fohr-mah-see-'ohn/lah 'sah-lah deh eh-'speh-rah]
Can I bring this as hand luggage?	¿Puedo llevar esto como equipaje de mano? ['pweh-doh yeh-'vahr 'eh-stoh 'koh-moh eh-kee-'pah-heh deh 'mah-noh]
Is the flight to…late?	¿Tiene retraso el avión a…? [tee-'eh-neh reh-'trah-soh ehl ah-vee-'ohn ah]
How late is it going to be?	¿Cuánto retraso tiene? ['kwahn-toh reh-'trah-soh tee-'eh-neh]
Has the flight from… already landed?	¿Ha aterrizado ya al avión de…? [ah ah-teh-rree-'sah-doh yah ehl ah-vee-'ohn deh]

Last call. Passengers for…, on flight number…, please go to gate…

Ultima llamada. Rogamos a los señores pasajeros con destino a, vuelo número…, que se dirijan a la salida… ['ool-tee-mah yah-'mah-dah. Roh-'gah-mohs ah lohs seh-'nyoh-rehs pah-sah-'heh-rohs kohn deh-'stee-noh ah…, 'vweh-loh 'noo-meh-roh…, keh seh dee-'ree-hahn ah lah sah-'lee-dah]

On Board

A bordo

No smoking, please. Fasten your seat belts, please.

¡Les rogamos apaguen sus cigarrillos! ¡Sujétense los cinturones de seguridad! [lehs roh-'gah-mohs ah-'pah-guen soos see-gah-'rree-yohs. Soo-'heh-tehn-seh lohs seen-too-'roh-nehs deh seh-goo-ree-'dahd]

What river/lake is that?

¿Qué río/lago es ése? [keh 'ree-oh/'lah-goh ehs 'eh-seh]

What mountain is that?

¿Qué montaña es ésa? [keh mohn-'tah-nyah ehs 'eh-sah]

Where are we now?

¿Dónde estamos ahora? ['dohn-deh eh-'stah-mohs ah-'oh-rah]

When do we land in…?

¿Cuándo aterrizamos en…? ['kwahn-doh ah-teh-rree-'sah-mohs ehn]

We'll be landing in about…minutes.

Aterrizaremos dentro de unos… minutos. [ah-teh-rree-sah-'reh-mohs 'dehn-troh deh 'oo-nohs mee-'noo-tohs]

What's the weather like in…?

¿Qué tiempo hace en…? [keh tee-'ehm-poh 'ah-seh ehn]

Arrival	**Llegada**

See also Chapter 9—Lost and Found

I can't find my luggage/ my suitcase.	No encuentro mi equipaje/mi maleta (*Am* valija). [noh ehn-'kwehn-troh mee eh-kee-'pah-heh/mee mah-'leh-tah (vah-'lee-hah)]
My luggage is missing.	Mi equipaje se ha perdido. [mee eh-kee-'pah-heh seh ah pehr-'dee-doh]
My suitcase is damaged.	Mi maleta (*Am* valija) está estropeada. [mee mah-'leh-tah (vah-'lee-hah) eh-'stah eh-stroh-peh-'ah-dah]
Where can I report it?	¿Dónde puedo reclamar? ['dohn-deh 'pweh-doh reh-klah-'mahr]
Where does the air terminal bus leave from?	¿De dónde sale el autobús para la terminal? [deh 'dohn-deh 'sah-leh ehl ow-toh-'boos 'pah-rah lah tehr-mee-'nahl]

Word List: Airplane	**See also Word List: Ship, Train**

airline	compañía aérea [kohm-pah-'nyee-ah ah-'eh-reh-ah]
airplane	el avión [ehl ah-vee-'ohn]
airplane door	puerta ['pwehr-tah]
airplane ticket	el billete (*Am* boleto) de avión [ehl bee-'yeh-teh (boh-'leh-toh) deh ah-vee-'ohn]
airport bus	el autobús del aeropuerto [ehl ow-toh-'boos dehl ah·eh-roh-'pwehr-toh]
airport tax	los derechos de aeropuerto [lohs deh-'reh-chohs dehl ah·eh-roh-'pwehr-toh]
air terminal	la terminal [lah tehr-mee-'nahl]
aisle	pasillo [pah-'see-yoh]
arrival	llegada [yeh-'gah-dah]
baggage	el equipaje [ehl eh-kee-'pah-heh]
baggage cart	carrito portaequipajes [kah-rree-toh pohr-tah-eh-kee-'pah-hehs]

baggage check-in — la facturación de equipajes [lah fahk-too-rah-see-'ohn deh eh-kee-'pah-hehs]

baggage claim — entrega de equipaje [ehn-'treh-gah deh eh-kee-'pah-heh]

boarding pass — tarjeta de embarque [tahr-'heh-tah deh ehm-'bahr-keh]

business class — la clase de negocios, la clase preferente [lah 'klah-seh deh neh-'goh-see·ohs, lah 'klah-seh preh-feh-'rehn-teh]

to cancel — anular [ah-noo-'lahr]

captain — el capitán [ehl kah-pee-'tahn]

to change the reservation/booking — cambiar el vuelo [kahm-bee-'ahr ehl 'vweh-loh]

delay — retraso [reh-'trah-soh]

charter flight — vuelo chárter ['vweh-loh 'chahr-tehr]

to check in — facturar [fahk-too-'rahr]

connection — el empalme (*train*), el enlace (*plane*) [ehl ehm-'pahl-meh, ehl ehn-'lah-seh]

crew — la tripulación [lah tree-poo-lah-see-'ohn]

destination — destino [deh-'stee-noh]

direct flight — vuelo directo ['vweh-loh dee-'rehk-toh]

domestic flight — vuelo nacional ['vweh-loh nah-see·oh-'nahl]

duty-free sale — venta libre de impuestos ['vehn-tah 'lee-breh deh eem-'pweh-stohs]

economy class — la clase económica, la clase turista [lah 'klah-seh eh-koh-'noh-mee-kah, lah 'klah-seh too-'ree-stah]

emergency chute — el tobogán de emergencia [ehl toh-boh-'gahn deh eh-mehr-'hehn-see·ah]

emergency exit — salida de emergencia [sah-'lee-dah deh eh-mehr-'hehn-see·ah]

emergency landing — el aterrizaje forzoso [ehl ah-teh-rree-'sah-heh fohr-'soh-soh]

fasten your seat belt — abrocharse el cinturón de seguridad [ah-broh-'chahr-seh ehl seen-too-'rohn deh seh-goo-ree-'dahd]

flight — vuelo ['vweh-loh]

flight attendant	auxiliar (*m/f*) de vuelo/(*f*) azafata (*Am* aeromoza) [ehl/lah owk-see-lee-'ahr deh 'vweh-loh/lah ah-sah-'fah-tah (ah-eh-roh-moh-'sah)]
flight insurance rate	tarifa de seguro de vuelo [tah-'ree-fah deh seh-'goo-roh deh 'vweh-loh]
flight route	ruta (de vuelo) ['roo-tah (deh 'vweh-loh)]
flight schedule	horario (de vuelo) [oh-'rah-ree·oh (deh 'vweh-loh)]
hand luggage, carry-on luggage	el equipaje de mano [ehl eh-kee-'pah-heh deh 'mah-noh]
helicopter	helicóptero [eh-lee-'kohp-teh-roh]
international flight	vuelo internacional ['vweh-loh een-tehr-nah-see-oh-'nahl]
jet, jet plane	el reactor, el avión a reacción [ehl reh-ahk-'tohr, ehl ah-vee-'ohn ah reh-ahk-see-'ohn]
to land	aterrizar [ah-teh-rree-'sahr]
landing	el aterrizaje [ehl ah-teh-rree-'sah-heh]
landing	el aterrizaje [ehl ah-teh-rree-'sah-heh]
last-minute flight	vuelo de última hora ['vweh-loh deh 'ool-tee-mah 'oh-rah]
life jacket	chaleco salvavidas [chah-'leh-koh sahl-vah-'vee-dahs]
line	cola ['koh-lah]
non-smokers	no fumadores [noh foo-mah-'doh-rehs]
on board	a bordo [ah 'bohr-doh]
passenger	pasajero [pah-sah-'heh-roh]
pilot	piloto [pee-'loh-toh]
regular flight	el avión de línea [ehl ah-vee-'ohn deh 'lee-neh-ah]
reservation, booking	reserva [reh-'sehr-vah]
to reserve, to book	reservar [reh-sehr-'vahr]
runway	pista ['pee-stah]
seat belt	el cinturón de seguridad [ehl seen-too-'rohn deh seh-goo-ree-'dahd]
security check	control (*m*) de seguridad [ehl kohn-'trohl deh seh-goo-ree-'dahd]
scheduled time of departure	salida regular [sah-'lee-dah reh-goo-'lahr]
smokers	fumadores [foo-mah-'doh-rehs]
stopover	escala [eh-'skah-lah]

tag	etiqueta [eh-tee-'keh-tah]
take off	el despegue (*m*) [ehl dehs-'peh-geh]
time of arrival	hora de llegada ['oh-rah deh yeh-'gah-dah]
window	ventanilla [vehn-tah-'nee-yah]
window seat	asiento junto a la/de ventanilla [ah-see-'ehn-toh 'hoon-toh ah lah/deh vehn-tah-'nee-yah]

Train
Ferrocarril/Tren

**At the Travel Agency/
At the Railroad Station**

**En la oficina de viajes/
En el estación**

A second/first class ticket to..., please.

Un billete (*Am* boleto) de segunda/de primera clase para ..., por favor. [oon bee-'yeh-teh (boh-'leh-toh) deh seh-'goon-dah/deh pree-'meh-rah 'klah-se 'pah-rah, pohr fah-'vohr]

Two round-trip tickets to..., please.

Dos billetes (*Am* boletos) de ida y vuelta a..., por favor. [dohs bee-'yeh-tehs (boh-'leh-tohs) deh 'ee-dah ee 'vwehl-tah ah, pohr fah-'vohr]

Do you have weekend discount rates?

¿Hay billetes (*Am* boletos) a precio reducido para fines de semana? ['ah·ee bee-'yeh-tehs (boh-'leh-tohs) ah 'preh-see·oh reh-doo-'see-doh 'pah-rah 'fee-nehs deh seh-'mah-nah]

Do you have discount rates for children/large families/students?

¿Hacen ustedes descuento para niños/familias numerosas/estudiantes? ['ah-sehn oo-'steh-dehs dehs-'kwehn-toh 'pah-rah 'nee-nyohs/fah-'mee-lee-ahs noo-meh-'roh-sahs/eh-stoo-dee-'ahn-tehs]

I'd like to make one reservation for the…train to…, please.

Una reserva de asiento para el tren de las…a…, por favor. ['oo-nah reh-'sehr-vah deh ah-see-'ehn-toh 'pah-rah ehl trehn de las a, pohr fah-'vohr]

A window seat?

¿Un asiento junto a la ventanilla? [oon ah-see-'ehn-toh 'hoon-toh ah lah vehn-tah-'nee-yah]

I'd like one sleeping-car ticket for the eight o'clock train to…, please.

Quisiera un billete (*Am* boleto) para el coche-cama (*Am* coche-dormitorio)/el coche-literas en el tren de las ocho a… [kee-see-'eh-rah oon bee-'yeh-teh (boh-'leh-toh) 'pah-rah ehl 'koh-cheh-'kah-mah ('koh-cheh-dohr-mee-'toh-ree·oh)/ ehl 'koh-cheh-lee-'teh-rahs ehn ehl trehn deh lahs 'oh-choh]

Is there a car train to…?

¿Hay un autotrén para…? ['ah·ee oon ow-toh-'trehn 'pah-rah]

How much is it for a car and four people?

¿Cuánto se paga por un coche con cuatro personas? ['kwahn-toh seh 'pah-gah pohr oon 'koh-cheh kohn 'kwah-troh pehr-'soh-nahs]

I'd like to check this suitcase.

Quisiera facturar esta maleta (*Am* valija). [kee-see-'eh-rah fahk-too-'rahr 'eh-stah mah-'leh-tah (vah-'lee-hah)]

Where can I check my bike?

¿Dónde puedo entregar mi bicicleta? ['dohn-deh 'pweh-doh ehn-treh-'gahr mee bee-see-'kleh-tah]

Would you like to insure your luggage?

¿Desea usted asegurar el equipaje? [deh-'seh-ah oo-'stehd ah-seh-goo-'rahr ehl eh-kee-'pah-heh]

Is the luggage leaving on the…train?

¿Sale el equipaje con el tren de las…? ['sah-leh ehl eh-kee-'pah-heh kohn ehl trehn deh lahs]

When will it arrive in…?

¿Cuándo llega a…? ['kwahn-doh 'yeh-gah ah]

Is the…train going to be late?

¿Tiene retraso el tren de…? [tee-'eh-neh reh-'trah-soh ehl trehn deh]

Is there a connection in... to.../with the ferry in...?	¿Hay enlace (*Am* combinación) en... para.../con el transbordador (*Am* ferry-boat) en...? [ah·ee ehn-'lah-seh (kohm-bee-nah-see-'ohn) ehn 'pah-rah/kohn ehl trahs-bohr-dah-'dohr (feh-rree-'boht) ehn]
(Where) Do I have to change?	¿(Dónde) Tengo que hacer transbordo? [('dohn-deh) 'tehn-goh keh ah-'sehr trahns-'bohr-doh]
Which platform does the...train leave from...?	¿De qué andén sale el tren para...? [deh keh ahn-'dehn 'sah-leh ehl trehn 'pah-rah]
Train number..., from... is now arriving in platform 1.	El tren número..., procedente de ... entra en el andén número uno. [ehl trehn 'noo-meh-roh, proh-seh-'dehn-teh deh 'ehn-trah ehn ehl ahn-'dehn 'noo-meh-roh 'oo-noh]
Train number... from... has a ten-minute delay.	El tren número..., procedente de ... tiene diez minutos de retraso. [ehl trehn 'noo-meh-roh, proh-seh-'dehn-teh deh tee-'eh-neh dee-'ehs mee-'noo-tohs deh reh-'trah-soh]
All aboard! Close the doors!	¡Atención! ¡Viajeros al tren! ¡Cierren las puertas! [ah-tehn-see-'ohn. vee-ah-'heh-rohs ahl trehn. see-'eh-rrehn lahs 'pwehr-tahs]

On the Train	**En el tren**
Excuse me, is this seat free?	Perdón, señora/señorita/señor, ¿está libre este asiento? [pehr-'dohn, seh-'nyoh-rah/seh-nyoh-'ree-tah/seh-'nyohr, eh-'stah 'lee-breh 'eh-steh ah-see-'ehn-toh]
Can you help me, please?	¿Puede usted ayudarme, por favor? ['pweh-deh oo-'stehd ah-yoo-'dahr-meh, pohr fah-'vohr]
Can I open/shut the window, please?	¿Puedo abrir/cerrar la ventanilla, por favor? ['pweh-doh ah-'breer/seh-'rrahr lah vehn-tah-'nee-yah, pohr fah-'vohr]

Excuse me, this is a nonsmoking compartment.	Perdone, señor/señora/señorita, éste es un departamento (*Am* compartimiento) para no fumadores. [pehr-'doh-neh, seh-'nyoh-rah/seh-nyoh-'ree-tah/seh-'nyohr, 'eh-steh ehs oon deh-pahr-tah-'mehn-toh (kohm-pahr-tee-mee-'ehn-toh) 'pah-rah noh foo-mah-'doh-rehs]
Excuse me, that's my seat. I have a reservation.	Perdón, este sitio es el mío. Tengo reserva de asiento. [pehr-'dohn, 'eh-steh 'see-tee-oh ehs ehl 'mee-oh. 'tehn-goh reh-'sehr-vah deh ah-see-'ehn-toh]
Tickets, please.	¡Billetes (*Am* boletos), por favor! [bee-'yeh-tehs (boh-'leh-tohs), pohr fah-'vohr]
Does this train stop in…?	¿Para este tren en…? ['pah-rah 'eh-steh trehn ehn..]
Where are we now?	¿Dónde estamos ahora? ['dohn-deh eh-'stah-mohs ah-'oh-rah]
How long are we stopping here?	¿Cuánto tiempo paramos aquí? ['kwahn-toh tee-'ehm-poh pah-'rah-mohs ah-'kee]
Are we arriving on time?	¿Llegaremos puntuales? [yeh-gah-'reh-mohs poon-too-'ah-lehs]

Signs and Information

Agua no potable	Water Not for Drinking
Andén/vía	Platform
Caballeros	Men
Lavabo	Washroom
Coche-cama (*Am* coche-dormitorio)	Sleeping car
Coche-litera	Couchette Car (four- to six-berth compartments)
Coche-restaurante	Restaurant Car

Consigna	Checkroom
Consigna automática	Locker
Despacho de billetes, (*Am* boletería)	Ticket Office
Freno de alarma	Emergency Brake
Fumadores	Smokers
Horario	Timetable
Información	Information
Jefe de estación	Stationmaster
Libre	Free
Llegada	Arrival
No fumadores	Nonsmokers
Ocupado	Busy
Paso a los andenes	Passage to Platforms
Paso subterráneo	Underground Passage
Refrescos	Refreshments, Cafeteria
Sala de espera	Waiting Room
Salida	Exit, Departure
Señoras	Women
Servicio sanitario (*Am* asistencia pública)	Restroom
W.C./lavabo	Toilet, Washroom

Word List: Train   See also Word Lists: Airplane, Ship

additional charge	suplemento [soo-pleh-'mehn-toh]
arrival	llegar [yeh-'gahr]
to board	subir [soo-'beer]
baggage cart	carrito portaequipajes [kah-'rree-toh pohr-tah-eh-kee-'pah-hehs]
baggage check, baggage room	consigna (de equipajes) [kohn-'seeg-nah (deh eh-kee-'pah-hehs)]
baggage claim check	el talón (*Am* boleto) (de equipajes) [ehl tah-'lohn (boh-'leh-toh) (deh eh-kee-'pah-hehs)]

baggage counter	ventanilla de equipajes [vehn-tah-'nee-yah deh eh-kee-'pah-hehs)]
baggage, luggage	el equipaje [ehl eh-kee-'pah-heh]
baggage rack	rejilla (de equipajes) [reh-'hee-yah (deh eh-kee-'pah-hehs)]
busy	ocupado [oh-koo-'pah-doh]
car number	número del vagón ['noo-meh-roh dehl vah-'gohn]
car train	el autotrén [ehl ow-toh-'trehn]
central station	la estación central [lah eh-stah-see-'ohn sehn-'trahl]
compartment	departamento (*Am* compar-timiento) [deh-pahr-tah-'mehn-toh (kohm-pahr-tee-mee-'ehn-toh]
corridor	pasillo [pah-'see-yoh]
couchette ticket (couchette: four- to six-berth compartment)	el billete (*Am* boleto) de coche-literas [ehl bee-'yeh-teh (boh-'leh-toh) deh 'koh-cheh-lee-'teh-rahs]
departure	salida, partida [sah-'lee-dah, pahr-'tee-dah]
departure time	hora de salida ['oh-rah deh sah-'lee-dah]
direct train	el tren directo [ehl trehn dee-'rehk-toh]
discount	descuento, la reducción [dehs-'kwehn-toh, lah reh-dook-see-'ohn]
EC (Eurocity)	EC (Eurocity) [eh-seh]
emergency brake	freno de alarma ['freh-noh deh ah-'lahr-mah]
express train	el tren expreso [ehl trehn ehk-'spreh-soh]
ferry	el transbordador (*Am* el ferry-boat) [ehl trahns-bohr-dah-'dohr (ehl feh-rree-'boht)]
free	libre ['lee-breh]
to get off	bajar [bah-'hahr]
group ticket	el billete colectivo [ehl bee-'yeh-teh koh-lehk-'tee-voh]
guidebook	la guía (de viaje) [lah 'gee-ah (deh vee-'ah-heh)]
half-fare, children's fare	el billete (*Am* boleto) infantil [ehl bee-'yeh-teh (boh-'leh-toh) een-fahn-'teel]

high-speed train	el tren de alta velocidad [ehl trehn deh 'ahl-tah veh-loh-see-'dahd]
IC (Intercity)	IC (Intercity) [ee-seh]
locker	consigna automática [kohn-'seeg-nah ow-toh-'mah-tee-kah]
locomotive	locomotora [loh-koh-moh-'toh-rah]
no-smoking compartment	departamento (*Am* compartimiento) de no fumadores [deh-pahr-tah-'men-toh (kohm-pahr-tee-mee-'ehn-toh) deh noh foo-mah-'doh-rehs]
open freight car	el vagón abierto de carga [ehl vah-'gohn ah-bee-'ehr-toh deh 'kahr-gah]
to pay an additional charge	pagar un suplemento [pah-'gahr oon soo-pleh-'mehn-toh]
platform	el andén [ehl ahn-'dehn]
platform pass	el billete de andén [ehl bee-'yeh-teh deh ahn-'dehn]
porter	mozo ['moh-soh]
reservation	reserva [reh-'sehr-vah]
restaurant car	el vagón-restaurante [ehl vah-'gohn-reh-stah·oo-'rahn-teh]
restrooms	los servicios, baño [lohs sehr-'vee-see·ohs, 'bah-nyoh]
round-trip ticket	el billete de ida y vuelta [ehl bee-'yeh-teh deh 'ee-dah ee 'vwehl-tah]
seat reservation	reserva de asiento [reh-'sehr-vah deh ah-see-'ehn-toh]
schedule	horario [oh-'rah-ree·oh]
sleeping-car ticket	el billete de coche-cama [ehl bee-'yeh-teh deh 'koh-cheh-'kah-mah]
smoking compartment	departamento (*Am* compartimiento) de fumadores [deh-pahr-tah-'mehn-toh (kohm-pahr-tee- mee-'ehn-toh) deh foo-mah-'doh-rehs]
station	la estación [lah eh-stah-see-'ohn]
station restaurant	el restaurante de la estación [ehl reh-stah-oo-'rahn-teh deh lah eh-stah-see-'ohn]
stop	parada [pah-'rah-dah]
subject to additional charge	sujeto a suplemento [soo-'heh-toh ah soo-pleh-'mehn-toh]
TAV (high-speed train)	TAV (tren de alta velocidad) [trehn deh 'ahl-tah veh-loh-see-'dahd]

ticket	el billete (*Am* boleto) [ehl bee-'yeh-teh (boh-'leh-toh)]
ticket check	el control de billetes (*Am* boletos) [ehl kohn-'trohl deh bee-'yeh-tehs (boh-'leh-tohs)]
ticket counter	ventanilla (*Am* boletería) [vehn-tah-'nee-yah (boh-leh-teh-'ree-ah)]
ticket price	precio del billete ['preh-see-oh dehl bee-'yeh-teh]
train	el ferrocarril, el tren [ehl feh-rroh-kah-'rreel, ehl trehn]
train staff	el personal del tren [ehl pehr-soh-'nahl dehl trehn]
waiting room	sala de espera ['sah-lah deh eh-'speh-rah]
washrooms	los lavabos [lohs lah-'vah-bohs]
window seat	asiento junto a la ventanilla [ah-see-'ehn-toh 'hoon-toh ah lah vehn-tah-'nee-yah]

Ship
Barco

Information	Información
How can I get to...by ship?	Por favor, ¿para ir en barco a...? [pohr fah-'vohr, 'pah-rah eer ehn 'bahr-koh ah]
Where/When does the next boat/ferry leave for...?	¿De dónde/Cuándo parte el próximo barco/el próximo transbordador (*Am* ferry/ferry-boat) para...? [deh 'dohn-deh/'kwahn-doh 'pahr-teh ehl 'prohk-see-moh 'bahr-koh/ehl 'prohk-see-moh trahns-bohr-dah-'dohr ('feh-ree, feh-ree-'boht) 'pah-rah]
How long is the trip?	¿Cuánto dura la travesía? ['kwahn-toh 'doo-rah lah trah-veh-'see-'ah]

What ports do we call in/stop in?	¿En qué puertos hacemos escala? [ehn keh 'pwehr-tohs ah-'seh-mohs eh-'skah-lah]
When do we arrive in…?/ dock in…?	¿Cuándo atracamos en…? ['kwahn-doh ah-trah-'kah-mohs ehn]
How long are we stopping at …?	¿Cuánto tiempo nos detenemos en…? ['kwahn-toh tee-'ehm-poh nohs deh-teh-'neh-mohs ehn]
I'd like a ticket to…	Quisiera un pasaje para… [kee-see-'eh-rah oon pah-'sah-heh 'pah-rah]
first class	de primera clase [deh pree-'meh-rah 'klah-seh]
tourist class	de clase turista [deh 'klah-seh too-'ree-stah]
a single cabin	un camarote individual [oon kah-mah-'roh-teh een-dee-vee-doo-'ahl]
a double cabin	un camarote doble [oon kah-mah-'roh-teh 'doh-bleh]
I'd like a ticket for the…excursion.	Quisiera un pasaje para la excursión de las… [kee-see-'eh-rah oon pah-'sah-heh 'pah-rah lah ehk-skoor-see-'ohn deh lahs]

On Board

A bordo

Where's cabin number…, please?	¿Puede decirme dónde está el camarote número…? ['pweh-deh deh-'seer-meh 'dohn-deh eh-'stah ehl kah-mah-'roh-teh 'noo-meh-roh]
Can I have a different cabin?	¿Me podrían dar otro camarote? [meh poh-'dree-ahn dahr 'oh-troh kah-mah-'roh-teh]
Where's my suitcase/ baggage?	¿Dónde está mi maleta (*Am* valija)/mi equipaje? ['dohn-deh eh-'stah mee mah-'leh-tah (vah-'lee-hah)/mee eh-kee-'pah-heh]
Where's the restaurant/ lounge?	¿Dónde está el comedor/el salón? ['dohn-deh eh-'stah ehl koh-meh-'dohr/ehl sah-'lohn]

At what time are meals served?	¿A qué hora se come? [ah keh 'oh-rah seh 'koh-meh]
Waiter, could I have a…, please?	Camarero, por favor, tráigame… [kah-mah-'reh-roh, pohr fah-'vohr, 'trah-ee-gah-meh]
I'm not feeling well.	No me siento bien. [noh me see-'ehn-toh 'bee·ehn]
Please call the ship's doctor.	Haga el favor de llamar al médico de bordo. ['ah-gah ehl fah-'vohr deh yah-'mahr ahl 'meh-dee-koh deh 'bohr-doh]
Could you give me something for seasickness, please?	¿Puede usted darme un remedio contra el mareo? ['pweh-deh oo-'stehd 'dahr-meh oon reh-'meh-dee·oh 'kohn-trah ehl mah-'reh-oh]

Word List: Ship	**See also Word Lists: Airplane, Train**
anchor	(el) ancla [(ehl) 'ahnk-lah]
oar	remo ['reh-moh]
bed surcharge	suplemento para cama [soo-pleh-'mehn-toh 'pah-rah 'kah-mah]
bow	proa ['proh-ah]
on board	a bordo [ah 'bohr-doh]
to board, to embark	embarcar(se) [eh-bahr-'kahr-seh]
boat connection	la conexión/el enlace de barcos [lah koh-nehk-see-'ohn/ehl ehn-'lah-seh deh 'bahr-kohs]
cabin	cabina [kah-'bee-nah]
to call at	hacer escala [ah-'sehr eh-'skah-lah]
captain	el capitán [ehl kah-pee-'tahn]
car ferry	el transbordador de automóviles [ehl trahns-bohr-dah-'dohr deh ow-toh-'moh-vee-lehs]
coast	costa ['koh-stah]
course	rumbo ['room-boh]
crew	la tripulación [lah tree-poo-lah-see-'ohn]
cruise	crucero [kroo-'seh-roh]
deck	cubierta [koo-bee-'ehr-tah]

Cape Tarifa, southernmost point of continental Europe

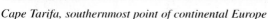

to disembark	**desembarcar** [dehs-ehm-bahr-'kahr]
to dock at	**atracar en** [ah-'trah-'kahr ehn]
excursion	**la excursión** [lah ehk-skoor-see-'ohn]
ferry	**el transbordador (*Am* el ferry/ferryboat)** [ehl trahns-bohr-dah-'dohr (ehl 'feh-rree/feh-rree-'boht)]
ferry bridge (a ferry-boat that carries trains)	**el transbordador de trenes** [ehl trahns-bohr-dah-'dohr deh 'treh-nehs]
harbor fees	**derechos portuarios** [deh-'reh-chohs pohr-too-'ah-ree-ohs]
hovercraft	**el aerodeslizador** [ehl ah-eh-roh-dehs-lee-sah-'dohr]
hydrofoil, jetfoil	**el hidroala, el hidrofoil** [ehl ee-droh-'ah-lah, ehl ee-droh-'foh-eel]
inside cabin	**cabina interior** [kah-'bee-nah een-teh-ree-'ohr]
knot	**nudo** ['noo-doh]
lifeboat	**el bote salvavidas** [ehl 'boh-teh sahl-vah-'vee-dahs]
life jacket	**chaleco salvavidas** [chah-'leh-koh sahl-vah-'vee-dahs]

life preserver	el salvavidas [ehl sahl-vah-'vee-dahs]
lighthouse	faro ['fah-roh]
lower deck	el entrepuente, entrecubierta [ehl ehn-treh-'pwehn-teh, ehn-treh-koo-bee-'ehr-tah]
mainland	tierra firme [tee-'eh-rrah 'feer-meh]
motorboat	(lancha) motora [('lahn-chah) moh-'toh-rah]
outside cabin	cabina exterior [kah-'bee-nah ehks-teh-ree-'ohr]
passenger	pasajero [pah-sah-'heh-roh]
pier	embarcadero [ehm-bahr-kah-'deh-roh]
pier	el muelle [ehl 'mweh-yeh]
port	puerto ['pwehr-toh]
port side	el babor [ehl bah-'bohr]
promenade deck	cubierta de paseo [koo-bee-'ehr-tah deh pah-'seh-oh]
reservation	reserva [reh-'sehr-vah]
rough sea	el oleaje [ehl oh-leh-'ah-heh]
rowboat	barca de remos ['bahr-kah deh 'reh-mohs]
to sail	salir del puerto [sah-'leer dehl 'pwehr-toh]
sailboat	barco de vela ['bahr-koh deh 'veh-lah]
sailor	marino [mah-'ree-noh]
seasickness	mareo [mah-'reh-oh]
starboard	el estribor [ehl eh-stree-'bohr]
steamer, steamship	el vapor [ehl vah-'pohr]
stern	popa ['poh-pah]
steward	camarero (de barco) [kah-mah-'reh-roh (deh 'bahr-koh)]
sundeck	cubierta solar [koo-bee-'ehr-tah soh-'lahr]
ticket	el billete (*Am* boleto) [ehl bee-'yeh-teh (boh-'leh-toh)]
voyage	travesía [trah-veh-'see-ah]
wave	ola ['oh-lah]
yacht	el yate [ehl 'yah-teh]

At the Border
En la frontera

Passport Check | **Control de pasaporte**

Your passport, please. | Su pasaporte, por favor. [soo pah-sah-'pohr-teh, pohr fah-'vohr]

Your passport has expired. | Su pasaporte está caducado. [soo pah-sah-'pohr-teh eh-'stah kah-doo-'kah-doh]

I'm with the...group. | Formo parte del grupo de... ['fohr-moh 'pahr-teh dehl 'groo-poh deh]

Let me see your dog's/cat's... | Déjeme ver el... de su perro/gato, por favor. ['deh-heh-meh vehr ehl deh soo 'peh-rroh/'gah-toh, pohr fah-'vohr]

   official veterinary's certificate | certificado veterinario oficial [sehr-tee-fee-'kah-doh veh-teh-ree-'nah-ree·oh oh-fee-see-'ahl]

   rabies vaccination certificate | certificado de vacunación contra la rabia [sehr-tee-fee-'kah-doh deh vah-koo-nah-see-'ohn 'kohn-trah lah 'rah-bee·ah]

Do you have a visa? | ¿Tiene usted un visado (Am una visa)? [tee-'eh-neh oo-'stehd oon vee-'sah-doh ('oo-nah 'vee-sah)]

Can I get a visa here? | ¿Puedo conseguir un visado (Am una visa) aquí mismo? ['pweh-doh kohn-seh-'geer oon vee-'sah-doh ('oo-nah 'vee-sah) ah-kee 'mees-moh]

Customs | **Aduana**

Do you have anything to declare? | ¿Tiene usted algo que declarar? [tee-'eh-neh 'ahl-goh keh deh-klah-'rahr]

No, I just have some presents. | No, sólo tengo algunos regalos. [noh, 'soh-loh 'tehn-goh ahl-'goo-nohs reh-'gah-lohs]

Pull over to the right/the left, please.	Aparque aquí a la derecha/a la izquierda, por favor. [ah-'pahr-keh ah-'kee ah lah deh-'reh-chah/ah lah ees-kee-'ehr-dah, pohr fah-'vohr]
Please open your trunk/ this suitcase.	Quiere abrir el portaequipajes (*Am* baúl)/esta maleta (*Am* vali-ja). [kee-'eh-reh ah-'breer ehl pohr-tah-eh-kee-'pah-hehs (bah-'ool)/ 'eh-stah mah-'leh-tah (vah-'lee-hah), pohr fah-'vohr]
Do I have to pay duty on this?	¿Hay que pagar derechos de aduana por esto? ['ah-ee keh pah-'gahr deh-'reh-chohs deh ah-'dwah-nah pohr 'eh-stoh]
How much duty do I have to pay?	¿Cuánto son los derechos de aduana? ['kwahn-toh sohn lohs deh-'reh-chohs deh ah-'dwah-nah]

Word List: At the Border

address	domicilio [doh-mee-'see-lee-oh]
border, border crossing	frontera [frohn-'teh-rah]
children's I.D./identity card	el carnet de identidad para menores de edad [ehl kahr-'neht deh ee-dehn-tee-'dahd 'pah-rah meh-'noh-rehs deh eh-'dahd]
citizenship	la nacionalidad, la ciudadanía [lah nah-see-oh-nah-lee-'dahd, lah see-oo-dah-dah-'nee-ah]
customs	aduana [ah-'dwah-nah]
customs check	el control de aduana [ehl kohn-'trohl deh ah-'dwah-nah]
customs office	oficina de aduanas [oh-fee-'see-nah deh ah-'dwah-nahs]
customs officer	funcionario de aduanas [foonk-see-oh-'nah-ree-oh deh ah-'dwah-nahs]
date of birth	fecha de nacimiento ['feh-chah deh nah-see-mee-'ehn-toh]
driver's license	permiso/el carnet de conducir [pehr-'mee-soh/ehl kahr-'neht deh kohn-doo-'seer]

duty	**los derechos de aduana** [lohs deh-'reh-chohs deh ah-'dwah-nah]
duty-free	**exento de derechos de aduana** [ehk-'sehn-toh deh deh-'reh-chohs deh ah-'dwah-nah]
to enter (the country)	**entrada (al pais)** [ehn-'trah-dah (ahl pah-'ees)]
export	**la exportación** [lah ehk-spohr-tah-see-'ohn]
first name	**el nombre (de pila)** [ehl 'nohm-breh (deh 'pee-lah)]
import	**la importación** [lah eem-pohr-tah-see-'ohn]
international vaccination certificate	**certificado internacional de vacunación** [sehr-tee-fee-'kah-doh een-tehr-nah-see-oh-'nahl deh vah-koo-nah-see-'ohn]
to leave (the country)	**salida/partida (del pais)** [sah-'lee-dah/pahr-'tee-dah (dehl pah-'ees)]
license plate	**(placa de) matrícula** [('plah-kah deh) mah-'tree-koo-lah]
maiden name	**el nombre de soltera** [ehl 'nohm-breh deh sohl-'teh-rah]
marital status	**estado civil** [eh-'stah-doh see-'veel]
married	**casado** [kah-'sah-doh]
passport	**el pasaporte** [ehl pah-sah-'pohr-teh]
passport check	**el control de pasaporte** [ehl kohn-'trohl deh pah-sah-'pohr-teh]
personal I.D., identity card	**el carnet/documento de identidad** (*Am* **cédula personal**) [ehl kahr-'neht/doh-koo-'mehn-toh deh ee-dehn-tee-'dahd ('seh-doo-lah pehr-soh-'nahl]
place of birth	**el lugar de nacimiento** [ehl loo-'gahr deh nah-see-mee-'ehn-toh]
prescriptions	**las prescripciones** [lahs preh-skreep-see-'oh-nehs]
rabies	**rabia** ['rah-bee-ah]
single	**soltero** [sohl-'teh-roh]
subject to customs duties	**sujeto a derechos de aduana** [soo-'heh-toh ah deh-'reh-chohs deh ah-'dwah-nah]

surname	el apellido [ehl ah-peh-'yee-doh]
valid	válido ['vah-lee-doh]
visa	el visado (*Am* la visa) [ehl vee-'sah-doh (lah 'vee-sah)]
widow, widower	viudo, viuda [vee-'oo-doh, vee-'oo-dah]

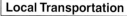

Local Transportation
Transportes urbanos

Which bus/tramway/subway line goes to...?	¿Qué autobús/tranvía/metro hay que tomar para ir a...? [keh ow-toh-'boos/trahn-'vee-ah/'meh-troh 'ah·ee keh toh-'mahr 'pah-rah eer ah]
Excuse me, where's the nearest...?	Por favor, ¿dónde está la próxima... [pohr fah-'vohr, 'dohn-deh eh-'stah lah 'prohk-see-mah]
bus stop?	parada del autobús? [pah-'rah-dah dehl ow-toh-'boos]
tram stop?	parada del tranvía? [pah-'rah-dah dehl trahn-'vee-ah]
subway stop/station?	parada/estación del metro? [pah-'ah-dah/eh-stah-see-'ohn dehl 'meh-troh]
Which line goes to..., please?	¿Cuál es la línea que va a..., por favor? [kwahl ehs lah 'lee-neh-ah keh vah ah, pohr fah-'vohr]
Is this bus going to...?	¿Es éste el autobús para...? [ehs 'eh-steh ehl ow-toh-'boos 'pah-rah]
What time does the bus leave?/Where does the bus leave from?	¿Cuándo/De dónde sale el autobús? ['kwahn-doh/deh 'dohn-deh 'sah-leh ehl ow-toh-'boos]
When is the first/last train leaving to...?	¿Cuándo sale el primer/último metro para...? ['kwahn-doh 'sah-leh ehl pree-'mehr/'ool-tee-moh 'meh-troh 'pah-rah]
Which way do I have to go?	¿Qué dirección tengo que tomar? [keh dee-rehk-see-'ohn 'tehn-goh keh toh-'mahr]

How many stops to...?	¿Cuántas paradas hay hasta...? ['kwahn-tahs pah-'rah-dahs 'ah-ee 'ah-stah]
Where do I get off/change?	¿Dónde tengo que bajar/cambiar? ['dohn-deh 'tehn-goh keh bah-'hahr/ kahm-bee-'ahr]
Please let me know where I get off.	Haga el favor de avisarme cuando tenga que bajar. ['ah-gah ehl fah-'vohr deh ah-vee-'sahr-meh 'kwahn-doh 'tehn-gah keh bah-'hahr]
Where can I buy a ticket?	¿Dónde puedo comprar el billete (*Am* boleto)? ['dohn-deh 'pweh-doh kohm-'prahr ehl bee-'yeh-teh (boh-'leh-toh)]
One ticket to..., please.	Un billete (*Am* boleto) a..., por favor. [oon bee-'yeh-teh (boh-'leh-toh) ah, pohr fah-'vohr]
Are there one-day/ weekly tickets?	¿Hay también billetes para varios viajes/billetes semanales? ['ah-ee tahm-bee-'ehn bee-'yeh-tehs 'pah-rah 'vah-ree·ohs vee-'ah-hehs/ bee-'yeh-tehs seh-mah-'nah-lehs]

Taxi

Taxi

Where's the nearest taxi stand?	Perdón, señora/señorita/señor, ¿dónde está la parada de taxis más cercana? [pehr-'dohn, seh-'nyoh-rah/seh-nyoh-'ree-tah/seh-'nyohr, 'dohn-deh eh-'stah lah pah-'rah-dah deh 'tahk-sees mahs sehr-'kah-nah]
To the station.	A la estación. [ah lah eh-stah-see-'ohn]
To the...hotel.	Al hotel... [ahl oh-'tehl]
To...street.	A la calle... [ah lah 'kah-yeh]
To..., please.	A..., por favor. [ah, pohr fah-'vohr]

How much is it to …?	¿Cuánto cuesta hasta…? ['kwahn-toh 'kweh-stah 'ah-stah]
Could you stop here, please?	¿Pare aquí, por favor? ['pah-reh ah-'kee, pohr fah-'vohr]
Could you wait here, please? I'll be back in five minutes.	Espere aquí, por favor. Vuelvo en cinco minutos. [eh-'speh-reh ah-'kee, pohr fah-'vohr. Vwehl-voh ehn 'seen-koh mee-'noo-tohs]
That's for you.	Para usted. ['pah-rah oo-'stehd]

On Foot
A pie

Excuse me, where's…, please?	Perdón, señora/señorita/señor, ¿dónde está…? [pehr-'dohn, seh-'nyoh-rah/seh-nyoh-'ree-tah/seh-'nyohr, 'dohn-deh eh-'stah]
Could you tell me how I can get to…, please?	¿Podría decirme cómo se va a…? [poh-'dree-ah deh-'seer-meh 'koh-moh seh vah ah]
I'm sorry, I don't know.	Lo siento, pero no lo sé. [loh see-'ehn-toh, 'peh-roh noh loh seh]
What's the quickest way to…?	¿Cuál es el camino más corto para ir a…? [kwahl ehs ehl kah-'mee-noh mahs 'kohr-toh 'pah-rah eer ah]
How far is it to...?	¿Cuánto se tarda en llegar a…? ['kwahn-toh seh 'tahr-dah ehn yeh-'gahr ah]
It's (not) far.	(No) está lejos. [(noh) eh-'stah 'leh-hohs]
It's very near.	Está muy cerca de aquí. [eh-'stah 'moo-ee 'sehr-kah deh ah-'kee]
Straight ahead.	Todo seguido (*Am* derecho). ['toh-doh seh-'gee-doh (deh-'reh-choh)]

Turn left/right.

Tuerza (*Am* Doble) a la izquierda/derecha. ['twehr-sah ('doh-bleh) ah lah ees-kee-'ehr-dah/deh-'reh-chah]

First/second street on the left/right.

La primera/segunda calle a la izquierda/a la derecha. [lah pree-'meh-rah/seh-'goon-dah 'kah-yeh ah lah ees-kee-'ehr-dah/ah lah deh-'reh-chah]

Cross…
the bridge.
the plaza.
the street.

Atraviese… [ah-trah-vee-'eh-seh]
el puente. [ehl 'pwehn-teh]
la plaza. [lah 'plah-sah]
la calle. [lah 'kah-yeh]

Then ask again.

Luego pregunte usted otra vez. ['lweh-goh preh-'goon-teh oo-'stehd 'oh-trah vehs]

You can't miss it.

No es posible equivocarse. [noh ehs poh-'see-bleh eh-kee-voh-'kahr-seh]

You can take...	Puede usted tomar... ['pweh-deh oo-'stehd toh-'mahr]
the bus.	el autobús. [ehl ow-toh-'boos]
the tram.	el tranvía. [ehl trahn-'vee-ah]
the suburban train.	el suburbano. [ehl soo-boor-'bah-noh]
the subway.	el metro. [ehl 'meh-troh]
the trolleybus.	el trolebús. [ehl troh-leh-'boos]

Word List: On the Go in Town

alley	calleja [kah-'yeh-hah]
building	edificio [eh-dee-'fee-see-oh]
bus	el autobús [ehl ow-toh-'boos]
bus (city)	el autobús (urbano) [ehl ow-toh-'boos (oor-'bah-noh)]
bus station	la estación de autobuses [lah eh-'stah-see-'ohn deh ow-toh-'boo-sehs]
to buy a ticket	sacar (un billete) [sah-'kahr (oon bee-'yeh-teh)]
cab driver	el/la taxista [ehl/lah tahk-'see-stah]
church	iglesia [ee-'gleh-see-ah]
city center/downtown area	centro (de la ciudad) ['sehn-troh (deh lah see-oo-'dahd)]
departure	salida [sah-'lee-dah]
direction	la dirección [lah dee-rehk-see-'ohn]
driver	el conductor (*Am* chofer) [ehl kohn-dook-'tohr (choh-'fehr)]
end of the line, last stop	la estación final [lah eh-stah-see-'ohn fee-'nahl]
to get off	bajar [bah-'hahr]
to get on	subir [soo-'beer]
house	casa ['kah-sah]
house number	número de la casa ['noo-meh-roh deh lah 'kah-sah]
inspector	el revisor [ehl reh-vee-'sohr]
intercity bus	el coche de línea, el autobús interurbano [ehl 'koh-cheh deh 'lee-neh-ah, ehl ow-toh-'boos een-tehr-oor-'bah-noh]

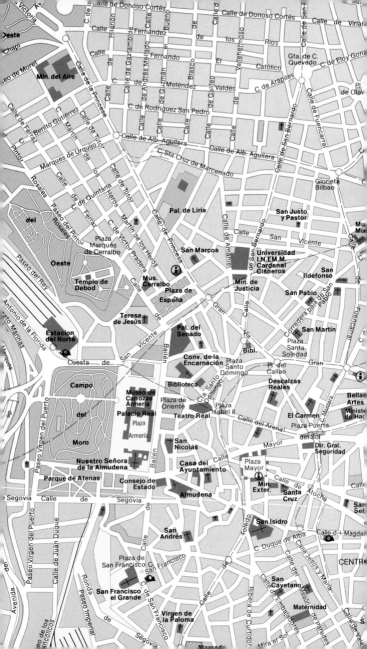

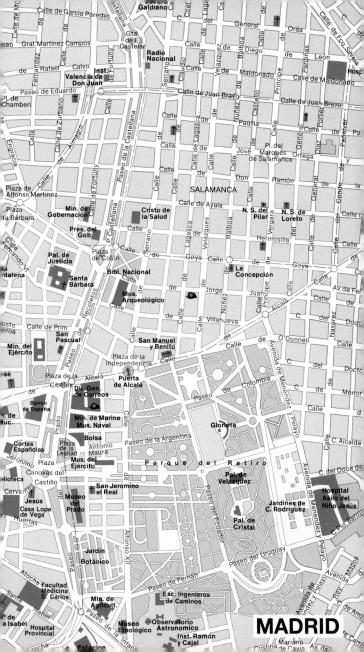

MADRID

main street	la calle principal [lah 'kah-yeh preen-see-'pahl]
neighborhood	barrio ['bah-rree-oh]
one-day transit card	abono diario, el billete válido para un solo día [ehl ah-'boh-noh dee-'ah-ree-oh, ehl bee-'yeh-teh 'vah-lee-doh 'pah-rah oon 'soh-loh 'dee-ah]
park	el parque [ehl 'pahr-keh]
pedestrian mall	zona peatonal ['soh-nah peh-ah-toh-'nahl]
rack railroad	el ferrocarril de cremallera [ehl feh-rroh-kah-'rreel deh kreh-mah-'yeh-rah]
rate per kilometer	precio por kilómetro ['preh-see·oh pohr kee-'loh-meh-troh]
receipt	recibo [reh-'see-boh]
schedule	horario [oh-'rah-ree-oh]
side street	la calle lateral [lah 'kah-yeh lah-teh-'rahl]
sidewalk	acera [ah-'seh-rah]
sightseeing tour (of the city)	visita de la ciudad [vee-'see-tah deh lah see-oo-'dahd]
the stop	parada [pah-'rah-dah]
to stop	parar [pah-'rahr]
street	la calle [lah 'kah-yeh]
suburb	suburbio, barrio periférico [soo-'boor-bee·oh, 'bah-rree·oh peh-ree-'feh-ree-koh]
suburban train	el tren de cercanías, el tren suburbano [ehl trehn deh sehr-kah-'nee-ahs, ehl trehn soo-boor-'bah-noh]
subway	metro ['meh-troh]
taxi stand	parada de taxis [pah-'rah-dah deh 'tahk-sees]
taxi van, taxi pool, collective taxi	el taxi colectivo [ehl 'tahk-see koh-lehk-'tee-voh]
ticket	el billete (*Am* boleto) [ehl bee-'yeh-teh (boh-'leh-toh)]
ticket canceling machine	máquina canceladora de billetes (*Am* boletos) ['mah-kee-nah kahn-seh-lah-'doh-rah deh bee-'yeh-tehs (boh-'leh-tohs)]

ticket price	**precio del billete** ['preh-see-oh dehl bee-'yeh-teh]
ticket selling machine	**máquina expendedora de billetes** (*Am* **boletos**) ['mah-kee-nah ehks-pehn-deh-'doh-rah deh bee-'yeh-tehs (boh-'leh-tohs)]
tip	**propina** [proh-'pee-nah]
total price	**precio global/total** ['preh-see·oh gloh-'bahl/toh-'tahl]
tramway	**el tranvía** [ehl trahn-'vee-ah]
travel/bus/subway card	**(tarjeta de) abono** [(tahr-'heh-tah deh) ah-'boh-noh]
travel card, weekly/ monthly ticket	**abono** [ah-'boh-noh]
trolleybus	**el trolebús** [ehl troh-leh-'boos]
weekly ticket	**el billete semanal** [ehl bee-'yeh-teh seh-mah-'nahl]

4 **Accommodations**
Alojamiento

Information
Información

Can you recommend… please?	Perdón, señor/señora/señorita. ¿Podría usted indicarme/recomendarme… [pehr-'dohn, seh-'nyoh-rah/seh-nyoh-'ree-tah/seh-'nyohr. poh-'dree-ah oo-'stehd een-dee-'kahr-meh/reh-koh-mehn-'dahr-meh]
a good hotel	un buen hotel? [oon bwehn oh-'tehl]
a cheap hotel	un hotel barato? [oon oh-'tehl bah-'rah-toh]
a guest house	una pensión? ['oo-nah pehn-see-'ohn]
a bed and breakfast	una habitación particular? ['oo-nah ah-bee-tah-see-'ohn pahr-tee-koo-'lahr]
Is it centrally located/ quiet/near the beach?	¿Está en un lugar central/tranquilo/ cerca de la playa? [eh-'stah ehn oon loo-'gahr sehn-'trahl/trahn-'kee-loh/'sehr-kah deh lah 'plah-yah]
How much is it per night?	¿Sabe usted cuánto costará aprox-imadamente una habitación? ['sah-beh oo-'stehd 'kwahn-toh koh-stah-'rah ah-prohk-see-mah-dah-'mehn-teh 'oo-nah ah-bee-tah-see-'ohn]
Is there a youth hostel/ camping site here?	¿Hay por aquí un albergue juvenil/ un cámping? ['ah·ee pohr ah-kee oon ahl-'behr-geh hoo-veh-'neel/oon 'kahm-peen]

Hotel/Guest House/Bed and Breakfast
Hotel/Pensión/Habitación particular

At the Reception Desk	**En la recepción**
I have a reservation. My name is …	He reservado aquí una habitación. Me llamo… [eh reh-sehr-'vah-doh ah-'kee 'oo-nah ah-bee-tah-see-'ohn. Meh 'yah-moh]

Do you have a room available?

¿Tienen ustedes habitaciones libres? [tee-'eh-nehn oo-'steh-dehs ah-bee-tah-see-'oh-nehs 'lee-brehs]

...for one night?

...para una noche. ['pah-rah 'oo-nah 'noh-cheh]

...for two days/one week?

... para dos días/una semana. ['pah-rah dohs 'dee-ahs/'oo-nah seh-'mah-nah]

I'm sorry, we're full.

Lo siento, señor/señora/señorita, está todo ocupado. [loh see-'ehn-toh, seh-'nyoh-rah/seh-nyoh-'ree-tah/seh-'nyohr, eh-'stah 'toh-doh oh-koo-'pah-doh]

Yes. What kind of room are you looking for?

Sí. ¿Qué clase de habitación desea usted? [see. keh 'klah-seh deh ah-bee-tah-see-'ohn deh-'seh-ah oo-'stehd]

a single room

una habitación individual ['oo-nah ah-bee-tah-see-'ohn een-dee-vee-doo-'ahl]

a double room (with two beds)

una habitación doble (de dos camas) ['oo-nah ah-bee-tah-see-'ohn 'doh-bleh (deh dohs 'kah-mahs)]

National Hotel called "Via de la Plata" in Mérida, Badajoz.

a double room with
a large bed/(Am)
double bed

una habitación doble con
cama matrimonial ['oo-nah
ah-bee-tah-see-'ohn 'doh-bleh
kohn 'kah-mah mah-tree-moh-
nee-'ahl]

a quiet room

una habitación tranquila ['oo-
nah ah-bee-tah-see-'ohn trahn-
'kee-lah]

a sunny room

una habitación soleada ['oo-
nah ah-bee-tah-see-'ohn soh-
leh-'ah-dah]

with hot and cold
running water

con agua corriente caliente y
fría [kohn 'ah-gwah koh-rree-
'ehn-teh kah-lee-'ehn-teh ee
'free-ah]

with a shower
with a bath
with a balcony/terrace

con ducha [kohn 'doo-chah]
con baño [kohn 'bah-nyoh]
con balcón/terraza [kohn bahl-
'kohn/teh-'rrah-sah]

with a view of the sea

con vistas al mar [kohn 'vee-
stahs ahl mahr]

at the front, facing
the street
  at the back, facing
  the courtyard/patio

que dé a la calle [keh deh ah
lah 'kah-yeh]
  que dé al patio [keh deh ahl
  'pah-tee·oh]

Can I see the room?

¿Podría ver la habitación? [poh-
'dree-ah vehr lah ah-bee-tah-see-
'ohn]

I don't like this room.
Could you show me
another one, please?

Esta habitación no me gusta.
¿Haga el favor de enseñarme otra?
['eh-stah ah-bee-tah-see-'ohn noh
meh 'goo-stah. 'ah-gah ehl fah-'vohr
deh ehn-seh-'nyahr-meh 'oh-trah]

This is a very nice room.
I'll take it.

Esta habitación es muy bonita.
Me quedo con ella. ['eh-stah ah-
bee-tah-see-'ohn ehs 'moo·ee boh-
'nee-tah. meh 'keh-doh kohn 'eh-yah]

Could you put another
bed/a cot in the room?

¿Pueden ustedes poner otra
cama/una cama para un niño?
['pweh-dehn oo-'steh-dehs poh-
'nehr 'oh-trah 'kah-mah/'oo-nah
'kah-mah 'pah-rah oon 'nee-nyoh]

How much is the room with…	¿Cuánto cuesta la habitación con… ['kwahn-toh 'kweh-stah lah ah-bee-tah-see-'ohn kohn]
breakfast?	desayuno? [deh-sah-'yoo-noh]
breakfast and dinner?	media pensión? ['meh-dee·ah pehn-see-'ohn]
full board?	pensión completa? [pehn-see-'ohn kohm-'pleh-tah]
Would you fill in the registration form, please?	¿Quiere hacer el favor de rellenar el formulario de inscripción? [kee-'eh-reh ah-'sehr ehl fah-'vohr deh reh-yeh-'nahr ehl fohr-moo-'lah-ree·oh deh een-skreep-see-'ohn]
May I see your passport/I.D.?	¿Puedo ver su pasaporte/carnet de identidad? ['pweh-doh vehr soo pah-sah-'pohr-teh/kahr-'neht deh ee-dehn-tee-'dahd]
Please have the luggage taken to my room.	Pueden llevar el equipaje a mi habitación. ['pweh-dehn yeh-'vahr ehl eh-kee-'pah-heh ah mee ah-bee-tah-see-'ohn]
Where can I park?	¿Dónde puedo aparcar el coche? ['dohn-deh 'pweh-doh ah-pahr-'kahr ehl 'koh-cheh]
In our garage/parking lot.	En nuestro garaje/esta-cionamiento. [ehn 'nweh-stroh gah-'rah-heh/eh-stah-see·oh-nah-mee-'ehn-toh]
Does the hotel have a pool/private beach?	¿Tiene el hotel una piscina/una playa propia? [tee-'eh-neh ehl oh-'tehl 'oo-nah pee-'see-nah/'oo-nah 'plah-yah 'proh-pee·ah]

Talking to the Hotel Staff	**Con el personal del hotel**
What time is breakfast?	¿A qué hora se puede desayunar? [ah keh 'oh-rah seh 'pweh-deh deh-sah-yoo-'nahr]

At what time do you serve meals?	¿A qué hora se sirven las comidas? [ah keh 'oh-rah seh 'seer-vehn lahs koh-'mee-dahs]
Where's the dining room?	¿Dónde está el comedor? ['dohn-deh eh-'stah ehl koh-meh-'dohr]
Where's the breakfast room?	¿Dónde se desayuna? ['dohn-deh seh deh-sah-'yoo-nah]
Downstairs.	Un piso más abajo. [oon 'pee-soh mahs ah-'bah-hoh]
Would you like breakfast in your room?	¿Desea que le sirvamos el desayuno en la habitación? [deh-'seh-ah keh leh seer-'vah-mohs ehl deh-sah-'yoo-noh ehn lah ah-bee-tah-see-'ohn]
I'd like breakfast in my room at..., please.	Lléveme por favor el desayuno a la habitación a las… ['yeh-veh-meh pohr fah-'vohr ehl deh-sah-'yoo-noh ah lah ah-bee-tah-see-'ohn ah lahs]
For breakfast, I want…	Para el desayuno tomo… ['pah-rah ehl deh-sah-'yoo-noh 'toh-moh]
black coffee.	café solo. [kah-'feh 'soh-loh]
coffee with milk.	café con leche. [kah-'feh kohn 'leh-cheh]
decaf coffee.	café descafeinado. [kah-'feh dehs-kah-feh·ee-'nah-doh]
tea with milk/lemon.	té con leche/limón. [teh kohn 'leh-cheh/lee-'mohn]
herbal tea.	una infusión (de hierbas)/una tisana. ['oo-nah een-foo-see-'ohn (deh 'yehr-bahs)/'oo-nah tee-'sah-nah]
hot chocolate.	chocolate. [choh-koh-'lah-teh]
juice.	un zumo de fruta. [ooon 'soo-moh deh 'froo-tah]
a soft-boiled egg.	un huevo pasado por agua. [oon 'weh-voh pah-'sah-doh pohr 'ah-gwah]
scrambled eggs.	huevos revueltos. ['weh-vohs reh-'vwehl-tohs]
ham and eggs.	huevos con jamón. ['weh-vohs kohn hah-'mohn]

bread/rolls/toast.	pan/panecillos/tostadas. [pahn/pah-neh-'see-yohs/toh-'stah-dahs]
croissant.	un croissant (*Am* una media luna). [oon kroh·ee-'sahnt ('oo-nah 'meh-dee·ah 'loo-nah)]
churros (Spanish-style fritters).	churros. ['choo-rrohs]
butter.	mantequilla (*Am* manteca). [mahn-teh-'kee-yah (mahn-'teh-kah)]
cheese.	queso. ['keh-soh]
sausage.	embutido. [ehm-boo-'tee-doh]
ham.	jamón. [hah-'mohn]
honey.	miel. [mee-'ehl]
jam/marmalade.	mermelada. [mehr-meh-'lah-dah]
yogurt.	un yogur. [oon yoh-'goor]
some fruit.	un poco de fruta. [oon 'poh-koh deh 'froo-tah]
Could I have a packed lunch tomorrow?	¿Me podrían preparar para mañana un paquete de comida? [meh poh-'dree-ahn preh-pah-'rahr 'pah-rah mah-'nyah-nah oon pah-'keh-teh deh koh-'mee-dah]
Please wake me at…in the morning.	Haga el favor de despertarme mañana a las… ['ah-gah ehl fah-'vohr deh dehs-pehr-'tahr-meh mah-'nyah-nah ah lahs]
Could you bring me…please?	¿Haga el favor de traerme…? ['ah-gah ehl fah-'vohr deh trah-'ehr-meh]
another towel	otra toalla ['oh-trah toh-'ah-yah]
a soap	una pastilla de jabón ['oo-nah pah-'stee-yah deh hah-'bohn]
some hangers	unas perchas ['oo-nahs 'pehr-chahs]
How does…work?	¿Cómo funciona…? ['koh-moh foonk-see-'oh-nah]
My key, please.	Mi llave, por favor. [mee 'yah-veh, pohr fah-'vohr]
Has anyone asked for me?	¿Ha preguntado alguien por mí? [ah preh-goon-'tah-doh 'ahl-gee·ehn pohr mee]

Do I have any mail?	¿Hay cartas para mí? ['ah·ee 'kahr-tahs 'pah-rah mee]
Do you have postcards/stamps?	¿Tienen ustedes postales/sellos (*Am* estampillas)? [tee-'eh-nehn oo-'steh-dehs poh-'stah-lehs/'seh-yohs (eh-stahm-'pee-yahs)]
Where can I mail this letter?	¿Dónde puedo echar esta carta? ['dohn-deh 'pweh-doh eh-'chahr 'eh-stah 'kahr-tah]
Where can I rent/borrow...?	¿Dónde puedo alquilar/tomar prestado...? ['dohn-deh 'pweh-doh ahl-kee-'lahr/toh-'mahr preh-'stah-doh]
Where can I make a phone call?	¿Dónde se puede llamar por teléfono? ['dohn-deh seh 'pweh-deh yah-'mahr pohr teh-'leh-foh-noh]
Can I keep my valuables in your safe?	¿Puedo depositar mis objetos de valor en su caja fuerte? ['pweh-doh deh-poh-see-'tahr mees ohb-'heh-tohs deh vah-'lohr ehn soo 'kah-hah 'fwehr-teh]
Can I leave my things here until I get back?	¿Puedo dejar aquí mis cosas hasta que vuelva? ['pweh-doh deh-'hahr ah-'kee mees 'koh-sahs 'ah-stah keh 'vwehl-vah]

Complaints	**Reclamaciones**
The room hasn't been cleaned.	La habitación no está limpia. [lah ah-bee-tah-see-'ohn noh eh-'stah 'leem-pee·ah]
The shower...	La ducha... [lah 'doo-chah]
The toilet...	El water/(*Am*) inodoro, servicio sanitario... [ehl 'oo·ah-tehr/een-oh-'doh-roh, sehr-'vee-see·oh sah-nee-'tah-ree·oh]
The heat...	La calefacción... [lah kah-leh-fahk-see-'ohn]
The light...	La luz... [lah loos]
The radio...	La radio... [lah 'rah-dee·oh]

The TV set...	El televisor… [ehl teh-leh-vee-'sohr]
doesn't work.	no funciona. [noh foonk-see-'oh-nah]
The faucet drips.	El grifo del agua gotea. [ehl 'gree-foh dehl 'ah-gwah goh-'teh-ah]
There's no (hot) water.	No sale agua (caliente). [noh 'sah-leh 'ah-gwah (kah-lee-'ehn-teh)]
The toilet/sink is clogged.	El wáter (*Am.* inodoro, servicio sanitario)/El lavabo está atascado (*Am* tapado). [ehl 'oo·ah-tehr (een-oh-'doh-roh, sehr-'vee-see·oh sah-nee-'tah-ree·oh)/ehl lah-vah-boh eh-'stah ah-tah-'skah-doh (tah-'pah-doh)]
I can't shut/open the window.	La ventana no se puede cerrar/abrir. [lah vehn-'tah-nah noh seh 'pweh-deh seh-'rrahr/ah-'breer]
The key doesn't fit.	La llave no va. [lah 'yah-veh noh vah]

Checking Out	**Partida**
I'm leaving this afternoon/evening at...	Me marcho esta tarde a las... [meh 'mahr-choh 'eh-stah 'tahr-deh ah lahs]
I'm leaving tomorrow at...	Me marcho mañana a las… [meh 'mahr-choh mah-'nyah-nah ah lahs]
At what time do I have to check out?	¿A qué hora tengo que dejar libre la habitación? [ah keh 'oh-rah 'tehn-goh keh deh-'hahr 'lee-breh lah ah-bee-tah-see-'ohn]
Can I have my bill, please?	Prepáreme la cuenta, por favor. [preh-'pah-reh-meh lah 'kwehn-tah, pohr fah-'vohr]
Separate bills, please.	Cuentas separadas, por favor. ['kwehn-tahs seh-pah-'rah-dahs, pohr fah-'vohr]
Do you take dollars/Eurochecks?	¿Aceptan ustedes dólares/eurocheques? [ah-'sehp-tahn oo-'steh-dehs 'doh-lah-rehs/eh·oo-roh-'cheh-kehs]

Please forward my mail to this address.	Haga el favor de mandarme las cartas a esta dirección. ['ah-gah ehl fah-'vohr deh mahn-'dahr-meh lahs 'kahr-tahs ah 'eh-stah dee-rehk-see-'ohn]
Would you please get my luggage down?	¿Pueden bajar mis maletas (*Am* valijas), por favor? ['pweh-dehn bah-'hahr mees mah-'leh-tahs (vah-'lee-hahs), pohr fah-'vohr]
Could you take my luggage to the (train) station/ (airport bus) terminal?	¿Pueden llevar mi equipaje a la estación (de trenes)/a la terminal (aérea)? ['pweh-dehn yeh-'vahr mee eh-kee-'pah-heh ah lah eh-stah-see-'ohn (deh 'treh-nehs)/ah lah tehr-mee-'nahl (ah-'eh-reh-ah)]
Could you call a taxi for me, please?	¿Puede pedirme un taxi, por favor? ['pweh-deh peh-'deer-meh oon 'tahk-see, pohr fah-'vohr]
Thanks for everything. Good-bye.	Muchas gracias por todo. Adiós. ['moo-chahs 'grah-see·ahs pohr 'toh-doh. ah-dee-'ohs]

Word List: Hotel/Guest House/Bed and Breakfast

air conditioning	el aire acondicionado [ehl 'ah·ee-reh ah-kohn-dee-see·oh-'nah-doh]
airport bus/van	el autobús/el microbús del/al aeropuerto [ehl ow-toh-'boos/ehl mee-kroh-'boos dehl/ahl ah-eh-roh-'pwehr-toh]
ashtray	cenicero [seh-nee-'seh-roh]
babysitting/child care service	guardería infantil [gwahr-deh-'ree-ah een-fahn-'teel]
balcony	el balcón [ehl bahl-'kohn]
barbecue, grill	barbacoa [bahr-bah-'koh-ah]
bathroom	cuarto de baño ['kwahr-toh deh 'bah-nyoh]
bathtub	bañera, baño [bah-'nyeh-rah, 'bah-nyoh]
bed	cama ['kah-mah]
bed linen	ropa de cama ['roh-pah deh 'kah-mah]

bidet	el bidé [ehl bee-'deh]
blanket	colcha; manta ['kohl-chah, 'mahn-tah]
bolster	travesero, cabezal [trah-veh-'seh-roh, kah-beh-'sahl]
breakfast	desayuno [deh-sah-'yoo-noh]
breakfast and dinner	media pensión ['meh-dee·ah pehn-see-'ohn]
breakfast room	sala de desayuno ['sah-lah deh deh-sah-'yoo-noh]
category	categoría [kah-teh-goh-'ree-ah]
children's cot	cama de niño ['kah-mah deh 'nee-nyoh]
to clean	limpiar [leem-pee-'ahr]
closet, armoire	armario (*Am* el closet, el escaparate) [ahr-'mah-ree·oh (ehl 'kloh-seht, ehl eh-skah-pah-'rah-teh)]
cold water	(el) agua fría [(ehl) 'ah-gwah 'free-ah]
connector, extension plug	el enchufe intermedio [ehl ehn-'choo-feh een-tehr-'meh-dee·oh]
dining room	el comedor [ehl koh-meh-'dohr]
dinner	cena ['seh-nah]
doorman, porter	portero [pohr-'teh-roh]
elevator	el ascensor [ehl ah-sehn-'sohr]
extension cord	el cordón/el cable de empalme [ehl kohr-'dohn/ehl 'kah-bleh deh ehm-'pahl-meh]
fan	el ventilador [ehl vehn-tee-lah-'dohr]
faucet	grifo (*Am* canilla, pluma, llave) ['gree-foh (kah-'nee-yah, 'ploo-mah, 'yah-veh)]
floor	piso ['pee-soh]
full board	la pensión completa [lah pehn-see-'ohn kohm-'pleh-tah]
glass of water	vaso de agua ['vah-soh deh 'ah-gwah]
guest house	la pensión [lah pehn-see-'ohn]
hanger	percha ['pehr-chah]
headrest	reposacabezas, apoyacabezas [reh-poh-sah-kah-'beh-sahs, ah-poh-yah-kah-'beh-sahs]
heating	la calefacción [lah kah-leh-fahk-see-'ohn]
high/peak season	temporada alta/principal [tehm-poh-'rah-dah 'ahl-tah/preen-see-'pahl]

hot water   (el) agua caliente [(ehl) 'ah-gwah kah-lee-'ehn-teh]

key   la llave [lah 'yah-veh]

lamp   lámpara ['lahm-pah-rah]

light switch   el interruptor, la llave de la luz [ehl een-teh-rroop-'tohr, lah 'yah-veh deh lah loos]

lobby   el hall (de entrada) (*Am.* el lobby/la recepción) [ehl jahl (deh ehn-'trah-dah), ehl 'loh-bee/lah reh-sehp-see-'ohn]

lodging   alojamiento [ah-loh-hah-mee-'ehn-toh]

lounge   sala de estar ['sah-lah deh eh-'stahr]

low/off season   temporada baja/secundaria [tehm-poh-'rah-dah 'bah-hah/seh-koon-'dah-ree·ah]

lunch   comida, almuerzo [koh-'mee-dah, ahl-'mwehr-soh]

maid/housekeeper (hotel)   camarera (del hotel) [kah-mah-'reh-rah (dehl oh-'tehl)]

mattress   el colchón [ehl kohl-'chohn]

minibar   el minibar [ehl mee-nee-'bahr]

mirror   espejo [eh-'speh-hoh]

motel   el motel [ehl moh-'tehl]

night lamp   lámpara de mesa de noche ['lahm-pah-rah deh 'meh-sah deh 'noh-cheh]

night table   mesita de noche [meh-'see-tah deh 'noh-cheh]

open buffet (for breakfast)   el bufete libre (para desayunar) [ehl boo-'feh-teh 'lee-breh ('pah-rah deh-sah-yoo-'nahr)]

outlet   caja del enchufe ['kah-hah dehl ehn-'choo-feh]

pillow   almohada [ahl-moh-'ah-dah]

playground   el parque de recreo infantil [ehl 'pahr-keh deh reh-'kreh-oh een-fahn-'teel]

plug   clavija de enchufe [klah-'vee-hah deh ehn-'choo-feh]

pool bar   el bar junto a la piscina [ehl bahr 'hoon-toh ah lah pee-'see-nah]

program of activities	el programa de actividades/animaciones [(ehl proh-'grah-mah deh) ahk-tee-vee-'dah-dehs/ah-nee-mah-see-'oh-nehs]
radio	la radio [lah 'rah-dee·oh]
reception/front desk	la recepción [lah reh-sehp-see-'ohn]
reservation	reserva [reh-'sehr-vah]
rocking chair	el sillón [ehl see-'yohn]
room	la habitación *(Am* pieza, cuarto) [lah ah-bee-tah-see-'ohn (pee-'eh-sah, 'kwahr-toh)]
room and board	comida y alojamiento [koh-'mee-dah ee ah-loh-hah-mee-'ehn-toh]
safe	caja fuerte ['kah-hah 'fwehr-teh]
sheet	sábana ['sah-bah-nah]
shower	ducha ['doo-chah]
sink	lavabo [lah-'vah-boh]
telephone	teléfono [teh-'leh-foh-noh]
terrace	terraza [teh-'rrah-sah]
toilet	los servicios, baño [lohs sehr-'vee-see·ohs, 'bah-nyoh]
toilet paper	el papel higiénico [ehl pah-'pehl ee-hee-'eh-nee-koh]
towel	toalla [toh-'ah-yah]
TV room	sala de televisión ['sah-lah deh teh-leh-vee-see-'ohn]
TV set	el televisor [ehl teh-leh-vee-'sohr]
wading pool	piscina para niños [pee-'see-nah 'pah-rah 'nee-nyohs]
wastebasket	papelera, cesta de papeles [pah-peh-'leh-rah, 'seh-stah deh pah-'peh-lehs]
water	(el) agua [(ehl)'ah-gwah]
window	ventana [vehn-'tah-nah]

Vacation Rentals: Houses/Apartments
Casas/Viviendas de vacaciones

Is electricity/water included in the rent?	¿Está incluido en el alquiler el precio de la electricidad/del agua? [eh-'stah een-kloo-'ee-doh ehn ehl ahl-kee-'lehr ehl 'preh-see·oh deh lah eh-lehk-tree-see-'dahd/dehl 'ah-gwah]

Do you allow pets?	¿Admiten ustedes animales domésticos? [ahd-'mee-tehn oo-'steh-dehs ah-nee-'mah-lehs doh-'meh-stee-kohs]
Where can we get the keys to the house?	¿Dónde nos entregan las llaves para la casa/la vivienda? ['dohn-deh nohs ehn-'treh-gahn lahs 'yah-vehs 'pah-rah lah 'kah-sah/lah vee-vee-'ehn-dah]
Do we have to return them to the same place?	¿Tenemos que devolverlas también allí? [teh-'neh-mohs keh deh-vohl-'vehr-lahs tahm-bee-'ehn ah-'yee]
Where are the garbage cans?	¿Dónde están los cubos de la basura? ['dohn-deh eh-'stahn lohs 'koo-bohs deh lah bah-'soo-rah]
Do we have to clean the place before we leave?	¿Tenemos que encargarnos nosotros de la limpieza final? [teh-'neh-mohs keh ehn-kahr-'gahr-nohs noh-'soh-trohs deh lah leem-pee-'eh-sah fee-'nahl]

Word List: Vacation Rentals: Houses/Apartments

additional costs	gastos adicionales ['gah-stohs ah-dee-see·oh-'nah-lehs]
apartment	apartamento (*Am* departamento) [ah-pahr-tah-'mehn-toh (deh-pahr-tah-'mehn-toh)]
bed/living room	sala-dormitorio, cuarto de estar-dormitorio ['sah-lah-dohr-mee-'toh-ree·oh, 'kwahr-toh deh eh-'stahr-dohr-mee-'toh-ree·oh]
bedroom	dormitorio [dohr-mee-'toh-ree·oh]
brochure	folleto, prospecto [foh-'yeh-toh, proh-'spehk-toh]
bungalow	el bungalow [ehl 'boon-gah-loh]
bunk beds	las literas [lahs lee-'teh-rahs]
central heating	la calefacción central [lah kah-leh-fahk-see-'ohn sehn-'trahl]
coffeemaker	cafetera [kah-feh-'teh-rah]

day of arrival	el día de llegada [ehl 'dee-ah deh yeh-'gah-dah]
dishwasher	el lavaplatos, el lavavajillas [ehl lah-vah-'plah-tohs, ehl lah-vah-vah-'hee-yahs]
electric range	cocina eléctrica [koh-'see-nah eh-'lehk-tree-kah]
electricity, power	la corriente, la electricidad [lah koh-rree-'ehn-teh, lah eh-lehk-tree-see-'dahd]
final cleaning (before checking out)	limpieza final [leem-pee-'eh-sah fee-'nahl]
flat rate for electricity	tarifa global de electricidad [tah-'ree-fah gloh-'bahl deh eh-lehk-tree-see-'dahd]
garbage	basura [bah-'soo-rah]
gas range	cocina de gas [koh-'see-nah deh gahs]
inn (government-run)	el parador (nacional) [ehl pah-rah-'dohr (nah-see-oh-'nahl)]
kitchen rag, dish towel	paño de cocina ['pah-nyoh deh koh-'see-nah]
kitchenette	el rincón-cocina [ehl reen-'kohn-koh-'see-nah]
landlord/landlady, owner	dueño/duena de la casa ['dweh-nyoh/'dweh-nyah deh lah 'kah-sah]
living room	sala, cuarto de estar ['sah-lah, 'kwahr-toh deh eh-'stahr]
pets	los animales domésticos [lohs ah-nee-'mah-lehs doh-'meh-stee-kohs]
refrigerator	nevera *(Am* refrigerador) [neh-'veh-rah (reh-free-heh-rah-'dohr)]
rent	el alquiler [ehl ahl-kee-'lehr]
to rent	alquilar [ahl-kee-'lahr]
small corner table (for dining)	rinconera (para comer) [reen-koh-'neh-rah ('pah-rah koh-'mehr)]
sofa bed	el sofá-cama [ehl soh-'fah-'kah-mah]
stove	cocina [koh-'see-nah]
studio	estudio [eh-'stoo-dee-oh]
toaster	el tostador [ehl toh-stah-'dohr]
vacation apartment	piso *(Am* apartamento) de vacaciones ['pee-soh (ah-pahr-tah-'mehn-toh) deh vah-kah-see-'oh-nehs]

vacation house	casa de vacaciones ['kah-sah deh vah-kah-see-'oh-nehs]
vacation village/community	la urbanización de vacaciones [lah oor-bah-nee-sah-see-'ohn deh vah-kah-see-'oh-nehs]
voltage	el voltaje [ehl vohl-'tah-heh]
washing machine	lavadora [lah-vah-'doh-rah]
water meter	contador de agua [kohn-tah-'dohr deh 'ah-gwah]

Camping
Cámping

Is there a campsite nearby?	¿Hay por aquí cerca un cámping? ['ah·ee pohr ah-'kee 'sehr-kah oon 'kahm-peen]
Do you have room for another mobile home (trailer)/tent?	¿Tienen ustedes sitio para un coche-vivienda (*Am* una casa rodante)/una tienda (*Am* una carpa)? [tee-'eh-nehn oo-'steh-dehs 'see-tee·oh 'pah-rah oon 'koh-cheh-vee-vee-'ehn-dah ('oo-nah 'kah-sah roh-'dahn-teh)/'oo-nah tee-'ehn-dah ('oo-nah 'kahr-pah)]
How much is it per day and per person?	¿Cuánto cuesta por día y por persona? ['kwahn-toh 'kweh-stah pohr 'dee-ah ee pohr pehr-'soh-nah]
How much is it for...	¿Cuánto se paga por... ['kwahn-toh seh 'pah-gah pohr]
the car?	un coche? [oon 'koh-cheh]
the trailer/camper?	un coche-vivienda (*Am* una casa rodante)? [oon 'koh-cheh vee-vee-'ehn-dah ('oo-nah 'kah-sah roh-'dahn-teh)]
the RV?	una autocaravana? ['oo-nah ow-toh-kah-rah-'vah-nah]
the tent?	una tienda (*Am* una carpa)? ['oo-nah tee-'ehn-dah ('oo-nah 'kahr-pah)]

Do you rent cabins/vacation homes/trailers/campers?	¿Alquilan cabañas/casas de vacaciones/coches-vivienda? [ahl-'kee-lahn kah-'bah-nyahs/'kah-sahs deh vah-kah-see-'oh-nehs/'koh-chehs vee-vee-'ehn-dah]
Where can I park...	¿Dónde puedo poner... ['dohn-deh 'pweh-doh poh-'nehr...]
my trailer/camper?	el coche-vivienda (*Am* la casa rodante)? [ehl 'koh-cheh vee-vee-'ehn-dah (lah 'kah-sah roh-'dahn-teh)]
my RV?	la autocaravana? [lah ow-toh-kah-rah-'vah-nah]
Where can I pitch my tent?	¿Dónde puedo montar la tienda (*Am* la carpa)? ['dohn-deh 'pweh-doh mohn-'tahr lah tee-'ehn-dah (lah 'kahr-pah)]
We plan to stay…days/weeks.	Pensamos quedarnos…días/semanas. [pehn-'sah-mohs keh-'dahr-nohs...'dee-ahs/seh-'mah-nahs]
Is there a grocery store nearby?	¿Hay aquí una tienda de comestibles? ['ah·ee ah-'kee 'oo-nah tee-'ehn-dah deh koh-meh-'stee-blehs]
Where are… the toilets?	¿Dónde están… ['dohn-deh eh-'stah] los servicios? [lohs sehr-'vee-see·ohs]
the washrooms?	los lavabos? [lohs lah-'vah-bohs]
the showers?	las duchas? [lahs 'doo-chahs]
Do you have electric power here?	¿Hay aquí corriente eléctrica? ['ah·ee ah-'kee koh-rree-'ehn-teh eh-'lehk-tree-kah]
Is it 220 or 110 volts?	¿La corriente es de 220 o de 110 voltios? [lah koh-rree-'ehn-teh ehs deh dohs-see-'ehn-tohs 'veh-een-teh oh deh see-'ehn-toh dee-'ehs 'vohl-tee·ohs]
Where can I refill/rent butane gas tanks?	¿Dónde puedo cambiar/alquilar botellas/bombonas de butano (*Am* garrafas de gas)? ['dohn-deh 'pweh-doh kahm-bee-'ahr/ahl-kee-

	'lahr boh-'teh-yahs/bohm-'boh-nahs deh boo-'tah-noh (gah-'rrah-fahs deh gahs)]
Is there a night watchman?	¿Está el cámping vigilado por la noche? [eh-'stah ehl 'kahm-peen vee-hee-'lah-doh pohr lah 'noh-cheh]
Is there a playground here?	¿Hay aquí parque infantil? ['ah·ee ah-'kee 'pahr-keh een-fahn-'teel]
Could you please lend me...?	¿Me puede prestar...? [meh 'pweh-deh preh-'stahr]

Youth Hostels
El albergue juvenil

Could you lend me some bed linen/a sleeping bag?	¿Me pueden prestar ropa de cama/un saco de dormir? [meh 'pweh-dehn preh-'stahr 'roh-pah deh 'kah-mah/oon 'sah-koh deh dohr-'meer]
The front door is locked at midnight.	La puerta de entrada se cierra a medianoche. [lah 'pwehr-tah deh ehn-'trah-dah seh see-'eh-rah ah meh-dee·ah-'noh-cheh]

Word List: Camping/Youth Hostels

to borrow	pedir prestado [peh-'deer preh-'stah-doh]
to camp	acampar, hacer cámping [ah-kahm-'pahr, ah-'sehr-'kahm-peen]
camping card/pass	el carnet de cámping [ehl kahr-'neht deh 'kahm-peen]
camping guide	guía de campings ['gee-ah deh 'kahm-peens]
camping stove	hornillo de gas [ohr-'nee-yoh deh gahs]
campsite	el cámping [ehl 'kahm-peen]
clothes drier	secadora [seh-kah-'doh-rah]
communal room	sala común ['sah-lah koh-'moon]
dormitory	dormitorio [dohr-mee-'toh-ree·oh]

drinking water	(el) agua potable [(ehl) 'ah-gwah poh-'tah-bleh]
electric power	la corriente, la electricidad [la koh-rree-'ehn-teh, lah eh-lehk-tree-see-'dahd]
farmhouse	casa de labranza (*Am* granja) ['kah-sah deh lah-'brahn-sah ('grahn-hah)]
gas canister	botella de gas [boh-'teh-yah deh gahs]
gas tank	bombona (*Am* garrafa) de gas [bohm-'boh-nah (gah-'rrah-fah) deh gahs]
kitchen sink	fregadero [freh-gah-'deh-roh]
to lend	prestar [preh-'stahr]
lounge	sala de estar ['sah-lah deh eh-'stahr]
membership card	tarjeta/el carnet de socio [tahr-'heh-tah/ehl kahr-'neht deh 'soh-see·oh]
oil lamp	lámpara de petróleo ['lahm-pah-rah deh peh-'troh-leh-oh]
outlet	(caja de) el enchufe/toma de corriente (*Am* el tomacorriente) [('kah-hah deh) ehl ehn-'choo-feh/ 'toh-mah deh koh-rree-'ehn-teh (ehl toh-mah-koh-rree-'ehn-teh]
playground	el parque de recreo infantil [ehl 'pahr-keh deh reh-'kreh-oh een-fahn-'teel]
plug	clavija de enchufe [klah-'vee-hah deh ehn-'choo-feh]
propane/butane gas	el gas propano/butano [ehl gahs proh-'pah-noh/boo-'tah-noh]
rental fee	(derechos de) alquiler [(deh-'reh-chohs deh) ahl-kee-'lehr]
rental fee, user's fee	tasa de utilización ['tah-sah deh oo-tee-lee-sah-see-'ohn]
RV	autocaravana [ow-toh-kah-rah-'vah-nah]
shared/multiple-bed room	la habitación compartida/de varias camas [lah ah-bee-tah-see-'ohn kohm-pahr-'tee-dah/deh 'vah-ree·ahs 'kah-mahs]
sleeping bag	saco de dormir ['sah-koh deh dohr-'meer]

student dormitory/college residence hall	residencia estudiantil, colegio mayor [reh-see-'dehn-see·ah eh-stoo-dee-ahn-'teel, koh-'leh-hee·oh mah-'yohr]
tank	el bidón (*Am* el tanque) [ehl bee-'dohn (ehl 'tahn-keh)]
tent	tienda de campaña (*Am* carpa) [tee-'ehn-dah deh kahm-'pah-nyah ('kahr-pah)]
tent peg	la estaquilla de la tienda [lah eh-stah-'kee-yah deh lah tee-'ehn-dah]
tent pole	palo de tienda (*Am* de carpa) ['pah-loh deh tee-'ehn-dah (deh 'kahr-pah)]
tent rope	cuerda de tienda (*Am* de carpa) ['kwehr-dah deh tee-'ehn-dah (deh 'kahr-pah)]
trailer, camper	el coche vivienda (*Am* casa rodante) [ehl 'koh-cheh vee-vee-'ehn-dah ('kah-sah roh-'dahn-teh)]
washrooms	los lavabos [lohs lah-'vah-bohs]
water	(el) agua [(ehl) 'ah-gwah]
youth group	grupo juvenil ['groo-poh hoo-veh-'neel]
youth hostel	el albergue juvenil [ehl ahl-'behr-geh hoo-veh-'neel]
youth hostel card/pass	el carnet de albergues juveniles [ehl kahr-'neht deh ahl-'behr-gehs hoo-veh-'nee-lehs]
youth hostel guide	guía de albergues juveniles ['gee-ah deh ahl-'behr-gehs hoo-veh-'nee-lehs]
youth hostel managers	los directores del albergue juvenil [lohs dee-rehk-'toh-rehs dehl ahl-'behr-geh hoo-veh-'neel

5 Eating and Drinking
Gastronomía

Eating Out

A comer

Is there...around here?	¿Dónde hay por aquí cerca... ['dohn-deh 'ah·ee·pohr ah-'kee 'sehr-kah]
a good restaurant	un buen restaurante? [oon bwehn reh-stah·oo-'rahn-teh]
a restaurant serving local cuisine	un restaurante típico? [oon reh-stah·oo-'rahn-teh 'tee-pee-koh]
an inexpensive restaurant	un restaurante no demasiado caro? [oon reh-stah·oo-'rahn-teh noh deh-mah-see-'ah-doh 'kah-roh]
a fast-food restaurant	un restaurante (de servicio) rápido? [oon reh-stah·oo-'rahn-teh (deh sehr-'vee-see·oh) 'rah-pee-doh]
Where can we eat well/ cheaply around here?	¿Dónde se puede comer bien/por poco dinero por aquí cerca? ['dohn-deh seh 'pweh-deh koh-'mehr 'bee·ehn/pohr 'poh-koh dee-'neh-roh pohr ah-'kee 'sehr-kah]

Some names to look out for:

el café (ehl kah-'feh) generally serves coffee, tea, hot chocolate, juices, soft drinks, pastries, and ice cream.

el bar (ehl bahr) can range from an American-style bar mostly serving alcoholic beverages (hotel bars, for example) to a wine bar, to a sort of café that also serves alcoholic beverages and snacks.

la cafetería (lah kah-feh-teh-'ree-ah) offers a limited food and drink menu, often including beer and wine; some are self-service.

la taberna (lah tah-'behr-nah) (also called **tasca** 'tah-skah) is very much like a pub, serving drinks and meals.

el (café-)restaurante (ehl kah-'feh reh-stah·oo-'rahn-teh) is a restaurant.

el chiringuito (ehl chee-reen-'gee-toh) is a small eatery or outdoor food stall; it can also be an outdoor bar.

la hamburguesería (lah ahm-boor-geh-seh-'ree-ah) serves hamburgers (hamburguesas), french fries, and the like.

At the Restaurant
En el restaurante

Can I reserve a table for four for tonight?

¿Puede reservarnos para esta noche una mesa para cuatro personas? ['pweh-deh reh-sehr-'vahr-nohs 'pah-rah 'eh-stah 'noh-cheh 'oo-nah 'meh-sah 'pah-rah 'kwah-troh pehr-'soh-nahs]

How late is the kitchen open?

¿Hasta qué hora sirven ustedes comida caliente? ['ah-stah keh 'oh-rah 'seer-vehn oo-'steh-dehs koh-'mee-dah kah-lee-'ehn-teh]

Is this table/seat free?

¿Está libre esta mesa/este asiento? [eh-'stah 'lee-breh 'eh-stah 'meh-sah/'eh-steh ah-see-'ehn-toh]

A table for two/three, please.

Una mesa para dos/tres personas, por favor. ['oo-nah 'meh-sah 'pah-rah dohs/trehs pehr-'soh-nahs, pohr fah-'vohr]

Where's the bathroom, please?

¿Dónde están los servicios, por favor? ['dohn-deh eh-'stahn lohs sehr-'vee-see·ohs, pohr fah-'vohr]

This way, please.

Por aquí. [pohr ah-'kee]

Ordering Breakfast   See also Chapter 4.
Pedido

Waiter,

Camarero (*Am* mozo), [kah-mah-'reh-roh ('moh-soh)]

  the menu

  la carta (*Am* el menú) [lah 'kahr-tah (ehl meh-'noo)]

  the wine list

  la carta de vinos [lah 'kahr-tah deh 'vee-nohs]

Can you recommend something?

¿Qué me recomienda usted? [keh meh reh-koh-mee-'ehn-dah oo-'stehd]

Do you have vegetarian dishes/low-calorie dishes?

¿Tienen ustedes comida vegetariana/de régimen? [tee-'eh-nehn oo-'steh-dehs koh-'mee-dah veh-heh-tah-ree-'ah-nah/deh 'reh-hee-mehn]

Do you have children's portions?	¿Tienen ustedes también platos especiales para niños? [tee-'eh-nehn oo-'steh-dehs tahm-bee-'ehn 'plah-tohs eh-speh-see-'ah-lehs 'pah-rah 'nee-nyohs]
Do you know what you want?	¿Ya han elegido ustedes? [yah ahn eh-leh-'hee-doh oo-'steh-dehs]

Seafood Casserole

What appetizer/dessert would you like?	¿Qué toman de aperitivo/de postre? [keh 'toh-mahn deh ah-peh-ree-'tee-voh/deh 'poh-streh]
I want…	Yo tomo… [yoh 'toh-moh]
As an appetizer/For dessert/As a main dish, I want…	De aperitivo/De postre/Como plato principal tomo… [deh ah-peh-ree-'tee-voh/deh 'poh-streh/'koh-moh 'plah-toh preen-see-'pahl 'toh-moh]
I don't want an appetizer, thank you.	Yo no tomo aperitivo, gracias. [yoh noh 'toh-moh ah-peh-ree-'tee-voh, 'grah-see·ahs]
I'm sorry, but we're out of…	Lo lamento, pero ya no tenemos … [loh lah-'mehn-toh, 'peh-roh yah noh teh-'neh-mohs]

That dish has to be ordered in advance.	Esa comida hay que pedirla por anticipado. ['eh-sah koh-'mee-dah 'ah·ee keh peh-'deer-lah pohr ahn-tee-see-'pah-doh]
Could I substitute…for…	¿Puede traerme…en lugar de…? ['pweh-deh trah-'ehr-meh ehn loo-'gahr deh]
I can't eat… Could you make my food without…?	…no me sienta bien. ¿Puede prepararme.la comida sin…? [noh meh see-'ehn-tah 'bee·ehn. 'pweh-deh preh-pah-'rahr-meh lah koh-'mee-dah seen]

How do you like your steak?	¿Como desea usted el filete? ['koh-moh deh-'seh-ah oo-'stehd ehl fee-'leh-teh]
well done	bien pasado ['bee·ehn pah-'sah-doh]
medium-rare	poco pasado ['poh-koh pah-'sah-doh]
rare	a la inglesa [ah lah een-'gleh-sah]
What would you like to drink?	¿Qué desea usted beber (*Am* tomar)? [keh deh-'seh-ah oo-'stehd beh-'behr (toh-'mahr)]
A glass of…, please.	Un vaso de…, por favor. [oon 'vah-soh de, pohr fah-'vohr]
A bottle/half a bottle of…, please.	Una botella/Media botella de…, por favor. ['oo-nah boh-'teh-yah/'meh-dee·ah boh-'teh-yah deh, pohr fah-'vohr]
With ice, please.	Con hielo, por favor. [kohn 'yeh-loh, pohr fah-'vohr]
Enjoy your meal.	¡Que aproveche! [keh ah-proh-'veh-cheh]
Is there anything else you want?	¿Desea usted algo más? [deh-'seh-ah oo-'stehd 'ahl-goh mahs]
Please, bring us…	Tráiganos …, por favor. ['trah·ee-gah-nohs, pohr fah-'vohr]
Could we get more bread/water/wine?	¿Puede traernos un poco más de pan/agua/vino? ['pweh-deh trah-'ehr-nohs oon 'poh-koh mahs deh pahn/'ah-gwah/'vee-noh]

Complaints
Reclamaciones

In Spain, all restaurants have a "libro de reclamaciones" (complaint book), which is regularly inspected by the Tourist Board. The book is usually placed at the entrance.

We need another...	Aquí falta un.../una... [ah-'kee 'fahl-tah oon/'oo-nah]
Did you forget my...?	¿Se ha olvidado usted de mi ...? [seh ah ohl-vee-'dah-doh oo-'stehd deh mee]
I didn't order this.	Yo no he pedido esto. [yoh noh eh peh-'dee-doh 'eh-stoh]
The food is cold/too salty.	La comida está fría/salada. [lah koh-'mee-dah eh-'stah 'free-ah/sah-'lah-dah]
The meat is tough/ too greasy.	La carne está dura/tiene demasi ada grasa. [lah 'kahr-neh eh-'stah 'doo-rah/tee-'eh-neh deh-mah-see-'ah-dah 'grah-sah]
This fish is not fresh.	Este pescado no es fresco. ['eh-steh peh-'skah-doh noh ehs 'freh-skoh]
Take it back, please.	Lléveselo, por favor. ['yeh-veh-seh-loh, pohr fah-'vohr]
Call the manager, please.	Llame al dueño, por favor. ['yah-meh ahl 'dweh-nyoh, pohr fah-'vohr]

The Check
La cuenta

Could I have the check, please?	¡La cuenta, por favor! [lah 'kwehn-tah, pohr fah-'vohr]
The check, please. We're in a hurry.	La cuenta, por favor. Tenemos prisa. [lah 'kwehn-tah, pohr fah-'vohr, teh-'neh-mohs 'pree-sah]

All together, please.	Todo junto, por favor. ['toh-doh 'hoon-toh, pohr fah-'vohr]
Separate checks, please.	Cuentas separadas, por favor. ['kwehn-tahs seh-pah-'rah-dahs, pohr fah-'vohr]
Is everything/the service/ the cover charge included?	¿Está todo/el servicio/el cubierto incluido? [eh-'stah 'toh-doh/ehl sehr-'vee-see·oh/ehl koo-bee-'ehr-toh een-kloo-'ee-doh]
Is the tax included or not?	¿El precio es con IVA o sin IVA? [ehl 'preh-see·oh ehs kohn 'ee-vah oh seen 'ee-vah]
I think there's a mistake in the check.	Me parece que hay un error en la cuenta. [meh pah-'reh-seh keh 'ah·ee oon eh-'rrohr ehn lah 'kwehn-tah]
I didn't have that. I had...	Esto no me lo ha servido. Yo tenía... ['eh-stoh noh meh loh ah sehr-'vee-doh. yoh teh-'nee-ah]
Did you enjoy your meal?	¿Le/Les ha gustado la comida? [leh/lehs ah goo-'stah-doh lah koh-'mee-dah]
The food was excellent.	La comida estaba excelente. [lah koh-'mee-dah eh-'stah-bah ehk-seh-'lehn-teh]
That's for you.	Para usted. ['pah-rah oo-'stehd]
Keep the change.	Está bien así. [eh-'stah 'bee·ehn ah-'see]

Service is included in the check in all Spanish restaurants and hotels; however, tipping is customary—usually 5% to 10% of the check.

As a Dinner Guest
Invitación a comer/Comer en compañia

Thank you very much for your invitation.	¡Muchas gracias por la invitación! ['moo-chahs 'grah-see·ahs pohr lah een-vee-tah-see-'ohn]

Help yourself!	¡Sírvase, sírvase! ['seer-vah-seh, 'seer-vah-seh]
Cheers!	¡Salud! [sah-'lood]
Could you pass me the…, please?	¿Me puede acercar/pasar…? [meh 'pweh-deh ah-sehr-'kahr/pah-'sahr]
Would you like some more…?	¿Un poco más de…? [oon 'poh-koh mahs deh]
No, thanks, I've eaten enough/I'm full.	No, gracias, he comido ya mucho/ya estoy satisfecho [noh, 'grah-see·ahs, eh koh-'mee-doh yah 'moo-choh/yah eh-'stoh·ee sah-tees-'feh-choh]
Do you mind if I smoke?	¿Puedo fumar? ['pweh-doh foo-'mahr]

Word List: Eating and Drinking

See also Unit 8.
Word Lists: Food and Drink

appetizers	los entremeses [lohs ehn-treh-'meh-sehs]
ashtray	cenicero [seh-nee-'seh-roh]
au gratin	gratinado [grah-tee-'nah-doh]
bay leaf	el laurel [ehl lah·oo'rehl]
beer	cerveza [sehr-'veh-sah]
beverage	bebida [beh-'bee-dah]
boil	cocer, hervir [koh-'sehr, ehr-'veer]
boiled	cocido, hervido [koh-'see-doh, ehr-'vee-doh]
bone	hueso ['weh-soh]
bread	el pan [ehl pahn]
breakfast	desayuno [deh-sah-'yoo-noh]
butter	mantequilla (*Am* manteca) [mahn-teh-'kee-yah (mahn-'teh-kah)]
carafe	garrafa [gah-'rrah-fah]
clove	clavo ['klah-voh]
coffeemaker	cafetera [kah-feh-'teh-rah]
cold	frío ['free-oh]
corkscrew	el sacacorchos [ehl sah-kah-'kohr-chohs]
to cook	cocinero [koh-see-'neh-roh]
course	plato ['plah-toh]

cumin	comino [koh-'mee-noh]
cup	taza ['tah-sah]
cutlery, place setting, silver	los cubiertos [lohs koo-bee-'ehr-tohs]
dessert	el postre [ehl 'poh-streh]
diabetic	diabético [dee-ah-'beh-tee-koh]
diet	dieta [dee-'eh-tah]
dinner	cena ['seh-nah]
dish	plato, comida ['plah-toh, koh-'mee-dah]
draft, on tap	de barril [deh bah-'rreel]
dressing	aliño [ah-'lee-nyoh]
dry	seco ['seh-koh]
egg cup	huevera [weh-'veh-rah]
fat	graso, gordo ['grah-soh, 'gohr-doh]
fishbone	espina [eh-'spee-nah]
fork	el tenedor [ehl teh-neh-'dohr]
french fries	las patatas fritas [lahs pah-'tah-tahs 'free-tahs]
fresh	fresco ['freh-skoh]
fried	frito ['free-toh]
garlic	ajo ['ah-hoh]

glass	vaso ['vah-soh]
grill	parrilla [pah-'rree-yah]
grilled	a la parrilla [ah lah pah-'rree-yah]
herbs	las hierbas [lahs 'yehr-bahs]
hot	caliente [kah-lee-'ehn-teh]
hot, spicy	picante [pee-'kahn-teh]
juicy	jugoso [hoo-'goh-soh]
knife	cuchillo [koo-'chee-yoh]
landlord	casero [kah-'seh-roh]
lean (meat)	magro ['mah-groh]
lemon	el limón [ehl lee-'mohn]
lunch	comida, almuerzo [koh-'mee-dah, ahl-'mwehr-soh]
lunch/dinner specials	el menú turístico [ehl meh-'noo too-'ree-stee-koh]
main meal/dish	comida/plato principal [koh-'mee-dah/'plah-toh preen-see-'pahl]
mayonnaise	mayonesa [mah-yoh-'neh-sah]
menu	carta (*Am* el menú) ['kahr-tah (ehl meh-'noo)]
menu of the day	el menú del día [ehl meh-'noo dehl 'dee-ah]
mustard	mostaza [moh-'stah-sah]
napkin	servilleta [sehr-vee-'yeh-tah]
nonalcoholic	sin alcohol [seen ahl-koh-'ohl]
nutmeg	la nuez moscada [lah noo-'ehs moh-'skah-dah]
oil	el aceite [ehl ah-'seh-ee-teh]
oil and vinegar set	las vinagreras [lahs vee-nah-'greh-rahs]
olive oil	el aceite de oliva [ehl ah-'seh-ee-teh deh oh-'lee-vah]
olives	las aceitunas [lahs ah-seh-ee-'too-nahs]
onion	cebolla [seh-'boh-yah]
to order	pedir [peh-'deer]
parsley	el perejil [ehl peh-reh-'heel]
pasta	pasta ['pah-stah]
pepper	pimienta [pee-mee-'ehn-tah]
pepper mill	pimentero [pee-mehn-'teh-roh]
pitcher	jarra, jarro ['hah-rrah, 'hah-rroh]
place setting	cubierto [koo-bee-'ehr-toh]
platter	la fuente [lah 'fwehn-teh]
portion	la ración [lah rah-see-'ohn]

potatoes	patatas [pah-'tah-tahs]
to put dressing (on the salad)	aliñar la ensalada [ah-lee-'nyahr lah ehn-sah-'lah-dah]
raw	crudo ['kroo-doh]
red pepper	el pimentón [ehl pee-mehn-'tohn]
rice	el arroz [ehl ah-'rrohs]
roast	asado [ah-'sah-doh]
saccharine	sacarina [sah-kah-'ree-nah]
salad	ensalada [ehn-sah-'lah-dah]
salad bar	el bufete de ensaladas diversas [ehl boo-'feh-teh deh ehn-sah-'lah-dahs dee-'vehr-sahs]
salt	la sal [lah sahl]
salt shaker	salero [sah-'leh-roh]
sauce	salsa ['sahl-sah]
saucer	plato pequeño ['plah-toh peh-'keh-nyoh]
to season	sazonar [sah-soh-'nahr]
to serve oneself	servirse [sehr-'veer-seh]
side dish	la guarnición [lah gwahr-nee-see-'ohn]
slice	*(bread)* rebanada; *(meat, fruit)* tajada; *(sausage, fruit)* rodaja [reh-bah-'nah-dah; tah-'hah-dah; roh-'dah-hah]
smoked	ahumado [ah-oo-'mah-doh]
soft	blando ['blahn-doh]
soup	sopa ['soh-pah]
soup dish	plato de sopa ['plah-toh deh 'soh-pah]
sour	agrio ['ah-gree·oh]
specialty	la especialidad [lah eh-speh-see·ah-lee-'dahd]
specialty of the day	plato del día ['plah-toh dehl 'dee-ah]
spice, condiment	especia, condimento [eh-'speh-see·ah, kohn-dee-'mehn-toh]
spit-roasted	en el asador [ehn ehl ah-sah-'dohr]
spoon	cuchara [koo-'chah-rah]
stain	mancha ['mahn-chah]
steamed	al vapor, rehogado [ahl vah-'pohr, reh-oh-'gah-doh]
stew	estofado [eh-stoh-'fah-doh]
straw	pajita [pah-'hee-tah]
stuffed, stuffing	relleno [reh-'yeh-noh]
sugar	el azúcar [ehl ah-'soo-kahr]

sweet	dulce ['dool-seh]
tablecloth	el mantel [ehl mahn-'tehl]
taste	el sabor [ehl sah-'bohr]
to taste	probar [proh-'bahr]
teaspoon	cucharilla de té [koo-chah-'ree-yah deh teh]
tender	tierno [tee-'ehr-noh]
the order	pedido [peh-'dee-doh]
tip	propina [proh-'pee-nah]
toasted	tostado [toh-'stah-doh]
toothpick	palillo de dientes [pah-'lee-yoh deh dee-'ehn-tehs]
tough	duro ['doo-roh]
to uncork	descorchar [dehs-kohr-'chahr]
vegetarian	vegetariano [veh-heh-tah-ree-'ah-noh]
vinegar	el vinagre [ehl vee-'nah-greh]
waiter/waitress	camarero/camarera [kah-mah-'reh-roh/kah-mah-'reh-rah]
water	(el) agua [(ehl) 'ah-gwah]
well-done	en su punto, bien cocido/asado [ehn soo 'poon-toh, 'bee·ehn koh-'see-doh/ah-'sah-doh]
wine	vino ['vee-noh]
wineglass	vaso para vino ['vah-soh 'pah-rah 'vee-noh]

Menu

Menú

Lunch/Dinner Specials Menú turístico

1. Noodle soup — Sopa de fideos ['soh-pah deh fee-'deh-ohs]

   Veal cutlet — Escalope de ternera [eh-skah-'loh-peh deh tehr-'neh-rah]

   Flan (Spanish-style custard) or coffee — Flan o café [flahn oh kah-'feh]

2. Consomme — Consomé [kohn-soh-'meh]
   Veal chops with potatoes and peas — Chuleta de ternera con patatas y guisantes [choo-'leh-tah deh tehr-'neh-rah kohn pah-'tah-tahs ee gee-'sahn-tehs]

   Dessert (flan or fruit in season) or coffee — Postre (flan o fruta del tiempo) ['poh-streh (flahn oh 'froo-tah dehl tee-'ehm-poh)]; o café [oh kah-'feh]

3. Gazpacho — Gazpacho [gahs-'pah-choh]
   Chicken cutlet or hake — Pechuga de pollo o merluza [peh-'choo-gah deh 'poh-yoh oh mehr-'loo-sah]

   Fruit in season — Fruta del tiempo ['froo-tah dehl tee-'ehm-poh]

Appetizers Entremeses

anchovies (fresh) — boquerones [boh-keh-'roh-nehs]
artichokes — alcachofas [ahl-kah-'choh-fahs]
boiled ham — jamón (de) york, jamón cocido [hah-'mohn (deh) yohrk, hah-'mohn koh-'see-doh]

In Spain, many restaurants offer a "menú turístico," consisting of fixed price meals.

chorizo	chorizo [choh-'ree-soh]
clams	almejas [ahl-'meh-hahs]
cold cuts	fiambre [fee-'ahm-breh]
crabs	cangrejos [kahn-'greh-hohs]
croquettes	croquetas [kroh-'keh-tahs]
garlic shrimp	gambas al ajillo ['gahm-bahs ahl ah-'hee-yoh]
grilled shrimp	gambas a la plancha ['gahm-bahs ah lah 'plahn-chah]
mussels	mejillones [meh-hee-'yoh-nehs]
olives	aceitunas [ah-seh·ee-'too-nahs]
Russian salad	ensaladilla rusa [ehn-sah-lah-'dee-yah 'roo-sah]
salami-type sausage	salchichón [sahl-chee-'chohn]
sardines	sardinas [sahr-'dee-nahs]
sausage	embutido [ehm-boo-'tee-doh]
seafood salad	salpicón de marisco [sahl-pee-'kohn deh mah-'ree-skoh]
serrano cured ham	jamón serrano [hah-'mohn seh-'rrah-noh]
shrimp	gambas ['gahm-bahs]
snails	caracoles [kah-rah-'koh-lehs]

Soups

Sopas

Asturian bean stew	fabada asturiana [fah-'bah-dah ah-stoo-ree-'ah-nah]
broth, bouillon	caldo ['kahl-doh]
consomme	consomé [kohn-soh-'meh]
cream of asparagus soup	crema de espárragos ['kreh-mah deh eh-'spah-rrah-gohs]
fish soup	sopa de pescado ['soh-pah deh peh-'skah-doh]
garlic soup	sopa de ajo ['soh-pah deh 'ah-hoh]
gazpacho	gazpacho [gahs-'pah-choh]
noodle soup	sopa de fideos ['soh-pah deh fee-'deh-ohs]
rice soup	sopa de arroz ['soh-pah deh ah-'rrohs]
vegetable soup	sopa de verduras (juliana, jardinera) ['soh-pah deh vehr-'doo-rahs (hoo-lee-'ah-nah, hahr-dee-'neh-rah)]

Fish and Seafood

Pescados y Mariscos

angler, angler fish	rapé [rah-'peh]
baby eel	angulas [ahn-'goo-lahs]
breaded squid	calamares a la romana [kah-lah-'mah-rehs ah lah roh-'mah-nah]
carp	carpa ['kahr-pah]
codfish	bacalao [bah-kah-'lah-oh]
dorado	dorada [doh-'rah-dah]
eel	anguila [ahn-'gee-lah]
fish in a tomato and parsley sauce	pescado a la marinera [peh-'skah-doh ah lah mah-ree-'neh-rah]
flounder	platija [plah-'tee-hah]
grilled fish platter	parrillada de pescado [pah-rree-'yah-dah deh peh-'skah-doh]
hake	merluza [mehr-'loo-sah]
herring	arenque [ah-'rehn-keh]
large lobster	bogavante [boh-gah-'vahn-teh]
lobster	langosta [lahn-'goh-stah]
mackerel	caballa [kah-'bah-yah]
Norway lobster	cigala [see-'gah-lah]
octopus	pulpo ['pool-poh]
paella	paella [pah-'eh-yah]
perch	perca ['pehr-kah]
prawn	langostino [lahn-goh-'stee-noh]
ray	raya ['rah-yah]
red bream, sea bream	besugo [beh-'soo-goh]
red mullet	salmonete [sahl-moh-'neh-teh]
salmon	salmón [sahl-'mohn]
sea bass	corvina [kohr-'vee-nah]; lubina [loo-'bee-nah]
seafood casserole	zarzuela de mariscos [sahr-soo-'eh-lah deh mah-'ree-skohs]
shrimp	gambas ['gahm-bahs]
sole	lenguado [lehn-'gwah-doh]
spider crab, large crab	centolla, centollo [sehn-'toh-yah, sehn-'toh-yoh]
squid casserole	calamares en su tinta [kah-lah-'mah-rehs ehn soo 'teen-tah]
swordfish	pez espada [pehs eh-'spah-dah]
trout	trucha ['troo-chah]
tuna	atún, bonito [ah-'toon, boh-'nee-toh]

| turbot | rodaballo [roh-dah-'bah-yoh] |
| whiting, small hake | pescadilla [peh-skah-'dee-yah] |

Meat and Poultry

Carne y Aves

beef	carne de vaca ['kahr-neh deh 'vah-kah]
boiled, cooked	cocido [koh-'see-doh]
brains	sesos ['seh-sohs]
chicken	pollo ['poh-yoh]
chicken breast	pechuga de pollo [peh-'choo-gah deh 'poh-yoh]
chop	chuleta (*Am* costeleta) [choo-'leh-tah (koh-steh-'leh-tah)]
chopped meat	carne picada ['kahr-neh pee-'kah-dah]
cutlet, scalopini	escalope [eh-skah-'loh-peh]
duck	pato ['pah-toh]
filet (steak)	filete [fee-'leh-teh]
grilled meats	parrillada de carne [pah-rree-'yah-dah deh 'kahr-neh]
hare	liebre [lee-'eh-breh]
kidneys	riñones [ree-'nyoh-nehs]
lamb	cordero lechal [kohr-'deh-roh leh-'chahl]
liver	hígado ['ee-gah-doh]
loin	lomo ['loh-moh]
meat pie	empanada [ehm-pah-'nah-dah]
mutton	cordero [kohr-'deh-roh]
paella (rice with meat, sausage, green vegetables)	paella [pah-'eh-yah]
partridge	perdiz [pehr-'dees]
pheasant	faisán [fah·ee-'sahn]
pigeon	pichón [pee-'chohn]
piglet, suckling pig	cochinillo [koh-chee-'nee-yoh]
pork	cerdo ['sehr-doh]
rabbit	conejo [koh-'neh-hoh]
roast	asado [ah-'sah-doh]
roast beef	rosbif [rohs-'beef]
sirloin	solomillo [soh-loh-'mee-yoh]
steak	bistec [bee-'stehk]

stew	guiso ['gee-soh]
stewed	guisado [gee-'sah-doh]
stewed or braised meat	estofado [eh-stoh-'fah-doh]
tongue	lengua ['lehn-gwah]
tripe	callos ['kah-yohs]
turkey	pavo ['pah-voh]
veal	ternera [tehr-'neh-rah]
young goat	cabrito, chivito [kah-'bree-toh, chee-'vee-toh]

Salads and Vegetables   Ensalada y Verduras

artichokes	alcachofas [ahl-kah-'choh-fahs]
asparagus	espárragos [eh-'spah-rrah-gohs]
Brussels sprouts	col de Bruselas [kohl de broo-'seh-lahs]
carrots	zanahorias [sah-nah-'oh-ree·ahs]
cauliflower	coliflor [koh-lee-'flohr]
chard	acelgas [ah-'sehl-gahs]
chick-peas	garbanzos [gahr-'bahn-sohs]
cucumber	pepino [peh-'pee-noh]
eggplant	berenjenas [beh-rehn-'heh-nahs]
escarole	escarola [eh-skah-'roh-lah]
french fries	patatas (*Am* papas) fritas [pah-'tah-tahs ('pah-pahs) 'free-tahs]
green beans, string beans	judías verdes, (*Am* habichuelas) [hoo-'dee-ahs 'vehr-dehs, ah-bee-choo-'eh-lahs]
lentils	lentejas [lehn-'teh-hahs]
lettuce	lechuga [leh-'choo-gah]
mixed salad	ensalada variada/mixta [ehn-sah-'lah-dah vah-ree-'ah-dah/'meek-stah]
mushrooms	setas ['seh-tahs]
onions	cebollas [seh-'boh-yahs]
peas	guisantes [gee-'sahn-tehs]
pepper	pimiento [pee-mee-'ehn-toh]
pisto (manchego): braised meat dish, with stuffed peppers, tomato, pumpkin, and other ingredients	pisto (manchego) ['pee-stoh (mahn-'cheh-goh)]

potatoes	patatas (*Am* papas) [pah-'tah-tahs ('pah-pahs)]
salad in season	ensalada de estación [ehn-sah-'lah-dah deh eh-stah-see-'ohn]
tomato	tomate [toh-'mah-teh]
watercress	berro ['beh-rroh]
white beans	judías blancas (alubias), (*Am* frijoles blancos) [hoo-'dee-ahs 'blahn-kahs (ah-'loo-bee·ahs), free-'hoh-lehs 'blahn-kohs]

Egg Dishes

Platos de Huevos

fried eggs	huevos al plato, huevos fritos ['weh-vohs ahl 'plah-toh, 'weh-vohs 'free-tohs]
hard-boiled eggs	huevos duros ['weh-vohs 'doo-rohs]
omelette with potatoes (and onion)	tortilla (a la) española [tohr-'tee-yah (ah lah) eh-spah-'nyoh-lah]
plain omelette	tortilla (a la) francesa [tohr-'tee-yah (ah lah) frahn-'seh-sah]
scrambled eggs	huevos revueltos (*Am* revoltillo) ['weh-vohs reh-'vwehl-tohs (reh-vohl-'tee-yoh)]
soft-boiled eggs	huevos pasados por agua ['weh-vohs pah-'sah-dohs pohr 'ah-gwah]

Dessert, Cheese, Fruit

Postres, Queso, Fruta

apple	manzana [mahn-'sah-nah]
apricots	albaricoques (*Am* damascos) [ahl-bah-ree-'koh-kehs (dah-'mah-skohs)]
banana	plátano (*Am* banana) ['plah-tah-noh (bah-'nah-nah)]
cherries	cerezas [seh-'reh-sahs]
compote	compota [kohm-'poh-tah]

custard	natillas [nah-'tee-yahs]
figs	higos ['ee-gohs]
flan (Spanish-style custard)	flan [flahn]
fruit salad	macedonia de frutas (*Am* ensalada de frutas) [mah-seh-'doh-nee·ah deh 'froo-tahs (ehn-sah-'lah-dah deh 'froo-tahs)]
goat cheese	queso de cabra ['keh-soh deh 'kah-brah]
grapefruit	toronja [toh-'rohn-hah]
grapes	uvas ['oo-vahs]
Gruyère or Emmenthal cheese	queso (de) Gruyère ['keh-soh (deh) groo-'yehr]
manchego cheese	queso manchego ['keh-soh mahn-'cheh-goh]
mandarin orange	mandarina [mahn-dah-'ree-nah]
melon	melón [meh-'lohn]
orange	naranja [nah-'rahn-hah]
peach	melocotón (*Am* durazno) [meh-loh-koh-'tohn (doo-'rahs-noh)]
pear	pera ['peh-rah]
pineapple	piña (*Am* ananás) ['pee-nyah (ah-nah-'nahs)]
prunes	ciruelas [see-roo-'eh-lahs]
rice pudding	arroz con leche [ah-'rrohs kohn 'leh-cheh]
sheep cheese	queso de oveja ['keh-soh deh oh-'veh-hah]
strawberries	fresas (*Am* frutilla) ['freh-sahs (froo-'tee-yah)]
tart	tarta ['tahr-tah]
watermelon	sandía [sahn-'dee-ah]

Ice Creams, etc.

Helados

assorted ice cream	helado variado [eh-'lah-doh vah-ree-'ah-doh]
chocolate ice cream	helado de chocolate [eh-'lah-doh deh choh-koh-'lah-teh]
ice cream cup	copa de helado ['koh-pah deh eh-'lah-doh]

ice cream cup with fruit	copa de helado con frutas [koh-pah deh eh-'lah-doh kohn 'froo-tahs]
iced coffee	café helado [kah-'feh eh-'lah-doh]
lemon ice cream	helado de limón [eh-'lah-doh deh lee-'mohn]
mantecado: milk, eggs, and sugar ice cream	mantecado [mahn-teh-'kah-doh]
strawberry ice cream	helado de fresa [eh-'lah-doh deh 'freh-sah]
vanilla ice cream	helado de vainilla [eh-'lah-doh deh vah·ee-'nee-yah]

Sweets   ## Dulces

apple tart	tarta de manzana ['tahr-tah deh mahn-'sah-nah]
cake, tart	tarta ['tahr-tah]; torta ['tohr-tah]
chocolate	chocolate [choh-koh-'lah-teh]
churros: Spanish-style fritters	churros ['choo-rohs]
crackers	galletas [gah-'yeh-tahs]
cream	nata ['nah-tah]
cream puffs/pastries	pastelillos de crema [pah-steh-'lee-yohs deh 'kreh-mah]
cream tart	tarta de crema ['tahr-tah deh 'kreh-mah]
fruit tart	tarta de frutas ['tahr-tah deh 'froo-tahs]
ice cream cake	tarta helada ['tahr-tah eh-'lah-dah]
pastries	pastas, pasteles ['pah-stahs, pah-'steh-lehs]
praline, chocolate candy	bombón [bohm-'bohn]
sweets (Am pastries)	dulces ['dool-sehs]
whipped cream	nata batida/montada ['nah-tah bah-'tee-dah/mohn-'tah-dah]

Beverages

Bebidas

Some Typical Spanish Wines

dry aperitif (Basque)

dry red or white wine from Catalonia
dry red or white wine from the La Mancha region
dry red table wine from Galicia
dry table wine
dry white wine

muscatel
Rioja (dry red or white wine)
sangria
sweet dessert wine
sweet sherry

Algunos Vinos Típicos Españoles

chacolí [chah-koh-'lee]; montilla [mohn-'tee-yah]
priorato [pree-oh-'rah-toh]

valdepeñas [vahl-deh-'peh-nyahs]

ribeiro [ree-'beh·ee-roh]

cariñena [kah-ree-'nyeh-nah]
manzanilla, moriles [mahn-sah-'nee-yah, moh-'ree-lehs]
moscatel [moh-skah-'tehl]
rioja [ree-'oh-hah]

sangría [sahn-'gree-ah]
málaga ['mah-lah-gah]
jerez dulce/oloroso [heh-'rehs 'dool-seh/oh-loh-'roh-soh]

Other Alcoholic Beverages

a strong brandy
anise
beer on tap

champagne

cognac
gin
hard apple cider
liqueur
rum and Coke
small glass of beer

Otras Bebidas Alcohólicas

aguardiente [ah-gwahr-dee-'ehn-teh]
anís [ah-'nees]
cerveza de barril [sehr-'veh-sah deh bah-'rreel]
champán, cava [chahm-'pahn, 'kah-vah]
coñac [koh-'nyahk]
ginebra [hee-'neh-brah]
sidra ['see-drah]
licor [lee-'kohr]
cuba libre ['koo-bah 'lee-breh]
caña de cerveza ['kah-nyah deh sehr-'veh-sah]

> Sidra, the hard apple cider from the northern Spanish region of Asturias, is a traditional holiday drink in many Latin American countries and Latino communities throughout the United States. This inexpensive alternative to champagne, with a 5% to 7% alcoholic content, is particularly popular for Christmas and weddings.

Nonalcoholic Beverages

Bebidas No Alcohólicas

almond drink	horchata de almendras [ohr-'chah-tah deh ahl-'mehn-drahs]
coffee with milk	café con leche [kah-'feh kohn 'leh-cheh]
decaffeinated coffee	café descafeinado [(kah-'feh) dehs-kah-feh·ee-'nah-doh]
espresso	café solo [kah-'feh 'soh-loh]
expresso with a small amount of milk	café cortado [(kah-'feh) kohr-'tah-doh]
fruit juice	zumo (Am jugo) de fruta ['soo-moh ('hoo-goh) deh 'froo-tah]
hot chocolate, cocoa	cacao [kah-'kah-oh]
large black coffee	café americano [(kah-'feh) ah-meh-ree-'kah-noh]
lemon juice	zumo (Am jugo) de limón, limón natural ['soo-moh ('hoo-goh) deh lee-'mohn, lee-'mohn nah-too-'rahl]
lemonade	limonada [lee-moh-'nah-dah]
milk	leche ['leh-cheh]
milk shake	batido [bah-'tee-doh]
mineral water	agua mineral ['ah-gwah mee-neh-'rahl]
orange drink	naranjada [nah-rahn-'hah-dah]
orange juice	zumo (Am jugo) de naranja ['soo-moh ('hoo-goh) deh nah-'rahn-hah]
seltzer	soda, (agua de) sifón ['soh-dah, ('ah-gwah deh) see-'fohn]
soda	gaseosa [gah-seh-'oh-sah]
tea	té [teh]
tonic water	agua tónica [('ah-gwah) 'toh-nee-kah]

6 **Culture and Nature**
Cultura y naturaleza

At the Visitor's (Tourist) Center
En la oficina de turismo

I'd like a map of…, please.

Quisiera un mapa de… [kee-see-'eh-rah oon 'mah-pah deh]

Do you have any brochure about…?

¿Tienen ustedes folletos de…? [tee-'eh-nehn oo-'steh-dehs foh-'yeh-tohs deh]

Do you have a weekly events program?

¿Tienen ustedes un programa de espectáculos para esta semana? [tee-'eh-nehn oo-'steh-dehs oon proh-'grah-mah deh eh-spehk-'tah-koo-'lohs 'pah-rah 'eh-stah seh-'mah-nah]

Are there sightseeing tours of the town (city)?

¿Hay visitas organizadas de la ciudad? ['ah·ee vee-'see-tahs ohr-gah-nee-'sah-dahs deh lah see·oo-'dahd]

How much is the ticket?

¿Cuánto cuesta el billete (*Am* boleto)? ['kwahn-toh' kweh-stah ehl bee-'yeh-teh (boh-'leh-toh)]

Places of Interest/Museums
Lugares dignos de verse y museos

What are the places of interest here?

¿Qué cosas dignas de verse hay aquí? [keh 'koh-sahs 'deeg-nahs deh 'vehr-seh 'ah·ee ah-'kee]

We would like to visit…

Nos gustaría visitar… [nohs goo-stah-'ree-ah vee-see-'tahr]

When is the museum open?

¿A qué horas está abierto el museo? [ah keh 'oh-rahs eh-'stah ah-bee-'ehr-toh ehl moo-'seh-oh]

When does the tour start?

¿A qué hora comienza la visita con guía? [ah keh 'oh-rah koh-mee-'ehn-sah lah vee-'see-tah kohn 'gee-ah]

Spain

1. *El Escorial*
2. *Post Office, Madrid*
3. *Plaza del Rey, Barcelona*
4. *Monasterio de Guadalupe*
5. *Alhambra, Granada*
6. *Scenic View, Toledo*

Is there a tour in English, too?	El guía, ¿da también explicaciones en inglés? [ehl gee-ah, dah tahm-bee-'ehn ehks-plee-kah-see-'oh-nehs ehn een-'glehs]
Can we take pictures here?	¿Se pueden tomar fotografías aquí? [seh 'pweh-dehn toh-'mahr foh-toh-grah-'fee-ahs ah-'kee]
What plaza/church is this?	¿Cómo se llama esta plaza/iglesia? ['koh-moh seh 'yah-mah 'eh-stah 'plah-sah/ee-'gleh-see-ah]
Is this (that)...?	¿Es éste el...?/¿Es ésta la...? [ehs 'eh-steh ehl/ehs 'eh-stah lah]
When was this built/restored?	¿Cuándo se construyó/De qué época es este edificio? ['kwahn-doh seh kohn-stroo-'yoh/deh keh 'eh-poh-kah ehs 'eh-steh eh-dee-'fee-see-oh]
When was this building restored?	¿Cuándo se restauró este edificio? ['kwahn-doh seh reh-stah·oo-'roh 'eh-steh eh-dee-'fee-see·oh]
Are there any other buildings by this architect in the city?	¿Hay también otras obras de este arquitecto en la ciudad? ['ah·ee tahm-bee-'ehn 'oh-trahs 'oh-brahs deh 'eh-steh ahr-kee-'tehk-toh ehn lah see·oo-'dahd]
Have they finished digging this site?	¿Ya han terminado las excavaciones? [yah ahn tehr-mee-'nah-doh lahs ehks-kah-vah-see-'oh-nehs]
Where are the artifacts (found here) being exhibited?	¿Dónde están expuestos los objetos hallados? ['dohn-deh eh-'stahn ehks-'pweh-stohs lohs ohb-'heh-tohs ah-'yah-dohs]
Who is the painter/sculptor?	¿Quién ha pintado este cuadro/hecho esta escultura? [kee-'ehn ah peen-'tah-doh 'eh-steh 'kwah-droh/'eh-choh 'eh-stah eh-skool-'too-rah]
Is there an exhibition catalog?	¿Hay un catálogo de la exposición? ['ah·ee oon kah-'tah-loh-goh deh lah ehks-poh-see-see-'ohn]

Latin America

1. *Los atlantes de Tula, Mexico*
2. *Machu Picchu, Incan ruins, Peru*
3. *San Augustin, precolombian artifacts, Colombia*
4. *University, Mexico*
5. *Temple del Gran Jaguar, Mayan temple, Guatemala*
6. *Machu Picchu, Incan ruins, Peru*

Do you have a poster/
postcard/slide of this
painting?

¿Tiene usted este cuadro en
póster/postal/diapositiva? [tee-
'eh-neh oo-'stehd 'eh-steh 'kwah-
droh ehn 'poh-stehr/poh-'stahl/dee-
ah-poh-see-'tee-vah]

Word List: Places of Interest/Museums

abbey	abadía [ah-bah-'dee-ah]
altar	el altar [ehl ahl-'tahr]
ambulatory	deambulatorio [deh-ahm-boo-lah-'toh-ree·oh]
ancestral home	casa patricia ['kah-sah pah-'tree-see-ah]
antique	antiguo [ahn-'tee-gwoh]
aqueduct	acueducto [ah-kweh-'dook-toh]
Arabic	árabe, morisco ['ah-rah-beh, moh-'ree-skoh]
arcade	arcada, los soportales [ahr-'kah-dah, lohs soh-pohr-'tah-lehs]
arch	arco ['ahr-koh]
arch of triumph	arco de triunfo ['ahr-koh deh tree-'oon-foh]
archaeology	arqueología [ahr-keh-oh-loh-'hee-ah]
architect	arquitecto [ahr-kee-'tehk-toh]
architecture	arquitectura [ahr-kee-tehk-'too-rah]
arts and crafts	artesanía [ahr-teh-sah-'nee-ah]
balustrade	balaustrada [bah-lah·oo-'strah-dah]
baptismal fountain	pila bautismal ['pee-lah bah·oo-tees-'mahl]
baroque	barroco [bah-'rroh-koh]
base of the cupola/dome	cimborio [seem-'boh-ree·oh]
bay	el mirador, el balcón salidizo [ehl mee-rah-'dohr, ehl bahl-'kohn sah-lee-'dee-soh]
bell	campana [kahm-'pah-nah]
birthplace	la ciudad de nacimiento [lah see-oo-'dahd deh nah-see-mee-'ehn-toh]
bishopric, diocesan town	la sede episcopal (*Am* el obispado) [lah 'seh-deh eh-pee-skoh-'pahl (ehl oh-bees-'pah-doh)]
bridge	el puente [ehl 'pwehn-teh]
bronze	el bronce [ehl 'brohn-seh]

Bronze Age	la edad del bronce [lah eh-'dahd dehl 'brohn-seh]
building	edificio [eh-dee-'fee-see-oh]
bullfighting arena	plaza de toros ['plah-sah deh'toh-rohs]
to burn, to incinerate	quemar, incinerar [keh-'mahr, een-see-neh-'rahr]
bust, half-length portrait	busto, retrato de medio cuerpo ['boo-stoh, reh-'trah-toh deh 'meh-dee·oh 'kwehr-poh]
buttress	el contrafuerte [ehl kohn-trah-'fwehr-teh]
candelabrum	candelabro [kah-deh-'lah-broh]
capital (headpiece of column)	el capitel [ehl kah-pee-'tehl]
carpet	alfombra [ahl-'fohm-brah]
castle	castillo [kah-'stee-yoh]
catacombs	las catacumbas [lahs kah-tah-'koom-bahs]
cathedral	la catedral [lah kah-teh-'drahl]
catholic	católico [kah-'toh-lee-koh]
cave paintings	pinturas rupestres [peen-'too-rahs roo-'peh-strehs]
ceiling	techo ['teh-choh]
ceiling frescoes	las pinturas del techo/del cielo raso [lahs peen-'too-rahs dehl 'teh-choh/dehl see-'eh-loh 'rah-soh]
celtic	celta ['sehl-tah]
cemetery	cementerio [seh-mehn-'teh-ree-oh]
century	siglo ['see-gloh]
ceramic	cerámica [seh-'rah-mee-kah]
changing of the guard	relevo de la guardia [reh-'leh-voh deh lah 'gwahr-dee·ah]
chapel	capilla [kah-'pee-yah]
choir	coro ['koh-roh]
choir stalls	sillería de coro [see-yeh-'ree-ah deh 'koh-roh]
Christian	cristiano [kree-stee-'ah-noh]
Christianity	Cristianismo [kree-stee-ah-'nees-moh]
church	iglesia [ee-'gleh-see-ah]
Cistersian (pertaining to the order of St. Bernard)	cisterciense [see-stehr-see-'ehn-seh]
citadel	ciudadela [see-oo-dah-'deh-lah]

city center	centro de la ciudad ['sehn-troh deh lah see·oo·'dahd]
city hall	ayuntamiento [ah-yoon-tah-mee-'ehn-toh]
cloister	claustro ['klah·oo-stroh]
column, pillar	columna, el pilar [koh-'loom-nah, ehl pee-'lahr]

Alhambra, Granada

copperplate (engraving)	grabado en cobre [grah-'bah-doh ehn 'koh-breh]
copy	copia ['koh-pee-ah]
Corinthian	corintio [koh-'reen-tee-oh]
convent church	iglesia conventual [ee-'gleh-see-ah kohn-vehn-too-'ahl]
covered indoor market	mercado (cubierto) [mehr-'kah-doh (koo-bee-'ehr-toh)]
cross	la cruz [lah kroos]
crossing (of the nave)	la intersección de la nave [lah een-tehr-sehk-see-'ohn deh lah 'nah-veh]
crucifix	crucifijo [kroo-see-'fee-hoh]
crypt	cripta ['kreep-tah]
cubism	cubismo [koo-'bees-moh]

cult of the dead	culto a los muertos ['kool-toh ah lohs 'mwehr-tohs]
cupola, dome	cúpula ['koo-poo-lah]
custom	la costumbre [lah koh-'stoom-breh]
denomination	la religion, la denominacion [lah reh-lee-hee-'ohn, lah deh-noh-mee-nah-see-'ohn]
design	diseño [dee-'seh-nyoh]
dig, excavation	las excavaciones [lahs ehk-skah-vah-see-'oh-nehs]
door, gates	puerta, el portón ['pwehr-tah, ehl pohr-'tohn]
Doric	dórico ['doh-ree-koh]
drawing	dibujo [dee-'boo-hoh]
dynasty	dinastía [dee-nah-'stee-ah]
early work	obra juvenil ['oh-brah hoo-veh-'neel]
Elizabethan	estilo isabelino [eh-'stee-loh eh-sah-beh-'lee-noh]
emblem, symbol	el emblema, símbolo [ehl ehm-'bleh-mah, 'seem-boh-loh]
engraving	grabado [grah-'bah-doh]
epoch	época ['eh-poh-kah]
etching	el aguafuerte [ehl ah-gwah-'fwehr-teh]
exhibition	la exposición [lah ehks-poh-see-see-'ohn]
facade	fachada [fah-'chah-dah]
Flemish	flamenco [flah-'mehn-koh]
folklore museum	museo del folklore [moo-'seh-oh dehl fohlk-lohr]
fortress, citadel	fortaleza; ciudadela [fohr-tah-'leh-sah; see·oo-dah-'deh-lah]
foundation	fundamento; los cimientos [foon-dah-'mehn-toh; lohs see-mee-'ehn-tohs]
fountain	la fuente [lah 'fwehn-teh]
Franciscan	franciscano [frahn-sees-'kah-noh]
fresco	fresco ['freh-skoh]
frieze	friso ['free-soh]
gable	frontispicio [frohn-tee-'spee-see-oh]
gallery	coro; galería alta ['koh-roh; gah-leh-'ree-ah 'ahl-tah]
goldworking	orfebrería [ohr-feh-breh-'ree-ah]
Gothic	gótico ['goh-tee-koh]

government building	edificio del gobierno [eh-dee-'fee-see·oh dehl goh-bee-'ehr-noh]
Greek	griego [gree-'eh-goh]
Greeks	los griegos [lohs gree-'eh-gohs]
guided tour	visita guiada [vee-'see-tah gee-'ah-dah]
height (heyday)	apogeo [ah-poh-'heh-oh]
high Gothic	alto gótico ['ahl-toh 'goh-tee-koh]

Güell Park, Barcelona

history	historia [ee-'stoh-ree·ah]
illustration	la ilustración [lah ee-loo-strah-see-'ohn]
impressionism	impresionismo [eem-preh-see-oh-'nees-moh]
india ink	tinta china ['teen-tah 'chee-nah]
industrial arts	las artes industriales [lahs 'ahr-tehs een-doo-stree-'ah-lehs]
influence	influencia [een-floo-'ehn-see·ah]
inlaid work	marquetería [mahr-keh-teh-'ree-ah]
inner courtyard	patio interior ['pah-tee·oh een-teh-ree-'ohr]
inscription	la inscripción [lah een-skreep-see-'ohn]

Ionic	jónico ['hoh-nee-koh]
Islamic	islámico [ees-'lah-mee-koh]
Jewish	judío [hoo-'dee-oh]
king/queen	el rey/la reina [ehl 'reh·ee/lah 'reh-ee-nah]
landscape painting	paisajismo, pintura de paisajes [pah·ee-sah-'hees-moh, peen-'too-rah deh pah·ee-'sah-hehs]
late Gothic	gótico tardío ['goh-tee-koh tahr-'dee-oh]
level (instrument)	plano horizontal ['plah-noh oh-ree-sohn-'tahl]
library	biblioteca [beeb-lee-oh-'teh-kah]
lithograph	litografía [lee-toh-grah-'fee-ah]
mannerism	manierismo [mah-nee-eh-'rees-moh]

manneristic	manierista [mah-nee-eh-'re-stah]
marble	el mármol [ehl 'mahr-mohl]
market	mercado [mehr-'kah-doh]
material	el material [ehl mah-teh-ree-'ahl]
mature/late work	obra tardía ['oh-brah tahr-'dee-ah]
mausoleum	mausoleo [mah-oo-soh-'leh-oh]
mayor	el alcalde/alcaldesa [ehl ahl-'kahl-deh/ahl-kah-'deh-sah]
medieval	medieval [meh-dee·eh-'vahl]
megalithic monument, dolmen	dolmen, monumento megalítico ['dohl-mehn, moh-noo-'mehn-toh meh-gah-'lee-tee-koh]
memorial site	el lugar conmemorativo [ehl loo-'gahr kohn-meh-moh-rah-'tee-voh]
menhir, monolith	el menhir [ehl mehn-'eer]
Middle Ages	la Edad Media [lah eh-'dahd 'meh-dee·ah]
minaret, tall slender tower of mosque	el minarete [ehl mee-nah-'reh-teh]
model	modelo [moh-'deh-loh]
modern	moderno [moh-'dehr-noh]
modernism, Art Nouveau	modernismo, Art Nouveau [moh-dehr-'nees-moh, ahrt noo-'voh]
monastery, convent	monasterio, convento [moh-nah-'steh-ree-oh, kohn-'vehn-toh]
monument (in burial places)	tumba, monumento fúnebre ['toom-bah; moh-noo-'mehn-toh 'foo-neh-breh]

monument preservation	la protección de los monumentos [lah proh-tehk-see-'ohn deh lohs moh-noo-'mehn-tohs]
monuments	los monumentos [lohs moh-noo-'mehn-tohs]
mosaic	mosaico [moh-'sah·ee-koh]
Moslem	el musulmán [(ehl) moo-sool-'mahn]
mosque	mezquita [meh-'skee-tah]
mozarab	mozárabe [moh-'sah-rah-beh]
mudéjar style	estilo mudéjar [eh-'stee-loh moo-'deh-hahr]
multimedia show	espectáculo de multivisión [eh-spehk-'tah-koo-loh deh mool-tee-vee-see-'ohn]

mural painting	pintura mural [peen-'too-rah moo-'rahl]
museum	museo [moo-'seh-oh]
nave	la nave [lah 'nah-veh]
nude	desnudo [dehs-'noo-doh]
object exhibited	objeto expuesto [ohb-'heh-toh ehks-'pweh-stoh]
objects found	los objetos hallados [lohs ohb-'heh-tohs ah-'yah-dohs]
oil painting	pintura al óleo [peen-'too-rah ahl 'oh-leh-oh]

Cathedral, Segovia

old city	la ciudad vieja [lah see·oo-'dahd vee-'eh-hah]
opera	ópera ['oh-peh-rah]
order (rel)	la orden (religiosa) [lah 'ohr-dehn (reh-lee-hee-'oh-sah)]
organ	órgano ['ohr-gah-noh]
original	el original [ehl oh-ree-hee-'nahl]
ornament	ornamento, adorno [ohr-nah-'mehn-toh, ah-'dohr-noh]
pagan	pagano [pah-'gah-noh]
painter	el pintor/la pintora [ehl peen-'tohr/lah peen-'toh-rah]
painting	pintura, cuadro [peen-'too-rah, 'kwah-droh]
painting collection	la colección de pintura [lah koh-lehk-see-'ohn deh peen-'too-rah]
painting on glass	pintura sobre cristal [peen-'too-rah 'soh-breh kree-'stahl]
painting on wood	pintura sobre madera [peen-'too-rah 'soh-breh mah-'deh-rah]
palace	palacio [pah-'lah-see·oh]
parchment	pergamino [pehr-gah-'mee-noh]
pastel	el pastel [ehl pah-'stehl]
pastor	el pastor [ehl pah-'stohr]
patio, courtyard	patio ['pah-tee·oh]
pavilion	el pabellón [ehl pah-beh-'yohn]
Phoenician	fenicio [feh-'nee-see-oh]
photography	fotografía [foh-toh-grah-'fee-ah]
photomontage	el fotomontaje [ehl foh-toh-mohn-'tah-heh]
pilgrim	peregrino/peregrina [peh-reh-'gree-noh/peh-reh-'gree-nah]
pilgrimage	la peregrinación [pah peh-reh-gree-nah-see-'ohn]
pilgrimage church	templo de peregrinación ['tehm-ploh deh peh-reh-gree-nah-see-'ohn]
pillage	saqueo [sah-'keh-oh]
pillar	el pilar [ehl pee-'lahr]
plaza	plaza ['plah-sah]
pointed arch	ojiva, arco ojival [oh-'hee-vah, 'ahr-koh oh-hee-'vahl]
porcelain	porcelana [pohr-seh-'lah-nah]
portal	el portal [ehl pohr-'tahl]
portrait	retrato [reh-'trah-toh]

poster	el cartel [ehl kahr-'tehl]
pottery	alfarería [ahl-fah-reh-'ree-ah]
prehistoric	prehistórico [preh-ee-'stoh-ree-koh]
priest	el sacerdote, el cura [ehl sah-sehr-'doh-teh, ehl 'koo-rah]
Protestant	el/la protestante [ehl/lah proh-teh-'stahn-teh]
pulpit	púlpito ['pool-pee-'toh]
realism	realismo [reh-ah-'lees-moh]
to reconstruct	reconstruir [reh-kohn-stroo-'eer]
relief	el relieve [ehl reh-lee-'eh-veh]
religion	la religión [lah reh-lee-hee-'ohn]
remains	restos ['reh-stohs]
Renaissance	renacimiento [reh-nah-see-mee-'ehn-toh]

restoration	la restauración [lah reh-stah·oo-rah-see-'ohn]
to restore	restaurar [reh-stah·oo-'rahr]
Roman	romano [roh-'mah-noh]
Romanesque	románico [roh-'mah-nee-koh]
Romanesque style	estilo románico [eh-'stee-loh roh-'mah-nee-koh]
roof	tejado [teh-'hah-doh]
rose window	el rosetón [ehl roh-seh-'tohn]
round arch	arco de medio punto ['ahr-koh deh 'meh-dee·oh 'poon-toh]
round-trip	recorrido, el viaje circular [reh-koh-'rree-doh, ehl vee-'ah-heh seer-koo-'lahr]
ruins	ruina [roo-'ee-nah]
sacred site	el lugar sagrado [ehl loo-'gahr sah-'grah-doh]
sacristy	sacristía [sah-kree-'stee-ah]
sandstone	piedra arenisca [pee-'eh-drah ah-reh-'nee-skah]
sarcophagus	sarcófago [sahr-'koh-fah-goh]
school	escuela [eh-'skweh-lah]
sculptor	el escultor [ehl ehs-kool-'tohr]
sculpture	escultura [eh-skool-'too-rah]
service, mass	culto, misa ['kool-toh; 'mee-sah]
sightseeing tour of the city/town	visita de la ciudad, excursiones [vee-'see-tah deh lah see·oo-'dahd, ehk-skoor-see-'oh-nehs]
silk-screen printing	serigrafía [seh-ree-grah-'fee-ah]
statue	estatua [eh-'stah-too-ah]

still life	naturaleza muerta, el bodegón [nah-too-rah-'leh-sah 'mwehr-tah, ehl boh-deh-'gohn]
Stone Age	la edad de piedra [lah eh-'dahd deh pee-'eh-drah]
stucco	estuco [eh-'stoo-koh]
style	estilo [eh-'stee-loh]
surrealism	surrealismo [soo-rreh-ah-'lees-moh]
symbolism	simbolismo [seem-boh-'lees-moh]
synagogue	sinagoga [see-nah-'goh-gah]
tapestry	el tapiz [ehl tah-'pees]
temple	templo ['tehm-ploh]
terracotta	terracota, barro cocido [teh-rrah-'koh-tah, 'bah-rroh koh-'see-doh]
theater	teatro [teh-'ah-troh]
tomb	tumba ['toom-bah]
tombstone	lápida (sepulcral) ['lah-pee-dah (seh-pool-'krahl)]
torso	torso ['tohr-soh]
tourist guide	el guía (turístico) [ehl 'gee-ah (too-'ree-stee-koh)]
tower, bell tower	la torre, campanario [lah 'toh-rreh, kahm-pah-'nah-ree-oh]
trading city	la ciudad comercial [lah see-oo-'dahd koh-mehr-see-'ahl]
transept	la nave transversal [lah 'nah-veh trahs-vehr-'sahl]
treasure chamber	cámara del tesoro [('kah-mah-rah dehl) teh-'soh-roh]
university	la universidad [lah oo-nee-vehr-see-'dahd]
vase, flowerpot	florero, el jarrón [floh-'reh-roh; ehl hah-'rrohn]
vault	bóveda ['boh-veh-dah]
Visigoth	visigodo [vee-see-'goh-doh]
visit	visita [vee-'see-tah]
wall	muro, la pared ['moo-roh, lah pah-'rehd]
walls (of the city)	muralla (de la ciudad) [moo-'rah-yah (deh lah see-oo-'dahd)]
watercolor	acuarela [ah-kwah-'reh-lah]
weaving	tejeduría, el arte de tejer [teh-heh-doo-'ree-ah; ehl 'ahr-teh deh teh-'hehr]
window	ventana [vehn-'tah-nah]

wing	(el) ala [(ehl) 'ah-lah]
wood carving	escultura en madera [eh-skool-'too-rah ehn mah-'deh-rah]
woodcut	grabado/talla en madera [grah-'bah-doh/'tah-yah ehn mah-'deh-rah]
work	obra ['oh-brah]

Excursions

Excursiones

Can we see the...from here?	¿Se puede ver...desde aquí? [seh 'pweh-deh vehr...'dehs-deh ah-'kee]
Which way is the...?	¿En qué dirección está...? [ehn keh dee-rehk-see-'ohn eh-'stah]
Are we going to pass the...?	¿Pasamos por...? [pah-'sah-mohs pohr]
Are we going to see the..., too?	¿Vamos a visitar también...? ['vah-mohs a vee-see-'tahr tahm-bee-'ehn]
How much free time do we have...?	¿Cuánto tiempo libre tenemos en...? ['kwahn-toh tee-'ehm-poh 'lee-breh teh-'neh-mohs ehn...]
When are we going back?	¿Cuándo regresamos? ['kwahn-doh reh-greh-'sah-mohs]
At what time do we get back?	¿A qué hora estaremos de vuelta? [ah keh 'oh-rah eh-stah-'reh-mohs deh 'vwehl-tah]

Word List: Excursions

amusement park
el parque de atracciones [ehl 'pahr-keh deh ah-trahk-see-'oh-nehs]

astronomical observatory
observatorio astronómico [ohb-sehr-vah-'toh-ree·oh ah-stroh-'noh-mee-koh]

bird preserve
reserva ornitológica [reh-'sehr-vah ohr-nee-toh-'loh-hee-kah]

botanical garden
el jardín botánico [ehl har-'deen boh-'tah-nee-koh]

cave
cueva ['kweh-vah]

cliff
escollo [eh-'skoh-yoh]

country house
quinta, residencia rural ['keen-tah, reh-see-'dehn-see·ah roo-'rahl]

day trip
la excursión de un día [lah ehk-skoor-see-'ohn deh oon 'dee-ah]

environs, surrounding area
los alrededores [lohs ahl-reh-deh-'doh-rehs]

fishing port
puerto de pescadores ['pwehr-toh deh peh-skah-'doh-rehs]

fishing spot
el lugar de pesca [ehl loo-'gahr deh 'peh-skah]

forest
el bosque [ehl 'boh-skeh]

forest fire
incendio forestal [een-'sehn-dee·oh foh-reh-'stahl]

gorge, ravine
desfiladero, barranco [dehs-fee-lah-'deh-roh; bah-'rrahn-koh]

grotto
gruta ['groo-tah]

guided tour of the island
visita (guiada) de la isla [vee-'see-tah (gee-'ah-dah) deh lah 'ees-lah]

hinterland
zona interior; el interior del país ['soh-nah een-teh-ree-'ohr; ehl een-teh-ree-'ohr dehl pah-'ees]

inhabited cave
cueva habitada ['kweh-vah ah-bee-'tah-dah]

lake
lago ['lah-goh]

landscape
el paisaje [ehl pah·ee-'sah-heh]

lava
lava ['lah-vah]

lookout
el mirador, punto de observación [ehl mee-rah-'dohr, 'poon-toh deh ohb-sehr-vah-see-'ohn]

market
mercado [mehr-'kah-doh]

mountain village	pueblo de montaña ['pweh-bloh deh mohn-'tah-nyah]
mountains	cordillera [kohr-dee-'yeh-rah]
national park	el parque nacional [ehl 'pahr-keh nah-see·oh-'nahl]
nature/ecological preserve	reserva natural/ecológica [reh-'sehr-vah nah-too-'rahl/eh-koh-loh-'hee-ah]
open-air museum	museo al aire libre [moo-'seh-oh ahl 'ah·ee-reh 'lee-breh]
panorama	el panorama, vista panorámica [ehl pah-noh-'rah-mah, 'vee-stah pah-noh-'rah-mee-kah]
passport	el pasaporte [ehl pah-sah-'pohr-teh]
place of pilgrimage	el lugar de peregrinación [ehl loo-'gahr deh peh-reh-gree-nah-see-'ohn]
planetarium	planetario [plah-neh-'tah-ree-oh]
plaza	plaza ['plah-sah]
reef	el arrecife [ehl ah-rreh-'see-feh]
safari park	el safari (park) [ehl sah-'fah-ree (pahrk)]
sea	el mar [ehl mahr]
sightseeing tour, excursion	la excursión [lah ehk-skoor-see-'ohn]
stalactite cave	cueva de estalactitas ['kweh-vah deh eh-stah-lahk-'tee-tahs]
suburb	barrio periférico; suburbio ['bah-rree-oh peh-ree-'feh-ree-koh; soo-'boor-bee-oh]
tour, course	recorrido, el viaje circular [reh-koh-'rree-doh, ehl vee-'ah-heh seer-koo-'lahr]
valley	el valle [ehl 'vah-yeh]
volcano	el volcán [ehl vohl-'kahn]
waterfall	catarata; cascada [kah-tah-'rah-tah; kah-'skah-dah]
wildlife preserve/ hunting preserve	reserva cinegética/de caza [reh-'sehr-vah see-neh-'heh-tee-kah/deh 'kah-sah]
windmill	molino de viento [moh-'lee-noh deh vee-'ehn-toh]
zoo	zoo, el parque zoológico [soh·oh, ehl 'pahr-keh soh-oh-'loh-hee-koh]

Events/Entertainment
Espectáculos/Diversiones

Theater/Concerts/Movies	Teatro/Conciertos/Cine

What's playing (at the theater) tonight?

¿Qué hay esta tarde (en el teatro)? [keh 'ah·ee 'eh-stah 'tahr-deh (ehn ehl teh-'ah-troh)]

What's playing at the movies tomorrow evening?

¿Qué hay mañana por la tarde en el cine? [keh 'ah·ee mah-'nyah-nah pohr lah 'tahr-deh ehn ehl 'see-neh]

Are there concerts in the cathedral?

¿Hay conciertos en la catedral? ['ah·ee kohn-see-'ehr-tohs ehn lah kah-teh-'drahl]

Can you recommend a good play?

¿Puede usted recomendarme una buena obra de teatro? ['pweh-deh oo-'stehd reh-koh-mehn-'dahr-meh 'oo-nah 'bweh-nah 'oh-brah deh teh-'ah-troh]

When does the performance start?

¿A qué hora comienza la representación? [ah keh 'oh-rah koh-mee-'ehn-sah lah reh-preh-sehn-tah-see-'ohn]

Where can I get tickets?

¿Dónde se pueden adquirir los billetes (*Am* boletos)? ['dohn-deh seh 'pweh-dehn ahd-kee-'reer lohs bee-'yeh-tehs (boh-'leh-tohs)]

Two tickets for this evening/tomorrow evening, please.

Dos entradas (*Am* boletos) para esta tarde/mañana por la tarde, por favor. [dohs ehn-'trah-dahs ('boh-leh-tohs) 'pah-rah 'eh-stah 'tahr-deh/mah-'nyah-nah pohr lah 'tahr-deh, pohr fah-'vohr]

Two tickets for ..., please.

Dos entradas para…, por favor. [dohs ehn-'trah-dahs 'pah-rah, pohr fah-'vohr]

Two adults and a child.

Dos adultos y un niño. [dohs ah-'dool-tohs ee oon 'nee-nyoh]

Can I have a program, please?

¿Me puede dar un programa? [meh 'pweh-deh dahr oon proh-'grah-mah]

| At what time does the performance end? | ¿Cuándo acaba la representación? ['kwahn-doh ah-'kah-bah lah reh-preh-sehn-tah-see-'ohn] |

| Where's the checkroom? | ¿Dónde está el guardarropa? ['dohn-deh eh-'stah ehl gwahr-dah-'rroh-pah] |

Word List: Theater/Concerts/Movies

accompaniment	acompañamiento [ah-kohm-pah-nyah-mee-'ehn-toh]
act	acto ['ahk-toh]
actor/actress	actor/actriz [ahk-'tohr/ahk-'trees]
admission ticket	entrada, el billete [ehn-'trah-dah, ehl bee-'yeh-teh]
advance sale	venta anticipada ['vehn-tah ahn-tee-see-'pah-dah]
balcony/circle	galería [gah-leh-'ree-ah]
ballet	el ballet [ehl bah-'yeht]
box (seats)	palco ['pahl-koh]
box office	caja ['kah-hah]
cabaret	el cabaré, el cabaret [ehl kah-bah-'reh, ehl kah-bah-'reht]
calendar of events	calendario de actos [kah-lehn-'dah-ree·oh deh 'ahk-tohs]
chamber music concert	concierto de cámara [kohn-see-'ehr-toh deh 'kah-mah-rah]
checkroom	el guardarropa [ehl gwahr-dah-'roh-pah]
choir	coro ['koh-roh]
circus	circo ['seer-koh]
comedy	comedia [koh-'meh-dee-ah]
composer	el compositor/compositora [ehl kohm-poh-see-'tohr/kohm-poh-see-'toh-rah]
concert	concierto [kohn-see-'ehr-toh]
conductor	el director (de orquesta) [ehl dee-rehk-'tohr (deh ohr-'keh-stah)]
curtain	cortina [kohr-'tee-nah]
dancer	bailarín/bailarina [bah-ee-lah-'reen, bah·ee-lah-'ree-nah]
direction	la dirección [lah dee-rehk-see-'ohn]
drama	el drama [ehl 'drah-mah]

drive-in cinema	el cine al aire libre [ehl 'see-neh ahl 'ah·ee·reh 'lee-breh]
festival	el festival [ehl feh-stee-'vahl]
intermission	entreacto, descanso [ehn-treh-'ahk-toh, deh-'skahn-soh]
jazz concert	concierto de jazz [kohn-see-'ehr-toh deh yahz]
main role	el papel principal [ehl pah-'pehl preen-see-'pahl]
movie actor/actress	el actor/la actriz de cine [ehl ahk-'tohr/lah ahk-'trees deh 'see-neh]
movie house	el cine [ehl 'see-neh]
movie, film	película, el film(e) [peh-'lee-koo-lah, ehl 'feelm (eh)]
music hall	teatro de variedades [teh-'ah-troh deh vah-ree-eh-'dah-dehs]
musical	comedia musical, el musical [koh-'meh-dee·ah moo-see-'kahl, ehl moo-see-'kahl]
nude	desnudo [dehs-'noo-doh]
open-air theater	teatro al aire libre [teh-'ah-troh ahl 'ah·ee·reh 'lee-breh]
opera	ópera ['oh-peh-rah]
opera glasses	los gemelos/los prismáticos de teatro [lohs heh-'meh-lohs/lohs prees-'mah-tee-kohs deh teh-'ah-troh]
operetta, zarzuela (Spanish operetta)	opereta, zarzuela [oh-peh-'reh-tah; sahr-soo-'eh-lah]
orchestra	orquesta [ohr-'keh-stah]
orchestra (seating)	platea [plah-'teh-ah]
original version	la versión original [lah vehr-see-'ohn oh-ree-hee-'nahl]
performance	la escenificación, espectáculo, teatro [lah eh-seh-nee-fee-kah-see-'ohn, eh-spehk-'tah-koo-loh, teh-'ah-troh]
play	obra de teatro ['oh-brah deh teh-'ah-troh]
pop concert	concierto de música pop [kohn-see-'ehr-toh deh 'moo-see-kah pohp]
premiere	estreno [eh-'streh-noh]
program	el programa [ehl proh-'grah-mah]
role	el papel, el rol [ehl pah-'pehl, ehl rohl]

sacred music concert	concierto de música sagrada [kohn-see-'ehr-toh deh 'moo-see-kah sah-'grah-dah]
show, performance	espectáculo, la representación, la sesión [eh-spehk-'tah-koo-'loh, lah reh-preh-sehn-tah-see-'ohn, lah seh-see-'ohn]
singer	el/la cantante [ehl/lah kahn-'tahn-teh]
soloist	el/la solista [ehl/lah soh-'lee-stah]
stage	escenario [eh-seh-'nah-ree-oh]
subtitle	subtítulo [soob-'tee-too-loh]
symphonic music concert	concierto sinfónico [kohn-see-'ehr-toh seen-'foh-nee-koh]
tragedy	tragedia [trah-'heh-dee-ah]

Bar/Discotheque/Nightclub

Bar/Discoteca/Club nocturno

What local shows can we go to in the evening?

¿Qué espectáculos típicos hay aquí por las tardes? [keh eh-spehk-'tah-koo-'lohs 'tee-pee-kohs 'ah·ee ah-'kee pohr lahs 'tahr-dehs]

Is there a nice bar around here?

¿Hay por aquí un bar/una taberna acogedor/a? ['ah·ee pohr ah-'kee oon bahr/'oo-nah tah-'behr-nah ah-koh-heh-'dohr (ah)]

Where can we go dancing?

¿Dónde se puede ir aquí a bailar? ['dohn-deh seh 'pweh-deh eer ah-'kee ah bah·ee-'lahr]

Is there a nightclub where they do flamenco?

¿Hay algún club nocturno donde bailen flamenco? ['ah·ee ahl-'goon kloob nohk-'toor-noh 'dohn-deh 'bah·ee-lehn flah-'mehn-koh]

Is it mostly geared to a young or to an older crowd?

¿Va allí un público joven o mayor? [vah ah-'yee oon 'poob-lee-koh 'hoh-vehn oh mah-'yohr]

Do you have to dress up to go there?

¿Hay que ir de etiqueta? ['ah·ee keh eer deh eh-tee-'keh-tah]

The admission price includes one drink.	La entrada incluye una bebida. [lah ehn-'trah-dah een-'kloo-yeh 'oo-nah beh-'bee-dah]
A beer, please.	Una cerveza, por favor. ['oo-nah sehr-'veh-sah, pohr fah-'vohr]
Another one, please.	Otra vez lo mismo. ['oh-trah vehs loh 'mees-moh]
This round's on me.	Esta ronda corre de mi cuenta. ['eh-stah 'rohn-dah 'koh-rreh deh mee 'kwehn-tah]
Another dance?	¿Bailamos (otra vez)? [bah·ee-'lah-mohs ('oh-trah vehs)]
Do you want to go for a walk?	¿Damos un paseíto? ['dah-mohs oon 'pah-seh-'ee-toh]

Word List: Bar/Discotheque/Nightclub

band	banda, conjunto ['bahn-dah, kohn-'hoon-toh]
bar	taberna, tasca, el bar [tah-'behr-nah, 'tah-skah, ehl bahr]
bouncer	portero [pohr-'teh-roh]
cash	dinero efectivo, moneda contante [dee-'neh-roh eh-fehk-'tee-voh, moh-'neh-dah kohn-'tahn-teh]
casino	casino [kah-'see-noh]
D.J.	el/la pinchadiscos [ehl/lah peen-chah-'dee-skohs]
to dance	bailar [bah·ee-'lahr]
dance band	orquesta de baile [ohr-'keh-stah deh 'bah·ee-leh]
dance music	música de baile ['moo-see-kah deh 'bah·ee-leh]
disco, discotheque	discoteca [dee-skoh-'teh-kah]
fashion show	el desfile de modas/modelos [ehl dehs-'fee-leh deh 'moh-dahs/moh-'deh-lohs]
flamenco	flamenco [flah-'mehn-koh]
folklore	el folklore [ehl fohlk-'lohr]
folkloric show	espectáculo folklórico [eh-speh-'tah-koo-'loh fohlk-'loh-ree-koh]

gambling arcade	el salón de juegos [ehl sah-'lohn deh 'hweh-gohs]
to go out	salir [sah-'leer]
live music	música en directo ['moo-see-kah ehn dee-'rehk-toh]
nightclub	el club nocturno [ehl kloob nohk-'toor-noh]
show	espectáculo [eh-spehk-'tah-koo-loh]

"Tapas," the assorted appetizers displayed on the counter of most Spanish bars, are usually eaten by patrons while they drink, standing at the bar. Increasingly popular abroad, a "tapa" can be any small, single-item dish that the cook chooses to put out. Olives, cheese, ham, anchovies, sardines, and cold omelette "tapas" are among the most popular.

7 **On the Beach/Sports**
En la Playa/Deportes

At the Swimming Pool/On the Beach
En la piscina/En la playa

Is there…here?	¿Hay aquí ['ah·ee ah-'kee]
an outdoor pool	una piscina al aire libre? ['oo-nah pee-'see-nah ahl 'ah·ee-reh 'lee-breh]
an indoor pool	una piscina cubierta? ['oo-nah pee-'see-nah koo-bee-'ehr-tah]
a thermal pool	una piscina termal? ['oo-nah pee-'see-nah tehr-'mahl]

One admission ticket (with changing room), please.

Por favor, una entrada (*Am* un boleto) (con derecho a cabina). [pohr fah-'vohr, 'oo-nah ehn-'trah-dah (oon boh-'leh-toh) (kohn deh-'reh-choh ah kah-'bee-nah)]

Swimmers only!

¡Sólo para nadadores! ['soh-loh 'pah-rah nah-dah-'doh-rehs]

No diving!

¡Prohibido saltar al agua/zambullirse! [proh-ee-'bee-doh sahl-'tahr ahl 'ah-gwah/sahm-boo-'yeer-seh]

No swimming!

¡Prohibido bañarse! [proh-ee-'bee-doh bah-'nyahr-seh]

Is the beach…	La playa… [lah 'plah-yah]
sandy?	¿es de arena? [ehs deh ah-'reh-nah]
pebbled?	¿es pedregosa? [ehs peh-dreh-'goh-sah]
rocky?	¿tiene rocas? [tee-'eh-neh 'roh-kahs]

Are there any sea urchins/jellyfish here?

¿Hay aquí erizos de mar/medusas? ['ah·ee ah-'kee eh-'ree-sohs deh mahr/meh-'doo-sahs]

How far can we swim?

¿Hasta dónde está permitido nadar? ['ah-stah 'dohn-deh eh-'stah pehr-mee-'tee-doh nah-'dahr]

Is there a strong current?

¿Es fuerte la corriente? [ehs 'fwehr-teh lah koh-rree-'ehn-teh]

Is it dangerous for kids?

¿Es peligroso para los niños?
[ehs peh-lee-'groh-soh 'pah-rah lohs 'nee-nyohs]

When is the high/low tide?

¿A qué hora es la marea baja/alta?
[ah keh 'oh-rah ehs lah mah-'reh-ah 'bah-hah/'ahl-tah]

I'd like to rent...

Quisiera alquilar ... [kee-see-'eh-rah ahl-kee-'lahr]

a boat.
a pair of water skis.

una barca. ['oo-nah 'bahr-kah]
un par de esquíes náuticos.
[oon pahr deh eh-'skee-ehs 'nah·oo-tee-kohs]

How much is it per hour/per day?

¿Cuánto cuesta por hora/por día?
['kwahn-toh 'kweh-stah pohr 'oh-rah/pohr 'dee-ah]

Sports
Deportes

What sports events do you have here?

¿Qué manifestaciones deportivas hay aquí? [keh mah-nee-feh-stah-see-'oh-nehs deh-pohr-'tee-vahs 'ah·ee ah-'kee]

What sports can one practice here?

¿Qué posibilidades hay aquí de hacer deporte? [keh poh-see-bee-lee-'dah-dehs 'ah·ee ah-'kee deh ah-'sehr deh-'pohr-teh]

Is there a golf course/a tennis court here?

¿Hay aquí un campo de golf/una pista (*Am* cancha) de tenis?
['ah·ee ah-'kee oon 'kahm-poh deh gohlf/'oo-nah 'pee-stah ('kahn-chah) deh 'teh-nees]

Where can I go fishing?

¿Dónde se puede pescar a caña?
['dohn-deh seh 'pweh-deh peh-'skahr ah 'kah-nyah]

I'd like to see the soccer game.

Quisiera ver el partido de fútbol.
[kee-see-'eh-rah vehr ehl pahr-'tee-doh deh 'foot-bohl]

When/Where is it?	¿Cuándo/Dónde es? ['kwahn-doh/'dohn-deh ehs]
How much is it to get in?	¿Cuánto cuesta la entrada (*Am* el boleto)? ['kwahn-toh 'kweh-stah lah ehn-'trah-dah (ehl boh-'leh-toh)]
Are there ski slopes in the mountains?	¿Hay pistas de esquí en las montañas? ['ah·ee 'pee-stahs deh eh-'skee ehn lahs mohn-'tah-nyahs]
When is the cable railway's last trip up/down?	¿A qué hora es la última subida/bajada del teleférico? [ah keh 'oh-rah ehs lah 'ool-tee-mah soo-'bee-dah/bah-'hah-dah dehl teh-leh-'feh-ree-koh]
I'd like to go mountain hiking.	Quisiera hacer una excursión por las montañas. [kee-see-'eh-rah ah-'sehr 'oo-nah ehk-skoor-see-'ohn pohr lahs mohn-'tah-nyahs]

Can you show me an interesting route on the map?	¿Puede usted indicarme en el mapa un itinerario interesante? ['pweh-deh oo-'stehd een-dee-'kahr-meh ehn ehl 'mah-pah oon ee-tee-neh-'rah-ree·oh een-teh-reh-'sahn-teh]
Where can I borrow…?	¿Dónde puedo tomar prestado …? ['dohn-deh 'pweh-doh toh-'mahr pre-'stah-doh]
I'd like to take a…course.	Me gustaría hacer un curso de … [meh goo-stah-'ree-ah ah-'sehr oon 'koor-soh deh]
What sport do you play?	¿Qué deporte practica usted? [keh deh-'pohr-teh prahk-'tee-kah oo-'stehd]
I play…	Juego a… ['hweh-goh ah]
I'm a…fan.	Soy aficionado a… ['soh·ee ah-fee-see·oh-'nah-doh ah]
I like to go to…	Me gusta ir a… [meh 'goo-stah eer ah]
Can I play too?	¿Puedo jugar yo también? ['pweh-doh hoo-'gahr yoh tahm-bee-'ehn]

Word List: Beach/Sports

active vacations
(las) vacaciones activas [(lahs) vah-kah-see-'oh-nehs ahk-'tee-vahs]

admission ticket
entrada, el billete (*Am* boleto) [ehn-'trah-dah, ehl bee-'yeh-teh (boh-'leh-toh)]

aerobics
(el) aerobic, el ejercicio aeróbico [(ehl) ah·eh-roh-'beek, ehl eh-hehr-'see-see·oh ah·eh-'roh-bee-koh]

air mattress
el colchón neumático [ehl kohl-'chohn neh·oo-'mah-tee-koh]

badminton
el badminton [ehl bahd-'meen-tohn]

ball
pelota, el balón [peh-'loh-tah, ehl bah-'lohn]

banderilla (barbed dart with flag used in bullfighting)
banderilla [bahn-deh-'ree-yah]

baseball
béisbol ['beh·ees-bohl]

basketball
baloncesto [bah-lohn-'seh-stoh]

bath attendant
bañero [bah-'nyeh-roh]

bath towel	toalla de baño [toh-'ah-yah deh 'bah-nyoh]
beach	playa ['plah-yah]
beach cove	cala con playa ['kah-lah kohn 'plah-yah]
beach umbrella	sombrilla (de playa) [sohm-'bree-yah (deh 'plah-yah)]
beginner	el/la principiante [ehl/lah preen-see-pee-'ahn-teh]
to bicycle	montar (*Am* andar) en bicicleta [mohn-'tahr (ahn-'dahr) ehn bee-see-'kleh-tah]
bicycle race	carrera ciclista [kah-'rreh-rah see-'klee-stah]
bicycle tour	la excursión en bici(cleta) [lah ehk-skoor-see-'ohn eh 'bee-see ('kleh-tah)]
bicycling	ciclismo [see-'klees-moh]
boat rental	el alquiler de barcas [ehl ahl-kee-'lehr deh 'bahr-kahs]
bocce	petanca, bocha [peh-'tahn-kah, 'boh-chah]
bowling	los bolos [lohs 'boh-lohs]
bowling alley	bolera [boh-'leh-rah]
bullfight	corrida de toros [koh-'rree-dah deh 'toh-rohs]
bullfighting arena	plaza de toros ['plah-sah deh 'toh-rohs]
canoe	canoa, piragua [kah-'noh-ah, pee-'rah-gwah]
chair lift	el telesilla [ehl teh-leh-'see-yah]
championship	campeonato [kahm-peh-oh-'nah-toh]
contest	la competición [lah kohm-peh-tee-see-'ohn]
course	curso ['koor-soh]
crew	equipo [eh-'kee-poh]
cross-country race	carrera de fondo [kah-'rreh-rah deh 'fohn-doh]
cross-country ski trails	pista de fondo ['pee-stah deh 'fohn-doh]
deck chair	tumbona, hamaca (*Am* perezosa) [toom-'boh-nah, ah-'mah-kah (peh-reh-'soh-sah)]

deep-sea fishing	pesca marítima/de altura ['peh-skah mah-'ree-tee-mah/deh ahl-'too-rah]
defeat	derrota [deh-'rroh-tah]
diving board	el trampolín [ehl trahm-poh-'leen]
diving mask	las gafas de buceo [lahs 'gah-fahs deh boo-'seh-oh]
doubles (tennis)	el doble [ehl 'doh-bleh]
downhill skiing	el esquí alpino [ehl eh-'skee ahl-'pee-noh]
dune	duna ['doo-nah]
figure skating	el patinaje artístico [ehl pah-tee-'nah-heh ahr-'tee-stee-koh]
fishing permit	licencia de pesca [lee-'sehn-see·ah deh 'peh-skah]
fishing rod	caña de pescar ['kah-nyah deh peh-'skahr]
fitness training	la preparación física [lah preh-pah-rah-see-'ohn 'fee-see-kah]
flippers	las aletas (de natación) [lahs ah-'leh-tahs (deh nah-tah-see-'ohn)]
freestyle wrestling	la lucha libre [lah 'loo-chah 'lee-breh]
fronton *(jai-alai court)*	el frontón [ehl frohn-'tohn]
funicular, cable railway	el funicular, teleférico [ehl foo-nee-koo-'lahr, teh-leh-'feh-ree-koh]
game	juego, partido ['hweh-goh, pahr-'tee-doh]
to go horseback riding	montar a caballo [mohn-'tahr ah kah-'bah-yoh]
to go sledding	montar en trineo [mohn-'tahr ehn tree-'neh-oh]
goal	portería [pohr-teh-'ree-ah]
goalkeeper	portero [pohr-'teh-roh]
golf	el golf [ehl gohlf]
golf club	raqueta de golf [rah-'keh-tah deh gohlf]
gymnastics	gimnasia [heem-'nah-see·ah]
half-time	primer/segundo tiempo [pree-'mehr/seh-'goon-doh tee-'ehm-poh]
handball	balonmano [bah-lohn-'mah-noh]
to hang glide	volar a vela [voh-'lahr ah 'veh-lah]
hang gliding	aladeltismo [ah-lah-dehl-'tees-moh]

hiking	excursionismo, pedestrismo [ehks-koor-see-oh-'nees-moh, peh-deh-'strees-moh]
hiking trail	sendero (para excursiones a pie) [sehn-'deh-roh ('pah-rah ehk-skoor-see-'oh-nehs ah 'pee-eh)]
horse	caballo [kah-'bah-yoh]
horse race	carrera de caballos [kah-'rreh-rah deh kah-'bah-yohs]
horseback ride	paseo a caballo [pah-'seh-oh ah kah-'bah-yoh]
ice hockey	el hockey sobre hielo [ehl 'joh-kee 'soh-breh 'yeh-loh]
ice rink	pista de hielo ['pee-stah deh 'yeh-loh]
ice skates	las botas de patinaje [lahs 'boh-tahs deh pah-tee-'nah-heh]
ice skating	el patinaje sobre hielo [ehl pah-tee-'nah-heh 'soh-breh 'yeh-loh]
indoor athletics	atletismo en sala [aht-leh-'tees-moh ehn 'sah-lah]
jai-alai	jai alai, juego de pelota vasca ['hah·ee ah-'lah·ee, 'hweh-goh deh peh-'loh-tah 'vah-skah]
jazz (dance)	(el baile de) jazz [(ehl 'bah·ee-leh deh) dyahz]
to jog	hacer/practicar jogging [ah-'sehr/prahk-tee-'kahr 'dyoh-geeng]
jogging	el jogging [ehl 'dyoh-geeng]
judo	judo ['hoo-doh]
karate	el karate [ehl kah-'rah-teh]
kayak	el kayak [(ehl) kah-'yahk]
life preserver, float	el flotador [ehl floh-tah-'dohr]
to lose	perder [pehr-'dehr]
marathon	maratón [mah-rah-'tohn]
minigolf	el minigolf [ehl mee-nee-'gohlf]
motorboat	motora (lancha) [moh-'toh-rah ('lahn-chah)]
motorcycling	motociclismo [moh-toh-see-'klees-moh]
mountain climbing	alpinismo [ahl-pee-'nees-moh]
net	la red [lah rehd]
ninepins, skittles	bolos (juego de) [('hweh-goh deh) 'boh-lohs]

nonswimmers	no nadadores [noh nah-dah-'doh-rehs]
nude beach	playa nudista ['plah-yah noo-'dee-stah]
one-day ticket	el billete (*Am* boleto) válido para un día [ehl bee-'yeh-teh (boh-'leh-toh) 'vah-lee-doh 'pah-rah oon 'dee-ah]
outdoor pool	piscina al aire libre [pee-'see-nah ahl 'ah·ee-reh 'lee-breh]
parachuting	paracaidismo [pah-rah-kah·ee-'dees-moh]
pebbles	los guijarros [lohs gee-'hah-rrohs]
pedal boat	barca de pedales ['bahr-kah deh peh-'dah-lehs]
Ping-Pong, table tennis	el ping-pong, el tenis de mesa [ehl peeng pohng, ehl 'teh-nees deh 'meh-sah]
private beach	playa privada/particular ['plah-yah pree-'vah-dah/pahr-tee-koo-'lahr]
program	el programa [ehl proh-'grah-mah]
race	carrera [kah-'rreh-rah]
racket	raqueta [rah-'keh-tah]
referee	árbitro ['ahr-bee-troh]
regatta, boat race	regata [reh-'gah-tah]
riding	la equitación [lah eh-kee-tah-see-'ohn]
rock climbing	escalada en roca [eh-skah-'lah-dah ehn 'roh-kah]
roller hockey	el hockey sobre patines [ehl 'hoh-kee 'soh-bree pah-'tee-nehs]
to row	remar [reh-'mahr]
rowboat	barca de remos ['bahr-kah deh 'reh-mohs]
rubber dinghy/boat	el bote neumático [ehl 'boh-teh neh·oo-'mah-tee-koh]
rugby	el rugby [ehl 'roog-bee]
to sail	la navegación a vela [lah nah-veh-gah-see-'ohn ah 'veh-lah]
sailboat	barco de vela ['bahr-koh deh 'veh-lah]
saltwater swimming pool	piscina de agua marina [pee-'see-nah deh 'ah-gwah mah-'ree-nah]
sand	arena [ah-'reh-nah]
sauna	sauna ['sah·oo-nah]

score	resultado [reh-sool-'tah-doh]
to scuba dive	bucear [boo-seh-'ahr]
scuba diving equipment	equipo de buceo [eh-'kee-poh deh boo-'seh-oh]
shower	ducha ['doo-chah]
shuttlecock, birdie	el rehilete, el volante [ehl reh-ee-'leh-teh, ehl voh-'lahn-teh]
singles (tennis)	(partido) individual [(pahr-'tee-doh) een-dee-vee-doo-'ahl]
skateboard	el monopatín [ehl moh-noh-pah-'teen]
ski	el esquí [ehl eh-'skee]
to ski	esquiar [eh-skee-'ahr]
ski goggles	las gafas de esquí [lahs 'gah-fahs deh eh-'skee]
ski poles	los bastones de esquí [lohs bah-'stoh-nehs deh eh-'skee]
ski straps	la fijación, atadura (de los esquíes) [lah fee-hah-see-'ohn, ah-tah-'doo-rah (deh lohs eh-'skee-ehs)]

ski tow	el telearrastre [ehl teh-leh-ah-'rrah-streh]
skiing course	curso de esquí ['koor-soh deh eh-'skee]
skiing instructor	el profesor de esquí [ehl proh-feh-'sohr deh eh-'skee]
sled	trineo [tree-'neh-oh]
snorkel	el (tubo) respirador [ehl ('too-boh) reh-spee-rah-dohr]
soccer	el fútbol [ehl 'foot-bohl]
soccer field	campo (*Am* cancha) de fútbol ['kahm-poh ('kahn-chah) deh 'foot-bohl]
soccer game	partido de fútbol [pahr-'tee-doh deh 'foot-bohl]
soccer team	equipo de fútbol [eh-'kee-poh deh 'foot-bohl]
solarium	solario [soh-'lah-ree·oh]
sports field	campo (*Am* cancha) de deportes ['kahm-poh ('kahn-chah) deh deh-'pohr-tehs]
sportsman/woman	el/la deportista [ehl/lah deh-pohr-'tee-stah]
squash	el squash [ehl skoo-'ahsh]

start	salida, partida [sah-'lee-dah, pahr-'tee-dah]
sunbathing area	zona para tenderse a tomar el sol ['soh-nah 'pah-rah tehn-'dehr-seh ah toh-'mahr ehl sohl]
surfboard	tabla deslizadora/de surf ['tah-blah dehs-lee-sah-'doh-rah/deh soorf]
to surf	practicar el surf [prahk-tee-'kahr ehl soorf]
surfing	el patinaje sobre las olas, el surfing [ehl pah-tee-'nah-heh 'soh-breh lahs 'oh-lahs, ehl 'soor-feeng]
swimmers	nadadores [nah-dah-'doh-rehs]
swimming	la natación [lah nah-tah-see-'ohn]
swimming pool	piscina (*Am* pileta) [pee-'see-nah (pee-'leh-tah)]
tennis	el tenis [ehl 'teh-nees]
tennis racket	raqueta (de tenis) [rah-'keh-tah (deh 'teh-nees)]
ticket office	caja, boletería ['kah-hah, boh-leh-teh-'ree-ah]
tied	empatado(s) [ehm-pah-'tah-doh(s)]
victory	victoria [veek-'toh-ree·ah]
volleyball	el balón-volea, el volibol [ehl bah-'lohn-voh-'leh-ah, ehl voh-lee-'bohl]
water polo	water polo ['wah-tehr 'poh-loh]
water wings	los flotadores [lohs floh-tah-'doh-rehs]
to win	ganar [gah-'nahr]
wrestling	lucha (grecorromana/libre) ['loo-chah (greh-koh-rroh-'mah-nah/'lee-breh)]

Questions/Prices
Preguntas/Precios

opening hours

horas de apertura ['oh-rahs deh ah-pehr-'too-rah]

open/closed/closed
for vacation

abierto/cerrado/cerrado por
vacaciones [ah-bee-'ehr-toh/seh-'rrah-doh/seh-'rrah-doh pohr vah-kah-see-'oh-nehs]

Where can I find…?

Por favor, ¿dónde hay…? [pohr fah-'vohr, 'dohn-deh 'ah·ee]

Can you recommend
a…shop?

¿Puede usted indicarme una
buena tienda de…? ['pweh-deh oo-'stehd een-dee-'kahr-meh 'oo-nah 'bweh-nah tee-'ehn-dah deh]

Are you being helped?

¿Ya le/la atienden? [yah leh/lah ah-tee-'ehn-dehn]

Thanks, I'm just browsing.

Gracias, sólo quiero mirar un
poco. ['grah-see·ahs, 'soh-loh kee-'eh-roh mee-'rahr oon 'poh-koh]

I'd like…

Quisiera…/Desearía…/Me gus-
taría… [kee-see-'eh-rah/deh-seh-ah-'ree-ah/meh goo-stah-'ree-ah]

Do you have…?

¿Tiene usted…? [tee-'eh-neh oo-'stehd]

Could I see…, please?

Enséñeme…, por favor. [ehn-'seh-nyeh-meh, pohr fah-'vohr]

Please…
   a pair of…
   a piece of…

Por favor… [pohr fah-'vohr]
   un par de… [oon pahr deh]
   un trozo de… [oon 'troh-soh deh]

Could you show me
another…, please?

¿Tiene usted otro/otra…, por
favor? [tee-'eh-neh oo-'stehd 'oh-troh/'oh-trah, pohr fah-'vohr]

Do you have anything
cheaper?

¿Tienen ustedes también algo
más barato? [tee-'eh-nehn oo-'steh-dehs tahm-bee-'ehn 'ahl-goh mahs bah-'rah-toh]

This is good. I'll take it.	Me gusta. Me lo llevo. [meh 'goo-stah. meh loh 'yeh-voh]
How much is it?	¿Cuánto cuesta? ['kwahn-toh 'kweh-stah]
Do you take…?	¿Aceptan ustedes… [ah-'sehp-tahn oo-'steh-dehs]
dollars?	dólares? ['doh-lah-rehs]
Eurochecks?	Eurocheques? [eh·oo-roh-'cheh-kehs]
credit cards?	tarjetas de crédito? [tahr-'heh-tahs deh 'kreh-dee-toh]
traveler's checks?	cheques de viaje? ['cheh-kehs deh vee-'ah-heh]
Could you wrap this for me?	¿Me lo puede empaquetar (*Am* empacar)? [meh loh 'pweh-deh ehm-pah-keh-'tahr (ehm-pah-'kahr]
I'd like to exchange this.	Quisiera cambiar esto. [kee-see-'eh-rah kahm-bee-'ahr 'eh-stoh]

Word List: Stores

antiques	las antigüedades [lahs ahn-tee-gweh-'dah-dehs]

appliance store	tienda de artículos eléctricos [(tee-'ehn-dah deh) ahr-'tee-koo-lohs eh-'lehk-tree-kohs]
art dealer	el/la comerciante de objetos de arte [(ehl/lah koh-mehr-see-'ahn-teh deh) ohb-'heh-tohs deh 'ahr-teh]
arts and crafts	tienda de artesanía [tee-'ehn-dah deh ahr-teh-sah-'nee-ah]
bakery	panadería [pah-nah-deh-'ree-ah]
beauty salon	instituto de belleza [een-stee-'too-toh deh beh-'yeh-sah]
bookstore	librería [lee-breh-'ree-ah]
boutique	la boutique [lah boh-'teek]
butcher shop	carnicería [kahr-nee-seh-'ree-ah]
candy store	confitería [kohn-fee-teh-'ree-ah]
cigar store	estanco (*Am* cigarrería) [eh-'stahn-koh (seh-gah-rreh-'ree-ah)]
dairy	lechería [leh-cheh-'ree-ah]
department store	los grandes almacenes [lohs 'grahn-dehs ahl-mah-'seh-nehs]
drugstore	droguería [droh-geh-'ree-ah]
dry cleaner	tintorería, limpieza en seco [teen-toh-reh-'ree-ah, leem-pee-'eh-sah ehn 'seh-koh]

fish market	pescadería [peh-skah-deh-'ree-ah]
flower shop	florería [floh-reh-'ree-ah]
fruit market/store	frutería [froo-teh-'ree-ah]
furniture store	el almacén de muebles [(ehl ahl-mah-'sehn deh) 'mweh-blehs]
furrier's	peletería [peh-leh-teh-'ree-ah]
grocery store	tienda de comestibles (*Am* el almacén) [tee-'ehn-dah deh koh-meh-'stee-blehs (ehl ahl-mah-'sehn)]
hair salon (women's, men's)	peluquería (de señoras, de caballeros) [peh-loo-keh-'ree-ah (deh seh-'nyoh-rahs, deh kah-bah-'yeh-rohs)]
hardware store	ferretería [feh-rreh-teh-'ree-ah]
health food store	tienda de productos dietéticos [(tee-'ehn-dah deh) proh-'dook-tohs dee-eh-'teh-tee-kohs]
housewares store	tienda de artículos domésticos [(tee-'ehn-dah deh) ahr-'tee-koo-lohs doh-'meh-stee-kohs]

jewelry	joyería [hoh-yeh-'ree-ah]
junk shop	rastro ['rah-stroh]
laundromat	lavandería automática/de autoservicio [lah-vahn-deh-'ree-ah ow-toh-'mah-tee-kah/deh ow-toh-sehr-'vee-see·oh]
laundry	lavandería [lah-vahn-deh-'ree-ah]
leather shop	(tienda de) artículos de piel/cuero [(tee-'ehn-dah deh) ahr-'tee-koo-lohs deh pee-'ehl/'kweh-roh]
liquor store	tienda de bebidas alcohólicas, vinos y licores [(tee-'ehn-dah deh) beh-'bee-dahs ahl-koh-'oh-lee-kahs, 'vee-nohs ee lee-'koh-rehs]
macrobiotic store	tienda macrobiótica [tee-'ehn-dah mah-kroh-bee-'oh-tee-kah]
market	mercado [mehr-'kah-doh]
music shop	tienda de artículos de música [(tee-'ehn-dah deh) ahr-'tee-koo-lohs deh 'moo-see-kah]
newspaper seller	el vendedor de periódicos [ehl vehn-deh-'dohr deh peh-ree-'oh-dee-kohs]
optician	óptico ['ohp-tee-koh]
pastry shop	pastelería, confitería [pah-steh-leh-'ree-ah, kohn-fee-teh-'ree-ah]
perfume shop	perfumería [pehr-foo-meh-'ree-ah]
pharmacy	farmacia [fahr-'mah-see·ah]
photo supply shop	tienda de artículos fotográficos [(tee-'ehn-dah deh) ahr-'tee-koo-lohs foh-toh-'grah-fee-kohs]
record shop	tienda de discos [tee-'ehn-dah deh 'dee-skohs]
second-hand/used bookstore	librería de segunda mano [lee-breh-'ree-ah deh seh-'goon-dah 'mah-noh]
second-hand/used goods store	artículos de segunda mano [ahr-'tee-koo-lohs deh seh-'goon-dah 'mah-noh]
self-service	autoservicio [ow-toh-sehr-'vee-see·oh]
shoe repair shop	zapatero [sah-pah-'teh-roh]
shoe store	zapatería [sah-pah-teh-'ree-ah]

souvenir shop	recuerdos, souvenirs [reh-'kwehr-dohs, soo-veh-'neers]
specialty food store/ delicatessen	tienda de comestibles finos (*Am* fiambrería) [(tee-'ehn-dah deh) koh-meh-'stee-blehs 'fee-nohs (fee-ahm-breh-'ree-ah)]
sports supplies store	tienda de artículos de deporte [(tee-'ehn-dah deh) ahr-'tee-koo-lohs deh deh-'pohr-teh]
stationery store	papelería [pah-peh-leh-'ree-ah]
supermarket	supermercado [soo-pehr-mehr-'kah-doh]
tailor/seamstress	el sastre/la modista [ehl 'sah-streh/ lah moh-'dee-stah]
toy store	juguetería, tienda de artículos de juguete [hoo-geh-teh-'ree-ah, (tee-'ehn-dah deh) ahr-'tee-koo-lohs deh hoo-'geh-teh]
travel agency	agencia de viajes [ah-'hehn-see·ah deh vee-'ah-hehs]
variety store	tienda de baratijas, el bazar [tee-'ehn-dah deh, bah-rah-'tee-hahs, ehl bah-'sahr]
vegetable market/shop, greengrocer	verdulería [vehr-doo-leh-'ree-ah]
watchmaker's	relojero [reh-loh-'heh-roh]
wine shop	(el almacén de) vinos, la bodega [(ehl ahl-mah-'sehn deh) 'vee-nohs, lah boh-'deh-gah]

Groceries
Productos alimenticios

What can I get you?	¿Qué desea? [keh deh-'seh-ah]
I'd like…, please	Déme…, por favor. ['deh-meh, pohr fah-'vohr]
a kilo of…	un kilo de… [oon 'kee-loh deh]
a pound of…	una libra de… ['oo-nah 'lee-brah deh]
ten slices of cheese	diez rebanadas de queso [dee-'ehs reh-bah-'nah-dahs deh 'keh-soh]

ten slices of salami	diez rodajas de salami [dee-'ehs roh-'dah-hahs deh sah-'lah-mee]
a piece of…	un trozo de… [oon 'troh-soh deh]
a package of…	un paquete de… [oon pah-'keh-teh deh]

a jar of…	un frasco de… [oon 'frahs-koh deh]
a can of…	un bote/una lata de… [oon 'boh-teh/'oo-nah 'lah-tah deh]
a bottle of…	una botella de… ['oo-nah boh-'teh-yah deh]
a bag of…	una bolsa… ['oo-nah 'bohl-sah]
Can I give you a little more?	¿Puedo ponerle un poquito más? ['pweh-doh poh-'nehr-leh oon poh-'kee-toh mahs]
Can I get you anything else?	¿Desea alguna cosa más? [deh-'seh-ah ahl-'goo-nah 'koh-sah mahs]
Could I try some of this, please?	¿Me permite probar un poco de esto? [meh pehr-'mee-teh proh-'bahr oon 'poh-koh deh 'eh-stoh]
That's all, thanks.	Eso es todo, gracias. ['eh-soh ehs 'toh-doh, 'grah-see·ahs]

Word List: Groceries

almonds	las almendras [lahs ahl-'mehn-drahs]
anchovies (fresh)	los boquerones [lohs boh-keh-'roh-nehs]
anchovies (canned)	las anchoas [lahs ahn-'choh-ahs]
angler fish	el rapé [ehl rah-'peh]
apples	las manzanas [lahs mahn-'sah-nahs]
apricots	los albaricoques [lohs ahl-bah-ree-'koh-kehs]
artichokes	las alcachofas [lahs ahl-kah-'choh-fahs]
asparagus	los espárragos [lohs eh-'spah-rrah-gohs]
avocado	el aguacate [ehl ah-gwah-'kah-teh]
baby food	los alimentos infantiles [lohs ah-lee-'mehn-tohs een-fahn-'tee-lehs]
bananas	los plátanos (*Am* las bananas) [lohs 'plah-tah-nohs (lahs bah-'nah-nahs)]
basil	albahaca [ahl-bah-'ah-kah]
beans	las judías, las habas (*Am* los frijoles, los porotos) [lahs hoo-'dee-ahs, lahs 'ah-bahs (lohs free-'hoh-lehs, lohs poh-'roh-tohs)]

beef	la carne de vaca [lah 'kahr-neh deh 'vah-kah]
beer	cerveza [sehr-'veh-sah]
blackberries	las moras [lahs 'moh-rahs]
blood sausage	morcilla [mohr-'see-yah]
boiled ham	el jamón de york, el jamón cocido [ehl hah-'mohn deh yohrk, ehl hah-'mohn koh-'see-doh]
bologna sausage	mortadela [mohr-tah-'deh-lah]
bread	el pan [ehl pahn]
brown bread	el pan moreno [ehl pahn moh-'reh-noh]
bun, roll	panecillo [pah-neh-'see-yoh]
butter	mantequilla (*Am* manteca) [mahn-teh-'kee-yah (mahn-'teh-kah)]
cabbage	col, repollo, berza [kohl, reh-'poh-yoh, 'behr-sah]
Camembert	el camembert [ehl kah-mehm-'behrt]
carrots	las zanahorias [lahs sah-nah-'oh-ree-ahs]

cauliflower	la coliflor [lah koh-lee-'flohr]
celery	apio ['ah-pee·oh]
champagne	el champán, el cava [ehl chahm-'pahn, ehl 'kah-vah]
chard	acelga [ah-'sehl-gah]
cheese	queso ['keh-soh]
cherries	las cerezas [lahs seh-'reh-sahs]
chestnut	las castañas [lahs kah-'stah-nyahs]
chick-peas	los garbanzos [lohs gahr-'bahn-sohs]
chicken	pollo ['poh-yoh]
chicory	endibia [ehn-'dee-bee·ah]
chocolate	el chocolate [ehl choh-koh-'lah-teh]
chocolate bar	barra/barrita de chocolate ['bah-rrah/bah-'rree-tah deh choh-koh-'lah-teh]
chop	costilla [koh-'stee-yah]
chopped meat	la carne picada [lah 'kahr-neh pee-'kah-dah]
coconut	el coco [ehl 'koh-koh]
cod	bacalao [bah-kah-'lah-oh]
cod (dried)	bacalao (seco) [bah-kah-'lah-oh ('seh-koh)]
coffee	el café [ehl kah-'feh]
cold cuts	el embutido, los fiambres variados [ehl ehm-boo-'tee-doh, lohs fee-'ahm-brehs vah-ree-'ah-dohs]
corn	el maíz [ehl mah-'ees]
corncob	mazorca/panocha de maíz (*Am* choclo) [mah-'sohr-kah/pah-'noh-chah deh mah-'ees ('choh-kloh)]
cottage cheese	el requesón [ehl reh-keh-'sohn]
crackers	las galletas [lahs gah-'yeh-tahs]
cream	crema, nata ['kreh-mah, 'nah-tah]
cream cheese	queso crema ['keh-soh 'kreh-mah]
cucumber	pepino [peh-'pee-noh]
cumin	comino [koh-'mee-noh]
dates	los dátiles [lohs 'dah-tee-lehs]
dorado	dorada [doh-'rah-dah]
dried meat	cecina [seh-'see-nah]
eel	anguila [ahn-'gee-lah]
eggplant	las berenjenas [lahs beh-rehn-'heh-nahs]
eggs	los huevos [lohs 'weh-vohs]
escarole	escarola [eh-skah-'roh-lah]

fennel	hinojo [ee-'noh-hoh]
figs	los higos [lohs 'ee-gohs]
fish	pescado [peh-'skah-doh]
flour	harina [ah-'ree-nah]
free-range eggs	los huevos de gallinas de corral [lohs 'weh-vohs deh gah-'yee-nahs deh koh-'rrahl]
fresh	fresco ['freh-skoh]
fruit	fruta ['froo-tah]
garlic	ajo ['ah-hoh]
goat cheese	queso de cabra ['keh-soh deh 'kah-brah]
goulash (Hungarian stew)	estofado (a la húngara) [eh-stoh-'fah-doh (ah lah 'oon-gah-rah)]
grapefruit	toronja, pomelo [toh-'rohn-hah, poh-'meh-loh]
grapes	las uvas [lahs 'oo-vahs]
green beans	las judías verdes (*Am* las habichuelas, las chauchas) [lahs hoo-'dee-ahs 'vehr-dehs (ah-bee-choo-'eh-lahs (ah-bee-choo-'eh-lahs)]
hake	merluza [mehr-'loo-sah]
ham	el jamón [ehl hah-'mohn]

hazelnuts	las avellanas [lahs ah-veh-'yah-nahs]
herring	el arenque [ehl ah-'rehn-keh]
home-grown vegetables	las legumbres de cosecha propia [lahs leh-'goom-brehs deh koh-'seh-chah 'proh-pee·ah]
honey	la miel [lah mee-'ehl]
honeydew melon	el melón dulce [ehl meh-'lohn 'dool-seh]
horchata de almendras (an almond drink)	horchata de almendras [ohr-'chah-tah deh ahl-'mehn-drahs]
horns, rolled wafers, (ice cream) cones	los barquillos [lohs bahr-'kee-yohs]
ice, ice cream	helado [eh-'lah-doh]
lamb	la carne de carnero/cordero [lah 'kahr-neh deh kahr-'neh-roh/kohr-'deh-roh]
leek	puerro ['pweh-rroh]
lemonade	limonada [lee-moh-'nah-dah]
lemons	los limones [lohs lee-'moh-nehs]
lentils	las lentejas [lahs lehn-'teh-hahs]
lettuce	lechuga [leh-'choo-gah]
licorice	el regaliz [ehl reh-gah-'lees]
liver paté	el paté de hígado [ehl pah-'teh deh 'ee-gah-doh]
low-fat milk	la leche semidesnatada [lah 'leh-cheh seh-mee-dehs-nah-'tah-dah]
mackerel	caballa [kah-'bah-yah]
mandarine	mandarina [mahn-dah-'ree-nah]
margarine	margarina [mahr-gah-'ree-nah]
marmalade	mermelada [mehr-meh-'lah-dah]
mayonnaise	mayonesa, mahonesa [mah-yoh-'neh-sah, mah-oh-'neh-sah]
meat	la carne [lah 'kahr-neh]
meatballs	las albóndigas [lahs ahl-'bohn-dee-gahs]
melon	el melón [ehl meh-'lohn]
milk	la leche [lah 'leh-cheh]
mineral water	(el) agua mineral [(ehl) 'ah-gwah mee-neh-'rahl]
mushrooms	las setas, los hongos, los champiñones [lahs 'seh-tahs, lohs 'ohn-gohs, lohs chahm-pee-'nyoh-nehs]

mussels	los mejillones, las almejas [lohs meh-hee-'yoh-nehs, lahs ahl-'meh-hahs]
mustard	mostaza [moh-'stah-sah]
nonalcoholic beer	cerveza sin alcohol [sehr-'veh-sah seen ahl-koh-'ohl]
noodles	los fideos [lohs fee-'deh-ohs]
oil	el aceite [ehl ah-'seh·ee·teh]
olive oil	el aceite de oliva [ehl ah-'seh·ee·teh deh oh-'lee-vah]
olives	las aceitunas [lahs ah-seh·ee-'too-nahs]
onions	las cebollas [lahs seh-'boh-yahs]
orange drink	naranjada [nah-rahn-'hah-dah]
orange juice	zumo/jugo de naranja ['soo-moh/'hoo-goh deh nah-'rahn-hah]
oranges	las naranjas [lahs nah-'rahn-hahs]
oregano	orégano [oh-'reh-gah-noh]
oysters	las ostras [lahs 'oh-strahs]
parsley	el perejil [ehl peh-reh-'heel]
partridge	la perdiz [lah pehr-'dees]
pasta	las pastas [lahs 'pah-stahs]
peaches	los melocotones [lohs meh-loh-koh-'toh-nehs]

peanuts	los cacahuetes (*Am* el maní) [lohs kah-kah-'weh-tehs (ehl mah-'nee)]
pear	las peras [lahs 'peh-rahs]
peas	los guisantes (*Am* las arvejas, las alverjas) [lohs gee-'sahn-tehs (lahs ahr-'veh-hahs, lahs ahl-'vehr-hahs]
pepper	pimiento [pee-mee-'ehn-toh]
pesticide-treated	tratado con pesticidas [trah-'tah-doh kohn peh-stee-'see-dahs]
pie	el pastel [ehl pah-'stehl]
pine nuts	los piñones [lohs pee-'nyoh-nehs]
pineapple	piña (*Am* el ananás) ['pee-nyah (ehl ah-nah-'nahs)]
pinto beans	las judías pintas (*Am* los frijoles/porotos pintos) [lahs hoo-'dee-ahs 'peen-tahs (lohs free-'hoh-lehs/poh-roh-tohs 'peen-tohs]
plums	las ciruelas [lahs see-roo-'eh-lahs]
pork	la carne de cerdo [lah 'kahr-neh deh 'sehr-doh]

potatoes	las patatas [lahs pah-'tah-tahs]
praline (chocolate candy)	los bombones [lohs bohm-'boh-nehs]
preserves	las conservas [lahs kohn-'sehr-vahs]
prickly pears	los higos chumbos [lohs 'ee-gohs 'choom-bohs]
puff pastry	el hojaldre [ehl oh-'hahl-dreh]
pumpernickel	el pan negro [ehl pahn 'neh-groh]
pumpkin	calabaza [kah-lah-'bah-sah]
quince, quince jelly	membrillo [mehm-'bree-yoh]
rabbit	conejo [koh-'neh-hoh]
raisins	las (uvas) pasas [lahs ('oo-vahs) 'pah-sahs]
red cabbage	lombarda, col roja [lohm-'bahr-dah, kohl 'roh-hah]
red currants	las grosellas rojas [lahs groh-'seh-yahs 'roh-hahs]
red pepper	el pimentón [ehl pee-mehn-'tohn]
red wine	vino tinto ['vee-noh 'teen-toh]
rice	el arroz [ehl ah-'rrohs]
rolled oats	los copos de avena [lohs 'koh-pohs deh ah-'veh-nah]
rosé wine	vino rosado ['vee-noh roh-'sah-doh]
rosemary	romero [roh-'meh-roh]
round Dutch Edam cheese	queso de bola ['keh-soh deh 'boh-lah]
saffron	el azafrán [ehl ah-sah-'frahn]
salad	ensalada [ehn-sah-'lah-dah]
salami	el salchichón (*Am* el salame) [ehl sahl-chee-'chohn (ehl sah-'lah-meh)]
salmon	el salmón [ehl sahl-'mohn]
salt	la sal [lah sahl]
sandwich	bocadillo (*Am* el sándwich) [boh-kah-'dee-yoh (ehl 'sahnd-weech)]
sardines	las sardinas [lahs sahr-'dee-nahs]
sausage	embutido, salchicha [ehm-boo-'tee-doh, sahl-'chee-chah]
seafood	los mariscos [lohs mah-'ree-skohs]
semolina	sémola ['seh-moh-lah]
serrano ham (Spanish cured ham)	el jamón serrano/crudo [ehl hah-'mohn seh-'rrah-noh/'kroo-doh]
sheep cheese	queso de oveja ['keh-soh deh oh-'veh-hah]
shrimp	las gambas, los camarones [lahs 'gahm-bahs, lohs kah-mah-'roh-nehs]

smoked meat	la carne ahumada [lah 'kahr-neh ah-oo-'mah-dah]
sole	lenguado [lehn-'gwah-doh]
soup	sopa ['soh-pah]
sour cream	nata agria ['nah-tah 'ah-gree·ah]
spaghetti	los espaguetis [lohs eh-spah-'geh-tees]
spinach	las espinacas [lahs eh-spee-'nah-kahs]
squid	los calamares, los chipirones, la sepia [lohs kah-lah-'mah-rehs, lohs chee-pee-'roh-nehs, lah 'seh-pee·ah]
strawberries	las fresas, los fresones (*Am* la frutilla) [lahs 'freh-sahs, lohs freh-'soh-nehs (lah froo-'tee-yah)]
sugar	el azúcar [ehl ah-'soo-kahr]
Swedish-style toast	el pan sueco [ehl pahn 'sweh-koh]
sweets	los dulces, las golosinas [lohs 'dool-sehs, lahs goh-loh-'see-nahs]
swordfish	el pez espada [ehl pehs eh-'spah-dah]

tapas (Spanish appetizers)	las tapas [lahs 'tah-pahs]
tart, pie, cake	la tarta [lah 'tahr-tah]
tea	el té [ehl teh]
teabag	bolsita de té [bohl-'see-tah deh teh]
thyme	tomillo [toh-'mee-yoh]
toast	tostada [toh-'stah-dah]
tomatoes	los tomates [lohs toh-'mah-tehs]
trout	trucha ['troo-chah]
tuna fish	el bonito, el atún [ehl boh-'nee-toh, ehl ah-'toon]
veal	la carne de ternera [lah 'kahr-neh deh tehr-'neh-rah]
vegetables	las verduras, las legumbres [lahs vehr-'doo-rahs, lahs leh-'goom-brehs]
vinegar	el vinagre [ehl vee-'nah-greh]
walnut	la nuez [lah noo-'ehs]
watercress	berro ['beh-rroh]
watermelon	la sandía [lah sahn-'dee-ah]
whipped cream	nata batida/montada ['nah-tah bah-'tee-dah/mohn-'tah-dah]
white beans	las judías blancas (*Am* los frijoles/porotos blancos) [lahs hoo-'dee-ahs 'blahn-kahs (lohs free-'hoh-lehs/poh-'roh-tohs 'blahn-kohs)]

white bread	el pan blanco [ehl pahn 'blahn-koh]
white wine	vino blanco ['vee-noh 'blahn-koh]
whole-wheat bread	el pan integral [ehl pahn een-teh-'grahl]
wine	vino ['vee-noh]
yogurt	el yogur [ehl yoh-'goor]
zucchini	el calabacín [ehl kah-lah-bah-'seen]

Drugstore Items
En la droguería-perfumería

Word List: Drugstore Items

after-shave	la loción para después de afeitar [lah loh-see-'ohn 'pah-rah deh-'spwehs deh ah-feh·ee-'tahr]
Band-Aid	esparadrapo [ehs-pah-rah-'drah-poh]
blusher, rouge	el colorete [ehl koh-loh-'reh-teh]
body lotion	crema para la piel ['kreh-mah 'pah-rah lah pee-'ehl]
bottle (for a baby)	el biberón [ehl bee-beh-'rohn]
brush	cepillo [seh-'pee-yoh]
clothes brush	cepillo de ropa [seh-'pee-yoh deh 'roh-pah]
cologne	el agua de colonia [ehl 'ah-gwah deh koh-'loh-nee·ah]
comb	el peine [ehl 'peh·ee-neh]
condom	preservativo [preh-sehr-vah-'tee-voh]
cotton	el algodón [ehl ahl-goh-'dohn]
cotton swab	bastoncillo de algodón [bah-stohn-'see-yoh deh ahl-goh-'dohn]
cream	crema ['kreh-mah]
cream for dry/normal/ oily skin	crema para piel seca/normal/grasa ['kreh-mah 'pah-rah pee-'ehl 'seh-kah/nohr-'mahl/'grah-sah]
curlers	rulos (*Am* rolos, ruleros) ['roo-lohs ('roh-lohs, roo-'leh-rohs)]
dandruff shampoo	el champú contra la caspa [ehl chahm-'poo 'kohn-trah lah 'kah-spah]
deodorant	el desodorante [ehl dehs-oh-doh-'rahn-teh]
diapers	los pañales [lohs pah-'nyah-lehs]

dishcloth	paño para fregar ['pah-nyoh 'pah-rah freh-'gahr]
dishwashing brush	cepillo para fregar [seh-'pee-yoh 'pah-rah freh-'gahr]
dishwashing liquid	el detergente [ehl deh-tehr-'hehn-teh]
eye shadow	sombra de ojos ['sohm-brah deh 'oh-hohs]
eyebrow pencil	el lápiz de cejas [ehl 'lah-pees deh 'seh-hahs]
eyeliner	el lápiz/líquido de ojos [ehl 'lah-pees/'lee-kee-doh deh 'oh-hohs]
face powder	los polvos de tocador [lohs 'pohl-vohs deh toh-kah-'dohr]
facial cleansing lotion/ make-up remover	crema desmaquilladora ['kreh-mah dehs-mah-kee-yah-'doh-rah]
hair gel	el gel para el pelo [ehl hehl 'pah-rah ehl 'peh-loh]
hair lotion, hair cream	el fijador [ehl fee-hah-'dohr]
hair remover	depilatorio [deh-pee-lah-'toh-ree-oh]
hair spray	el spray para el pelo [ehl eh-'spreh 'pah-rah ehl 'peh-loh]
hairband	elástico/goma para el pelo [eh-'lah-stee-koh/'goh-mah 'pah-rah ehl 'peh-loh]
hairbrush	cepillo del pelo [seh-'pee-yoh dehl 'peh-loh]
hairpins	las horquillas [lahs ohr-'kee-yahs]
hand cream	crema para las manos ['kreh-mah 'pah-rah lahs 'mah-nohs]
lipstick	el lápiz de labios [ehl 'lah-pees deh 'lah-bee·ohs]
mascara	el rímel [ehl 'ree-mehl]
mirror	espejo [eh-'speh-hoh]
moisturizing cream	crema hidratante ['kreh-mah ee-drah-'tahn-teh]
mouthwash	(el) agua dentífrica [(ehl) 'ah-gwah dehn-'tee-free-kah]
nail brush	cepillo de uñas [seh-'pee-yoh deh 'oo-nyahs]
nail cutter/scissors	tijera de uñas [tee-'heh-rah deh 'oo-nyahs]
nail file	lima de uñas ['lee-mah deh 'oo-nyahs]

nail polish	laca de uñas ['lah-kah deh 'oo-nyahs]
nail polish remover	el quitaesmaltes [ehl 'kee-tah-ehs-'mahl-tehs]
pacifier	el chupete [ehl choo-'peh-teh]
perfume	el perfume [ehl pehr-'foo-meh]
powder	los polvos [lohs 'pohl-vohs]
razor blade	cuchilla de afeitar [koo-'chee-yah deh ah-feh·ee-'tahr]
razor, electric razor	maquinilla de afeitar; (electric) afeitadora (eléctrica), máquina de afeitar [mah-kee-'nee-yah deh ah-feh·ee-'tahr; ah-feh·ee-tah-'doh-rah (eh-'lehk-tree-kah), 'mah-kee-nah deh ah-feh·ee-'tahr]
safety pins	los imperdibles [lohs eem-pehr-'dee-blehs]
sanitary napkins	los paños higiénicos [lohs 'pah-nyohs ee-hee-'eh-nee-kohs]
shampoo	el champú [ehl chahm-'poo]
shampoo for oily/ normal/dry hair	el champú para pelo graso/ normal/seco [ehl chahm-'poo 'pah-rah 'peh-loh 'grah-soh/nohr-'mahl/ 'seh-koh]
shaving brush	brocha de afeitar ['broh-chah deh ah-feh·ee-'tahr]
shaving soap/cream	el jabón/la crema de afeitar [ehl hah-'bohn/lah 'kreh-mah deh ah-feh·ee-'tahr]
shower gel	el gel de ducha [ehl hehl deh 'doo-chah]
soap	el jabón [ehl hah-'bohn]
sponge	esponja [eh-'spohn-hah]
stain remover	el quitamanchas [ehl kee-tah-'mahn-chahs]
styling mousse	la espuma fijapelo [lah eh-'spoo-mah fee-hah-'peh-loh]
suntan lotion	crema solar ['kreh-mah soh-'lahr]
suntan oil	el aceite solar [ehl ah-'seh·ee-teh soh-'lahr]
tampon	el tampón [ehl tahm-'pohn]
tissue	los pañuelos de papel [lohs pah-nyoo-'eh-lohs deh pah-'pehl]
toilet paper	el papel higiénico [ehl pah-'pehl ee-hee-'eh-nee-koh]

toiletries bag	**el neceser (de viaje)** [ehl neh-seh-'sehr (deh vee-'ah-heh)]
toothbrush	**cepillo de dientes** [seh-'pee-yoh deh dee-'ehn-tehs]
toothpaste	**pasta de dientes** ['pah-stah deh dee-'ehn-tehs]
towelette	**toallita refrescante** [toh-ah-'yee-tah reh-freh-'skahn-teh]
tweezers	**las pinzas** [lahs 'peen-sahs]
UV protection rate (sunscreen)	**(el) factor de protección solar** [(ehl) fahk-'tohr deh proh-tehk-see-'ohn soh-'lahr]
washcloth	**manopla de baño, el guante de tocador** [mah-'noh-plah deh 'bah-nyoh, ehl 'gwahn-teh deh toh-kah-'dohr]

Tobacco Products

En el estanco (*Am* En la tabaquería)

A pack/carton of... with/without filter, please.	**Un paquete/Un cartón de cigarrillos… con/sin filtro, por favor.** [oon pah-'keh-teh/oon kahr-'tohn deh see-gah-'rree-yohs kohn/seen 'feel-troh, pohr fah-'vohr]
Do you have American/menthol cigarettes?	**¿Tiene usted cigarrillos norteamericanos/mentolados?** [tee-'eh-neh oo-'stehd see-gah-'rree-yohs nohr-teh-ah-meh-ree-'kah-nohs/mehn-toh-'lah-dohs]
Which brand (of light/strong cigarettes) would you recommend?	**¿Qué marca (de cigarrillos suaves/fuertes) me recomienda?** [keh 'mahr-kah (deh see-gah-'rree-yohs 'swah-vehs/'fwehr-tehs) meh reh-koh-mee-'ehn-dah]
Two cigars/small cigars, please.	**Déme dos puros (*Am* cigarros), tabacos/puritos (*Am* cigarros pequeños, tabaquitos), por favor.** ['deh-meh dohs 'poo-rohs (see-'gah-rrohs, tah-'bah-kohs/poo-'ree-tohs (see-'gah-rrohs peh-'keh-nyohs, tah-bah-'kee-tohs), pohr fah-'vohr]

A pouch/tin of cigarette/ pipe tobacco, please.

Un paquete/Una caja de tabaco/ de tabaco de pipa, por favor. [oon pah-'keh-teh/'oo-nah 'kah-hah deh tah-'bah-koh/deh tah-'bah-koh deh 'pee-pah, pohr fah-'vohr]

A matchbox/A lighter, please.

Una caja de cerillas (*Am* fós- foros)/Un mechero (*Am* encendedor, fosforera), por favor. ['oo-nah 'kah-hah deh seh-'ree-yahs ('fohs-foh-rohs)/oon meh-'cheh-roh (ehn-sehn-deh-'dohr, fohs-foh-'reh-rah), pohr fah-'vohr]

Clothing/Leather Goods/Dry Cleaning See Chapter 1: Colors
Vestidos/Peletería/Tintorerí

Can you show me…?

Puede usted enseñarme…? ['pweh-deh oo-'stehd ehn-seh-'nyahr-meh]

Do you have a particular color in mind?

¿Desea usted un color determi- nado? [deh-'seh-ah oo-'stehd oon koh-'lohr deh-tehr-mee-'nah-doh]

I would like something in…

Quisiera algo en… [kee-see-'eh-rah 'ahl-goh ehn]

I would like something to match this.

Quisiera algo que vaya bien con esto. [kee-see-'eh-rah 'ahl-goh keh 'vah-yah bee-ehn kohn 'eh-stoh]

Can I try it on?

¿Puedo probármelo? ['pweh-doh proh-'bahr-meh-loh]

What size are you?

¿Qué talla tiene usted? [keh 'tah-yah tee-'eh-neh oo-'stehd]

It's too…

Me resulta demasiado… [meh reh-'sool-tah deh-mah-see-'ah-doh]

    tight/big.

    estrecho (*Am* angosto)/ancho. [eh-'streh-choh (ahn-'goh-stoh)/'ahn-choh]

    short/long.
    small/big.

    corto/largo. ['kohr-toh/'lahr-goh]
    pequeño/grande. [peh-'keh-nyoh/'grahn-deh]

It fits fine. I'll take it.

Me va muy bien. Me lo llevo.
[meh vah 'moo·ee 'bee'ehn. meh loh 'yeh-voh]

It's not quite what I wanted.

No es exactamente lo que yo quería. [noh ehs ehk-sahk-tah-'mehn-teh loh keh yoh keh-'ree-ah]

I want a pair of…shoes.

Quiero un par de zapatos… [kee-'eh-roh oon pahr deh sah-'pah-tohs]

I wear size…

Calzo el número… ['kahl-soh ehl 'noo-meh-roh]

They're a little tight.

Me aprietan un poco. [meh ah-pree-'eh-tahn oon 'poh-koh]

They're too narrow/wide.

Son demasiado estrechos/anchos. [sohn deh-mah-see-'ah-doh eh-'streh-chohs/'ahn-chohs]

I also need a tube of shoe polish and a pair of shoelaces, please.

Déme también, por favor, un tubo de betún/unos cordones de zapatos. ['deh-meh tahm-bee-'ehn, pohr fah-'vohr, oon 'too-boh deh beh-'toon/'oo-nohs kohr-'doh-nehs deh sah-'pah-tohs]

Can you resole these shoes?

¿Puede poner medias suelas nuevas a estos zapatos? ['pweh-deh poh-'nehr 'meh-dee·ahs 'sweh-lahs noo-'eh-vahs ah 'eh-stohs sah-'pah-tohs]

Can you fix the heels, please?

¿Puede usted arreglar los tacones? ['pweh-deh oo-'stehd ah-rreh-'glahr lohs tah-'koh-nehs]

I'd like to have these dry cleaned/washed.

Quisiera que me limpiaran en seco/que me lavaran esta ropa. [kee-see-'eh-rah keh meh leem-pee-'ah-rahn ehn 'seh-koh/keh meh lah-'vah-rahn 'eh-stah 'roh-pah]

When will it be ready?

¿Cuándo estará lista? ['kwahn-doh eh-stah-'rah 'lee-stah]

Word List: Clothing/Leather Goods/Dry Cleaning

bag	bolso ['bohl-soh]
bathrobe, wrap	el albornoz [ehl ahl-bohr-'nohs]
beach sandals	las playeras, las zapatillas de playa [lahs plah-'yeh-rahs, lahs sah-pah-'tee-yahs deh 'plah-yah]
belt	el cinturón [ehl seen-too-'rohn]
bikini	el bikini [ehl bee-'kee-nee]
blazer	el blazer [ehl bleh·ee-'sehr]
blouse	blusa ['bloo-sah]
boots	las botas [lahs 'boh-tahs]
bow tie	pajarita [pah-hah-'ree-tah]
bra	el sujetador, el sostén (*Am* el brasier, el ajustador) [ehl soo-heh-tah-'dohr, ehl soh-'stehn (ehl brah-'seer, ehl ah-hoo-stah-'dohr]
briefs	(men) el calzoncillo, los calzoncillos [ehl kahl-sohn-'see-yoh, lohs kahl-sohn-'see-yohs]
button	el botón [ehl boh-'tohn]
cap	gorra ['goh-rrah]
cardigan	chaqueta de punto, rebeca (*Am* saco tejido) [chah-'keh-tah deh 'poon-toh, reh-'beh-kah ('sah-koh teh-'hee-doh)]
children's shoes	los zapatos de niño [lohs sah-'pah-tohs deh 'nee-nyoh]
coat	abrigo [ah-'bree-goh]
collar	cuello ['kweh-yoh]
color	el color [ehl koh-'lohr]
cotton	el algodón [ehl ahl-goh-'dohn]
dress	vestido [veh-'stee-doh]
dry cleaning	limpiar en seco [leem-pee-'ahr ehn 'seh-koh]
dungarees, jumpsuit, overalls	mono ['moh-noh]
evening dress	vestido/el traje de noche [veh-'stee-doh/ehl 'trah-heh deh 'noh-cheh]
flip-flops, beach sandals	las chancletas, las chanclas [lahs chahn-'kleh-tahs, lahs 'chahn-klahs]
fur coat	abrigo de piel [ah-'bree-goh deh pee-'ehl]
fur jacket	chaqueta de piel [chah-'keh-tah deh pee-'ehl]

gloves	los guantes [lohs 'gwahn-tehs]
handbag	cartera, bolsa (de mano) [kahr-'teh-rah, 'bohl-sah (deh 'mah-noh)]
handkerchief	pañuelo [pah-nyoo-'eh-loh]
hat	sombrero [sohm-'breh-roh]
housecoat	la bata de casa [lah 'bah-tah deh 'kah-sah]
jacket	chaqueta, (*Am*) saco [chah-'keh-tah, 'sah-koh]
jeans	los tejanos, los vaqueros [lohs teh-'hah-nohs, lohs vah-'keh-rohs]
jogging/track suit	el chándal, el traje de entre-namiento [ehl 'chahn-dahl, ehl 'trah-heh deh ehn-treh-nah-mee-'ehn-toh]
knapsack	mochila [moh-'chee-lah]
knee socks	los calcetines altos, las medias altas [lohs kahl-seh-'tee-nehs 'ahl-tohs, lahs 'meh-dee·ahs 'ahl-tahs]
leather coat	abrigo de cuero [ah-'bree-goh deh 'kweh-roh]
leather jacket	chaqueta de cuero [chah-'keh-tah deh 'kweh-roh]
leather pants	el pantalón de cuero [ehl pahn-tah-'lohn deh 'kweh-roh]
linen	lino ['lee-noh]
lining	forro ['foh-rroh]
machine washable	lavable en lavadora [lah-'vah-bleh ehn lah-vah-'doh-rah]
male swimsuit, swimming trunks	el pantalón de baño [ehl pahn-tah-'lohn deh 'bah-nyoh]
miniskirt	minifalda [mee-nee-'fahl-dah]
nightgown	el camisón [ehl kah-mee-'sohn]
pajama	el pijama [ehl pee-'hah-mah]
panties	braga, (*Am*) los panties, los pan-taloncitos ['brah-gah, lohs 'pahn-tees, lohs pahn-tah-lohn-'see-tohs]
pants	el pantalón [ehl pahn-tah-'lohn]
pantyhose	los leotardos, el panty [lohs leh-oh-'tahr-dohs, ehl 'pahn-tee]
parka	el anorak [ehl ah-noh-'rahk]
plaid	a cuadros [ah 'kwah-drohs]
pullover, sweater	el jersey (*Am* el pulóver, el suéter) [ehl hehr-'seh (ehl pool-'oh-vehr, ehl 'sweh-tehr)

raincoat	el impermeable [ehl eem-pehr-meh-'ah-bleh]
rubber boots	las botas de goma [lahs 'boh-tahs deh 'goh-mah]
sandals	las sandalias [sahn-'dah-lee-ahs]
scarf	pañuelo de cuello/(winter) bufanda [pah-nyoo-'eh-loh deh 'kweh-yoh/boo-'fahn-dah]
shawl	el chal [ehl chahl]
shirt	camisa [kah-'mee-sah]
shoe brush	cepillo del calzado [seh-'pee-yoh dehl kahl-'sah-doh]
shoe polish	el betún [ehl beh-'toon]
shoe size	número ['noo-meh-roh]
shoes	los zapatos [lohs sah-'pah-tohs]
shorts	el pantalón corto [ehl pahn-tah-'lohn 'kohr-toh]
shoulder bag	(bolsa en) bandolera [('bohl-sah ehn) bahn-doh-'leh-rah]
silk	seda ['seh-dah]
silk panties	pantys de seda ['pahn-tees deh 'seh-dah]
silk stockings	medias de seda ['meh-dee·ahs deh 'seh-dah]
ski boots	las botas de esquí [lahs 'boh-tahs deh eh-'skee]
ski pants	el pantalón de esquí [ehl pahn-tah-'lohn deh eh-'skee]
skirt	falda ['fahl-dah]
sleeve	manga ['mahn-gah]
slip	el refajo, la combinación [ehl reh-'fah-hoh, lah kohm-bee-nah-see-'ohn]
slippers	las zapatillas, las pantuflas [lahs sah-pah-'tee-yahs, lahs pahn-'too-flahs]
sneakers	las zapatillas de deporte, (*Am*) los (zapatos) tenis [lahs sah-pah-'tee-yahs deh deh-'pohr-teh (lohs sah-'pah-tohs) 'teh-nees]
socks	los calcetines [lohs kahl-seh-'tee-nehs]
sole	suela ['sweh-lah]
stockings	las medias [lahs 'meh-dee·ahs]

striped	**a rayas, rayado** [ah 'rah-yahs, rah-'yah-doh]
suede coat	**abrigo de ante** [ah-'bree-goh deh 'ahn-teh]
suede jacket	**chaqueta de ante** [chah-'keh-tah deh 'ahn-teh]
suit	**el traje** [ehl 'trah-heh]
suit (women's)	**el traje de chaqueta** [ehl 'trah-heh deh chah-'keh-tah]
suitcase	**maleta** [lah mah-'leh-tah]
summer dress	**vestido de verano** [veh-'stee-doh deh veh-'rah-noh]
swimming cap	**gorro de baño** ['goh-rroh deh 'bah-nyoh]
swimsuit	**el traje de baño, el bañador** [ehl 'trah-heh deh 'bah-nyoh, ehl bah-nyah-'dohr]
synthetic fiber	**fibra sintética** ['fee-brah seen-'teh-tee-kah]
T-shirt	**camiseta** [kah-mee-'seh-tah]
terry cloth	**tejido de rizo** [(teh-'hee-doh deh) 'ree-soh]
tie	**corbata** [kohr-'bah-tah]
to iron	**planchar** [plahn-'chahr]
travel bag	**bolsa de viaje** ['bohl-sah deh vee-'ah-heh]
umbrella	**el paraguas** [ehl pah-'rah-gwahs]
undershirt	**camiseta** [kah-mee-'seh-tah]
underwear	**ropa interior** ['roh-pah een-teh-ree-'ohr]
vest	**chaleco** [chah-'leh-koh]
wash and wear, no ironing needed	**no necesita plancha** [noh neh-seh-'see-tah 'plahn-chah]
wool	**lana** ['lah-nah]
zipper	**cremallera** (*Am* el cierre relámpago) [kreh-mah-'yeh-rah (ehl see-'eh-rreh reh-'lahm-pah-goh]

Books and Stationery
En la librería/En la papelería

I'd like…	Quisiera… [kee-see-'eh-rah]
an American newspaper.	un periódico americano. [oon peh-ree-'oh-dee-koh ah-meh-ree-'kah-noh]
a magazine.	una revista. ['oo-nah reh-'vee-stah]
a guide book.	una guía. ['oo-nah 'gee-ah]

Word List: Books and Stationery

adhesive tape	cinta celo (*Am* cinta adhesiva) ['seen-tah 'seh-loh ('seen-tah ahd-eh-'see-vah)]
ballpoint pen	bolígrafo (*Am* lapicero de bolilla) [boh-'lee-grah-foh (lah-pee-'seh-roh deh boh-'lee-yah)]
colored pencil	el lápiz de color [ehl 'lah-pees deh koh-'lohr]
coloring book	libro para colorear ['lee-broh 'pah-rah koh-loh-reh-'ahr]
crime novel, mystery novel	novela policiaca [noh-'veh-lah poh-lee-see-'ah-kah]
envelope	el sobre [ehl 'soh-breh]
eraser	goma de borrar ['goh-mah deh boh-'rrahr]
gift wrap	el papel de regalo [ehl pah-'pehl deh reh-'gah-loh]
glue	la goma, el pegamín [lah 'goh-mah, ehl peh-gah-'meen]
magazine	revista [reh-'vee-stah]
map	el mapa [ehl 'mah-pah]
marker, felt-tip pen	el rotulador [ehl roh-too-lah-'dohr]
newspaper	periódico [peh-ree-'oh-dee-koh]
notebook	agenda, libreta de apuntes [ah-'hehn-dah, lee-'breh-tah deh ah-'poon-tehs]
notepad	el bloc/la libreta de apuntes [ehl blohk/lah lee-'breh-tah deh ah-'poon-tehs]

novel	novela [noh-'veh-lah]
paper	el papel [ehl pah-'pehl]
paper clip	la presilla, el clip, el sujetapapeles [lah preh-'see-yah, ehl kleep, ehl soo-heh-tah-pah-'peh-lehs]
pen, fountain pen	pluma (estilográfica), (*Am*) plumafuente ['ploo-mah (eh-stee-loh-'grah-fee-kah), ploo-mah-'fwehn-teh]
pencil	el lápiz lapicero [ehl 'lah-pees lah-pee-'seh-roh]
pencil sharpener	el sacapuntas [ehl sah-kah-'poon-tahs]
playing cards	las cartas, baraja [lahs 'kahr-tahs, bah-'rah-hah]
pocket book	libro de bolsillo ['lee-broh deh bohl-'see-yoh]
postcard	la postal [lah poh-'stahl]
road map	el mapa de carreteras [ehl 'mah-pah deh kah-rreh-'teh-rahs]
sketchbook	el bloc/el cuaderno de dibujo [ehl blohk/ehl kwah-'dehr-noh deh dee-'boo-hoh]
stamp	sello (*Am* estampilla) ['seh-yoh (eh-stahm-'pee-yah)]
stationery	el papel de escribir [ehl pah-'pehl deh eh-skree-'beer]
thumb tacks	las chinchetas [lahs cheen-'cheh-tahs]
town map	plano de la ciudad ['plah-noh deh lah see-oo-'dahd]

Household Items
Artículos domésticos

Word List: Household Items

aluminum foil	el papel de estaño [ehl pah-'pehl deh eh-'stah-nyoh]
bottle opener	el abrebotellas [ehl ah-breh-boh-teh-yahs]
broom	escoba [eh-'skoh-bah]

brush	escobilla [eh-skoh-'bee-yah]
bucket	cubo (*Am* el balde) ['koo-boh (ehl 'bahl-deh)]
camp chair	silla de cámping ['see-yah deh 'kahm-peen]
camp table	mesa de cámping ['meh-sah deh 'kahm-peen]
can opener	el abrelatas [ehl ah-breh-'lah-tahs]
candles	velas ['veh-lahs]
charcoal	el carbón de parrilla [ehl kahr-'bohn deh pah-'rree-yah]
clothesline	cuerda de la ropa ['kwehr-dah deh lah 'roh-pah]
clothespins	las pinzas de la ropa [lahs 'peen-sahs deh lah 'roh-pah]
cooler	el refrigerador portátil [ehl reh-free-heh-rah-'dohr pohr-'tah-teel]
corkscrew	el sacacorchos [ehl sah-kah-'kohr-chohs]
cutlery	los cubiertos [lohs koo-bee-'ehr-tohs]
dustpan	el recogedor [ehl reh-koh-heh-'dohr]
garbage bag	bolsa de la basura ['bohl-sah deh lah bah-'soo-rah]
glass	vaso ['vah-soh]
grill	parrilla, barbacoa [pah-'rree-yah, bahr-bah-'koh-ah]
ice bag	bolsita de hielo [bohl-'see-tah deh 'yeh-loh]
matchbox	caja de fósforos ['kah-hah deh 'fohs-foh-rohs]
methyl alcohol	el alcohol de quemar [ehl ahl-koh-'ohl deh keh-'mahr]
paper cups	los vasos de cartón [lohs 'vah-sohs deh kahr-'tohn]
paper napkins	las servilletas de papel [lahs sehr-vee-'yeh-tahs deh pah-'pehl]
paper plates	los platos de cartón [lohs 'plah-tohs deh kahr-'tohn]
plastic bag	bolsa de plástico ['bohl-sah deh 'plah-stee-koh]
pocketknife	navaja [nah-'vah-hah]
pot	cazuela, puchero [kah-soo-'eh-lah, poo-'cheh-roh]

thermos	termo ['tehr-moh]
umbrella	sombrilla [sohm-'bree-yah]
wax paper	el papel de conservación fresca [ehl pah-'pehl deh kohn-sehr-vah-see-'ohn 'freh-skah]

Electrical Goods and Photographic Supplies
Artículos eléctricos y Fotográficos

I'd like…

Quisiera…/Desearía…/Me gustaría… [kee-see-'eh-rah/deh-seh-ah-'ree-ah/me goo-stah-'ree-ah]

a roll of film for this camera.

una película para esta cámara. ['oo-nah peh-'lee-koo-'lah 'pah-rah 'eh-stah 'kah-mah-rah]

a roll of color film for prints/slides.

una película en color para reproducciones en papel/para diapositivas. ['oo-nah peh-'lee-koo-lah ehn koh-'lohr 'pah-rah reh-proh-dook-see-'oh-nehs ehn pah-'pehl/'pah-rah dee-ah-poh-see-'tee-vahs]

a roll of film with 36/24/12 exposures.

un carrete de 36/24/12 fotografías. [oon kah-'rreh-teh deh 'treh·een-tah ee 'seh·ees/veh-een-teh-ee 'kwah-troh/'doh-seh foh-toh-grah-'fee-ahs]

Could you put the film in the camera for me, please?

¿Puede usted colocarme el carrete? ['pweh-deh oo-'stehd koh-loh-'kahr-meh ehl kah-'rreh-teh]

Would you develop this film, please?

¿Pueden ustedes revelarme esta película? ['pweh-dehn oo-'steh-dehs reh-veh-'lahr-meh 'eh-stah peh-'lee-koo-lah]

I'd like one print of each of these negatives, please.

Hágame una copia de cada uno de estos negativos, por favor. ['ah-gah-meh 'oo-nah 'koh-pee·ah deh 'kah-dah 'oo-noh deh 'eh-stohs neh-gah-'tee-vohs, pohr fah-'vohr]

What size?

¿Qué tamaño desea? [keh tah-'mah-nyoh deh-'seh-ah]

Seven by ten./Nine by nine.	Siete por diez./Nueve por nueve. [see-'eh-teh pohr 'dee·ehs/noo-'eh-veh pohr noo-'eh-veh]
Glossy or matte?	¿Brillante o mate? [bree-'yahn-teh oh 'mah-teh]
When can I pick up the photos?	¿Cuándo puedo retirar las fotos? ['kwahn-doh 'pweh-doh reh-tee-'rahr lahs 'foh-tohs]
The viewfinder/shutter doesn't work.	El visor/El disparador no funciona. [ehl vee-'sohr/ehl dee-spah-rah-'dohr noh foonk-see-'oh-nah]
This is broken. Can you fix it?	Está estropeado. ¿Podrían arreglármelo? [eh-'stah eh-stroh-peh-'ah-doh. poh-'dree-ahn ah-rreh-'glahr-meh-loh]

Word List: Electrical Goods and Photographic Supplies

adapter	el adaptador [ehl ah-dahp-tah-'dohr]
aperture	el diafragma [ehl dee-ah-'frahg-mah]
audiocassette	la/el casete [lah/ehl kah-'seh-teh]
battery	batería [bah-teh-'ree-ah]
black and white film	película en blanco y negro [peh-'lee-koo-lah ehn 'blahn-koh ee 'neh-groh]
camera	cámara fotográfica ['kah-mah-rah foh-toh-'grah-fee-kah]
cassette film	el carrete (en casete) [ehl kah-'rreh-teh (ehn kah-'seh-teh)]
cassette recorder	grabadora [grah-bah-'doh-rah]
CD, compact disc	el DC, disco compacto [ehl deh-seh, 'dee-skoh kohm-'pahk-toh]
extension cord	el cordón/el cable de empalme [ehl kohr-'dohn/ehl 'kah-bleh deh ehm-'pahl-meh]
film speed	la sensibilidad [lah sehn-see-bee-lee-'dahd]
film winder	el arrastre [ehl ah-'rrah-streh]
flash	el flash [ehl flahsh]
flashbulb	cubo de flash ['koo-boh deh flahsh]
flashlight	linterna [leen-'tehr-nah]

hair dryer	el secador de pelo [ehl seh-kah-'dohr deh 'peh-loh]
headphones	los auriculares [lohs ah·oo-ree-koo-'lah-rehs]
lens	la lente, el objetivo [lah 'lehn-teh, ehl ohb-heh-'tee-voh]
light bulb	bombilla [bohm-'bee-yah]
light meter	fotómetro [foh-'toh-meh-troh]
passport photo	la foto (para) pasaporte [lah 'foh-toh ('pah-rah) pah-sah-'pohr-teh]
plug	clavija de enchufe [klah-'vee-hah deh ehn-'choo-feh]
pocket calculator	calculadora de bolsillo [kahl-koo-lah-'doh-rah deh bohl-'see-yoh]
record	disco ['dee-skoh]
self-timer	el disparador automático [ehl dee-spah-rah-'dohr ow-toh-'mah-tee-koh]
shutter	el obturador, el cierre [ehl ohb-too-rah-'dohr, ehl see-'eh-rreh]
shutter release	el disparador [ehl dee-spah-rah-'dohr]
speaker	el altavoz (*Am* el altoparlante) [ehl ahl-tah-'vohs (ehl ahl-toh-pahr-'lahn-teh)]
super 8 film	el film/la película súper-8 [ehl feelm/lah peh-'lee-koo-lah 'soo-pehr 'oh-choh]
telephoto	teleobjetivo [teh-leh-ohb-heh-'tee-voh]
tripod	el trípode [ehl 'tree-poh-deh]
video camera	cámara de vídeo, filmadora ['kah-mah-rah deh 'vee-deh-oh, feel-mah-'doh-rah]
videocassette, video recorder	la/el videocasete [lah/ehl vee-deh-oh-kah-'seh-teh]
videotape	película vídeo [peh-'lee-koo-lah 'vee-deh-oh]
viewfinder	el visor [ehl vee-'sohr]
walkman	el walkman [ehl 'oo·ahlk-mahn]

At the Optician

En el establecimiento de óptica

Could you fix these glasses/ the frame for me, please?	¿Puede usted arreglarme estas gafas (*Am* estos anteojos/lentes/ espejuelos)/la montura, por favor? ['pweh-deh oo-'stehd ah-rreh-'glahr-meh 'eh-stahs 'gah-fahs ('eh-stohs ahn-teh-'oh-hohs/'lehn-tehs/eh-speh-hoo-'eh-lohs)/lah mohn-'too-rah, pohr fah-'vohr]
One of the lenses is broken.	Se me ha roto un cristal de las gafas (*Am* de los lentes). [seh meh ah 'roh-toh oon kree-'stahl deh lahs 'gah-fahs (deh lohs 'lehn-tehs)]
I'm near-sighted/far-sighted.	Soy miope/présbita. ['soh-ee mee-'oh-peh/'prehs-bee-tah]
What is your eye prescription?	¿Cuál es su potencia visual? [kwahl ehs soo poh-'tehn-see·ah vee-soo-'ahl]
Plus/minus…in the right eye,… in the left eye.	A la derecha más/menos…, a la izquierda… [ah lah deh-'reh-chah mahs/'meh-nohs, ah lah ees-kee-'ehr-dah]
When can I pick up the glasses?	¿Cuándo puedo recoger las gafas? ['kwahn-doh 'pweh-doh reh-koh-'hehr lahs 'gah-fahs]

I need…
    contact lens preserver/ preserving solution.
	Necesito… [neh-seh-'see-toh]
	    líquido para conservar lentillas. ['lee-kee-doh 'pah-rah kohn-sehr-'vahr lehn-'tee-yahs]

cleaning solution for hard/soft contact lenses.	detergente para lentes de contacto duras/blandas. [deh-tehr-'hehn-teh 'pah-rah 'lehn-tehs deh kohn-'tahk-toh 'doo-rahs/'blahn-dahs]

I'm looking for…
    sunglasses.
	Quisiera… [kee-see-'eh-rah]
	    unas gafas de sol. ['oo-nahs 'gah-fahs deh sohl]

binoculars.	unos prismáticos. ['oo-nohs prees-'mah-tee-kohs]

At the Watchmaker/Jeweler
En la relojería/Joyería

My watch doesn't work. Could you take a look at it?	Mi reloj no funciona. ¿Puede usted mirar lo que tiene? [mee reh-'loh noh foonk-see-'oh-nah. 'pweh-deh oo-'stehd mee-'rahr loh keh tee-'eh-neh]
I'd like a nice souvenir/present.	Quisiera un recuerdo/un regalo bonito. [kee-see-'eh-rah oon reh-'kwehr-doh/oon reh-'gah-loh boh-'nee-toh]
How much do you want to spend?	¿Cuánto quiere usted gastar aproximadamente? ['kwahn-toh kee-'eh-reh oo-'stehd gah-'stahr ah-prohk-see-mah-dah-'mehn-teh]
I'd like something that's not too expensive.	Quisiera algo que no sea demasiado caro. [kee-see-'eh-rah 'ahl-goh keh noh 'seh-ah deh-mah-see-'ah-doh 'kah-roh]

Word List: Watchmaker/Jeweler

bracelet	pulsera, el brazalete [pool-'seh-rah, ehl brah-sah-'leh-teh]
brooch	el broche [ehl 'broh-cheh]
chain	el collar, cadena [ehl koh-'yahr, kah-'deh-nah]
coral	el coral [ehl koh-'rahl]
costume jewelry	bisutería [bee-soo-teh-'ree-ah]
crystal	el cristal (de roca) [ehl kree-'stahl (deh 'roh-kah)]
earrings	los pendientes (*Am* los aretes) [lohs pehn-dee-'ehn-tehs (lohs ah-'reh-tehs)]
gold	oro ['oh-roh]
jewelry	las joyas [lahs 'hoh-yahs]
pearl	perla ['pehr-lah]
pendant	el colgante [ehl kohl-'gahn-teh]
ring	anillo [ah-'nee-yoh]
silver	plata ['plah-tah]

turquoise	turquesa [toor-'keh-sah]
wristwatch	el reloj de pulsera [ehl reh-'loh deh pool-'seh-rah]

At the Hairdresser/Barber
En la peluquería

Can I make an appointment for tomorrow?	¿Puede usted darme hora (*Am* un turno) para mañana? ['pweh-deh oo-'stehd 'dahr-meh 'oh-rah (oon 'toor-noh) 'pah-rah mah-'nyah-nah]
How do you like your hair done?	¿Cómo quiere (que le arregle) el pelo? ['koh-moh kee-'eh-reh (keh leh ah-'rrehg-leh) ehl 'peh-loh]
Shampoo and blow dry/set, please.	Lavar y secar/marcar, por favor. [lah-'vahr ee seh-'kahr/mahr-'kahr, pohr fah-'vohr]
Wash and cut/Cut only, please.	Cortar y lavar/Cortar sin lavar, por favor. [kohr-'tahr ee lah-'vahr/kohr-'tahr seen lah-'vahr, pohr fah-'vohr]
I'd like…please.	Quisiera…/Desearía…, por favor. [kee-see-'eh-rah/deh-seh-ah-'ree-ah, pohr fah-'vohr]
a perm	una permanente ['oo-nah pehr-mah-'nehn-teh]
to color/highlight my hair	teñirme el pelo/unos reflejos [teh-'nyeer-meh ehl 'peh-loh/'oo-nohs reh-'fleh-hohs]
Leave it long, please.	Déjelo largo, por favor. ['deh-heh-loh 'lahr-goh, pohr fah-'vohr]
Just trim the ends.	Sólo las puntas. ['soh-lohs lahs 'poon-tahs]
Not too short/Very short/A little shorter, please.	No demasiado corto/Muy corto/Un poco más corto, por favor. [noh deh-mah-see-'ah-doh 'kohr-toh/'moo·ee 'kohr-toh/oon 'poh-koh mahs 'kohr-toh, pohr fah-'vohr]

A bit off the back/front/top/sides, please.

Corte un poco por detrás/por delante/arriba/a los lados, por favor. ['kohr-teh oon 'poh-koh pohr deh-'trahs/pohr deh-'lahn-teh/ah-'rree-bah/ah lohs 'lah-dohs, pohr fah-'vohr]

Cut above/below the ears.

Que no me tape/Que me cubra las orejas. [keh noh meh 'tah-peh/keh me 'koo-brah lahs oh-'reh-hahs]

The part on the left/right, please.

La raya a la izquierda/a la derecha, por favor. [lah 'rah-yah ah lah ees-kee-'ehr-dah/ah lah deh-'reh-chah, pohr fah-'vohr]

A razor cut, please.

Un corte de pelo a navaja, por favor. [oon 'kohr-teh deh 'peh-loh ah nah-'vah-hah, pohr fah-'vohr]

Could you fluff it, please?

Cardar (*Am* Batir) el pelo, por favor. [kahr-'dahr (bah-'teer) ehl 'peh-loh, pohr fah-'vohr]

No/Not too much hairspray, please.

No me ponga laca/Sólo un poco de laca, por favor. [noh meh 'pohn-gah 'lah-kah/'soh-loh oon 'poh-koh deh 'lah-kah, pohr fah-'vohr]

I'd like a shave, please.

Afeitar, por favor. [ah-feh·ee-'tahr, pohr fah-'vohr]

Would you trim my beard, please?

Córteme un poco/Arrégleme la barba, por favor. ['kohr-teh-meh oon 'poh-koh/ah-'rreh-gleh-meh lah 'bahr-bah, pohr fah-'vohr]

Could you give me a manicure?

¿Puede hacerme la manicura? ['pweh-deh ah-'sehr-meh lah mah-nee-'koo-rah]

Thank you. That's fine.

Muchas gracias. Está muy bien así. ['moo-chahs 'grah-see·ahs. eh-'stah 'moo·ee 'bee-ehn ah-'see]

Word List: Hairdresser/Barber

bangs	flequillo [fleh-'kee-yoh]
beard	barba ['bahr-bah]
blond	rubio ['roo-bee-oh]
to color, dye	teñir [teh-'nyeer]
to comb	peinar [peh·ee-'nahr]
curler	rulo (*Am* rulero) ['roo-loh (roo-'leh-roh)]
curls	los rizos (*Am* los rulos) [lohs 'ree-sohs (lohs 'roo-lohs)]
to cut	cortar [kohr-'tahr]
dandruff	caspa ['kah-spah]
dry	secar [seh-'kahr]
dry hair	pelo seco ['peh-loh 'seh-koh]
eyebrows	las cejas [lahs 'seh-hahs]
hair	pelo ['peh-loh]
hair fall	caída de pelo [kah-'ee-dah deh 'peh-loh]
hair style	peinado [peh·ee-'nah-doh]
hair tonic	tónico para el pelo ['toh-nee-koh 'pah-rah ehl 'peh-loh]
haircut	el corte de pelo [ehl 'kohr-teh deh 'peh-loh]
hairpiece	peluca, el bisoñé [peh-'loo-kah, ehl bee-soh-'nyeh]
hairspray	el spray para el pelo [ehl 'spreh 'pah-rah ehl 'peh-loh]
to have a shave	afeitarse [ah-feh·ee-'tahr-seh]
to highlight	dar reflejos [dahr reh-'fleh-hohs]
mustache	el bigote [ehl bee-'goh-teh]
oily hair	pelo graso ['peh-loh 'grah-soh]
part	raya ['rah-yah]
perm	la permanente [lah pehr-mah-'nehn-teh]
to set	marcar [mahr-'kahr]
shampoo	el champú [ehl chahm-'poo]
sideburns	las patillas [lahs pah-'tee-yahs]
wig	peluca [peh-'loo-kah]

Money Matters
Asuntos de dinero

Where's the nearest bank/
money changing office?

Por favor, ¿dónde hay por aquí
un banco/una oficina de cambio?
[pohr fah-'vohr, 'dohn-deh 'ah·ee
pohr ah-'kee oon 'bahn-koh/'oo-nah
oh-fee-'see-nah deh 'kahm-bee·oh]

What time does the bank
open/close?

¿A qué hora se abre/cierra el
banco? [ah keh 'oh-rah seh 'ah-
breh/see-'eh-rah ehl 'bahn-koh]

I'd like to change…dollars
(pounds/shillings/marks/
francs) into pesetas (pesos).

Quisiera cambiar… dólares
(libras esterlinas/chelines/marcos/
francos) en pesetas (pesos). [kee-
see-'eh-rah kahm-bee-'ahr...'doh-lah-
rehs ('lee-brahs, eh-stehr-'lee-nahs,
cheh- 'lee-nehs, 'mahr-kohs, 'frahn-
kohs) ehn peh-'seh-tahs ('peh-sohs)]

What's the current exchange
rate?

¿Cómo está hoy el cambio?
['koh-moh eh-'stah 'oh·ee ehl
'kahm-bee·oh]

How many pesetas
(pesos) do I get for
$100/100 pounds?

¿Cuántas pesetas (Cuántos
pesos) dan por cien dólares/
libras esterlinas? ['kwahn-tahs
peh-'seh-tahs ('kwahn-tohs 'peh-
sohs) dahn pohr 'see·ehn 'doh-lah-
rehs/'lee-brahs eh-stehr-'lee-nahs]

I'd like to cash this
traveler's check/Eurocheck/
money order.

Quisiera cobrar este cheque de
viaje/eurocheque/este giro postal.
[kee-see-'eh-rah koh-'brahr 'eh-steh
'cheh-keh deh vee-'ah-heh/eh·oo-
roh-'cheh-keh/'eh-steh 'hee-roh
poh-'stah!]

What's the biggest check
I can cash?

¿Cuál es el importe máximo
posible? [kwahl ehs ehl eem-'pohr-
teh 'mahk-see-moh poh-'see-bleh]

Can I see your passport/ID?

¿Puedo ver su pasaporte/carnet
de identidad? ['pweh-doh vehr soo
pah-sah-'pohr-teh/kahr-'neht deh
ee-dehn-tee-'dahd]

Can I see your bank/
check card, please?

Su tarjeta bancaria/de cheques,
por favor. [soo tahr-'heh-tah bahn-
'kah-ree-ah/deh 'cheh-kehs, pohr
fah-'vohr]

Sign here, please.

¿Quiere firmar aquí, por favor?
[kee-'eh-reh feer-'mahr ah-'kee,
pohr fah-'vohr]

I want to withdraw…
dollars/pesetas from my
checking/savings account.

Quisiera retirar…dólares/pesetas
de mi cuenta corriente/de ahorro.
[kee-see-'eh-rah reh-tee-'rahr 'doh-
lah-rehs/peh-'seh-tahs deh mee
'kwehn-tah koh-rree-'ehn-teh/deh
ah-'oh-rroh]

Has any money been
transferred to my account/
to me?

¿Ha llegado dinero a mi cuenta/
para mí? [ah yeh-'gah-doh dee-
'neh-roh ah mee 'kwen-tah/'pah-rah
mee]

Go to the cashier, please.

Vaya/Pase a la caja. ['vah-yah,
'pah-seh ah lah 'kah-hah]

How do you want the
money?

¿Cómo quiere el dinero? ['koh-
moh kee-'eh-reh ehl dee-'neh-roh]

Bills only, please.

Solamente en billetes, por favor.
[soh-lah-'mehn-teh ehn bee-'yeh-
tehs, pohr fah-'vohr]

Some change too, please.

Un poco de dinero suelto también, por favor. [oon 'poh-koh deh
dee-'neh-roh 'swehl-toh tahm-bee-
'ehn, pohr fah-'vohr]

Give me three 1000 peseta
(peso) bills and the rest in
change, please.

Déme tres billetes de mil pesetas
(pesos) y el resto en moneda,
por favor. ['deh-meh trehs bee-
'yeh-tehs deh meel peh-'seh-tahs
('peh-sohs) ee ehl 'reh-stoh ehn
moh-'neh-dah, pohr fah-'vohr]

I lost my traveler's checks.
What do I have to do now?

He perdido mis cheques de
viaje. ¿Qué es lo que tengo que
hacer? [eh pehr-'dee-doh mees
'cheh-kehs deh vee-'ah-heh. keh
ehs loh keh 'tehn-goh keh ah-'sehr]

Word List: Money Matters

account	cuenta ['kwehn-tah]
amount	el importe, suma [ehl eem-'pohr-teh, 'soo-mah]
bank	banco ['bahn-koh]
bank account	cuenta bancaria ['kwehn-tah bahn-'kah-ree-ah]
bank charges	los derechos de banco [lohs deh-'reh-chohs deh 'bahn-koh]
bank code number	la clave bancaria [lah 'klah-veh bahn-'kah-ree-ah]
bill	el billete (de banco) [ehl bee-'yeh-teh (deh 'bahn-koh)]
Canadian/Australian/ New Zealand dollar	dólar canadiense/australiano/de Nueva Zelandia ['doh-lahr kah-nah-dee-'ehn-seh, owh-strah-lee-'ah-noh/deh noo-'eh-vah seh-'lahn-dee-ah]
cash	dinero efectivo/contante [dee-'neh-roh eh-fehk-'tee-voh/kohn-'tahn-teh]
to cash a check	pagar/saldar un cheque [pah-'gahr/sahl-'dahr oon 'cheh-keh]
cash (payment), *(to pay)* cash	al contado, en efectivo [ahl kohn-'tah-doh, ehn eh-fehk-'tee-voh]
cash machine	cajero automático [kah-'heh-roh ah·oo-toh-'mah-tee-koh]
to change	cambiar [kahm-bee-'ahr]
change office	oficina de cambio [oh-fee-'see-nah deh 'kahm-bee·oh]
check	el cheque [ehl 'cheh-keh]
check card	tarjeta de cheques [tahr-'heh-tah deh 'cheh-kehs]
checkbook	talonario de cheques [tah-loh-'nah-ree·oh deh 'cheh-kehs]
coins, change	las monedas, dinero suelto [(lahs) moh-'neh-dahs, dee-'neh-roh 'swehl-toh]
to credit	ingresar [een-greh-'sahr]
credit card	tarjeta de crédito [tahr-'heh-tah deh 'kreh-dee-toh]
currency	moneda [moh-'neh-dah]

Eurocheck	el eurocheque [ehl eh·oo-roh-'cheh-keh]
exchange	cambio ['kahm-bee-oh]
exchange rate	tipo de cambio [('tee-poh deh) 'kahm-bee·oh]
fee (per check)	la comisión (por cheque) [lah koh-mee-see-'ohn (pohr 'cheh-keh)]
foreign currency	las divisas [lahs dee-'vee-sahs]
form	impreso, formulario [eem-'preh-soh, fohr-moo-'lah-ree·oh]
French franc	franco ['frahn-koh]
money	dinero [dee-'neh-roh]
money order	giro ['hee-roh]
to pay	pagar [pah-'gahr]
payment	pago ['pah-goh]
payment order	la orden de pago [lah 'ohr-dehn deh 'pah-goh]
PIN (personal identification number)	número secreto, la clave ['noo-meh-roh seh-'kreh-toh, lah 'klah-veh]
post office savings bank	caja postal de ahorros ['kah-hah poh-'stahl deh ah-'oh-rrohs]
post office savings passbook	libreta de la caja (postal) de ahorros [lee-'breh-tah deh lah 'kah-hah (poh-'stahl) deh ah-'oh-rrohs]
postal money order	giro postal [hee-'roh poh-'stahl]
postal money order form	impreso para giro postal [eem-'preh-soh 'pah-rah 'hee-roh poh-'stahl]
receipt	recibo [reh-'see-boh]
savings account	cuenta de ahorros ['kwehn-tah deh ah-'oh-rrohs]
savings bank	caja de ahorros ['kah-hah deh ah-'oh-rrohs]
savings book	libreta de ahorro [lee-'breh-tah deh ah·'oh-rroh]
signature	firma ['feer-mah]
Swiss franc	franco suizo ['frahn-koh 'swee-soh]
traveler's check	el cheque de viaje [ehl 'cheh-keh deh vee-'ah-heh]
U.S. dollar	dólar ['doh-lahr]
window	la ventanilla (*Am* boletería) [lah vehn-tah-'nee-yah (boh-leh-teh-'ree-ah)]

wired money order	giro telegráfico ['hee-roh teh-leh-'grah-fee-koh]
to withdraw	retirar [reh-tee-'rahr]
to write a check	extender/librar un cheque [ehks-tehn-'dehr/lee-'brahr oon 'cheh-keh]

At the Post Office
En correos

Where is the nearest post office/mailbox?	¿Dónde está la oficina de correos más cercana/el buzón más cercano? ['dohn-deh eh-'stah lah oh-fee-'see-nah deh koh-'rreh-ohs mahs sehr-'kah-nah/ehl boo-'sohn mahs sehr-'kah-noh]
How much does it cost to send a postcard/letter…	¿Cuánto cuesta una carta/una postal… ['kwahn-toh 'kweh-stah 'oo-nah 'kahr-tah/'oo-nah poh-'stahl]
to the United States?	para Estados Unidos? ['pah-rah eh-'stah-dohs oo-'nee-dohs]
to England/Britain?	para Inglaterra/Gran Bretaña? ['pah-rah een-glah-'teh-rrah/grahn breh-'tah-nyah]

to Switzerland?	para Suiza? ['pah-rah 'swee-sah]
to Canada?	para el Canadá? ['pah-rah ehl kah-nah-'dah]
to Australia?	para Australia? ['pah-rah ow-'strah-lee-ah]
to New Zealand?	para Nueva Zelandia? ['pah-rah noo-'eh-vah seh-'lahn-dee-ah]
to Hong Kong?	para Hong Kong? ['pah-rah hohng kohng]
to India?	para la India? ['pah-rah lah 'een-dee-ah]
to Taiwan?	para Taiwán? ['pah-rah tah-ee-'wahn]
Three…-peseta stamps, please.	Tres sellos (*Am* estampillas) de … pesetas, por favor. [trehs 'seh-yohs (eh-stahm-'pee-nahs) deh peh-'seh-tahs, pohr fah-'vohr]

I'd like to send this letter...

Quisiera enviar esta carta... [kee-see-'eh-rah ehn-vee-'ahr 'eh-stah 'kahr-tah]

  registered.

  certificada (*Am* registrada). [sehr-tee-fee-'kah-dah (reh-hee-'strah-dah)]

  airmail.

  por correo aéreo. [pohr koh-'rreh-oh ah-'eh-reh-oh]

  express.

  urgente. [oor-'hehn-teh]

How long does a letter to the United States take?

¿Cuánto tarda en llegar una carta a los Estados Unidos? ['kwahn-toh 'tahr-dah ehn yeh-'gahr 'oo-nah 'kahr-tah ah los eh-'stah-dohs oo-'nee-dohs]

Do you have collector's/special issues stamps?

¿Tiene usted sellos (*Am* estampillas) especiales? [tee-'eh-neh oo-'stehd 'seh-yohs (eh-stahm-'pee-yahs) eh-speh-see-'ah-lehs]

This set/One stamp of each set, please.

Esta serie/Un sello (*Am* Una estampilla) de cada serie, por favor. ['eh-stah 'seh-ree-eh/oon 'seh-yoh ('oo-nah eh-stahm-'pee-yah) deh 'kah-dah 'seh-ree-eh, pohr fah-'vohr]

Held Mail

Lista de correos (*Am* cartas detenidas)

Do I have any mail? My name is...

¿Hay correo para mí? Me llamo ... ['ah-ee koh-'rreh-oh 'pah-rah mee? meh 'yah-moh]

No, there's nothing for you.

No, no hay nada. [noh, noh 'ah-ee 'nah-dah]

Yes, there's something. Do you have any ID, please?

Sí, hay algo. ¿Tiene usted algún documento personal, por favor? [see, 'ah-ee 'ahl-goh/ tee-'eh-neh oo-'stehd ahl-'goon doh-koo-'mehn-toh pehr-soh-'nahl, pohr fah-vohr]

Telegrams/Faxes	**Telegrama/(tele)fax**

I'd like to send a telegram.

Quisiera enviar un telegrama.
[kee-see-'eh-rah ehn-vee-'ahr oon teh-leh-'grah-mah]

Can you help me fill this out?

¿Podría usted ayudarme a rellenarlo? [poh-'dree-ah oo-'stehd ah-yoo-'dahr-meh ah reh-yeh-'nahr-loh]

How much is it per word?

¿Cuánto cuesta por palabra?
['kwahn-toh 'kweh-stah pohr pah-'lah-brah]

Up to ten words it's...;
each extra word is...

Hasta diez palabras cuesta ...;
por cada palabra más se paga...
['ah-stah dee-'ehs pah-'lah-brahs 'kweh-stah, pohr 'kah-dah pah-'lah-brah mahs seh 'pah-gah]

Will the telegram be
delivered today in...?

¿Llegará el telegrama hoy mismo a...? [yeh-gah-'rah ehl teh-leh-'grah-mah 'oh·ee 'mees-moh ah]

Can I send a fax to... ?

¿Puedo enviar desde aquí un (tele)fax a ...? ['pweh-doh ehn-vee-'ahr 'dehs-deh ah-'kee oon (teh-leh) fahks ah]

Word List: Post Office	**See also Word List: Money Matters**

address

la dirección [lah dee-rehk-see-'ohn]

addressee

destinatario [deh-stee-nah-'tah-ree-oh]

by air mail

por correo aéreo [pohr koh-'rreh-oh ah-'eh-reh-oh]

cash on delivery (COD)

contra reembolso ['kohn-trah reh-ehm-'bohl-soh]

collection

recogida [reh-koh-'hee-dah]

customs declaration

la declaración de aduana [lah deh-klah-rah-see-'ohn deh ah-'dwah-nah]

declaration of value

la declaración de valor [lah deh-klah-rah-see-'ohn deh vah-'lohr]

destination

destino [deh-'stee-noh]

envelope

el sobre [ehl 'soh-breh]

express letter	carta urgente, expreso ['kahr-tah oor-'hehn-teh, ehk-'spreh-soh]
fee	tarifa [tah-'ree-fah]
form	impreso, formulario [eem-'preh-soh, fohr-moo-'lah-ree·oh]
to forward	hacer seguir (el correo) [ah-'sehr seh-'geer (ehl koh-'rreh-oh)]
held mail	lista de correos (*Am* cartas detenidas) ['lee-stah deh koh-'rreh-ohs ('kahr-tahs deh-teh-'nee-dahs)]
letter	carta ['kahr-tah]
mailbox	el buzón [ehl boo-'sohn]
main post office	Oficina Central de Correos [oh-fee-'see-nah sehn-'trahl deh koh-'rreh-ohs]
opening hours	horario de apertura [oh-'rah-ree·oh deh ah-pehr-'too-rah]
parcel/package (small)	el paquete (pequeño) [ehl pah-'keh-teh (peh-'keh-nyoh)]
post office	oficina de correos [oh-fee-'see-nah deh koh-'rreh-ohs]
postage	franqueo [frahn-'keh-oh]
postcard	la postal [lah poh-'stahl]
postman/-woman	cartero/cartera [kahr-'teh-roh/kahr-'teh-rah]
printed matter	impreso [eem-'preh-soh]
proof of delivery	el acuse de recibo [ehl ah-'koo-seh deh reh-'see-boh]
to put stamps (on letter/ package)	franquear [frahn-keh-'ahr]
registered letter	carta certificada ['kahr-tah sehr-tee-fee-'kah-dah]
to send	enviar, expedir [ehn-vee-'ahr, ehks-peh-'deer]
sender	el/la remitente [ehl/lah reh-mee-'tehn-teh]
stamp	sello (*Am* estampilla) ['seh-yoh (eh-stahm-'pee-yah)]
stamp machine	el expendedor automático de sellos [ehl ehks-pehn-deh-'dohr ow-toh-'mah-tee-koh deh 'seh-yohs]
telex	el télex [ehl 'teh-lehks]
weight	peso ['peh-soh]

window, counter	la ventanilla (*Am* boletería) [lah vehn-tah-'nee-yah (boh-leh-teh-'ree-ah)]
zip code	código postal ['koh-dee-goh poh-'stahl]

Telephoning
Teléfonos

Can I use your phone, please?	¿Podría utilizar su teléfono, por favor? [poh-'dree-ah oo-tee-lee-'sahr soo teh-'leh-foh-noh, pohr fah-'vohr]
Where's the nearest phone booth?	¿Dónde está la cabina telefónica más próxima? ['dohn-deh eh-'stah lah kah-'bee-nah teh-leh-'foh-nee-kah mahs 'prohk-see-mah]
Can I have a token/phone card, please?	¿Me puede dar una ficha (telefónica)/una tarjeta telefónica? [meh 'pweh-deh dahr 'oo-nah 'fee-chah (teh-leh-'foh-nee-kah)/'oo-nah tahr-'heh-tah teh-leh-'foh-nee-kah]
Could you give me some change? I need it for the phone.	¿Me puede cambiar? Es que necesito dinero suelto (*Am* sencillo) para telefonear. [meh 'pweh-deh kahm-bee-'ahr? ehs keh neh-seh-'see-toh dee-'neh-roh 'swehl-toh (sehn-'see-yoh) 'pah-rah teh-leh-foh-neh-'ahr]
Do you have a…phone book?	¿Tienen aquí una guía telefónica de…? [tee-'eh-nehn ah-'kee 'oo-nah 'gee-ah teh-leh-'foh-nee-kah deh]
What's the country code/area code for…?	¿Cuál es el prefijo/el código territorial de…? [kwahl ehs ehl preh-'fee-hoh/ehl 'koh-dee-goh teh-rree-toh-ree-'ahl deh]
Information, please. Can I have the number for…	Información, por favor, ¿me puede dar el número de…? [een-fohr-mah-see-'ohn, pohr fah-'vohr, meh 'pweh-deh dahr ehl 'noo-meh-roh deh]

I'd like to make a long-distance call to...	Una llamada a larga distancia con…, por favor. ['oo-nah yah-'mah-dah ah 'lahr-gah dee-'stahn-see·ah kohn, pohr fah-'vohr]
I'd like to make a collect call to...	Una llamada a cobro revertido con…, por favor. ['oo-nah yah-'mah-dah ah 'koh-broh reh-vehr-'tee-doh kohn, pohr fah-'vohr]
Can you connect me with…, please?	¿Puede usted comunicarme con…? ['pweh-deh oo-'stehd koh-moo-nee-'kahr-meh kohn]
Go to booth number...	Pase a la cabina número… ['pah-seh ah lah kah-'bee-nah 'noo-meh-roh]
The line's busy.	Está ocupado. [eh-'stah oh-koo-'pah-doh]
There's no reply.	No contestan. [noh kohn-'teh-stahn]
Stay on the line, please.	No se retire, por favor. [noh seh reh-'tee-reh, pohr fah-'vohr]
This is…	Soy… ['soh·ee]
Hello, who is this, please?	¿Con quién hablo? [kohn kee-'ehn 'ah-bloh]
Can I speak to Mr./Mrs., Ms./Miss…, please?	¿Puedo hablar con el señor/la señora/la señorita…? ['pweh-doh ah-'blahr kohn ehl seh-'nyohr/lah seh-'nyoh-rah/lah seh-nyoh-'ree-tah]
Speaking.	Al aparato. (*Am* Al habla.) [ahl ah-pah-'rah-toh (ahl 'ah-blah)]
I'll put you through/connect you.	Le comunico. [leh koh-moo-'nee-koh]
I'm sorry, he's/she's not here/home.	Lo siento, no está aquí/en casa. [loh see-'ehn-toh, noh eh-'stah ah-'kee/ehn 'kah-sah]
When is she/he coming back?	¿Cuándo volverá? ['kwahn-doh vohl-veh-'rah]
Can he/she call you back?	¿Puede él/ella volver a llamar/llamar de vuelta? ['pweh-deh ehl/'eh-yah vohl-'vehr ah yah-'mahr/yah-'mahr deh 'vwehl-tah]

There are public telephone booths in almost every town in Spain. The directions for use are posted in several languages inside the booths. To use these phones, you need coins in denominations of 5, 25, 50, or 100 pesetas. No limit is placed on the duration of the call. In addition, in all the larger cities there are public telephone offices that are open all day.

For international long-distance calls, dial 07. After you hear the continuous tone, dial the prefix for the country and city in question, then the number of the party you wish to reach.

The code for dialing Spain from outside the country is 34.

Yes, my number's…	Sí, mi número es… [see, mee 'noo-meh-roh ehs]
Would you like to leave a message?	¿Desea usted dejar algún recado? [deh-'seh-ah oo-'stehd deh-'hahr ahl-'goon reh-'kah-doh]
Can you tell him/her that I called?	¿Podría decirle que he llamado? [poh-'dree-ah deh-'seer-leh keh eh yah-'mah-doh]
Could you give her/him a message?	¿Podría darle un recado? [poh-'dree-ah 'dahr-leh oon reh-'kah-doh]
I'll call back later.	Volveré a llamar más tarde. [vohl-veh-'reh ah yah-'mahr mahs 'tahr-deh]
Sorry, wrong number.	Se ha equivocado de número. [seh ah eh-kee-voh-'kah-doh deh 'noo-meh-roh]
That number doesn't exist.	Ese número no existe. ['eh-seh 'noo-meh-roh noh ehk-'see-steh]

Word List: Telephoning

to answer the phone	descolgar [dehs-kohl-'gahr]
answering machine	el contestador automático [ehl kohn-teh-stah-'dohr ow-toh-'mah-tee-koh]
area code	prefijo [preh-'fee-hoh]
busy	ocupado [oh-koo-'pah-doh]
busy signal	la señal de línea ocupada [lah seh-'nyahl deh 'lee-neh-ah oh-koo-'pah-dah]
buzz	zumbido [soom-'bee-doh]
to call	llamar por teléfono, telefonear [yah-'mahr pohr teh-'leh-foh-noh, teh-leh-foh-neh-'ahr]
collect call	llamada a cobro revertido [yah-'mah-dah ah 'koh-broh reh-vehr-'tee-doh]
communication	la comunicación [lah koh-moo-nee-kah-see-'ohn]
conference call	conferencia con preaviso [kohn-feh-'rehn-see·ah kohn preh-ah-'vee-soh]

conversation	la conversación [lah kohn-vehr-sah-see-'ohn]
to dial	marcar (el número) [mahr-'kahr (ehl 'noo-meh-roh)]
to dial direct	llamar directamente [yah-'mahr dee-rehk-tah-'mehn-teh]
dial tone	la señal para marcar [lah seh-'nyahl 'pah-rah mahr-'kahr]
directory information	la información [lah een-fohr-mah-see-'ohn]
international call	llamada internacional [yah-'mah-dah een-tehr-nah-see·oh-'nahl]
local call	llamada urbana [yah-'mah-dah oor-'bah-nah]
long-distance call	llamada interurbana/de larga distancia [yah-'mah-dah een-tehr-oor-'bah-nah/deh 'lahr-gah dee-'stahn-see·ah]
operator	centralita de teléfonos, la central (*Am* operadora) [sehn-trah-'lee-tah deh teh-'leh-foh-nohs, lah sehn-'trahl (oh-peh-rah-'doh-rah)]
phone book	guía telefónica ['gee-ah teh-leh-'foh-nee-kah]
phone booth	cabina telefónica [kah-'bee-nah teh-leh-'foh-nee-kah]
phone call	llamada telefónica [yah-'mah-dah teh-leh-'foh-nee-kah]
phone card	tarjeta telefónica [tahr-'heh-tah teh-leh-'foh-nee-kah]
phone company office	oficina de teléfonos [oh-fee-'see-nah deh teh-'leh-foh-nohs]
phone number	número de teléfono ['noo-meh-roh deh teh-'leh-foh-noh]
rate	tarifa [tah-'ree-fah]
receiver	el receptor [ehl reh-sehp-'tohr]
repair service	servicio de averías [sehr-'vee-see·oh deh ah-veh-'ree-ahs]
telephone, phone	teléfono [teh-'leh-foh-noh]
token (phone)	ficha (telefónica) ['fee-chah (teh-leh-'foh-nee-kah)]

unit rate	tarifa telefónica (por unidad) [tah-'ree-fah teh-leh-'foh-nee-kah (pohr oo-nee-'dahd)]
yellow pages	el índice comercial, las páginas amarillas [ehl 'een-dee-seh koh-mehr-see-'ahl, lahs 'pah-hee-nahs ah-mah-'ree-yahs]

At the Police Station
En la comisaría (de policía)

Where's the nearest police station, please?	Por favor, ¿dónde está la comis aría de policía más cercana? [pohr fah-'vohr, 'dohn-deh eh-'stah lah koh-mee-sah-'ree-ah deh poh-lee-'see-ah mahs sehr-'kah-nah]
I'd like to report a robbery/ a loss/an accident.	Quiero denunciar un robo/una pérdida/un accidente. [kee-'eh-roh deh-noon-see-'ahr oon 'roh-boh/'oo-nah 'pehr-dee-dah/oon ahk-see-'dehn-teh]

My...has been stolen.	Me han robado... [meh ahn roh-'bah-doh]
handbag	el bolso. [ehl 'bohl-soh]
wallet	la cartera. [lah kahr-'teh-rah]
camera	mi cámara fotográfica. [mee 'kah-mah-rah foh-toh-'grah-fee-kah]
car/bicycle	mi coche/mi bicicleta. [mee 'koh-cheh/mee bee-see-'kleh-tah]
They broke into my car.	Me han forzado la puerta del coche. [meh ahn fohr-'sah-doh lah 'pwehr-tah dehl 'koh-cheh]
They stole...from my car.	Me han robado del coche... [meh ahn roh-'bah-doh dehl 'koh-cheh]
I lost...	He perdido... [eh pehr-'dee-doh]
My daughter/son has been missing since...	Mi hija/hijo ha desaparecido desde... [mee 'ee-hah/'ee-hoh ah dehs-ah-pah-reh-'see-doh 'dehs-deh]

This man is harassing me.

Este hombre me está molestando. ['eh-steh 'ohm-breh meh eh-'stah moh-leh-'stahn-doh]

Can you help me, please?

¿Puede usted ayudarme, por favor? ['pweh-deh oo-'stehd ah-yoo-'dahr-meh, pohr fah-'vohr]

When exactly did it happen?

¿A qué hora exactamente ha sucedido? [ah keh 'oh-rah ehk-sahk-tah-'mehn-teh ah soo-seh-'dee-doh]

We'll take care of it.

Nosotros nos ocuparemos de ello. [noh-'soh-trohs nohs oh-koo-pah-'reh-mohs deh 'eh-yoh]

I've nothing to do with it.

Yo no tengo nada que ver con eso. [yoh noh 'tehn-goh 'nah-dah keh vehr kohn 'eh-soh]

Your name and address, please.

Por favor, su nombre y dirección. [pohr fah-'vohr, soo 'nohm-breh ee dee-rehk-see-'ohn]

Get in touch with the American/Canadian/British/Australian consulate, please.

Por favor, diríjase al consulado americano/canadiense/británico/australiano. [pohr fah-'vohr, dee-'ree-hah-seh ahl kohn-soo-'lah-doh ah-meh-ree-'kah-noh/kah-nah-dee-'ehn-seh/bree-'tah-nee-koh/ow-strah-lee-'ah-noh]

Word List: Police   See also Chapter 3—A Road Accident

to arrest	arrestar [ah-rreh-'stahr]
attorney	abogado [ah-boh-'gah-doh]
to beat up	golpear, pegar [gohl-peh-'ahr, peh-'gahr]
to break into/open	forzar, violentar [fohr-'sahr, vee-oh-lehn-'tahr]
car keys	las llaves del coche [lahs 'yah-vehs dehl 'koh-cheh]
car radio	la autorradio [lah ow-toh-'rrah-dee·oh]
check	el cheque [ehl 'cheh-keh]

check cashing card	tarjeta de cheques [tahr-'heh-tah deh 'cheh-kehs]
to confiscate	confiscar [kohn-fee-'skahr]
court	el tribunal [ehl tree-boo-'nahl]
crime	el delito (*however, murder is "el crimen"*) [ehl deh-'lee-toh, ehl 'kree-mehn]
documents, papers	los documentos [lohs doh-koo-'mehn-tohs]
driver's license	permiso de conducir/manejar [pehr-'mee-soh deh kohn-doo-'seer/mah-neh-'hahr]
drugs	las drogas [lahs 'droh-gahs]
guilt	culpa ['kool-pah]
to harass	molestar, hostigar, importunar [moh-leh-'stahr, oh-stee-'gahr, eem-pohr-too-'nahr]
ID	el carnet de identidad [ehl kahr-'neht deh ee-dehn-tee-'dahd]
jail	la cárcel [lah 'kahr-sehl]
judge	el juez [ehl hoo-'ehs]
key	la llave [lah 'yah-veh]
to lose	perder [pehr-'dehr]
to make a complaint, denounce	denunciar [deh-noon-see-'ahr]

money	dinero [dee-'neh-roh]
mugging	la agresión; el asalto [lah ah-greh-see-'ohn; ehl ah-'sahl-toh]
murder	el crimen, el asesinato [ehl 'kree-mehn, ehl ah-seh-see-'nah-toh]
passport	el pasaporte [ehl pah-sah-'pohr-teh]
police	policía [poh-lee-'see-ah]
police car	el coche de policía [ehl 'koh-cheh deh poh-lee-'see-ah]
police officer	el/la policía [ehl/lah poh-lee-'see-ah]
preventive detention, protective custody	la prisión preventiva [lah pree-see-'ohn preh-vehn-'tee-vah]
purse	monedero [moh-neh-'deh-roh]
rape	la violación [lah vee·oh-lah-see-'ohn]
smuggled goods	contrabando [kohn-trah-'bahn-doh]
theft, robbery	robo [ehl 'roh-boh]
thief	ratero, el ladrón [rah-'teh-roh, ehl lah-'drohn]

Lost and Found

Oficina de objetos perdidos

Where's the lost and found office, please?

Por favor, ¿dónde está la oficina de objetos perdidos? [pohr fah-'vohr, 'dohn-deh eh-'stah lah oh-fee-'see-nah deh ohb-'heh-tohs pehr-'dee-dohs]

I've lost...

He perdido… [eh pehr-'dee-doh]

I left my bag on the train.

He olvidado mi bolso en el tren. [eh ohl-vee-'dah-doh mee 'bohl-soh ehn ehl trehn]

Please let me know if someone returns/finds it.

Haga el favor de avisarme si lo devuelven/encuentran. ['ah-gah ehl fah-'vohr deh ah-vee-'sahr-meh see loh deh-'vwehl-vehn/ehn-'kwehn-trahn]

Here's the address of my hotel/my home address.

Aquí tiene la dirección de mi hotel/de mi casa. [ah-'kee tee-'eh-neh mee dee-rehk-see-'ohn deh mee oh-'tehl/deh mee 'kah-sah]

10 Health
La salud

At the Pharmacy
En la farmacia

Where's the nearest (all-night) pharmacy, please?

¿Dónde está la farmacia (de guardia) más cercana, por favor? ['dohn-deh eh-'stah lah fahr-'mah-see·ah (deh 'gwahr-dee·ah) mahs sehr-'kah-nah, pohr fah-'vohr]

Could you give me something for…

¿Me puede dar algo contra…, por favor? [meh 'pweh-deh dahr 'ahl-goh 'kohn-trah, pohr fah-'vohr]

You need a prescription for this medicine.

Para esa medicina se necesita una receta. ['pah-rah 'eh-sah meh-dee-'see-nah seh neh-seh-'see-tah 'oo-nah reh-'seh-tah]

Can I wait?

¿Puedo esperar? ['pweh-doh eh-speh-'rahr]

When can I pick it up?

¿Cúando puedo venir a recogerlo (*Am* buscarlo)? ['kwahn-doh 'pweh-doh veh-'neer ah reh-koh-'hehr-loh (boo-'skahr-loh)]

Word List: Pharmacy ➤ See also Word List: Doctor/Dentist/Hospital

after meals

después de las comidas [deh-'spwehs deh lahs koh-'mee-dahs]

antibiotic

antibiótico [ahn-tee-bee-'oh-tee-koh]

antidote

antídoto [ahn-'tee-doh-toh]

aspirin

aspirina [ah-spee-'ree-nah]

Band-Aid, adhesive tape

esparadrapo [ehs-pah-rah-'drah-poh]

before meals

antes de las comidas ['ahn-tehs deh lahs koh-'mee-dahs]

birth control pill

píldora anticonceptiva ['peel-doh-rah ahn-tee-kohn-sehp-'tee-vah]

camomile

manzanilla [mahn-sah-'nee-yah]

cardiac stimulant

medicamento para la circulación de la sangre [meh-dee-kah-'mehn-toh 'pah-rah lah seer-koo-lah-see-'ohn deh lah 'sahn-greh]

charcoal tablets

las pastillas de carbono [lahs pah-'stee-yahs deh kahr-'boh-noh]

condom	preservativo [preh-sehr-vah-'tee-voh]
cotton	el algodón [ehl ahl-goh-'dohn]
cough syrup	el jarabe (contra la tos) [ehl hah-'rah-beh ('kohn-trah lah tohs)]
disinfectant	el desinfectante [ehl dehs-een-fehk-'tahn-teh]
drops	las gotas [lahs 'goh-tahs]
eardrops	las gotas para los oídos [lahs 'goh-tahs 'pah-rah lohs oh-'ee-dohs]
elastic bandage	venda elástica ['vehn-dah eh-'lah-stee-kah]
eyedrops	las gotas para los ojos [lahs 'goh-tahs 'pah-rah lohs 'oh-hohs]
for external use	para uso externo ['pah-rah 'oo-soh ehk-stehr-noh]
for internal use	para uso interno ['pah-rah 'oo-soh een-'tehr-noh]
gargles	el agua para gargarismos [(ehl) 'ah-gwah 'pah-rah gahr-gah-'rees-mohs]
gauze bandage	gasa ['gah-sah]
glucose	glucosa [gloo-'koh-sah]
headache tablets/pills	las pastillas para el dolor de cabeza [lahs pah-'stee-yahs 'pah-rah ehl doh-'lohr deh kah-'beh-sah]
insecticide	el insecticida [ehl een-sehk-tee-'see-dah]
insulin	insulina [een-soo-'lee-nah]
iodine	tintura de yodo [teen-'too-rah deh 'yoh-doh]
laxative	el laxante [ehl lahk-'sahn-teh]
to let it dissolve in your mouth	dejar deshacerse en la boca [deh-'hahr dehs-ah-'sehr-seh ehn lah 'boh-kah]
lozenges	las pastillas para la garganta [lahs pah-'stee-yahs 'pah-rah lah gahr-'gahn-tah]
medicine, drug, medication	medicina, medicamento [meh-dee-'see-nah, meh-dee-kah-'mehn-toh]
ointment	pomada [poh-'mah-dah]
ointment for burns	pomada para quemaduras [poh-'mah-dah 'pah-rah keh-mah-'doo-rahs]
on an empty stomach	en ayunas [ehn ah-'yoo-nahs]
painkiller (tablets/pills)	las pastillas contra el dolor [lahs pah-'stee-yahs 'kohn-trah ehl doh-'lohr]

powder	los polvos [lohs 'pohl-vohs]
prescription	la receta [lah reh-'seh-tah]
remedy	remedio [reh-'meh-dee·oh]
side effects	los efectos secundarios [lohs eh-'fehk-tohs seh-koon-'dah-ree-ohs]
sleeping pills	los somníferos [lohs sohm-'nee-feh-rohs]
stomachache drops	las gotas para el dolor de estómago [lahs 'goh-tahs 'pah-rah ehl doh-'lohr deh eh-'stoh-mah-goh]
sunburn	quemadura por el sol [keh-mah-'doo-rah pohr ehl sohl]
suppositories	los supositorios [lohs soo-poh-see-'toh-ree·ohs]
tablet	pastilla, comprimido [pah-'stee-yah, kohm-pree-'mee-doh]
to take	tomar [toh-'mahr]
thermometer	termómetro [tehr-'moh-meh-troh]
tranquilizer	el tranquilizante [ehl trahn-kee-lee-'sahn-teh]

At the Doctor

En la consulta del médico

Could you recommend a good…?	¿Puede usted indicarme un buen …? ['pweh-deh oo-'stehd een-dee-'kahr-meh oon bwehn]

doctor	médico ['meh-dee-koh]
eye doctor, optometrist	oculista [oh-koo-'lee-stah]
gynecologist	ginecólogo [hee-neh-'koh-loh-goh]
ear, nose, and throat specialist	otorrinolaringólogo [oh-toh-rree-noh-lah-reen-'goh-loh-goh]
dermatologist	dermatólogo [dehr-mah-'toh-loh-goh]
alternative medicine practitioner	curandero (naturista) [koo-rahn-'deh-roh (nah-too-'ree-stah)]
internist	internista [een-tehr-'nee-stah]
pediatrician	puericultor, pediatra [poo-ehr-ee-kool-'tohr, peh-dee-'ah-trah]
neurologist	neurólogo [neh-oo-'roh-loh-goh]
general practitioner	médico (general) ['meh-dee-koh (heh-neh-'rahl)]

urologist	urólogo [oo-'roh-loh-goh]
dentist	dentista [dehn-'tee-stah]
Where's the office?	¿Dónde está la consulta (*Am* el consultorio)? ['dohn-deh eh-'stah lah kohn-'sool-tah (ehl kohn-sool-'toh-ree oh]
What are the office hours?	¿A qué hora tiene consulta? [ah keh 'oh-rah tee-'eh-neh kohn-'sool-tah]
What's the trouble?	¿Qué molestias siente? [keh moh-'leh-stee·ahs see-'ehn-teh]
I'm not feeling well.	No me siento bien. [noh meh see-'ehn-toh 'bee-ehn]
I have a fever.	Tengo fiebre. ['tehn-goh fee-'eh-breh]
I can't sleep.	No puedo dormir. [noh 'pweh-doh dohr-'meer]
I often feel sick./I feel nauseated/dizzy.	Me siento mal con frecuencia./Me mareo. [meh-see-'ehn-toh mahl kohn freh-'kwehn-see·ah/meh mah-'reh-oh]
I fainted.	Me he desmayado. [meh eh dehs-mah-'yah-doh]
I have a bad cold.	Estoy muy resfriado. [eh-'stoh·ee 'moo·ee rehs-free-'ah-doh]
I have…	Tengo… ['tehn-goh]
a headache.	dolor de cabeza. [doh-'lohr deh kah-'beh-sah]
a sore throat.	dolor de garganta. [doh-'lohr deh gahr-'gahn-tah]
a cough.	tos. [tohs]
I've been stung/bitten.	Tengo una picadura/mordedura. ['tehn-goh 'oo-nah pee-kah-'doo-rah/mohr-deh-'doo-rah]
I have an upset stomach.	Tengo una indigestión. ['tehn-goh 'oo-nah een-dee-heh-stee-'ohn]
I have diarrhea./I'm constipated.	Tengo colitis/estreñimiento. ['tehn-goh koh-'lee-tees/eh-streh-nyee-mee-'ehn-toh]

The food/the heat is making me sick.

La comida/El calor no me sienta bien. [lah koh-'mee-dah/ehl kah-'lohr noh meh see-'ehn-tah 'bee-ehn]

I hurt myself.

Me he hecho una herida. [meh eh 'eh-choh 'oo-nah eh-'ree-dah]

I fell down.

Me he caído. [meh eh kah-'ee-doh]

I think I've broken/ sprained...

Creo que me he roto/dislocado... ['kreh-oh keh meh eh 'roh-toh/dees-loh-'kah-doh]

Where does it hurt?

¿Dónde le duele? ['dohn-deh leh 'dweh-leh]

It hurts here.

Me duele aquí. [meh 'dweh-leh ah-'kee]

Does that hurt?

¿Le duele aquí? [leh 'dweh-leh ah-'kee]

I have high/low blood pressure.

Tengo presión sanguínea alta/baja. ['tehn-goh preh-see-'ohn sahn-'gee-neh-ah 'ahl-tah/'bah-hah]

I'm diabetic.

Soy diabético. ['soh-ee dee-ah-'beh-tee-koh]

I'm pregnant.

Estoy embarazada. [eh-'stoh-ee ehm-bah-rah-'sah-dah]

I had...recently.

Hace poco tuve... ['ah-seh 'poh-koh 'too-veh]

Undress yourself./Roll up your sleeve, please.

Quítese la ropa/Súbase la manga, por favor. ['kee-teh-seh lah 'roh-pah/'soo-bah-seh lah 'mahn-gah, pohr fah-'vohr]

Take a deep breath. Hold it.

Respire profundamente. Contenga la respiración. [reh-'spee-reh proh-foon-dah-'mehn-teh. kohn-'tehn-gah lah reh-spee-rah-see-'ohn]

Open your mouth.

Abra la boca. ['ah-brah lah 'boh-kah]

Let me see your tongue.

Saque la lengua. ['sah-keh lah 'lehn-gwah]

Cough, please.

Tosa. ['toh-sah]

How long have you been feeling ill?	¿Desde cuándo se siente usted mal? ['dehs-deh 'kwahn-doh seh see-'ehn-teh oo-'stehd mahl]
How's your appetite?	¿Tiene usted apetito? [tee-'eh-neh oo-'stehd ah-peh-'tee-toh]
I've lost my appetite.	No tengo apetito. [noh 'tehn-goh ah-peh-'tee-toh]
Do you have a vaccination card?	¿Tiene un certificado de vacunación? [tee-'eh-neh oon sehr-tee-fee-'kah-doh deh vah-koo-nah-see-'ohn]
I've been vaccinated against…	Estoy vacunado contra… [eh-'stoh·ee vah-koo-'nah-doh 'kohn-trah]
We'll need to do some tests.	Hay que hacerle unos análisis. ['ah·ee keh ah-'sehr-leh 'oo-nohs ah-'nah-lee-sees]
We'll need to do a blood/urine test.	Es necesario un análisis de sangre/de orina. [ehs neh-seh-'sah-ree·oh oon ah-'nah-lee-sees deh 'sahn-greh/deh oh-'ree-nah]
I'll have to send you to a specialist.	Hay que consultar a un especialista. ['ah·ee keh kohn-sool-'tahr ah oon eh-speh-see·ah-'lee-stah]
You need surgery.	Es necesario operarle/operarla. [ehs neh-seh-'sah-ree·oh oh-peh-'rahr-leh/oh-peh-'rahr-lah]
You need a few days in bed.	Debe quedarse en cama unos días. ['deh-beh keh-'dahr-seh ehn 'kah-mah 'oo-nohs 'dee-ahs]
It's nothing serious.	No es nada grave. [noh ehs 'nah-dah 'grah-veh]
Could you give me/prescribe something for me for…?	¿Podría usted darme/recetarme algo contra…? [poh-'dree-ah oo-'stehd 'dahr-meh/reh-seh-'tahr-meh 'ahl-goh 'kohn-trah]
I usually take…	Normalmente tomo… [nohr-mahl-'mehn-teh 'toh-moh]

Take a tablet/pill before going to bed.

Tome un comprimido antes de acostarse. ['toh-meh oon kohm-pree-'mee-doh 'ahn-tehs deh ah-koh-'stahr-seh]

Here's my international health insurance form.

Aquí tiene mi volante del seguro internacional. [ah-'kee tee-'eh-neh mee voh-'lahn-teh dehl seh-'goo-roh een-tehr-nah-see·oh-'nahl]

Could you give me a medical certificate?

¿Podría usted darme un certifica do médico? [poh-'dree-ah oo-'stehd 'dahr-meh oon sehr-tee-fee-'kah-doh 'meh-dee-koh]

At the Dentist
En la consulta del dentista

I have a toothache.

Tengo dolor de muelas. ['tehn-goh doh-'lohr deh 'mweh-lahs]

This tooth (at the top/bottom/front/back) hurts.

Me duele este diente (arriba/abajo/delante/atrás). [meh 'dweh-leh 'eh-steh dee-'ehn-teh (ah-'rree-bah/ah-'bah-hoh/deh-'lahn-teh/ah-'trahs)]

I've lost a filling.

Se me ha perdido un empaste (*Am* una tapadura). [seh meh ah pehr-'dee-doh oon ehm-'pah-steh ('oo-nah tah-pah-'doo-rah)]

I broke a tooth.

Se me ha roto un diente. [seh meh ah 'roh-toh oon dee-'ehn-teh]

I'll have to fill it.

Tengo que empastárselo. ['tehn-goh keh ehm-pah-'stahr-seh-loh]

I'll just do a temporary job.

Voy a hacer solamente una cura provisional. ['voh-ee ah-'sehr soh-lah-'mehn-teh 'oo-nah 'koo-rah proh-vee-see-oh-'nahl]

It'll have to come out.

Tengo que sacárselo. ['tehn-goh keh sah-'kahr-seh-loh]

I need a crown on this tooth.	Tengo que poner una corona en este diente. ['tehn-goh keh poh-'nehr 'oo-nah koh-'roh-nah ehn 'eh-steh dee-'ehn-teh]
I want/I don't want an injection.	Póngame/No me ponga una inyección. ['pohn-gah-meh/noh meh 'pohn-gah 'oo-nah een-yehk-see-'ohn]
Rinse well, please.	Enjuáguese bien, por favor. [ehm-hoo-'ah-geh-seh 'bee-ehn, pohr fah-'vohr]
Can you fix these dentures?	¿Podría usted arreglarme esta dentadura postiza? [poh-'dree-ah oo-'stehd ah-rreh-'glahr-meh 'eh-stah dehn-tah-'doo-rah poh-'stee-sah]
Come back in a couple of days so I can see how you're doing.	Vuelva dentro de dos días para comprobar cómo va. ['vwehl-vah 'dehn-troh deh dohs 'dee-ahs 'pah-rah kohm-proh-'bahr 'koh-moh vah]
See your dentist when you get home.	Cuando vuelva a casa, vaya a ver a su dentista. [kwahn-doh 'vwehl-vah ah 'kah-sah, 'vah-yah a vehr a soo dehn-'tee-stah]

At the Hospital
En el hospital

How long will I have to stay here?	¿Cuánto tiempo tendré que quedarme aquí? ['kwahn-toh tee-'ehm-poh tehn-'dreh keh keh-'dahr-meh ah-'kee]
I'm in pain./I can't sleep. Can you give me a painkiller/sleeping pill?	Tengo dolores/No puedo dormirme. ¿Podría darme un calmante/somnífero? ['tehn-goh doh-'loh-rehs/noh 'pweh-doh dohr-'meer-meh. poh-'dree-ah 'dahr-meh oon kahl-'mahn-teh/sohm-'nee-feh-roh]
When can I get up?	¿Cuándo podré levantarme? ['kwahn-doh poh-'dreh leh-vahn-'tahr-meh]

Could you give me a certificate showing how long I was in the hospital and also the diagnosis?

¿Puede darme un certificado con la duración de la estancia en el hospital y con el diagnóstico? ['pweh-deh 'dahr-meh oon sehr-tee-fee-'kah-doh kohn lah doo-rah-see-'ohn deh lah eh-'stahn-see-ah ehn ehl oh-spee-'tahl ee kohn ehl dee-ahg-'noo-stee-koh]

Word List: Doctor/Dentist/Hospital

abdomen — el vientre, el abdomen [ehl vee-'ehn-treh, ehl ahb-'doh-mehn]

abscess — absceso [ahb-'seh-soh]

AIDS — el SIDA [ehl 'see-dah]

allergy — alergia [ah-'lehr-jee·ah]

anesthesia — anestesia [ah-neh-'steh-see·ah]

angina — angina [ahn-'hee-nah]

ankle — tobillo [toh-'bee-yoh]

apoplexy, cerebral hemorrhage — apoplejía, hemorragia cerebral [ah-poh-pleh-'hee-ah, eh-moh-'rrah-hee·ah seh-reh-'brahl]

appendicitis — la apendicitis [(lah) ah-pehn-dee-'see-tees]

appendix — el apéndice [ehl ah-'pehn-dee-seh]

arm — brazo ['brah-soh]

artificial limb — la prótesis [lah 'proh-teh-sees]

asthma — el asma [ehl 'ahs-mah]

attack — el ataque [ehl ah-'tah-keh]

back — espalda [eh-'spahl-dah]

backache — los dolores de espalda [(lohs) doh-'loh-rehs deh eh-'spahl-dah]

to bandage — vendar [vehn-'dahr]

bandages — (los) vendajes [(lohs) vehn-'dah-hehs]

to be allergic to — ser alérgico contra [sehr ah-'lehr-hee-koh 'kohn-trah]

to be hoarse — estar ronco [eh-'stahr 'rohn-koh]

bladder — vejiga [veh-'hee-gah]

to bleed — sangrar [sahn-'grahr]

blood — la sangre [lah 'sahn-greh]

blood group — grupo sanguíneo ['groo-poh sahn-'gee-neh-oh]

blood poisoning	la intoxicación de la sangre [lah een-tohk-see-kah-see-'ohn deh lah 'sahn-greh]
blood pressure, high/low	la presión de la sangre, alta/baja [lah preh-see-'ohn deh lah 'sahn-greh, 'ahl-tah/'bah-hah]
blood test	el análisis de sangre [ehl ah-'nah-lee-sees deh 'sahn-greh]
blood transfusion	la transfusión de sangre [lah trahs-foo-see-'ohn deh 'sahn-greh]
bone	hueso ['weh-soh]
bowel movement	la deposición [lah deh-poh-see-see-'ohn]
brain	cerebro [seh-'reh-broh]
to breathe	respirar [reh-spee-'rahr]
broken	roto ['roh-toh]
bronchial tubes	los bronquios [lohs 'brohn-kee-ohs]
bronchitis	la bronquitis [lah brohn-'kee-tees]
bruise	el hematoma [ehl eh-mah-'toh-mah]
burn	quemadura [keh-mah-'doo-rah]
bypass	el bypass [ehl 'bah·ee-pahs]
cancer	el cáncer [ehl 'kahn-sehr]
cardiologist	cardiólogo [kahr-dee-'oh-loh-goh]
to catch a cold	resfriarse [rehs-free-'ahr-seh]
cavity *(tooth)*	agujero (en el diente) [ah-goo-'heh-roh (ehn ehl dee-'ehn-teh)]
certificate	certificado [sehr-tee-fee-'kah-doh]
chest	pecho ['peh-choh]
chicken pox	varicela [vah-ree-'seh-lah]
chills	escalofríos [eh-skah-loh-'free-ohs]
cholera	el cólera [ehl 'koh-leh-rah]
circulatory disorder	los trastornos de la circulación (lohs) trahs-'tohr-nohs]
clinic	la clínica [lah 'klee-nee-kah]
cold	resfriado, constipado, *(Am)* resfrío, catarro [rehs-free-'ah-doh, kohn-stee-'pah-doh, rehs-'free-oh, kah-'tah-rroh]
colic	cólico ['koh-lee-koh]
collarbone	clavícula [klah-'vee-koo-lah]
concussion	la conmoción cerebral [lah kohn-moh-see-'ohn seh-reh-'brahl]
constipation	estreñimiento [eh-streh-nyee-mee-'ehn-toh]

contagious	contagioso [kohn-tah-hee-'oh-soh]
contusion, bruise	la contusión, magulladura [lah kohn-too-see-'ohn, mah-goo-yah-'doo-rah]
cough	la tos [lah tohs]
cramp	el calambre, espasmo [ehl kah-'lahm-breh, eh-'spahs-moh]
crown *(tooth)*	corona [koh-'roh-nah]
cut	el corte [ehl 'kohr-teh]
diabetes	la diabetes [lah dee-ah-'beh-tehs]
diagnosis	el diagnóstico [ehl dee-ahg-'noh-stee-koh]
diarrhea	diarrea [dee-ah-'rreh-ah]
diet	la dieta, el régimen [lah dee-'eh-tah, ehl 'reh-hee-mehn]
difficulty breathing	las dificultades de respiración [(lahs) dee-fee-kool-'tah-dehs deh reh-spee-rah-see-'ohn]
digestion	la digestión [lah dee-heh-stee-'ohn]
diphtheria	difteria [deef-'teh-ree·ah]
to disinfect	desinfectar [dehs-een-fehk-'tahr]
dizziness, vertigo	mareo, vértigo [mah-'reh-oh, 'vehr-tee-goh]
doctor's office	consulta [kohn-'sool-tah]
ear	oreja, oído [oh-'reh-hah, oh-'ee-doh]
eardrum	tímpano ['teem-pah-noh]
elbow	codo ['koh-doh]
examination	el examen [ehl ehk-'sah-mehn]
to extract *(tooth)*	sacar [sah-'kahr]
eyes	ojos ['oh-hohs]
face	cara, rostro ['kah-rah, 'roh-stroh]
to faint	desmayarse [dehs-mah-'yahr-seh]
to faint, to be unconscious	desmayado, desvanecido [dehs-mah-'yah-doh, dehs-vah-neh-'see-doh]
to fester	supurar [soo-poo-'rahr]
fever	la fiebre [lah fee·'eh-breh]
filling *(tooth)*	el empaste, *(Am* la tapadura) [ehl ehm-'pah-steh (lah tah-pah-'doo-rah)]
finger	dedo ['deh-doh]
flatulence, gas	flato ['flah-toh]
flu	la gripe [lah 'gree-peh]
food poisoning	la intoxicación [lah een-tohk-see-kah-see-'ohn]
foot	el pie [ehl 'pee-eh]

fracture	fractura [frahk-'too-rah]
gallbladder	la vesícula [lah veh-'see-koo-'lah]
German measles	rubeola [roo-beh-'oh-lah]
gland	glándula ['glahn-doo-lah]
gullet, esophagus	esófago [eh-'soh-fah-goh]
gum	encía [ehn-'see-ah]
hand	la mano [lah 'mah-noh]
hay fever	la fiebre del heno [lah fee-'eh-breh dehl 'eh-noh]
head	cabeza [kah-'beh-sah]
headache	dolor de cabeza [doh-'lohr deh kah-'beh-sah]
heart	el corazón [ehl koh-rah-'sohn]
heart attack	el ataque/el infarto cardíaco [ehl ah-'tah-keh/ehl een-'fahr-toh kahr-'dee-ah-koh]
heart defect	defecto cardíaco [deh-'fehk-toh kahr-'dee-ah-koh]
heart trouble	los trastornos cardíacos [(lohs) trahs-'tohr-nohs kahr-'dee-ah-kohs]
heartburn	el ardor de estómago [ehl ahr-'dohr deh eh-'stoh-mah-goh]
hemorrhage	hemorragia [eh-moh-'rrah-hee·ah]
hemorrhoids	las hemorroides [(lahs) eh-moh-'rroh·ee-dehs]
hernia	hernia ['ehr-nee·ah]
hip	cadera [kah-'deh-rah]
hospital	el hospital [ehl oh-spee-'tahl]
to hurt	doler [doh-'lehr]
incisor	el (diente) incisivo [ehl (dee-'ehn-teh) een-see-'see-voh]
indigestion	la indigestión [lah een-dee-heh-stee-'ohn]
infection	la infección [lah een-fehk-see-'ohn]
inflammation	la inflamación [lah een-flah-mah-see-'ohn]
infusion	la infusión [lah een-foo-see-'ohn]
injection, shot	la inyección [lah een-yehk-see-'ohn]
insomnia	insomnio [een-'sohm-nee·oh]
intestine	intestino [een-teh-'stee-noh]
jaundice	ictericia [eek-teh-'ree-see·ah]
jaw	mandíbula [mahn-'dee-boo-lah]
joint	la articulación [lah ahr-tee-koo-lah-see-'ohn]

kidney	el riñón [ehl ree-'nyohn]
kidney stone	cálculo renal ['kahl-koo-loh reh-'nahl]
knee	rodilla [roh-'dee-yah]
lack of appetite	falta de apetito ['fahl-tah deh ah-peh-'tee-toh]
leg	pierna [pee-'ehr-nah]
limbs	los miembros [lohs mee-'ehm-brohs]
lip	el labio [ehl 'lah-bee-oh]
liver	hígado ['ee-gah-doh
lumbago	lumbago [loom-'bah-goh]
lung	el pulmón [ehl pool-'mohn]
malaria	el paludismo, la malaria [ehl pah-loo-'dees-moh, lah mah-'lah-ree·ah]
measles	el sarampión [ehl sah-rahm-pee-'ohn]
medical insurance	seguro de enfermedad [seh-'goo-roh deh ehn-fehr-meh-'dahd]
medical insurance form	el volante del seguro [ehl voh-'lahn-teh dehl seh-'goo-roh]
menstruation, period	la menstruación, el período [lah mehn-stroo-ah-see-'ohn, ehl peh-'ree-oh-doh]
middle ear infection	la otitis media [lah oh-'tee-tees 'meh-dee·ah]
migraine	jaqueca [hah-'keh-kah]
miscarriage	aborto no provocado [ah-'bohr-toh noh proh-voh-'kah-doh]
molar	muela ['mweh-lah]
mouth	boca ['boh-kah]
mumps	las paperas [lahs pah-'peh-rahs]
muscle	músculo ['moo-skoo-loh]
nausea	las náuseas [(lahs) 'nah·oo-seh-ahs]
neck	cuello ['kweh-yoh]
nephritis	la nefritis [lah neh-'free-tees]
nerve	nervio ['nehr-vee·oh]
nervous	nervioso [nehr-vee-'oh-soh]
nose	la nariz [lah nah-'rees]
nosebleed	hemorragia nasal [eh-moh-'rrah-hee·ah nah-'sahl]
nurse	la enfermera, el enfermero [lah ehn-fehr-'meh-rah, ehl ehn-fehr-'meh-roh]
office hours	horas de consulta ['oh-rahs deh kohn-'sool-tah]

pacemaker	el marcapasos [ehl mahr-kah-'pah-sohs]
pain	los dolores [lohs doh-'loh-rehs]
paralysis	la parálisis [lah pah-'rah-lee-sees]
pneumonia	pulmonía [pool-moh-'nee-ah]
poisoning	el envenenamiento, la intoxicación [ehl ehn-veh-nah-mee-'ehn-toh, lah een-tohk-see-kah-see-'ohn]
polio	la polio (mielitis) [lah 'poh-lee·oh (mee-eh-'lee-tees)]
pregnancy	embarazo [ehm-bah-'rah-soh]
to prescribe	recetar, prescribir [reh-seh-'tahr, preh-skree-'beer]
pulled ligament/muscle	la distensión (de ligamentos/muscular) [lah dee-stehn-see-'ohn (deh lee-gah-'mehn-tohs/moo-skoo-'lahr)]
pulse	pulso ['pool-soh]
pus	el pus [ehl poos]
rash	la erupción cutánea [lah eh-roop-see-'ohn koo-'tah-neh-ah]
rheumatism	el reuma [ehl reh-'oo-mah]
rib	costilla [koh-'stee-yah]
salmonella	las salmonelas [(lahs) sahl-moh-'neh-lahs]
scar	la cicatriz [lah see-kah-'trees]
scarlet fever	escarlatina [eh-skahr-lah-'tee-nah]
sciatica	ciática [see-'ah-tee-kah]
sexual organs	los órganos genitales [lohs 'ohr-gah-nohs heh-nee-'tah-lehs]
shin	tibia, espinilla ['tee-bee·ah, eh-spee-'nee-yah]
shoulder	hombro ['ohm-broh]
sick person	enfermo [ehn-'fehr-moh]
sickness, disease, illness	la enfermedad [lah ehn-fehr-meh-'dahd]
side stitches, sharp pain in the side	puntadas en el costado [poon-'tah-dahs ehn ehl koh-'stah-doh]
sinusitis	la sinusitis [lah see-noos-'ee-tees]
skin	la piel [lah pee-'ehl]
skin condition	la enfermedad de la piel [lah ehn-fehr-meh-'dahd deh lah pee-'ehl]
skull	cráneo ['krah-neh-oh]
smallpox	viruela [vee-roo-'eh-lah]

sore throat	el dolor de garganta [ehl doh-'lohr deh gahr-'gahn-tah]
specialist	el especialista [ehl eh-speh-see·ah-'lee-stah]
spine	columna vertebral [koh-'loom-nah vehr-teh-'brahl]
splint	tablilla, férula [tah-'blee-yah, 'feh-roo-lah]
sprained	dislocado [dees-loh-'kah-doh]
station	la sección [lah sehk-see-'ohn]
sting, prick	picadura; pinchazo [pee-kah-'doo-rah; peen-'chah-soh]
to stitch up	coser (*Am* dar puntos) [koh-'sehr (dahr 'poon-tohs)]
stomach	el vientre, el estómago [ehl vee-'ehn-treh, ehl eh-'stoh-mah-goh]
stomachache	el dolor de estómago [ehl doh-'lohr deh eh-'stoh-mah-goh]
sunstroke	la insolación [lah een-soh-lah-see-'ohn]
surgeon	cirujano/cirujana [see-roo-'hah-noh/see-roo-'hah-nah]
surgery	la operación [lah oh-peh-rah-see-'ohn]
sweat	el sudor [ehl soo-'dohr]
to sweat	sudar [soo-'dahr]
swelling	la hinchazón [lah een-chah-'sohn]
swollen	hinchado [een-'chah-doh]
tetanus	tétano ['teh-tah-noh]
thorax	la caja torácica, el tórax [lah 'kah-hah toh-'rah-see-kah, ehl 'toh-rahks]
toe	el dedo del pie [ehl 'deh-doh dehl 'pee-eh]
tongue	lengua ['lehn-gwah]
tonsillitis	la amigdalitis [(lah) ah-meeg-dah-'lee-tees]
tonsils	las amígdalas [lahs ah-'meeg-dah-lahs]
tooth	el diente [ehl dee-'ehn-teh]
toothache	el dolor de muelas [ehl doh-'lohr deh 'mweh-lahs]
torn ligament	rotura de ligamentos [roh-'too-rah deh lee-gah-'mehn-tohs]
throat	garganta ['gahr-'gahn-tah]

tumor	el tumor [ehl too-'mohr]
typhoid fever	el tifus [ehl 'tee-foos]
ulcer	úlcera ['ool-seh-rah]
ultrasound examination	reconocimiento con ultrasonido [reh-koh-noh-see-mee-'ehn-toh kohn ool-trah-soh-'nee-doh]
ultraviolet lamp	lámpara de cuarzo/de rayos, ultravioletas ['lahm-pah-rah deh 'kwahr-soh/deh 'rah-yohs, ool-trah-vee·oh-'leh-tahs]
urine	orina [oh-'ree-nah]
to vaccinate	vacunar [vah-koo-'nahr]
vaccination card	el carnet de vacunación [ehl kahr-'neht deh vah-koo-nah-see-'ohn]
vaccine	vacuna [vah-'koo-nah]
vein	vena ['veh-nah]
venereal disease, sexually transmitted disease	la enfermedad venérea [lah ehn-fehr-meh-'dahd veh-'neh-reh-ah]
virus	el virus [ehl 'vee-roos]
visiting hours	horario de visita [oh-'rah-ree·oh deh vee-'see-tah]
to vomit/throw up	vomitar, devolver [voh-mee-'tahr, deh-vohl-'vehr]
waiting room	sala de espera ['sah-lah deh eh-'speh-rah]
whooping cough	tosferina, (*Am* la tos convulsa) [tohs-feh-'ree-nah (lah tohs kohn-'vool-sah)]
wound	la herida [lah eh-'ree-dah]
to wound	herir [eh-'reer]
X-rays; to X-ray	radiografía; hacer una radiografía [rah-dee·oh-grah-'fee-ah; ah-'sehr 'oo-nah rah-dee·oh-grah-'fee-ah]
yellow fever	la fiebre amarilla [lah fee-'eh-breh ah-mah-'ree-yah]

At a Health Resort
En el balneario

Is this spa covered by medical insurance?	¿Está subvencionado este balneario por el seguro? [eh-'stah soob-vehn-see·oh-'nah-doh 'eh-steh bahl-neh-'ah-ree·oh pohr ehl seh-'goo-roh]
What's your doctor's diagnosis?	¿Qué diagnóstico ha hecho su médico? [keh dee·ahg-'noh-stee-koh ah 'eh-choh soo 'meh-dee-koh]
How many treatment sessions do I still have?	¿Cuántos tratamientos me quedan? ['kwahn-tohs trah-tah-mee-'ehn-tohs meh 'keh-dahn]
I'd like some extra...	Quisiera algunos suplementarios … [kee-see-'eh-rah ahl-'goo-nohs soo-pleh-mehn-'tah-ree·ohs]
I'd like to reschedule my appointment.	¿Podría cambiarme la cita para otro día? [poh-'dree-ah kahm-bee-'ahr-meh lah 'see-tah 'pah-rah 'oh-troh 'dee-ah]

Word List: Health Resort

1000-calorie diet	dieta de 1000 calorías [dee-'eh-tah deh meel kah-loh-'ree-ahs]
analgesic therapy	terapia analgésica [teh-'rah-pee·ah ah-nahl-'heh-see-kah]
autogenous (self-treatment)	entrenamiento autógeno [ehn-treh-nah-mee-'ehn-toh ow-'toh-heh-noh]
bath	baño ['bah-nyoh]
climatic station	la estación climática [lah eh-stah-see-'ohn klee-'mah-tee-kah]
connnective tissue massage	el masaje del tejido conjuntivo [ehl mah-'sah-heh dehl teh-'hee-doh kohn-hoon-'tee-voh]
cure	cura ['koo-rah]
to detoxify, to clean	desintoxicar, fango [dehs-een-tohk-see-'kahr, 'fahn-goh]
diet	dieta, el régimen [dee-'eh-tah, ehl 'reh-hee-mehn]

follow-up treatment	tratamiento ulterior [trah-tah-mee-'ehn-toh ool-teh-ree-'ohr]
foot bath	baño de pies ['bah-nyoh deh 'pee-ehs]
to give a massage	dar masaje(s) [dahr mah-'sah-heh(s)]
hot air	el aire caliente [ehl 'ah-ee-reh kah-lee-'ehn-teh]
hydrotherapeutic treatment	tratamiento hidroterápico [trah-tah-mee-'ehn-toh ee-droh-teh-'rah-pee-koh]
hydrotherapy pool	piscina para hidroterapia [pee-'see-nah 'pah-rah ee-droh-teh-'rah-pee·ah]
inhalation	la inhalación [lah een-ah-lah-see-'ohn]
to inhale	inhalar [eehn-ah-'lahr]
live cell therapy	terapia de células frescas [teh-'rah-pee·ah deh 'seh-loo-lahs 'freh-skahs]
massage	el masaje [ehl mah-'sah-heh]
masseur/masseuse	el/la masajista [ehl/lah mah-sah-'hee-stah]
medical treatment	tratamiento médico [trah-tah-mee-'ehn-toh 'meh-dee-koh]
medicinal bath	baño medicinal ['bah-nyoh meh-dee-see-'nahl]
medicinal waters	(las) aguas medicinales [(lahs) 'ah-gwahs meh-dee-see-'nah-lehs]
medicine	remedio, medicina [reh-'meh-dee·oh, meh-dee-'see-nah]
mineral water pool	piscina de agua mineral [pee-'see-nah deh 'ah-gwah mee-neh-'rahl]
mineral water spring	el manantial de agua mineral [ehl mah-nahn-tee-'ahl deh 'ah-gwah mee-neh-'rahl]
mud, mudbath	fango, baño de fango ['fahn-goh; 'bah-nyoh deh 'fahn-goh]
mudwrap	envoltura de fango [ehn-vohl-'too-rah deh 'fahn-goh]
naturist therapeutic method	método terapéutico naturista ['meh-toh-doh teh-rah-'peh-oo-tee-koh nah-too-'ree-stah]
physical therapy	fisioterapia [fee-see·oh-teh-'rah-pee·ah]
radiotherapy	radioterapia [rah-dee·oh-teh-'rah-pee·ah]

respiratory therapy | terapia respiratoria [teh-'rah-pee·ah reh-spee-rah-'toh-ree·ah]

rest cure | cura de reposo ['koo-rah deh reh-'poh-soh]

salt water bath | baño de agua salada ['bah-nyoh deh 'ah-gwah sah-'lah-dah]

sanatorium | sanatorio [sah-nah-'toh-ree-oh]

sea spa | balneario marítimo [bahl-neh-'ah-ree-oh mah-'ree-tee-moh]

spa clinic | clínica del balneario ['klee-nee-kah dehl bahl-neh-'ah-ree·oh]

spa physician | médico del balneario ['meh-dee-koh dehl bahl-neh-'ah-ree·oh]

steambath | baño turco/de vapor ['bah-nyoh 'toor-koh/deh vah-'pohr]

stimulating climate | el clima estimulante [ehl 'klee-mah eh-stee-moo-'lahn-teh]

thermal pool/bath/station | el baño/la piscina/la estación termal [ehl 'bah-nyoh/lah pee-'see-nah/lah eh-stah-see-'ohn tehr-'mahl]

treatment | tratamiento [trah-tah-mee-'ehn-toh]

ultrasound | ultrasonido [ool-trah-soh-'nee-doh]

ultraviolet lamp | lámpara de cuarzo/de rayos ultravioletas ['lahm-pah-rah deh 'kwahr-soh/deh 'rah-yohs ool-trah-vee-oh-'leh-tahs]

underwater massage | el masaje subacuático [ehl mah-'sah-heh soob-ah-'kwah-tee-koh]

whirlpool | bañera de remolinos [bah-'nyeh-rah deh reh-moh-'lee-nohs]

yoga | el yoga [ehl 'yoh-gah]

11 **A Business Trip**
Viaje de negocios

On the Way to a Business Meeting
A la reunión de negocios

How do I get to..., please?	Por favor, ¿cómo se va a...? [pohr fah-'vohr, 'koh-moh seh vah ah]
Where's the main entrance?	¿Dónde está la entrada principal? ['dohn-deh eh-'stah lah ehn-'trah-dah preen-see-'pahl]
My name is... I'm with...	Me llamo... Trabajo en la empresa... [meh 'yah-moh. trah-'bah-hoh ehn lah ehm-'preh-sah]
May I speak to... please?	¿Puedo hablar con..., por favor? ['pweh-doh ah-'blahr kohn, pohr fah-'vohr]
Could you tell... that I'm here?	¿Puede decir a... que estoy aquí? ['pweh-deh deh-'seer ah keh eh-'stoh·ee ah-'kee]
I have an appointment with...	Tengo una cita con... ['tehn-goh 'oo-nah 'see-tah kohn]
...is expecting you.	...ya le/la está esperando. [yah leh/lah eh-'stah eh-speh-'rahn-doh]
She's/He's still at a meeting.	Está todavía en una reunión. [eh-'stah toh-dah-'vee-ah ehn 'oo-nah reh-oo-nee-'ohn]
I'll take you to see...	Yo le acompaño a ver a... [yoh leh ah-kohm-'pah-nyoh ah vehr ah]
I'm sorry I'm late.	Perdone el retraso. [pehr-'doh-neh ehl reh-'trah-soh]
Please sit down.	Siéntese, por favor. [see-'ehn-teh-seh, pohr fah-'vohr]
Would you like something to drink?	¿Quiere tomar algo? [kee-'eh-reh toh-'mahr 'ahl-goh]
Did you have a good trip?	¿Ha tenido un viaje agradable? [ah teh-'nee-doh oon vee-'ah-heh ah-grah-'dah-bleh]
How much time do we have?	¿De cuánto tiempo disponemos? [deh 'kwahn-toh tee-'ehm-poh dees-poh-'neh-mohs]

When is your flight leaving?	¿Cuándo sale su avión? ['kwahn-doh 'sah-leh soo ah-vee-'ohn]
I need an interpreter.	Necesito un intérprete. [neh-seh-'see-toh oon een-'tehr-preh-teh]

Word List: Business Meeting

building	edificio [eh-dee-'fee-see·oh]
company	empresa, firma [ehm-'preh-sah, 'feer-mah]
conference	conferencia [kohn-feh-'rehn-see·ah]
conference center	centro de conferencias ['sehn-troh deh kohn-feh-'rehn-see·ahs]
conference room	sala de conferencias ['sah-lah deh kohn-feh-'rehn-see·ahs]
date	fecha ['feh-chah]
department	departamento [deh-pahr-tah-'mehn-toh]
doorman	portero [pohr-'teh-roh]
entrance	entrada [ehn-'trah-dah]
floor	piso ['pee-soh]
interpreter, translator	el/la intérprete; traductor/traductora [ehl/lah een-'tehr-preh-teh; trah-dook-'tohr/trah-dook-'toh-rah]
office	oficina [oh-fee-'see-nah]
reception	la recepción [lah reh-sehp-see-'ohn]
secretary/assistant	secretario/secretaria [seh-kreh-'tah-ree·oh/seh-kreh-'tah-ree·ah]
secretary's/assistant's office	secretariado [seh-kreh-tah-ree-'ah-doh]
session	la sesión [lah seh-see-'ohn]

Negotiations/Conferences/Trade Fairs
Negociación/Reunión/Feria

I'm looking for the…booth.	Busco el stand/puesto de la empresa… ['boo-skoh ehl eh-'stahnd/'pweh-stoh deh lah ehm-'preh-sah]
Go to room…, booth number…	Vaya a la sala…, stand número… ['vah-yah ah lah 'sah-lah, eh-'stahnd 'noo-meh-roh]

We manufacture…	Somos fabricantes de… ['soh-mohs fah-bree-'kahn-tehs deh]
We deal in...	Hacemos negocios con... [ah-'seh-mohs neh-'goh-see·ohs kohn]
Do you have information on…?	¿Tienen ustedes material de información sobre…? [tee-'eh-nehn oo-'steh-dehs mah-teh-ree-'ahl deh een-fohr-mah-see-'ohn 'soh-breh.]
We can send you detailed information on…	Podemos enviarle material abundante sobre… [poh-'deh-mohs ehn-vee-'ahr-leh mah-teh-ree-'ahl ah-boon-'dahn-teh 'soh-breh]
Who is in charge of…?	¿Quién es el encargado de…? [kee-'ehen ehs ehl ehn-kahr-'gah-doh deh]
Could you make us an offer?	¿Podrían ustedes hacernos una oferta? [poh-'dree-ahn oo-'steh-dehs ah-'sehr-nohs 'oo-nah oh-'fehr-tah]
We should arrange a meeting.	Deberíamos ponernos de acuerdo en una fecha para vernos. [deh-beh-'ree-ah-mohs poh-'nehr-nohs deh ah-'kwehr-doh ehn 'oo-nah 'feh-chah 'pah-rah 'vehr-nohs]
Here's my business card.	Aquí tiene mi tarjeta de visita. [ah-'kee tee-'eh-neh mee tahr-'heh-tah deh vee-'see-tah]

Word List: Negotiations/Conferences/Trade Fairs

advertising	la publicidad [lah poo-blee-see-'dahd]
advertising campaign	campaña publicitaria [kahm-'pah-nyah poo-blee-see-'tah-ree·ah]
advertising material	el material publicitario [ehl mah-teh-ree-'ahl poo-blee-see-'tah-ree·oh]
agenda	el orden del día [ehl 'ohr-dehn dehl 'dee-ah]
agent	la representación [lah reh-preh-sehn-tah-see-'ohn]

authorized dealer	concesionario oficial [kohn-seh-see·oh-'nah-ree·oh oh-fee-see-'ahl]
bill of sale	contrato de compra [kohn-'trah-toh deh 'kohm-prah]
brochure, prospectus	folleto, prospecto [foh-'yeh-toh, proh-'spehk-toh]
budget	presupuesto [preh-soo-'pweh-stoh]
business card	tarjeta de visita [tahr-'heh-tah deh vee-'see-tah]
business connections	las relaciones comerciales [lahs reh-lah-see-'oh-nehs koh-mehr-see-'ah-lehs]
business partner/associate	socio comercial ['soh-see·oh koh-mehr-see-'ahl]
catalog	catálogo [kah-'tah-loh-goh]
client	el cliente/clienta [ehl klee-'ehn-teh/klee-'ehn-tah]
concern	consorcio [kohn-'sohr-see·oh]
condition	la condición [lah kohn-dee-see-'ohn]
conference	conferencia [kohn-feh-'rehn-see·ah]
contact person	encargado, el responsable [ehn-kahr-'gah-doh, ehl reh-spohn-'sah-bleh]
contract	contrato [kohn-'trah-toh]
cooperation	la cooperación [lah koh-oh-peh-rah-see-'ohn]
costs	los costos [lohs 'koh-stohs]
discount	descuento, rebaja [dehs-'kwehn-toh, reh-'bah-hah]
distribution	la distribución [lah dees-tree-boo-see-'ohn]
distribution network	la red de distribución [lah rehd deh dees-tree-boo-see-'ohn]
exhibitor	el expositor [ehl ehks-poh-see-'tohr]
export	la exportación [lah ehks-pohr-tah-see-'ohn]
exporter	el exportador [ehl ehks-pohr-tah-'dohr]
financing	la financiación [lah fee-nahn-see·ah-see-'ohn]
freight	carga, el flete ['kahr-gah, ehl 'fleh-teh]
guarantee	garantía [gah-rahn-'tee-ah]
hall	sala ['sah-lah]
hall layout	plano de la sala ['plah-noh deh lah 'sah-lah]

import	la importación [lah eem-pohr-tah-see-'ohn]
importer	el importador [ehl eem-pohr-tah-'dohr]
industrial trade fair	feria industrial ['feh-ree·ah een-doo-stree-'ahl]
information	el material informativo [ehl mah-teh-ree-'ahl een-fohr-mah-'tee-voh]
information booth	el stand/puesto de información [ehl eh-'stahnd/'pweh-stoh deh een-fohr-mah-see-'ohn]
insurance	seguro [seh-'goo-roh]
interested in, to be	estar interesado en [eh-'stahr een-teh-reh-'sah-doh ehn]
invoice	factura [fahk-'too-rah]
joint venture	joint-venture [dyoh·'eent 'vehn-toor]
leasing	el leasing [ehl 'lee-seeng]
licensing (agreement)	contrato de licencia [(kohn-'trah-toh deh) lee-'sehn-see·ah]
list of exhibitors	catálogo de expositores [kah-'tah-loh-goh deh ehks-poh-see-'toh-rehs]
main office	la central [lah sehn-'trahl]
manufacturer	el/la fabricante [ehl/lah fah-bree-'kahn-teh]
marketing	el marketing [ehl mahr-keh-'teeng]
meeting	encuentro, la reunión [ehn-'kwehn-troh, lah reh-oo-nee-'ohn]
meeting point	el lugar de encuentro [ehl loo-'gahr deh ehn-'kwehn-troh]
minutes (of a meeting)	acta (de una reunión) ['ahk-tah (deh 'oo-nah reh-oo-nee-'ohn)]
offer	oferta [oh-'fehr-tah]
order	encargo, pedido [ehn-'kahr-goh, peh-'dee-doh]
order confirmation	la confirmación del pedido [lah kohn-feer-mah-see-'ohn dehl peh-'dee-doh]
packing	el embalaje [ehl ehm-bah-'lah-heh]
price	precio ['preh-see·oh]
price list	lista de precios ['lee-stah deh 'reh-see·ohs]
product	mercancía (*Am* mercadería) [mehr-kahn-'see·ah (mehr-kah-deh-'ree-ah)]

product list	lista de mercancías (*Am* mercaderías) ['lee-stah deh mehr-kahn-'see·ahs (mehr-kah-deh-'ree-ahs)]
production	la producción [lah proh-dook-see-'ohn]
public relations	las relaciones públicas [lahs reh-lah-see-'oh-nehs 'poo-blee-kahs]
retailer	el/la comerciante al por menor, el/la minorista [ehl/lah koh-mehr-see-'ahn-teh ahl pohr meh-'nohr, ehl/lah mee-noh-'ree-stah]
sales	la venta/las ventas [lah 'vehn-tah/lahs 'vehn-tahs]
sales promotion	la promoción de ventas [lah proh-moh-see-'ohn deh 'vehn-tahs]
sales representative	el/la representante [ehl/lah reh-preh-sehn-'tahn-teh]
sales tax	impuesto sobre el tráfico de empresas (*Am* sobre la cifra de negocios) [eem-'pweh-stoh 'soh-breh ehl 'trah-fee-koh deh ehm-'preh-sahs ('soh-breh lah 'see-frah deh neh-'goh-see·ohs)]
salesperson	el vendedor/la vendedora [ehl vehn-deh-'dohr/lah vehn-deh-'doh-rah]
sample	muestra ['mweh-strah]
subsidiary	la (sociedad) filial [lah (soh-see-eh-'dahd) fee-lee-'ahl]
supplier	el proveedor, el suministrador [ehl proh-veh-eh-'dohr, ehl soo-mee-nee-strah-'dohr]
supply	entrega [ehn-'treh-gah]
supply schedule	plazo de entrega ['plah-soh deh ehn-'treh-gah]
terms of a contract	las condiciones del contrato [lahs kohn-dee-see-'oh-nehs dehl kohn-'trah-toh]
terms of payment	las condiciones de pago [lahs kohn-dee-see-'oh-nehs deh 'pah-goh]
terms of supply	las condiciones de entrega [lahs kohn-dee-see-'oh-nehs deh ehn-'treh-gah]
trade fair	feria comercial ['feh-ree·ah koh-mehr-see-'ahl]

trade fair booth/stall	el stand/puesto de la feria [ehl eh-'stahnd/'pweh-stoh deh lah 'feh-ree-ah]
trade fair center	punto central de la feria ['poon-toh sehn-'trahl deh lah 'feh-ree-ah]
trade fair discount	descuento de la feria [dehs-'kwehn-toh deh lah 'feh-ree-ah]
trade fair hostess	azafata de la feria [ah-sah-'fah-tah deh lah 'feh-ree-ah]
trade fair management	la dirección de la feria [lah dee-rehk-see'ohn deh lah 'feh-ree-ah]
trade fair pass	el pase para la feria [ehl 'pah-seh 'pah-rah lah 'feh-ree-ah]
trade fair service	servicio de la feria [sehr-'vee-see-oh deh lah 'feh-ree-ah]
training	la formación, entrenamiento [lah fohr-mah-see-'ohn, ehn-treh-nah-mee-'ehn-toh]
transportation	el transporte [ehl trahns-'pohr-teh]
traveling salesperson	el/la representante de comercio [ehl/lah reh-preh-sehn-'tahn-teh deh koh-'mehr-see-oh]
type of business	forma de negocio ['fohr-mah deh neh-'goh-see-oh]
value added tax *(VAT)*	impuesto sobre el valor adjunto *(Am* añadido) *(IVA)* [eem-'pweh-stoh 'soh-breh ehl vah-'lohr ahd-'hoon-toh (ah-nyah-'dee-doh) ('ee-vah)]
wholesaler	el/la mayorista, el/la comerciante al por mayor [ehl/lah mah-yoh-'ree-stah, ehl/lah koh-mehr-see-'ahn-teh ahl pohr mah-'yohr]

Business Equipment
Dotación

Could you make some copies of this for me, please?	¿Me podría hacer unas copias? [meh poh-'dree-ah ah-'sehr 'oo-nahs 'koh-pee·ahs]
I need an overhead projector for my talk.	Necesito un retroproyector para mi conferencia. [neh-seh-'see-toh oon reh-troh-proh-yehk-'tohr 'pah-rah mee kohn-feh-'rehn-see·ah]
Could you get me…, please?	¿Podría usted proporcionarme…? [poh-'dree-ah oo-'stehd proh-pohr-see·oh-'nahr-meh]

Word List: Business Equipment

catalog	catálogo [kah-'tah-loh-goh]
copier *(color)*	fotocopiadora *(en color)* [foh-toh-koh-pee·ah-'doh-rah]
copy	copia ['koh-pee·ah]
disk	la/el diskete, disquete [lah/ehl dee-'skeh-teh, dee-'skeh-teh]
display material	el material de exposición [ehl mah-teh-ree-'ahl deh ehk-spoh-see-see-'ohn]
extension cord	el cordón/el cable de empalme [ehl kohr-'dohn/ehl 'kah-bleh deh ehm-'pahl-meh]
fax	el telefax [ehl teh-leh-'fahks]
flip chart	el trípode con papel [ehl 'tree-poh-deh kohn pah-'pehl]
lectern	tribuna de oradores [tree-'boo-nah deh oh-rah-'doh-rehs]
marker	el rotulador [ehl roh-too-lah-'dohr]
microphone	micrófono [mee-'kroh-foh-noh]
modem	(el) modem [ehl 'moh-dehm]
notepad	el bloc/cuaderno de notas [ehl blohk/kwah-'dehr-noh deh 'noh-tahs]
overhead projector	el retroproyector [ehl reh-troh-proh-yehk-'tohr]

overhead projector marker	el rotulador para retroproyector [ehl roh-too-lah-'dohr 'pah-rah reh-troh-proh-yehk-'tohr]
PC	el ordenador personal [ehl ohr-deh-nah-'dohr pehr-soh-'nahl]
pen; pencil	lapicero; el lápiz [lah-pee-'seh-roh; ehl 'lah-pees]
phone	teléfono [teh-'leh-foh-noh]
printer	impresora [eem-preh-'soh-rah]
telex	el télex [ehl 'teh-lehks]
video recorder	aparato de vídeo [ah-pah-'rah-toh deh 'vee-deh-oh]
word processor	el sistema de procesamiento de datos [ehl see-'steh-mah deh proh-seh-sah-mee-'ehn-toh deh 'dah-tohs]

A Short Grammar

Articles

	Singular and Plural Definite Article **the** *el, la, los, las*	Indefinite articles: **a, an, some** *un, una, unos, unas*
singular masculine feminine	**el** amigo the friend **la** rosa the rose	**un** amigo a friend **una** rosa a rose
plural masculine feminine	**los** amigos the friends **las** rosas the roses	**unos** amigos some friends **unas** rosas some roses

Neuter *lo* is used before a masculine singular adjective, a past participle, or a possessive to form abstract nouns:
lo bueno (what is good); **lo** acordado (what is/was agreed); **lo** mío (what is mine); Es bonito ver **lo** bien y **lo** de prisa que trabaja. It's great to see how well and fast he works.

Definite articles are used in the:

● Hour   ● Day   ● Date

a **las 7** at 7 o'clock Son **las 10.** It's 10 o'clock.	**El miércoles** viene Juan. Juan is arriving on Wednesday. **Los lunes** no trabajo. I don't work on Mondays.	**el año pasado** last year **la semana que viene** next week

● In generic expressions:

¿Le gusta **el vino tinto**? **Los perros** son fieles.	Do you like red wine? Dogs are loyal.

● Hobbies   ● Sports   ● Sports teams

tocar **la guitarra** to play the guitar	jugar **al tenis** to play tennis	**el Barcelona, el Real Madrid** the Barcelona team, the Real Madrid team

- With nouns that express title, rank, or condition (but not when addressing a person directly):

el señor García	Mr. García	Buenos días, profesor.
el profesor Ruiz	Professor Ruiz	Good morning, professor.

- With the names of many countries and cities:

La Habana, La Paz **El Cairo**	**(el)** Uruguay, **(el)** Brasil, **(el)** Japón, **(el)** Canadá, **(la)** Argentina, **(la)** India

Do not use articles:

- When the person's title comes first
- When addressing the person directly

don José	¿Qué tal, **señorita**?	How are you, Miss?
doña Isabel	¿Un café, **doctor**?	Coffee, doctor?

- Also: en **febrero** in February; **diciembre** December
- For means of transportation, use the preposition *en*:
  ir en **tren** / en **taxi**   take the train / take a taxi

The indefinite article is not used
before *otro,* and seldom before *medio* and *parte:*

otro libro	another book
dentro de **media** hora	in half an hour
parte de los alumnos	part of the students

Nouns: Gender and Number

In Spanish, nouns can be masculine or feminine:

● For masculine nouns ending in -o, feminine in -a, the plural is + -s;

● For masculine or feminine nouns ending in -e, the plural is + -s.

● The plural of nouns ending in consonants and in -í, -ú is -es;
  (most masculine nouns end in -ón, -l, -r);
  (most feminine nouns end in -ión, -ad, -z):

Singular		Plural	
el libro	the book	los libros	the books
la mesa	the table	las mesas	the tables
el coche	the car	los coches	the cars
la lente	the lens	las lentes	the lenses
el árbol	the tree	los árboles	the trees
la verdad	the truth	las verdades	the truths
el rubí	the ruby	los rubíes	the rubies
el pastor	the shepherd	los pastores	the shepherds
la nación	the nation	las naciones	the nations

● The plural of nouns ending in -s is indicated by the article that precedes them: el martes Tuesday, los martes; el cumpleaños the birthday, los cumpleaños; el paraguas the umbrella, los paraguas.

Exceptions

● There are some masculine nouns that end in -a:

el poeta	the poet	el telegrama	the telegram
el día	the day	el programa	the program
el mapa	the map	el tema	the subject
el clima	the climate	el poema	the poem

● There are some feminine nouns that end in -o:

la mano	the hand	la radio	the radio
la foto	the photo	la moto	the motorcycle

- Nouns that end in -*ista* are both feminine and masculine:

| el turista, la turista | the tourist(s) | los turistas, las turistas |
| el artista, la artista | the artist(s) | los artistas, las artistas |

Special characteristics

- Some nouns have a different meaning in the plural:

el padre	the father	los padres	the parents
la letra	the letter (of the alphabet) the handwriting	las letras	literature
la esposa	the wife	las esposas	the handcuffs

- Some nouns are used only in the plural:
  las gafas the glasses; los alrededores the surrounding area
  (some are only singular: la gente people)

- The letters of the alphabet are always feminine:
  la **a**, la **x** (equis)
  Numerals, rivers and almost all trees are masculine:
  el nueve nine; el Amazonas; el roble the oak

- Newspaper names are often masculine:
  "El País", el "Independiente"; but: "La Vanguardia"

- Some nouns have a different meaning according to their gender:

el frente	the front	la frente	the forehead
el capital	the capital (money)	la capital	the capital (of a country)
el cura	the priest	la cura	the cure
el policía	the policeman	la policía	the police/ policewoman

- Feminine nouns that begin with a stressed *a* use the article *el* in singular, and *las* in plural:
  el alma the soul, las almas; el águila the eagle, las águilas

Suffixes (Noun Endings)

- The diminutive suffixes -*ito*, -*cito*, -*ico*, -*illo* may indicate size, affection, admiration, appreciation, or pity:

paja**rito**, paja**rico**, paja**rillo**	little bird
un coche**cito**	a small stroller/car
affectionate connotation	
¡Hola, Pedrito!	Hi, Peter!

- The augmentative suffixes -*ón, -tón, -azo, -ote* may indicate size, admiration or appreciation:
  hombr**ón**, hombr**ote** big man, hunk

- The pejorative suffixes -*aco, -acho, -ucho* indicate lack of worth or dignity:
  libr**aco** worthless book

Prepositions
(Four Cases)

Subject (Who? What?)	**El coche** corre.	The car runs.
Direct Object (What?)	Juan compra **el coche**.	Juan buys the car.
Personal Direct Object (Who? To Whom?)	Doy la mano **a mi amigo**.	I shake my friend's hand.
Posession (Of Who/Whom?)	El piso **de María** es caro.	Maria's apartment is expensive.

Preposition *a*

- The preposition *a* (or *para*) expresses motion, beginning, or purpose; time, distance, or price; manner; and destination. A personal direct object is usually preceded by the personal *a*. Some verbs, such as *tener, buscar, necesitar,* and *encontrar,* usually don't take the personal *a*.

Acompaño **a** Pilar.	I accompany Pilar.
Tengo muchos amigos.	I have many friends.
¿Entiendes **al** profesor?	Do you understand the teacher?
Necesitamos un médico.	We need a doctor.

a + **el** = **al**	Voy **al** cine.	I'm going to the movies.
de + **el** = **del**	Viene **del** jardín.	(He/She) is coming from the garden.

Preposition *de*

● The preposition *de* expresses posesssion, matter or material, identification, origin, cause, and amount or content.

● Possession:

la mesa **de** Juanita	Juanita's table
las novelas **de** Cervantes	the novels of Cervantes

● Matter or material:

mesa **de** mármol	marble table

● Identification:

la dama **del** collar **de** perlas	the lady with the pearl necklace
el mes **de** junio	the month of June

● Origin:

Soy **de** Valencia.	I'm from Valencia.

● Cause:

María tiembla **de** miedo.	Maria shudders with fear.

● Amount or content:

dos kilos **de** manzanas	two kilos of apples
un litro **de** leche	a liter of milk
una taza **de** té	a cup of tea

Adjectives

Singular and Plural

● Adjective endings in *-o* change to *-a* to form the feminine *-a*:

un jardín hermos**o**	a beautiful garden
una muchacha hermos**a**	a beautiful girl

● Masculine adjectives ending in *-án, -ón,* and *-or* add *-a* to form the feminine:

trabajad**or**, trabajad**ora**	worker
harag**án**, harag**ana**	lazy
burl**ón**, burl**ona**	teaser

● Adjectives of nationality also add an *-a* to form the feminine (except when ending in *-í, -e*):

inglés, ingles**a**	English
español, español**a**	Spanish
marroqu**í**; árab**e**	Moroccan; Arab

● All other adjectives are the same for both genders:

el tiempo / la vida brev**e**	life is short
el traje / la camisa gri**s**	the gray suit/shirt

● The plural of adjectives is formed by adding an *-s* to those ending in a vowel and *-es* to those ending in a consonant:

las plant**as** bonit**as**	the beautiful plants
los zapat**os** azul**es**	the blue shoes
los chic**os** grand**es**	the big boys

Agreement between Noun and Adjective

An adjective agrees in number and in gender with the noun or pronoun it modifies:

el muchacho	**rubio**	the blond boy
la muchacha	**rubia**	the blond girl
los muchachos	**rubios**	the blond boys
las muchachas	**rubias**	the blond girls

Carlos es **rubio**.	Carlos is blond.
¿Conoces a esa chica **rubia**?	Do you know that blond girl?
Esos chicos son **rubios**.	Those boys are blond.
Anita y Cristina son **rubias**.	Anita and Cristina are blond.

Position of Adjectives

● A descriptive adjective usually follows the noun:

el traje negro / azul / gris	the black / blue / gray suit
un abrigo alemán / inglés	a German / an English coat

● Some adjectives have different meanings according to their position in relation to the noun:

la ahorrativa hormiga — the thrifty ant
un **pobre** hombre — a poor man (pity)
However: un hombre **pobre** — a poor man (finances)

● *Bueno* and *malo* drop the final *-o* if placed before a noun in the singular, either masculine or feminine:
un **buen** comienzo a good beginning; un **mal** día a bad day

● When it means great, *grande* precedes the noun and drops *-de* before a singular noun of either gender:
un gran hombre, una **gran** mujer a great man, a great woman

● However: un libro grande a big book

● *Mucho, poco* and *otro* change according to the noun they qualify:
mucha / poca suerte lots of / little luck; **otro** vaso another glass;
otra mujer another woman

Adverbs

● Some adverbs do not have a corresponding adjective. They can express time (*hoy, nunca, temprano, siempre*), place (*arriba, encima, delante, lejos*), quantity (*casi, demasiado, más, menos*). There are also adverbial phrases, like *sin embargo* (however) and *de repente* (suddenly):

Juan llegará **pronto**.	Juan will arrive soon.
A la larga no lo hará.	In the long run, he won't do it.

- Many adverbs are formed by adding the ending *-mente* to the feminine form of an adjective, if there is one:

Lo he hecho **rápidamente**.	I've done it quickly.
un día **terriblemente** frío	a terribly cold day
Leo **principalmente** novelas.	I mostly read novels.

- *muy* (very) is used before an adjective or adverb; with verbs or by itself, *mucho* is used:

Es un vino **muy** bueno.	It's a very good wine.
Hemos llegado **muy** tarde.	We arrived very late.
Marisa escribe **mucho**.	Marisa writes a lot.
Ha escrito **muchas** novelas.	He has written many novels.

Comparison of Adjectives and Adverbs

caro	**más caro**	**el más caro**	**carísimo**
expensive	more expensive	the most expensive	extremely expensive

Las rosas son **más caras** que los claveles.
Roses are more expensive than carnations.
Estas rosas son **carísimas / las más caras**.
These roses are extremely expensive/the most expensive ones.

- *tan... como* (as... as); *tanto como* (as much as)
  tanto/tanta/tantos/tantas... como (as many... as):

tan before adverb	Cose **tan** bien **como** tú.	(He/She) sews as well as you.
before adjective	Es **tan** alta **como** Juan.	She is as tall as Juan.
tanto as adverbial phrase	Gana **tanto** **como** él.	(He/She) earns as much as him.
tanto, tanta, tantos, tantas as adjective	**tantos** amigos y **tanta** suerte **como** Julia as many friends and as much luck as Julia. **tanto** not as many/much	

● *el mismo/la misma …que* (the same …as)
  lo mismo/igual que (the same):

los mismos problemas **que** tú	the same problems as you
lo mismo/igual que hoy	the same as today

● *más… que, menos… que* (more… than, less… than) is used
  after an affirmative or negative statement.
  However: **más de** (before exact date, hour, payment) **más que**
  (more than):

Luis trabaja **más que** tú.	Luis works more than you.
Gana **más de** 50.000 pesetas.	(He/She) earns more than 50 000 pesetas.
No hay **más que** dos botellas.	There are just/only two bottles.

Irregular Comparisons

● Adverbs: *bien, mejor,* muy bien; *mal, peor,* muy mal:
  Me siento **mejor** / muy mal. I feel better/very bad.

● Adjectives: bueno, malo, grande, pequeño:

bueno	**mejor**/más bueno	buenísimo/**óptimo**	el **mejor**
malo	**peor**/más malo	malísimo/**pésimo**	el **peor**
grande	**mayor**/más grande	grandísimo/**máximo**	el **mayor**
pequeño	**menor**/más pequeño	pequeñísimo/**mínimo**	el **menor**

● Spelling and phonetic changes of adjectives ending in *-ble, -co,
  -go, -guo*:

ama**ble**	más/muy/el más amable	amab**ilísimo**
ri**co**	más/muy/el más rico	ri**quísimo**
anti**guo**	más/muy/el más antiguo	anti**quísimo**
amar**go**	más/muy/el más amargo	amar**guísimo**

!

Verbs

a) Regular verbs

All Spanish verbs are classified as verbs of the first, second, or third conjugation according to the ending of the infinitive

	-ar		**-er**	**-ir**
	hablar speak/talk		comprender understand	recibir receive
yo tú	habl**o** habl**as**	I speak/talk you (*fam*) speak/talk	comprend**o** comprend**es**	recib**o** recib**es**
él ella usted	habl**a**	he speaks/ talks she speaks/ talks you (*polite*) speak/talk	comprend**e**	recib**e**
nosotros, -as	habl**amos**	we speak/ talk	comprend**emos**	recib**imos**
vosotros, -as	habl**áis**	you (*pl*) speak/talk	comprend**éis**	recib**ís**
ellos ellas ustedes	habl**an**	they speak/ talk they speak/ talk they speak/ talk	comprend**en**	recib**en**
	habl**ado**	spoken/ talked	comprend**ido**	recib**ido**

b) ser – estar; haber – tener

- *Ser* and *estar:* to be. *Ser* expresses permanent characteristics; *estar* expresses temporary ones. *Haber* and *tener:* to have. *Haber* is used as an auxiliary verb to form all compound verb tenses.

	ser	**estar**	to be	**haber**	**tener**	to have
yo	soy	estoy	I am	he	tengo	I have
tú	eres	estás	You are	has	tienes	You have
él ella usted	es	está	He/she /it is	ha	tiene	He/she/it has
nosotros, -as	somos	estamos	We are	hemos	tenemos	We have
vosotros, -as	sois	estáis	You are	habéis	tenéis	You have
ellos ellas ustedes	son	están	They are	han	tienen	They have

- (See conjugation of *ser* and *estar* pp. 291, 292.)

- *Haber* as an auxiliary verb forms compound tenses with the past participle of the main verbs (see also the impersonal *hay*, p. 293): **Hemos** comido bien. We have eaten well.

- *Tener* (to have): ¿**Tienes** dinero? Do you have money?

- Personal pronouns are usually omitted because verb endings indicate the person referred to; they are used when needed to clarify the meaning of the sentence.

- The polite forms of address (*usted, ustedes*) take a third person singular or plural verb:
  ¿Qué tal **está** usted, señor Pérez?   How are you, Mr. Pérez?
  ¿**Tienen** ustedes todavía tiempo?   Do you still have time?/ Do you have any time left?

!

c) Verbs with diphthongs

Every verb is composed of a stem and an ending. There is a group of verbs in which the *e* of the stem changes to *ie* and the *o* to *ue*:
empezar (to begin/start): emp**ie**zo, emp**ie**zas, emp**ie**za, empezamos, empezáis, emp**ie**zan.
volver (to return/turn): v**ue**lvo, v**ue**lves, v**ue**lve, volvemos, volvéis, v**ue**lven.

Other verbs in this group are:

cerrar	to close	entender	to understand
pensar	to think	perder	to lose
despertarse	to wake up	querer	to want, to love
sentarse	to sit (down)	poder	can, to be able to
encontrar	to find	doler	to ache
costar	to cost	preferir	to prefer
contar	to count	sentir	to feel
acostarse	to lie down, to go to bed	dormir	to sleep

d) Irregular participles

abrir	open	abierto	morir	dead	muerto
cubrir	covered	cubierto	resolver	solved	resuelto
escribir	written	escrito	romper	broken	roto

Imperfect, Preterite, and Perfect Indicative

There are two past tenses in Spanish: the imperfect and the preterite. The imperfect is used to express an action going on in the past. The preterite expresses the past as a completed action.

	habl**ar**	comprend**er**	recib**ir**
Imperfect	habl**aba**	comprend**ía**	recib**ía**
	habl**abas**	comprend**ías**	recib**ías**
	habl**aba**	comprend**ía**	recib**ía**
	habl**ábamos**	comprend**íamos**	recib**íamos**
	habl**abais**	comprend**íais**	recib**íais**
	habl**aban**	comprend**ían**	recib**ían**

	hablar	comprender	recibir
Preterite	hablé hablaste habló hablamos hablasteis hablaron	comprendí comprendiste comprendió comprendimos comprendisteis comprendieron	recibí recibiste recibió recibimos recibisteis recibieron

● The imperfect and the preterite often appear in the same sentence, to express that something happened while something else was going on:

Imperfect	Preterite
Cuando **iba** a dormirme, When I was about to fall asleep,	**sonó** el teléfono. the phone rang.
Quería ser médico He wanted to be a doctor,	pero no **terminó** la carrera. but he did not finish medical school.
Sabías mis señas You knew my address,	pero no **escribiste.** but you did not write.

Siempre **llamaba** por teléfono cuando **estábamos** durmiendo.
(He/She) always phoned us when we were sleeping.
Ayer **llamó** por teléfono cuando **estábamos** durmiendo.
Yesterday, (he/she) phoned when we were sleeping.

Perfect Indicative and Preterite

● The perfect indicative is formed with the present indicative of *haber* and the past participle of the main verb. Like the English present perfect, it refers to a recent action that still has an impact on the present:

Perfect indicative
he hablado I have talked
he comprendido I have understood
he recibido I have received

- The perfect indicative and the preterite both express the past as a concluded event, but in two different ways: as still having repercussions on the present (perfect indicative) and as frozen history (preterite).

Perfect indicative	Preterite
Este año **he tenido** suerte. This year, I've been lucky.	Ayer **vi** a Juan en el concierto. Yesterday, I saw Juan at a concert.
¿Ya **ha venido** Anita? Has Anita arrived?	El sábado pasado **dormimos** hasta las 10. Last Saturday we slept until ten.

The Future

The future tense has a single set of endings for all three conjugations.

hablar	leer	escribir
hablar**é** hablar**ás** hablar**á** hablar**emos** hablar**éis** hablar**án**	leer**é** leer**ás** leer**á** leer**emos** leer**éis** leer**án**	escribir**é** escribir**ás** escribir**á** escribir**emos** escribir**éis** escribir**án**

Another way to express the future is with the verb *ir* + a + *infinitive:*

Voy a hablar con Pedro.   I'm going to speak/talk to Pedro.
¿**Vas a leer** pronto el libro?   Are you going to read this book soon?
Vamos a escribir a Pilar.   We're going to write to Pilar.

The Conditional

The conditional has the same set of endings for all three conjugations.

hablar	leer	escribir
hablaría	leería	escribiría
hablarías	leerías	escribiría
hablaría	leería	escribiría
hablaríamos	leeríamos	escribiríamos
hablaríais	leeríais	escribiríais
hablarían	leerían	escribirían

The conditional is also used for polite requests:

¿**Podría** usted ayudarme?	Would you help me?
Querría pedirle algo.	I would like to ask you something.
Si lo tuviera, te lo **daría**.	If I had it, I would give it to you.

Imperative

a) affirmative commands

	hablar speak/talk	comer eat	escribir write
you *(fam, sing)*	habla	come	escribe
you *(pl)*	hablad	comed	escribid
you *(polite, sing)*	hable	coma	escriba
they	hablen	coman	escriban

- In colloquial language, the final *-d* of the second-person plural—i.e., cerrad, hablad, comed, escribid—may sound like an *-r*, as if an infinitive is being used:
  Cerrar *(coll)* la puerta, por favor. Close the door, please.

- In Latin America, *ustedes* is used instead of *vosotros*:
  No **hablen** tan alto, niños. Don't talk so loud, children.
  ¿**Han** venido en coche? Did you drive here?

b) negative commands

you (*sing*)	no hables	no comas	no escribas
you (*pl*)	no habléis	no comáis	no escribáis
you (*polite, sing.*)	no hable (usted)	no coma	no escriba
they	no hablen (ustedes)	no coman	no escriban

Gerund

cantar	cantando	reír (se)	riendo (riéndose)	pedir	pidiendo
comer	comiendo	leer	leyendo	sentir	sintiendo
escribir	escribiendo	oír	oyendo	dormir	durmiendo

(See also below.)

Siempre **está cantando**.	(He/she) is always singing.
¿Todavía **estás comiendo**?	Are you still eating?
¡Siga usted **leyendo**!	Go on reading!
¿Por qué (te)**estás riendo**?	Why are you laughing?
Leyendo se aprende mucho.	You can learn much by reading.

Gerund + *estar, ir, seguir* is a continuous form similar to the present participle in English.

Main Irregular Verbs (See also p. 283.)

andar to go, to be

Preterite:	anduve, anduviste, anduvo, anduvimos, etc.

caber to fit (in/into); to be possible

Present:	quepo, cabes, cabe, cabemos, cabéis, caben
Future:	cabré, cabrás, cabrá, cabremos, cabréis, cabrán
Preterite:	cupe, cupiste, cupo, cupimos, cupisteis, cupieron
Conditional:	cabría, cabrías, cabría, cabríamos, etc.

caer(se) fallen

Present:	caigo, caes, cae, caemos, caéis, caen
Imperative:	no te caigas, no os caigáis, no se caiga, etc.

coger to take; to catch; to get

Present:	cojo, coges, coge, cogemos, cogéis, cogen
Imperative:	coge/no cojas, coged/no cojáis, (no) coja, etc.

conducir to conduct; to direct; to drive

Present:	conduzco, conduces, conduce, conducimos, etc.
Preterite:	conduje, condujiste, condujo, condujimos, etc.
Imperative:	conduce/no conduzcas, conducid/no conduzcáis, (no) conduzca, (no) conduzcan.

Insert z before the endings -co, -ca:
producir to produce, **traducir** to translate

conocer to know; to meet; **agradecer** danken

Present:	conozco, conoces, conoce, conocemos, etc.
	agradezco, agradeces, etc.

dar to give

Present:	doy, das, da, damos, dais, dan
Preterite:	di, diste, dio, dimos, disteis, dieron

decir to say   dicho said   Gerund: diciendo

Present:	digo, dices, dice, decimos, decís, dicen
Future:	diré, dirás, dirá, diremos, diréis, dirán
Preterite:	dije, dijiste, dijo, dijimos, dijisteis, dijeron
Conditional:	diría, dirías, diría, diríamos, diríais, dirían
Imperative:	di/no digas, decid/no digáis, (no) diga, (no) digan

estar to be (See also pp. 281, 282, 291, 292.)

Present:	estoy, estás, está, estamos, estáis, están
Preterite:	estuve, estuviste, estuvo, estuvimos, etc.

!

haber   to have (as auxiliary verb: *he* estado, see also p. 282)

Present:	he, has, ha, hemos, habéis, han
Future:	habré, habrás, habrá, habremos, habréis, habrán
Preterite:	hube, hubiste, hubo, hubimos, hubisteis, hubieron
Conditional:	habría, habrías, habría, habríamos, etc.

hacer   to do; to make   hecho   done; made

Present:	hago, haces, hace, hacemos, hacéis, hacen
Future:	haré, harás, hará, haremos, haréis, harán
Preterite:	hice, hiciste, hizo, hicimos, hicisteis, hicieron
Conditional:	haría, harías, haría, haríamos, haríais, harían
Imperative:	haz/no hagas, haced/no hagáis, (no) haga, etc.

ir   to go   ido   gone   Gerund: yendo

Present:	voy, vas, va, vamos, vais, van
Preterite:	fui, fuiste, fue, fuimos, fuisteis, fueron
Imperfect:	iba, ibas, iba, íbamos, ibais, iban
Imperative:	ve/no vayas, id/no vayáis, (no) vaya, (no) vayan

oír   to hear   Gerund: oyendo

Present:	oigo, oyes, oye, oímos, oís, oyen
Preterite:	oí, oíste, oyó, oímos, oísteis, oyeron
Imperative:	oye/no oigas, oíd/no oigáis, (no) oiga, (no) oigan

poder   to be able to   Gerund: pudiendo

Present:	puedo, puedes, puede, podemos, podéis, pueden
Future:	podré, podrás, podrá, podremos, podréis, podrán
Preterite:	pude, pudiste, pudo, pudimos, etc.
Conditional:	podría, podrías, podría, podríamos, etc.

poner   to put   puesto   put

Present:	pongo, pones, pone, ponemos, ponéis, ponen
Future:	pondré, pondrás, pondrá, pondremos, etc.
Preterite:	puse, pusiste, puso, pusimos, etc.
Conditional:	pondría, pondrías, pondría, pondríamos, etc.
Imperative:	pon/no pongas, poned/no pongáis, (no) ponga, (no) pongan

querer   to want; to love

Present:	quiero, quieres, quiere, queremos, queréis, quieren
Future:	querré, querrás, querrá, querremos, etc.
Preterite:	quise, quisiste, quiso, quisimos, etc.
Conditional:	querría, querrías, querría, querríamos, etc.

reír(se)   to laugh   Gerund: laughing

Present:	río, ríes, ríe, reímos, reís, ríen
Preterite:	reí, reíste, rió, reímos, reísteis, rieron
Imperative:	ríe/no rías, reíd/no riáis, (no) ría, (no) rían

saber   to know

Present:	sé, sabes, sabe, sabemos, sabéis, saben
Future:	sabré, sabrás, sabrá, sabremos, sabréis, sabrán
Preterite:	supe, supiste, supo, supimos, etc.
Conditional:	sabría, sabrías, sabría, sabríamos, etc.

salir   to leave; to go (out)

Present:	salgo, sales, sale, salimos, salís, salen
Future:	saldré, saldrás, saldrá, saldremos, etc.
Conditional:	saldría, saldrías, saldría, saldríamos, etc.
Imperative:	sal/no salgas, salid/no salgáis, (no) salga, etc.

seguir   to follow; to continue; to go on   Gerund: siguiendo

Present:	sigo, sigues, sigue, seguimos, seguís, siguen
Preterite:	seguí, seguiste, siguió, seguimos, seguisteis, siguieron
Imperative:	sigue/no sigas, seguid/no sigáis, (no) siga, etc.

ser   to be   (See also pp. 281, 282.) sido been   Gerund: Siendo

Present:	soy, eres, es, somos, sois, son
Preterite:	fui, fuiste, fue, fuimos, fuisteis, fueron
Imperfect:	era, eras, era, éramos, erais, eran
Imperative:	sé/no seas, sed/no seáis, (no) sea, (no) sean

tener   to have;   **tener que**   to have to

Present:	tengo, tienes, tiene, tenemos, tenéis, tienen
Future:	tendré, tendrás, tendrá, tendremos, etc.
Preterite:	tuve, tuviste, tuvo, tuvimos, etc.
Conditional:	tendría, tendrías, tendría, tendríamos, etc.
Imperative:	ten/no tengas, tened/no tengáis, (no) tenga, etc.

traer   to bring   Gerund: bringing

Present:	traigo, traes, trae, traemos, traéis, traen
Indefinite:	traje, trajiste, trajo, trajimos, etc.
Imperative:	trae/no traigas, traed/no traigáis, (no) traiga, etc.

venir   to come   Gerund: coming

Present:	vengo, vienes, viene, venimos, venís, vienen
Future:	vendré, vendrás, vendrá, vendremos, etc.
Preterite:	vine, viniste, vino, vinimos, etc.
Conditional:	vendría, vendrías, vendría, vendríamos, etc.
Imperative:	ven/no vengas, venid/no vengáis, (no) venga, etc.

ver   to see **verse**   to see oneself   visto   seen

Present:	veo, ves, ve, vemos, veis, ven
Imperfect:	veía, veías, veía, veíamos, veíais, veían

volver to return; to come back; to turn   vuelto   returned; turned

Present:	vuelvo, vuelves, vuelve, volvemos, volvéis, vuelven
Imperative:	vuelve/no vuelvas, volved/no volváis, (no) vuelva, (no) vuelvan

Ser and estar (to be)   (conjugation, see pp. 288, 290)

- *Ser* = what something is, its essence or permanent characteristics;
  Ser = with adjectives that refer to something permanent;
  Ser = to state time, part of day, day of week or month, seasons, profession, religion, nationality, identification, state of being, appearance, character, size, color, material, etc.:

Juan **es inteligente**.	Juan is intelligent.
La puerta **es de madera**.	The door is made of wood.
Vámonos, ya **es la una**.	Let's go, it's already one o'clock.
Mañana **es domingo**, ¡qué bien!	Tomorrow is Sunday—that's great.
Carmen **es médica.**	Carmen is a doctor.
¿Tú **eres español** o argentino?	Are you Spanish or Argentinian?

- *Estar* = expresses temporary or accidental characteristics, such as place (both spatial and subjective);
  Estar = with adjectives that refer to something that is not permanent;
  Estar = to state location or position; to express mood or temporary conditions; to form the present and past continuous tenses:

Fernando **está en Chile.**	Fernando is in Chile.
Segovia **está en España.**	Segovia is in Spain.
Marisa **está** hoy **mejor**.	Marisa is better today.
¿Por qué **está** Luisa **triste**?	Why is Luisa sad?
La puerta **está abierta.**	The door is open.
La sopa **está** muy **salada**.	The soup is very salty.
Estoy bailando.	I'm dancing.
Estaban saltando.	They were jumping.

● **Other differences between ser and estar**

ser = general	*estar* = specific; here and now
Luis **es un hombre enfermo**. Luis is a sick man. Luis **es generoso**. Luis is generous. Luis **es joven**. Luis is young.	Maria **está enferma**. Maria is sick. María **está** muy **generosa**. Maria is very generous (these days). María **está joven**. Maria looks young.

!

Hay ("there + to be") (see also p. 282)

- *Hay* is the present indicative form of the verb *haber*, in its impersonal sense. Only the third-person **singular** is used in **all** cases: *hay* there is/are; *había* there was/ were, etc.
  Hay has no definite subject.
  Hay expresses existence.

- *Hay que* + infinitive = one has to; expresses idea of obligation or need.

- *Hay* is often used in weather idioms.

¿Qué **hay** hoy para comer?	What's for dinner today?/What is there to eat today?
Ayer **hubo** una huelga.	There was a strike yesterday.
Habrá muchos problemas.	There will be many problems.
Hay que comprar fruta.	We have to buy fruit.
Hay mucho frío.	It's very cold.

- *Hay* is used in many idioms:

No *hay* de qué.	You're welcome.
¿Qué *hay*?	How are you?
Aquí *hay* de todo.	They have everything here.
Sobre gustos no *hay* nada escrito.	To each their own.

Personal Pronouns
(See also Prepositions, p. 275.)

Direct Object Pronouns		Indirect Object Pronouns		Prepositional Pronouns	
me	me	**me**	to me	sobre **mí**	about me
te	you	**te**	to you	sobre **ti**	about you you (fam)
le	you (pol.)	**le**	to them	sobre **él**	about him
lo	him				
la	her			sobre **ella**	about her

Direct Object Pronouns	Indirect Object Pronouns	Prepositional Pronouns	
it		sobre **usted**	about you
nos us	**le, lo** to it	sobre **nosotros**	about us
	nos to us	sobre **vosotros**	about you
os you *(fam)*	**os** to you	sobre **ellos**	about them
		sobre **ellas**	about them
les } you	**les** to you, them	sobre **ustedes**	about them
los } them			
las			
	les { to them to you		

- The masculine *le, les* is generally used in Spain, while *lo, los* is more frequent in Latin America.

- An object pronoun (direct, indirect, or reflexive), generally precedes the conjugated verb:

¿Quién **me** llama?	Who is calling me?
Siempre **me lo** dice.	He/she always tells me.

- Object pronouns are sometimes emphasized by adding *a mí, a ti, a él, a ella,* etc. In the case of third person pronouns, this clarification may be sometimes necessary:

Alberto **me** escribe **a mí**.	Alberto writes to me.
A ti te lo dice.	He tells it to you.
A él no **le** conozco.	I don't know him.

- The preposition *con* (with) and *mí, ti,* and *sí* form the words *conmigo* (with me), *contigo* (with you), and *consigo* (with yourself, himself, herself, yourselves, themselves):

Ana viene hoy **conmigo**.	Ana comes with me today.
¿Puedo ir el domingo **contigo**?	Can I go with you on Sunday?

- When following a preposition, personal pronouns use the subject forms, except for the first and second persons singular, which become *mí* and *ti*:

Todos **menos tú**.	All but you.
Entre ella y yo no hay secretos.	Between she and I there are no secrets.
Esta canción es **para mí**.	This song is for me.

- The weaker object pronoun must be added when a sentence begins emphatically with a prepositional pronoun or with a noun that is a direct or indirect object of a verb:

A Juan no **le** he dado dinero.	I haven't given money to Juan.
La maleta **la** lleva Pedro.	Pedro carries the suitcase.
El pan **lo** compras después.	You buy the bread later.

- When an infinitive is the object of another verb, the object pronouns can be placed either before the first verb or joined to the infinitive at the end; however, they must be joined to the verb in the case of infinitives, gerunds, and imperative verbs in the second person:

¿Quieres ver**lo**? ¿**Lo** quieres ver?	Do you want to see it?
Está haciéndo**lo**./**Lo** está haciendo.	He/She is doing it.
¡Dá**me**lo, por favor!	Give it to me, please!

- When there are two object pronouns, the indirect precedes the direct, and the reflexive precedes any other pronoun. If both pronouns begin with the letter *l*, the first one is changed to *se* (*se lo* instead of *le lo*, *se las* instead of *les las*, etc):

Mañana **se** lo doy.	I'll give it to you/him/her tomorrow.
Se las daré a Luis.	I'll give them to Luis.
¿La llave? **Se** la he dado a tu hermano.	The key? I gave it to your brother.

- *Ello* often follows a preposition:
  por ello that's why, **con ello** with it, **para ello** for it.

Reflexive Pronouns and Reflexive Verbs

acostumbrarse   to be accustomed to

yo	**me** acostumbro	I accustom myself
tú	**te** acostumbras	you accustom yourself
él, ella }	**se** acostumbra	{ he, she accustom himself/herself
usted		you accustom yourself
nosotros, -as	**nos** acostumbramos	we accustom ourselves
vosotros, -as	**os** acostumbráis	you accustom yourselves
ellos, ellas } ustedes }	**se** acostumbran	{ they accustom themselves you accustom yourselves

- A reflexive pronoun always goes with a reflexive verb;

- A reflexive verb expresses an action done by the subject to himself or herself. A reflexive verb always has *se* attached to its infinitive.

Pedro no **se** quiere peinar.	Pedro doesn't want to comb his hair.
¿**Se** ha levantado ya Luis?	Is Luis up yet?
¿No quieres afeitar**te**? ¿No **te** quieres afeitar? }	You don't want to shave?
Isabel está levantándo**se**. Isabel **se** está levantando. }	Isabel is getting up.
Tranquilíza**te**, hombre!	Calm down, man!

- Some verbs are reflective in Spanish but not in English:
  Ella se quita el sombrero.   She takes off her hat.

- The passive form is less common in Spanish than in English. Instead, the "reflexive passive" is used, an impersonal construction with *se* and a verb in the third person:

Aquí **se respira** mucho mejor.	One can breathe much better here.
Uno **se siente** cansado.	It's tiring.
Se alquilan coches.	Cars are rented here.
Esas casas **se venden**.	Those houses are for sale.

Possessive Pronouns

Possessive Form			Independent Possessive Form	
mi	trabajo	my work/job	**mío, mía, míos, mías**	{ mine
tu	amigo	your friend	**tuyo, tuya, -os, -as**	{ yours
su	jardín	{ your/his/her garden		
			suyo, suyas, -os, -as	{ yours, his, hers
nuestro	padre	our father	**nuestro, nuestra, -os, -as**	ours
vuestro	tren	your train	**vuestro, vuestra, -os, -as**	your train
su	coche	your car	**suyo, suya, -os, -as**	{ yours, theirs

● Possessive pronouns are always preceded by a definite article, except after the verb *ser*, when it may be omitted. These pronouns agree in gender and number with the thing possessed:

Tengo unas cartas **tuyas**.	I have some of your letters.
Ese diccionario es **mío**.	That dictionary is mine.

Relative Pronouns

● *Que* may refer to persons or things, except after a preposition when it refers only to things.

● *El que, la que, los que, las que* may replace *que*, especially when used with certain prepositions or when there is a need to clarify:

Tengo el libro **que** buscas.	I have the book you're looking for.
El diccionario **con el que** traduzco.	The dictionary with which I translate.

● *Quien, quienes* (persons only): when used with a preposition, it means whom.

● *Lo que* = what, that which:

El amigo **con quien** viajo.	The friend with whom I travel.
Dice siempre **lo que** piensa.	He/she always says what he/she thinks.

● *el cual, la cual, los cuales, las cuales* replace *que* or *quien*, referring to persons or things, both for the sake of clarity and when they are used with some prepositions.

Demonstrative Adjectives and Pronouns

este / ese / aquel	libro	this/that/that book
esta / esa / aquella	flor	this/that/that flower
estos / esos / aquellos	vasos	these/those/those glasses
estas / esas / aquellas	blusas	these/those/those blouses

Pronoun only:

esto / eso / aquello	this/that/that

● Demonstrative adjectives precede the noun they modify and agree with it in gender and number. They do not have a written accent;

● Demonstrative pronouns have a written accent over the *e* of the stressed syllable, to distinguish them from the corresponding adjectives. They agree in number and gender with the noun they replace.

¿Te gusta **esta** camisa?	Do you like this shirt?
¿Cuál, **ésa**?	Which one—that one?
¿Ves **aquel** molino?	Do you see that windmill?
¿**Aquél** grande?	That big one?

● *Esto, eso, aquello* (neuter pronouns) do not have written accents, because they have no corresponding adjectives:

¿Qué es **eso**?	What is that?
¿**Esto**? Una piedra.	This? A stone.

Interrogative Adjectives, Pronouns, and Adverbs

¿quién? who?	**¿Quién** ha llamado? **¿A quién** esperas? **¿Por quién** ha preguntado?	Who has called? Who are you waiting for? Who did you ask for?
¿qué? what?	**¿Qué** has dicho? **¿De qué** se trata? **¿Qué** hora es?	What did you say? What is the matter? What time is it?
¿cuánto? how much?	**¿Cuánto** dinero necesitas? **¿Cuántas** chaquetas tienes? **¿Cuánto** dura la película?	How much money do you need? How many jackets do you have? How long is this movie?
¿dónde? where?	**¿Dónde** estudias español? **¿Dónde** está la parada?	Where do you study Spanish? Where is the stop?
¿adónde? (to) where?	**¿Adónde** quieren ir ustedes? **¿Adónde** vas con tanta prisa?	Where do you want to go? Where are you going so fast?
¿de dónde? (from) where?	**¿De dónde** vienes? **¿De dónde** es esa muchacha?	Where do you come from? Where is that girl from?
¿cuál? what?	**¿Cuál** es la capital? **¿Cuál** de las dos quieres?	What is the capital? Which one of the two you want?
¿cómo? how?	**¿Cómo** te llamas? **¿Cómo** está su señora?	What is your name? How is your wife?
¿por qué? why?	**¿Por qué** os vais ya? No sé **por qué** está tan triste.	Why are you leaving already? I don't know why he/she is so sad.

!

- Interrogative and exclamatory adjectives, pronouns, and adverbs always have a written accent:

  ¡qué bonito!   how pretty!

  ¿Qué noticias traes?   What's the latest?

Indefinite Adjectives and Pronouns

algo something, anything *nada* nothing	Mejor es **algo** que **nada**.	Something is better than nothing.
	¿Por qué no dices **nada**?	Why don't you say something?
alguien someone *nadie* no one	¿Ha llamado **alguien**?	Has someone called?
	No, no ha llamado **nadie**.	No, no one has called
alguno some, any (of a specific group) *ninguno* none (of a specific group)	¿Vive aquí **algún** médico?	Is there any doctor living here?
	No, aquí no vive **ninguno**.	No, there's none living here.
	¿**Alguno** de vosotros lo sabe?	Does any of you know it?
	Aquí no hay **ningún** libro.	There's no book here.

- *Alguno, ninguno* (adj **or** pron, sing m) = *algún, ningún* (adj **only**, sing m). (See *nada, nadie, ninguno* p. 301.)

- Some indefinites are **only** pronouns: *alguien* somebody, anybody; *nadie* nobody, anybody; *algo* something, anything; *nada* nothing. *Algo* and *nada* may also be used as adverbs. Two related concepts, *todo* all, whole, and *cada* every, each, are invariable adjectives: **Todo** hombre es mortal. All men are mortal. However, *todo* may also be used as a noun or a pronoun, meaning all, everything, everybody.

todo all, everything	Aquí **todo** está limpio. ¿Has comido **todo el** pan?	It's all clean in here. Have you eaten all the bread?
	Inés limpia **todos los** días **toda la** casa.	Ines cleans the whole house every day.
cada, *cada uno*	Por **cada** buena acción tendrá **cada uno** su premio.	For every good deed, every one each, each one

Negatives

- *No* always precedes the verb and any of its preceding object pronouns;

- When words such as *nadie* nobody, *nada* nothing, *nunca/jamás* never, *ningún/ninguno* no/none, etc., follow the verb, **no** must precede it.

Pablo **no** volverá hoy.	Pablo will not come back today.
Este chico **no** aprende **nada**.	This kid doesn't learn anything.
Laura **no** volverá **nunca** más. **Nunca** más volverá Laura. Mi	Laura will never come back.
hija **no** me lo ha dado.	My daughter hasn't given it to me.
¿**No** tienes **ninguna** foto de él?	Don't you have a pictur of him?

Word Order

- The word order of statements in Spanish is generally the same as in English:
 Fernando lee un libro. Fernando reads a book.

- Regular Spanish sentence structure: subject—verb—direct object—indirect object:
 Fernando presta un libro a Luisa. Fernando lends Luisa a book.

● Some variations of this regular structure:
  — in dependent clauses, the subject usually comes at the end, after the verb:
  No se cuándo llegará Ana.   I don't know when will Ana get here.
  — if an adverbial phrase opens the sentence, the subject comes after the verb:
  A última hora, llegó Ana.   Ana arrived at the last minute.
  — adverbs and adverbial phrases often come between the verb and its object:
  Fernando habla muy bien el inglés.   Fernando speaks English very well.

● (See also Personal Pronouns, p. 293.)

ENGLISH-SPANISH DICTIONARY

A

a little, a bit un poco [oon 'poh-koh]

abbreviation abreviatura [ah-breh-vee-ah-'too-rah]

able capaz [kah-'pahs]

able to, to be *(v)* ser capaz de [sehr kah-'pahs deh]

about alrededor de, en torno a; hacia [ahl-reh-deh-'dohr deh, ehn 'tohr-noh ah, 'ah-see-ah]

above arriba, encima, sobre [ah-'rree-bah, ehn-'see-mah, 'soh-breh]

abroad el extranjero [ehl eh-strahn-'heh-roh]

absent ausente [ow-'sehn-teh]

absolutely *(adv)* sin falta, absolutamente [seen 'fahl-tah, ahb-soh-loo-tah-'mehn-teh]

abundant abundante [ah-boon-'dahn-teh]

accelerate *(v)* acelerar [ah-seh-leh-'rahr]

accent acento [ah-'sehn-toh]

accept *(v)* aceptar [ah-sehp-'tahr]

accident accident [ahk-see-'dehn-teh]

accommodations alojamiento [ah-loh-hah-mee-'ehn-toh]

accompany *(v)* acompañar [ah-kohm-pah-'nyahr]; **in the company of** en compañía de [ehn kohm-pah-'nyee-ah deh]

acquaintance el conocido, la conocida [ehl koh-noh-'see-doh, lah koh-noh-'see-dah]

across (to/from) enfrente de, frente a [ehn-'frehn-teh deh, 'frehn-teh ah]

act *(v)* actuar, obrar [ahk-too-'ahr, oh-'brahr]

action la acción [lah ahk-see-'ohn]

activity la actividad [lah ahk-tee-vee-'dahd]

actually en realidad [ehn reh-ah-lee-'dahd]

ad anuncio, *(Am)* aviso [ah-'noon-see-oh, ah-'vee-soh]

adapted adaptado [ah-dahp-'tah-doh]

add *(v)* añadir, sumar [ah-nyah-'deer, soo-'mahr]

addition suma ['soo-mah]; **additional** adicional [ah-dee-see-oh-'nahl]; **in addition to** además de [ah-deh-'mahs deh]

additional suplementario, adicional [soo-pleh-mehn-'tah-ree-oh, ah-dee-see-oh-'nahl]

address *(v)* poner las señas/la dirección [poh-'nehr lahs 'seh-nyahs/lah dee-rehk-see-'ohn]

address las señas, la dirección [lahs 'seh-nyahs, lah dee-rehk-see-'ohn]

administration la administración [lah ahd-mee-nee-strah-see-'ohn]

admire *(v)* admirar [ahd-mee-'rahr]

admission charge/ticket precio/boleto de entrada ['preh-see-oh/boh-'leh-toh deh ehn-'trah-dah]

adult adulta, adulto [ah-'dool-toh, ah-'dool-tah]

advantage ventaja [vehn-'tah-hah]

advantageous ventajoso [vehn-tah-'hoh-soh]

advice consejo [kohn-'seh-hoh]

advise *(v)* aconsejar [ah-kohn-seh-'hahr]

affectionate cariñoso [kah-ree-'nyoh-soh]

afraid of, to be *(v)* tener miedo de [teh-'nehr mee-'eh-doh deh]

after después [deh-'spwehs]

after(wards) después, luego [deh-'spwehs, loo-'eh-goh]

afternoon la tarde [lah 'tahr-deh]; **por la(s) tarde(s)** [pohr lah(s) 'tahr-deh(s)]

again otra vez, de nuevo ['oh-trah vehs, deh noo-'eh-voh]

against contra, en contra de ['kohn-trah, ehn 'kohn-trah deh]

age la edad [lah eh-'dahd]

agency agencia [ah-'hehn-see-ah]

agree *(v)* convenir, acordar, estar de acuerdo/conforme(s), ponerse de acuerdo [kohn-veh-'neer, ah-kohr-'dahr, eh-'stahr deh ah-'kwehr-doh, kohn-'fohr-meh(s), poh-'nehr-seh deh ah-'kwehr-doh]

agreement convenio, acuerdo [kohn-'veh-nee-oh, ah-'kwehr-doh]

aid ayuda, auxilio [ah-'yoo-dah, owk-'see-lee-oh]; **first aid** los primeros auxilios [lohs pree-'meh-rohs owk-'see-lee-ohs]

air *(v)* ventilar [vehn-tee-'lahr]; **(air) draft** la corriente de aire [lah koh-rree-'ehn-teh deh 'ah-ee-reh]

A/Z

air el aire [ehl 'ah·ee·reh]

alarm clock el despertador [ehl deh-spehr-tah-'dohr]

alcohol el alcohol [ehl ahl-koh-'ohl];
  cooking alcohol alcohol de quemar [ahl-koh-'ohl deh keh-'mahr]

algae las algas [lahs 'ahl-gahs]

alive vivo ['vee-voh]

all todos ['toh-dohs]

alley calleja [kah-'yeh-hah]

alliance alianza [ah-lee-'ahn-sah]

allow (v) permitir, autorizar [pehr-mee-'teer, ow-toh-ree-'sahr]

allowed lícito, permitido ['lee-see-toh, pehr-mee-'tee-doh]

almost casi ['kah-see]

alone solo ['soh-loh]

along a lo largo de [ah loh 'lahr-goh deh]

already ya [yah]

also también [tahm-bee-'ehn]

although aunque ['ah·oon-keh]

always cada vez, siempre ['kah-dah vehs, see-'ehm-preh]

always siempre [see-'ehm-preh]

ambulance ambulancia [ahm-boo-'lahn-see·ah]

among entre ['ehn-treh]

amount el importe, suma [ehl eem-'pohr-teh, 'soo-mah]

and so on etcétera [eht-'seh-teh-rah]

Andalusia Andalucía [ahn-dah-loo-'see-ah]

Andalusian andaluz [ahn-dah-'loos]

anger enfado, cólera [ehn-'fah-doh, 'koh-leh-rah]

angry furioso, rabioso [foo-ree-'oh-soh, rah-bee-'oh-soh]

angry with/about, to be enfadarse con/por, encolerizarse con/por [ehn-fah-'dahr-seh kohn/pohr, ehn-koh-leh-ree-'sahr-seh kohn/pohr]

animal el animal [ehl ah-nee-'mahl]

announce (v) anunciar, avisar [ah-noon-see-'ahr, ah-vee-'sahr]

announcement el anuncio, la comunicación, (Am) aviso [ehl ah-'noon-see·oh, lah koh-moo-nee-kah-see-'ohn, ah-'vee-soh]

annoying pesado, molesto [peh-'sah-doh, moh-'leh-stoh]

annual(ly) (adj) anual [ah-noo-'ahl];
  (adv) al año, anualmente [ahl 'ah-nyoh, ah-noo-ahl-'mehn-teh]

annul (v) anular [ah-noo-'lahr]

answer (v) responder, contestar [reh-spohn-'dehr, kohn-teh-'stahr]

answer respuesta, la contestación [reh-'spweh-stah, lah kohn-teh-stah-see-'ohn]

any cualquiera, cualquier [kwahl-kee-'eh-rah, kwahl-kee-'ehr]

anything cualquier cosa [kwahl-kee-'ehr 'koh-sah]

apartment piso, (Am) departamento, apartamento ['pee-soh, deh-pahr-tah-'mehn-toh, ah-pahr-tah-'mehn-toh];
  furnished apartment piso amueblado ['pee-soh ah-mweh-'blah-doh]

apologize/to excuse oneself (v) disculparse, pedir perdón [dee-skool-'pahr-seh, peh-'deer pehr-'dohn] **excuse me, please** ¡perdone! [pehr-'doh-neh]

apology excusa [ehk-'skoo-sah]; **my apologies** lo siento/me disculpo/perdón [loh see-'ehn-toh/meh dee-'skool-poh/pehr-'dohn]

apparently aparentemente, por lo visto [ah-pah-rehn-teh-'mehn-teh, pohr loh 'vee-stoh]

appear (v) aparecer [ah-pah-reh-'sehr]

appearance vista, aspecto ['vee-stah, ah-'spehk-toh]

appetite apetito [ah-peh-'tee-toh]

applause aplauso [ah-'plah·oo-soh]

appointment cita ['see-tah]

approach (v) acercarse [ah-sehr-'kahr-seh]

approve (v) aprobar [ah-proh-'bahr]

approximate aproximado [ah-prohk-see-'mah-doh]

Aragon Aragón [ah-rah-'gohn]

area zona ['soh-nah]

Argentina Argentina [ahr-hehn-'tee-nah]

Argentine Argentino [ahr-hehn-'tee-noh]

around alrededor [ahl-reh-deh-'dohr]

arrive (v) llegar [yeh-'gahr]

article artículo [ahr-'tee-koo-loh]

ask (v) pedir, preguntar [peh-'deer, preh-goon-'tahr]

ask someone for something (v) pedir algo a alguien [peh-'deer 'ahl-goh ah 'ahl-gee-ehn]

assault (v) asaltar, atracar [ah-sahl-'tahr, ah-trah-'kahr]

association la asociación, la sociedad [lah ah-soh-see·ah-seh-'ohn, lah soh-see-eh-'dahd]

assume (v) suponer [soo-poh-'nehr]

assumption la suposición [lah soo-poh-see-see-'ohn]

assure *(v)* asegurar [ah-seh-goo-'rahr]
at home en casa [ehn 'kah-sah]
at least por lo/al menos [pohr loh 'meh-nohs, ahl 'meh-nohs]
Atlantic Atlántico [aht-'lahn-tee-koh]
attempt *(v)* probar, intentar [proh-'bahr, een-tehn-'tahr]
attempt prueba, intento [proo-'eh-bah, een-'tehn-toh]
attention la atención, cuidado [lah ah-tehn-see-'ohn, kwee-'dah-doh]
attentive atento [ah-'tehn-toh]
aunt tía ['tee-ah]
authorities la autoridad pública, las autoridades [lah ow-toh-ree-'dahd 'poo-blee-kah, lahs ow-toh-ree-'dah-dehs]
automatic automático [ow-toh-'mah-tee-koh]
available obtenible, en venta [ohb-teh-'nee-bleh, ehn 'vehn-tah]
average promedio, medio, mediano, por término medio [proh-'meh-dee-oh, 'meh-dee-oh, meh-dee-'ah-noh, pohr 'tehr-mee-noh 'meh-dee-oh]
avoid *(v)* evitar [eh-vee-'tahr]
awaken *(v)* despertar(se) [deh-spehr-'tahr(seh)]
awaken despierto [deh-spee-'ehr-toh]
aware, conscious consciente [kohn-see-'ehn-teh]
away fuera, ausente ['fweh-rah, ow-'sehn-teh]

B

baby el bebé [ehl beh-'beh]
backwards retrógrado, atrasado, al revés, hacia atrás [reh-'troh-grah-doh; ah-trah-'sah-doh, ahl reh-'vehs, 'ah-see-ah ah-'trahs]
bad *(adj)* malo, mal ['mah-loh, mahl]; *(adv)* mal [mahl]; **bad** malo, mal ['mah-loh, mahl]; **I feel bad about it** lo siento mucho [loh see-'ehn-toh 'moo-choh]; **bad weather** mal tiempo [mahl tee-'ehm-poh]
balance *(financial)* balanza [bah-'lahn-sah]
Baleares Islands las islas Baleares [lahs 'ee-slahs bah-leh-'ah-rehs]
ball pelota [peh-'loh-tah]; *(fest)* el baile [ehl 'bah-ee-leh]
ballroom sala de baile ['sah-lah deh 'bah-ee-leh]

ban *(v)* prohibir [proh-ee-'beer]
ban la prohibición [lah proh-ee-bee-see-'ohn]; **banned** prohibido [proh-ee-'bee-doh]
band banda, orquesta ['bahn-dah, ohr-'keh-stah]
bandage el vendaje [ehl vehn-'dah-heh]
bank banco ['bahn-koh]
barrier barrera [bah-'rreh-rah]
bars rejas ['reh-hahs]
basket cesta ['seh-stah]
Basque *(lang)* vasco, vascuence ['vah-skoh, vah-'skwehn-seh]
Basque region las Vascongadas [lahs vah-skohn-'gah-dahs]
Basque vasco, vasca ['vah-skoh, 'vah-skah]
bath baño ['bah-nyoh]
battery batería [bah-teh-'ree-ah]
bay bahía [bah-'ee-ah]
be (located at a place) *(v)* encontrarse [ehn-kohn-'trahr-seh]
be *(v)* ser, estar [sehr, eh-'stahr]; **be friends with** *(v)* ser amigo de [sehr ah-'mee-goh deh]; **be/feel sick** *(v)* estar/sentirse enfermo, estar malo/sentirse mal [eh-'stahr/sehn-'teer-seh ehn-'fehr-moh, eh-'stahr 'mah-loh/sehn-'teer-seh mahl]
beach playa ['plah-yah]
beam rayo ['rah-yoh]
bear *(v)* soportar [soh-pohr-'tahr]
beautiful hermoso, bello, lindo [ehr-'moh-soh, 'beh-yoh, 'leen-doh]
beauty belleza, hermosura [behl-'yeh-sah, ehr-moh-'soo-rah]
because porque, pues ['pohr-keh, pwehs]; **because of** a causa de [ah 'kah-oo-sah deh]
become *(v)* volverse, convertirse en, llegar a ser [vohl-'vehr-seh, kohn-vehr-'teer-seh ehn, yeh-'gahr a sehr]
bed cama ['kah-mah]
bee abeja [ah-'beh-hah]
before antes, delante de, antes de ['ahn- tehs, deh-'lahn-teh deh, 'ahn-tehs deh]; **before anything** sobre todo, ante todo ['soh-breh 'toh-doh, 'ahn-teh 'toh-doh]; **beforehand** de antemano [deh ahn-teh-'mah-noh]
begin *(v)* empezar, comenzar [ehm-peh-'sahr, koh-mehn-'sahr]
beginning principio, comienzo [preen-'see-pee-oh, koh-mee-'ehn-soh]; **beginning, start** comienzo [koh-mee-'ehn-soh]

A/Z

behavior, conduct comportamiento, conducta [kohm-pohr-tah-mee-'ehn-toh, kohn-'dook-tah]

behind detrás [deh-'trahs]; **at the back** detrás [deh-'trahs]

Belgian el /la belga [ehl/lah 'behl-gah]

Belgium Bélgica ['behl-hee-kah]

believe creer [kreh-'ehr]

bell el timbre [ehl 'teem-breh]

belong to pertenecer a, ser de [pehr-teh-neh-'sehr ah, sehr deh]

besides por otra parte, además; aparte de eso [pohr 'oh-trah 'pahr-teh, ah-deh-'mahs, ah-'pahr-teh deh 'eh-soh]

best, the la/el/lo mejor [lah/ehl/loh meh-'hohr]

bet (v) apostar [ah-poh-'stahr]

bet apuesta [ah-'pweh-stah]

better mejor [meh-'hohr]

between entre ['ehn-treh]

beyond al otro lado de, más allá de [ahl 'oh-troh 'lah-doh deh, mahs ah-'yah deh]

bicycle la bici(cleta) [lah 'bee-see('kleh-tah)]

binoculars los prismáticos, los gemelos [lohs prees-'mah-tee-kohs, lohs heh-'meh-lohs]

bird pájaro ['pah-hah-roh]

birth nacimiento [nah-see-mee-'ehn-toh]

birthday el cumpleaños [ehl koom-pleh-'ah-nyohs]

bite (v) morder [mohr-'dehr]

bite mordida [mohr-'dee-dah]

bitter amargo [ah-'mahr-goh]

blanket manta, colcha ['mahn-tah, 'kohl-chah]

blind ciego [see-'eh-goh]

blocked atascado, bloqueado [ah-tah-'skah-doh, bloh-keh-'ah-doh]

bloom (v) florecer [floh-reh-'sehr]

board (v) embarcarse, subir a bordo [ehm-bahr-'kahr-seh, soo-'beer ah 'bohr-doh]

boat barca, el bote, lancha ['bahr-kah, ehl 'boh-teh, 'lahn-chah] ·

body cuerpo ['kwehr-poh]

boil (v) hervir, cocer [ehr-'veer, koh-'sehr]

Bolivia Bolivia [boh-'lee-vee-ah]

Bolivian boliviano [boh-lee-vee-'ah-noh]

bolt cerrojo [seh-'rroh-hoh]

book libro ['lee-broh]

book, reserve (v) reservar [reh-sehr-'vahr]

border frontera, el límite [frohn-'teh-rah, ehl 'lee-mee-teh]

boring aburrido [ah-boo-'rree-doh]

born in, whose birthplace is natural de [nah-too-'rahl deh]

born nacido [nah-'see-doh]

borrow (v) tomar/pedir prestado [toh-'mahr, peh-'deer preh-'stah-doh]

boss el director, el jefe/la directora, la jefa [ehl dee-rehk-'tohr, ehl 'heh-feh/lah dee-rehk-'toh-rah, lah 'heh-fah]

both ambos, los dos ['ahm-bohs, lohs dohs]

bother (v) molestar, fastidiar [moh-leh-'stahr, fah-stee-dee-'ahr]

bottle botella [boh-'teh-yah]

box caja ['kah-hah]

boy muchacho, chico, joven [moo-'chah-choh, 'chee-koh, 'hoh-vehn]

boyfriend/girlfriend el novio/la novia [ehl 'noh-vee-oh/lah 'noh-vee-ah]

branch (office) la sucursal [lah soo-koor-'sahl]

brand marca ['mahr-kah]

break (v) romper [rohm-'pehr]

break open (v) forzar, violentar [fohr-'sahr, vee-oh-lehn-'tahr]

breakfast desayunar [deh-sah-yoo-'nahr]

breath, breathing la respiración [lah reh-spee-rah-see-'ohn]

bridge el puente [ehl 'pwehn-teh]

brief breve, corto ['breh-veh, 'kohr-toh]

briefcase carpeta, maletín, cartera [kahr-'peh-tah, mah-leh-'teen, kahr-'teh-rah]

bright claro ['klah-roh]

bright, shining luminoso, brillante [loo-mee-'noh-soh, bree-'yahn-teh]

brilliant brillante [bree-'yahn-teh]

bring (v) traer [trah-'ehr]; **bring back** devolver [deh-vohl-'vehr]

broad ancho ['ahn-choh]

broken averiado, roto, estropeado [ah-veh-ree-'ah-doh, 'roh-toh, eh-stroh-peh-'ah-doh]

brother hermano [ehr-'mah-noh]

brother-in-law cuñado [koo-'nyah-doh]

brown marrón [mah-'rrohn]; (hair) castaño [kah-'stah-nyoh]; (complexion) moreno, tostado [moh-'reh-noh, toh-'stah-doh]

brush (v) cepillar [seh-pee-'yahr]

brush cepillo [seh-'pee-yoh]

build (v) construir [kohn-stroo-'eer]

building edificio [eh-dee-'fee-see-oh]

bull toro ['toh-roh]

bunch *(people)* montón [mohn-'tohn]; *(flowers, fruits)* ramo, racimo ['rah-moh, rah-'see-moh]

burn *(v)* arder, quemar [ahr-'dehr, keh-'mahr]

burn quemadura [keh-mah-'doo-rah]

burst *(v)* reventar, estallar [reh-vehn-'tahr, eh-stah-'yahr]

bush mata, matorral ['mah-tah, mah-toh-'rrahl]; *(wilderness)* selva ['sehl-vah]

business negocio [neh-'goh-see-oh]

busy ocupado [oh-koo-'pah-doh]

but pero ['peh-roh]

button el botón [ehl boh-'tohn]

buy *(v)* comprar [kohm-'prahr]

buyer el comprador [ehl kohm-prah-'dohr]; *(customer)* el cliente [ehl klee-'ehn-teh]

by *(place)* junto a, cerca de ['hoon-toh ah, 'sehr-kah deh]; **by day/night** de día/noche [deh 'dee-ah/'noh-cheh]

by por, de [pohr, deh]; **by the way** por lo demás, por otra parte [pohr loh deh-'mahs, pohr 'oh-trah 'pahr-teh]

C

cabin cabina, el camarote [kah-'bee-nah, ehl kah-mah-'roh-teh]

café el café [ehl kah-'feh]

cafeteria cafetería, el bar [kah-feh-teh-'ree-ah, ehl bahr]

calculate *(v)* calcular [kahl-koo-'lahr]

call *(v)* llamar [yah-'mahr]

call for, pick up *(v)* ir a buscar, recoger [eer ah boo-'skahr, reh-koh-'hehr]; **have someone pick it up** *(v)* mandar a buscar [mahn-'dahr ah boo-'skahr]

calm oneself down *(v)* calmarse, tranquilizarse [kahl-'mahr-seh, trahn-kee-lee-'sahr-seh]

camera máquina de fotografías, cámara ['mah-kee-nah deh foh-toh-grah-'fee-ahs, 'kah-mah-rah]

can opener abrelata [ah-breh-'lah-tah]

canal el canal [ehl kah-'nahl]

Canary Islands Islas Canarias ['ees-lahs kah-'nah-ree-ahs]

cancel *(v)* cancelar [kahn-seh-'lahr]

candle vela ['veh-lah]

capable hábil, capaz ['ah-beel, kah-'pahs]

capital la capital [lah kah-pee-'tahl]

car el coche, el automóvil [ehl koh-cheh, ehl owh-toh-'moh-veel]

card tarjeta [tahr-'heh-tah]; **postcard** tarjeta postal [tahr-'heh-tah poh-'stahl]

care *(v)* atender, cuidar [ah-tehn-'dehr, kwee-'dahr]; **take care of** *(v)* cuidar a [kwee-'dahr ah]; **be careful of** *(v)* tener cuidado de [teh-'nehr kwee-'dah-doh deh]

care cuidado, esmero [kwee-'dah-doh, ehs-'meh-roh]

careful cuidadoso, esmerado [kwee-dah-'doh-soh, ehs-meh-'rah-doh]

careless descuidado [dehs-kwee-'dah-doh]

carry out *(v)* realizar, ejecutar; acabar [reh-ah-lee-'sahr, eh-heh-koo-'tahr, ah-kah-'bahr]

case suceso, caso [soo-'seh-soh, 'kah-soh]

castanets las castañuelas [lahs kah-stah-nyoo-'eh-lahs]

Castille Castilla [kah-'stee-yah]

Castillian castellano [kah-steh-'yah-noh]

castle palacio, castillo [pah-'lah-see-oh, kah-'stee-yoh]

cat gato ['gah-toh]

catalog catálogo [kah-'tah-loh-goh]

Catalonia Cataluña [kah-tah-'loo-nyah]; **Catalonian** el catalán, la catalana [ehl kah-tah-'lahn, lah]; *(lang)* **Catalonian** (el) catalán [ehl kah-tah-'lahn]

catch *(v)* coger, *(Am)* agarrar [koh-'hehr, ah-gah-'rrahr]

cause *(v)* causar [kah-oo-'sahr]

cause causa ['kah-oo-sah]

caution la precaución [lah preh-kah-oo-see-'ohn]; **caution!** ¡cuidado!, ¡atención! [kwee-'dah-doh, ah-tehn-see-'ohn]

cautious prudente, cuidadoso [proo-'dehn-teh, kwee-dah-'doh-soh]

cemetery cementerio [seh-mehn-'teh-ree-oh]

center centro ['sehn-troh]

central central [sehn-'trahl]

ceramic cerámica [seh-'rah-mee-kah]

certain(ly) *(adj)* determinado, cierto, seguro [deh-tehr-mee-'nah-doh, see-'ehr-toh, seh-'goo-roh]; *(adv)* ciertamente [see-ehr-tah-'mehn-teh]

certify *(v)* certificar [sehr-tee-fee-'kahr]

chain cadena [kah-'deh-nah]; *(necklace)* el collar [ehl koh-'yahr]

chair silla ['see-yah]

chance *(n)* la casualidad [lah kah-soo-ah-lee-'dahd], la oportunidad; *(adj)* casual [lah oh-pohr-too-nee-'dahd]

change *(v)* cambiar [kahm-bee-'ahr]

change cambio ['kahm-bee-oh]

A/Z

changeable inestable, inconstante [een-eh-'stah-bleh, een-kohn-'stahn-teh]
chapel capilla [kah-'pee-yah]
characteristic característica [kah-rahk-teh-'ree-stee-kah]
charming encantador [ehn-kahn-tah-'dohr]
chat (v) charlar [chahr-'lahr]
chat charla ['chahr-lah]
cheap barato [bah-'rah-toh]
cheat (v) engañar, defraudar, mentir, estafar [ehn-gah-'nyahr, deh-frah·oo-'dahr, mehn-'teer, eh-stah-'fahr]
check (v) revisar, comprobar [reh-vee-'sahr, kohm-proh-'bahr]
check cheque ['cheh-keh]
cheerful alegre, de buen humor [ah-'leh-greh, deh bwehn oo-'mohr]
chef el chef [ehl chehf]
chewing gum el chicle [ehl 'chee-kleh]
child niño ['nee-nyoh]
Chilean chileno/a [chee-'leh-noh]
choir coro ['koh-roh]
choose (v) escoger, elegir [eh-skoh-'hehr, eh-leh-'heer]
cigar cigarro, puro [see-'gah-rroh, 'poo-roh]
cigarette cigarrillo [see-gah-'rree-yoh]
circumstances las circunstancias [lahs seer-koon-'stahn-see-ahs]
city la ciudad [lah see·oo-'dahd]; **city map** plano de la ciudad ['plah-noh deh lah see·oo-'dahd]
class la clase [lah 'klah-seh]
clean (v) limpiar [leem-pee-'ahr]
clean limpio ['leem-pee-oh]
clear claro ['klah-roh]
clearance sale la liquidación, saldo [lah lee-kee-dah-see-'ohn, 'sahl-doh]
clever listo, inteligente, astuto ['lee-stoh, een-teh-lee-'hehn-teh, ah-'stoo-toh]
client el/la cliente, (Am) el marchante [ehl/lah klee-'ehn-teh, ehl mahr-'chan-teh]
climate el clima [ehl 'klee-mah]
climb (v) subir, trepar [soo-'beer, treh-'pahr]
clock el reloj de pared [ehl reh-'loh deh pah-'rehd]
clogged obstruido [ohb-stroo-'ee-doh]
closed cerrado [seh-'rrah-doh]
clotheshanger percha, perchero ['pehr-chah, pehr-'cheh-roh]
clothing ropa, los vestidos ['roh-pah, lohs veh-'stee-dohs]

cloudy (liquid) turbio ['toor-bee·oh]; (weather) nublado [noo-'blah-doh]
clue pista ['pee-stah]
coal el carbón [ehl kahr-'bohn]
coalition la coalición [lah koh-ah-lee-see-'ohn]
coast costa ['koh-stah]
cockroach cucaracha [koo-kah-'rah-chah]
coffee el café [ehl kah-'feh]
coin moneda [moh-'neh-dah]
cold frío ['free-oh]
cold, to be (v) tener/pasar frío [teh-'nehr/pah-'sahr 'free-oh]
colleague el/la colega [ehl/lah koh-'leh-gah]
collect (v) coleccionar; recoger [koh-lehk-see-oh-'nahr, reh-koh-'hehr]
collection la colección [lah koh-lehk-see-'ohn]
collision el choque [ehl 'choh-keh]
Colombia Colombia [koh-'lohm-bee-ah]
Colombian colombiano [koh-loom-bee-'ah-noh]
color el color [ehl koh-'lohr]
colored en/de colores, de color [ehn/deh koh-'loh-rehs, deh koh-'lohr]
colorful de colores, multicolor [deh koh-'loh-rehs, mool-tee-koh-'lohr]
come (v) venir, ir [veh-'neer, eer]; **come back** volver, regresar [vohl-'vehr, reh-greh-'sahr]; **come from** (v) venir (de), proceder de [veh-'neer (deh), proh-seh-'dehr deh]
come in (v) entrar [ehn-'trahr]
come in! ¡adelante!, ¡pase! [ah-deh-'lahn-teh, 'pah-seh]
comfort la comodidad [lah koh-moh-dee-'dahd]
comfortable cómodo ['koh-moh-doh]
common corriente, vulgar [koh-rree-'ehn-teh, vool-'gahr]
communicate (v) comunicar [koh-moo-nee-'kahr]
company la sociedad, compañía, empresa [lah soh-see-eh-'dahd, kohm-pah-'nyee-ah, ehm-preh-sah]
compare comparar [kohm-pah-'rah]
comparison la comparación [lah kohm-pah-rah-see-'ohn]
compass brújula ['broo-hoo-lah]
compensation la indemnización [lah een-dehm-nee-sah-see-'ohn]
competition competencia; concurso [kohm-peh-'tehn-see·ah; kohn-'koor-soh]

complain (v) quejarse [keh-'hahr-seh]; **(about/of)** (v) quejarse (de) [keh-'hahr-seh (deh)]

complaint queja, la reclamación [keh-'hahr, lah reh-klah-mah-see-'ohn]; (police) denuncia [deh-'noon-see-ah]

complete (v) completare, terminar, acabar [kohm-pleh-'tah-reh, tehr-mee-'nahr, ah-kah-'bahr]

complete(ly) completo, (adv) completamente [kohm-'pleh-toh, kohm-pleh-tah-'mehn-teh]

concerning relativo a, tocante a [reh-lah-'tee-voh ah, toh-'kahn-teh ah]

condition la condición [lah kohn-dee-see-'ohn]

condolence(s) el pésame [ehl 'peh-sah-meh]

condom preservativo, el condón [preh-sehr-vah-'tee-voh, ehl kohn-'dohn]

conductor (bus) el conductor, el cobrador [ehl koon-dook-'tohr, ehl koh-brah-'dohr]

cone cono ['koh-noh]

confident seguro de sí mismo, confiado en sí mismo [seh-'goo-roh deh see 'mees-moh, kohn-fee-'ah-doh ehn see 'mees-moh]

confirme (v) confirmar [kohn-feer-'mahr]

confuse (v) confundir [kohn-foon-'deer]

congested congestionado [kohn-heh-stee-oh-'nah-doh]

congratulations la felicitación, enhorabuena [lah feh-lee-see-tah-see-'ohn, ehn-oh-rah-'bweh-nah]; **to congratulate** (v) felicitar [feh-lee-see-'tahr]

connect (v) unir [oo-'neer]; (tel) conectar, poner en comunicación [kohn-nehk-'tahr, poh-'nehr ehn koh-moo-nee-kah-see-'ohn]

connection la relación, contacto [lah reh-lah-see-'ohn, kohn-'tahk-toh]; (tel) la comunicación [lah koh-moo-nee-kah-see-'ohn]

conscientious(ly) concienzudo [kohn-see-ehn-'soo-doh]; (adv) concienzudamente [kohn-see-ehn-soo-dah-'mehn-teh]

consider (v) considerar como [kohn-see-deh-'rahr 'koh-moh]

considerable considerable [kohn-see-deh-'rah-bleh]

consideration la consideración [lah kohn-see-deh-rah-see-'ohn]; **considerate** considerado [kohn-see-deh-'rah-doh]

consist of (v) constar de [kohn-'stahr deh]

constitution la constitución [lah kohn-stee-too-see-'ohn]

consulate consulado [kohn-soo-'lah-doh]

consult (v) consultar [kohn-sool-'tahr]

consume (v) consumir, gastar [kohn-soo-'meer, gah-'stahr]

consumption consumo [kohn-'soo-moh]

contact contacto [kohn-'tahk-toh]

contain (v) contener [kohn-teh-'nehr]

container vasija, el recipiente [vah-'see-hah, ehl reh-see-pee-'ehn-teh]

content contenido [kohn-teh-'nee-doh]

continue (v) continuar [kohn-tee-noo-'ahr]

contraceptive anticonceptivo [ahn-tee-kohn-sehp-'tee-voh]

contract contrato [kohn-'trah-toh]

contrary lo contrario [loh kohn-'trah-ree-oh]; **on the contrary** al contrario [ahl kohn-'trah-ree-oh]

control (v) controlar [kohn-troh-'lahr]

control control [kohn-'trohl]

conversation la conversación [lah kohn-vehr-sah-see-'ohn]

cook (v) cocinar, hacer la comida [koh-see-'nahr, ah-'sehr lah koh-'mee-dah]

cooked cocido, cocinado [koh-'see-doh, koh-see-'nah-doh]; **well-cooked/-done** bien cocido [bee-ehn koh-'see-doh]

cool fresco ['freh-skoh]

copy copia ['koh-pee-ah]

cordial cordial [kohr-dee-'ahl]

cordiality la cordialidad [lah kohr-dee-ah-lee-'dahd]

corner el rincón, esquina [ehl reen-'kohn, eh-'skee-nah]; (street) la esquina [lah eh-'skee-nah]

corporation empresa [ehm-'preh-sah]

correct (v) corregir [koh-rreh-'heer]

correct correcto [koh-'rrehk-toh]

correspondence correspondencia [koh-rreh-spohn-'dehn-see-ah]

corrupt corrupto, corrompido [koh-'roop-toh, koh-rrohm-'pee-doh]

cost (v) costar, valer [koh-'stahr, vah-'lehr]

cost costo, gasto ['koh-stoh, 'gah-stoh]; **cost-free** gratis, gratuito ['grah-tees, grah-too-'ee-toh]

Costa Rican costarricense [koh-stah-ree-'sehn-seh]

costly caro, costoso ['kah-roh, koh-'stoh-soh]

cough (v) toser [toh-'sehr]

count (v) contar [kohn-'tahr]

country el país [ehl pah-'ees]

A/Z

country house casa de campo ['kah-sah deh 'kahm-poh]

countryman el compatriota, *(Am)* el connacional [ehl kohm-pah-tree-'oh-tah, ehl koh-nah-see-oh-'nahl]

couple un par [oon pahr]; *(relationship)* pareja, matrimonio [pah-'reh-hah, mah-tree-'moh-nee-oh]

coupon el talón, *(Am)* el boletín, el cupón [ehl tah-'lohn, ehl boh-leh-'teen, ehl koo-'pohn]

course curso ['koor-soh]

court el tribunal [ehl tree-boo-'nahl]

courtyard patio ['pah-tee-oh]

cousin el primo/la prima [ehl 'pree-moh/lah 'pree-mah]

cover *(v)* tapar [tah-'pahr]

cover cubrir [koo-'breer]

cow vaca ['vah-kah]

crazy loco ['loh-koh]

create *(v)* crear [kreh-'ahr]

creative creativo [kreh-ah-tee-voh]

credit crédito ['kreh-dee-toh]

crew la tripulación [lah tree-poo-lah-see-'ohn]

criticize *(v)* criticar [kree-tee-'kahr]

cross *(v)* cruzar, atravesar [kroo-'sahr, ah-trah-veh-'sahr]

cross cruz [kroos]

crossing paso, el pasaje ['pah-soh, ehl pah-'sah-heh]

crossroads el cruce [ehl 'kroo-seh]

crowd la multitud, la muchedumbre [lah mool-tee-'tood, lah moo-cheh-'doom-breh]

cry *(v)* llorar [yoh-'rahr]

Cuba Cuba ['koo-bah]

Cuban cubano [koo-'bah-noh]

culture cultura [kool-'too-rah]

curious curioso [koo-ree-'oh-soh]

current la corriente [lah koh-rree-'ehn-teh]

curtain cortina [kohr-'tee-nah]

curve curva ['koor-vah]

cushion el cojín [ehl koh-'heen]

customs aduana [ah-'dwah-nah]; **customs officer** funcionario de aduanas, aduanero [foonk-see-oh-'nah-ree-oh deh ah-'dwah-nahs, ah-dwah-'neh-roh]

cut *(v)* cortar [kohr-'tahr]

cute lindo, gracioso ['leen-doh, grah-see-'oh-soh]

D

daily *(adj)* diario, cotidiano [dee-'ah-ree-oh, koh-tee-dee-'ah-noh]; *(adv)* a diario, diariamente [ah dee-'ah-ree-oh, dee-ah-ree-ah-'mehn-teh]

damage *(v)* dañar, estropear, echar a perder, hacer daño [dah-'nyahr, eh-stroh-peh-'ahr, eh-'chahr ah pehr-'dehr, ah-'sehr 'dah-nyoh]

damage daño ['dah-nyoh]

dance el baile [ehl 'bah-ee-leh]

danger peligro [peh-'lee-groh]

dangerous peligroso [peh-lee-'groh-soh]

dare *(v)* atreverse a [ah-treh-'vehr-seh ah]

dark oscuro [oh-'skoo-roh]

darling querido, cariño [keh-'ree-doh, kah-'ree-nyoh]

date fecha ['feh-chah]

daughter hija ['ee-hah]

day el día [ehl 'dee-ah]

dead muerto ['mwehr-toh]

deadline plazo ['plah-soh]

dear querido [keh-'ree-doh]

death muerte ['mwehr-teh]

debt deuda [deh-'oo-dah]

decide *(v)* decidir, resolver, acordar [deh-see-'deer, reh-sohl-'vehr, ah-kohr-'dahr]; **to decide (oneself)** *(v)* decidirse [deh-see-'deer-seh]

decision la decisión, la resolución [lah deh-see-see-'ohn, lah reh-soh-loo-see-'ohn]

declare *(v)* declarar [deh-klah-'rahr]

deep profundo, hondo [proh-'foon-doh, 'ohn-doh]

defective defectuoso [deh-fehk-too-'oh-soh]

defend *(v)* defender [deh-fehn-'dehr]

definite(ly) *(adj)* definitivo [deh-fee-nee-'tee-voh]; *(adv)* definitivamente [deh-fee-nee-tee-vah-'mehn-teh]

degree grado ['grah-doh]

delay *(v)* aplazar, prorrogar, retardar [ah-plah-'sahr, proh-rroh-'gahr, reh-tahr-'dahr]

delay aplazamiento, prórroga [ah-plah-sah-mee-'ehn-toh, 'proh-rroh-gah]

delighted *(adj)* encantado [ehn-kahn-'tah-doh]

delightful encantador [ehn-kahn-tah-'dohr]

deliver *(v)* entregar [ehn-treh-'gahr]

demand *(v)* exigir [ehk-see-'heer]

demand exigencia [ehk-see-'hehn-see-ah]

demonstrate (v) demostrar [deh-moh-'strahr]

dense denso ['dehn-soh]

deny (v) negar [neh-'gahr]

department store los (grandes) almacenes [lohs ('grahn-dehs) ahl-mah-'seh-nehs]

departure salida, partida [sah-'lee-dah, pahr-'tee-dah]

deposit (v) depositar [deh-poh-see-'tahr]

deposit depósito [deh-'poh-see-toh]

describe (v) describir [deh-skree-'beer]

deserve (v) merecer, ameritar [meh-reh-'sehr, ah-meh-ree-'tahr]

desperate desesperado [dehs-eh-speh-'rah-doh]

despicable sinvergüenza, descarado [seen-vehr-'gwehn-sah, dehs-kah-'rah-doh]

destroy (v) destruir [deh-stroo-'eer]

detail el detalle [ehl deh-'tah-yeh]

detailed (adj) detallado, amplio [deh-tah-'yah-doh, 'ahm-plee·oh]; (adv) detalladamente [deh-tah-yah-dah-'mehn-teh]

determined, to be (v) estar/ser decidido [eh-'stahr/sehr deh-see-'dee-doh]

detour rodeo [roh-'deh-oh]

develop (v) desarrollar; (foto) revelar [dehs-ah-rroh-'yahr ('foh-toh) reh-veh-'lahr]

development desarrollo; (foto) revelado [dehs-ah-'rroh-yoh; ('foh-toh) reh-veh-'lah-doh]

diagnosis diagnóstico [dee-ahg-'noh-stee-koh]

dice dado ['dah-doh]

die (v) morir [moh-'reer]

differ (v) estar en desacuerdo con [eh-'stahr ehn dehs-ah-'kwehr-doh kohn]

difference diferencia [dee-feh-'rehn-see·ah]

different distinto, diferente [dee-'steen-toh, dee-feh-'rehn-teh]; **differently** de otra manera/forma [deh 'oh-trah mah-'neh-rah/fohr-mah]

difficult difícil [dee-'fee-seel]

difficulty la dificultad [lah dee-fee-kool-'tahd]

diminish (v) disminuir; [dees-mee-noo-'eer]

direct(ly) (adj) directo, inmediato [dee-'rehk-toh, een-meh-dee-'ah-toh]; (adv) directamente, inmediatamente [dee-rehk-tah-'mehn-teh, een-meh-dee-ah-tah-'mehn-teh]

direction la dirección [lah dee-rehk-see-'ohn]

directory directorio, lista [dee-rehk-'toh-ree·oh, 'lee-stah]

dirt la suciedad, barro [lah soo-see-eh-'dahd, 'bah-rroh]

dirty sucio ['soo-see·oh]

disadvantage desventaja, el inconveniente [dehs-vehn-'tah-hah, ehl een-kohn-veh-nee-'ehn-teh]

disappear (v) desaparecer [dehs-ah-pah-reh-'sehr]

disappointed (adj) desilusionado [dehs-ee-loo-see-oh-'nah-doh]

discount rebaja, descuento [reh-'bah-hah, dehs-'kwehn-toh]

discover (v) descubrir [deh-skoo-'breer]

dish plato ['plah-toh]

disorder el desorden [ehl dehs-'ohr-dehn]

dispatch (v) enviar, remitir [ehn-vee-'ahr, reh-mee-'teer]

disruption interrupción [een-teh-rroop-see-'ohn]

distance distancia [dee-'stahn-see·ah]

distant distante, alejado [dee-'stahn-teh, ah-leh-'hah-doh]

distinguished distinguido [dee-steen-'gee-doh]

distribute (v) distribuir [dee-stree-boo-'eer]

distribution la distribución [lah dee-stree-boo-see-'ohn]

disturb (v) molestar, estorbar [moh-leh-'stahr, eh-stohr-'bahr]

disturbance, commotion tumulto [too-'mool-toh]

divide (v) partir, dividir [pahr-'teer, dee-vee-'deer]

dizzy mareado [mah-reh-'ah-doh]

do (v) hacer [ah-'sehr]

dock muelle, dársena ['mweh-yeh, 'dahr-seh-nah]

doctor, physician el doctor, médico [ehl dohk-'tohr, 'meh-dee-koh]

document documento [doh-koo-'mehn-toh]

dog perro ['peh-rroh]

doll muñeca [moo-'nyeh-kah]

donkey burro, asno ['boo-rroh, 'ahs-noh]

door puerta ['pwehr-tah]

double, twice doble ['doh-bleh]

doubt (v) dudar [doo-'dahr]

doubt duda ['doo-dah]

doubtful dudoso, incierto [doo-'doh-soh; een-see-'ehr-toh]

doubtless sin duda, indudable(mente) [seen 'doo-dah, een-doo-dah-bleh-'mehn-teh]

A/Z

down abajo, hacia abajo [ah-'bah-hoh, 'ah-see·ah ah-'bah-hoh]

down payment fianza, la caución [fee-'ahn-sah, lah kah·oo-see-'ohn]

downhill cuesta abajo ['kweh-stah ah-'bah-hoh]

draw (v) dibujar [dee-boo-'hahr]

dream (v) soñar [soh-'nyahr]

dream sueño ['sweh-nyoh]

dress (v) vestir [veh-'steer]; **to get dressed** (v) vestirse [veh-'steer-seh]

dress el traje, el vestido [ehl 'trah-heh, ehl veh-'stee-doh]

drink (v) beber, tomar [beh-'behr, toh-'mahr]

drinking water agua potable ['ah-gwah poh-'tah-bleh]

drip (v) gotear [goh-teh-'ahr]

drip gotera [goh-'teh-rah]

drive (v) conducir, (Am) manejar [kohn-doo-'seer, mah-neh-'hahr]

driver el conductor, el chófer, (Am) el chofer [ehl kohn-dook-'tohr, ehl 'choh-fehr, ehl choh-'fehr]

drop gota ['goh-tah]

drunk borracho, (Am) apimpado; (lightly) alegre, bebido, (Am) alegrón [boh-'rrah-choh, ah-peem-'pah-doh; ah-'leh-greh, beh-'bee-doh, ah-leh-'grohn]

dry (v) secar [seh-'kahr]

dry seco ['seh-koh]

dry cleaner tintorería [teen-toh-reh-'ree-ah]

dumb tonto, estúpido, bobo, (Am) zonzo ['tohn-toh, eh-'stoo-pee-'doh, 'boh-boh, 'sohn-soh]

durable duradero [doo-rah-'deh-roh]

duration la duración [lah doo-rah-see-'ohn]

dust polvo ['pohl-voh]

duty la obligación, el deber [lah ohb-lee-gah-see-'ohn, ehl deh-'behr]

E

each other uno(s) a otro(s), entre sí, mutuamente ['oo-noh(s) ah 'oh-troh(s), 'ehn-treh see, moo-too-ah-'mehn-teh]

earlier antes ['ahn-tehs]; **early** temprano [tehm-'prah-noh]

earn (v) ganar [gah-'nahr]

earnings ganancias [gah-'nahn-see·ahs]

earth tierra [tee-'eh-rrah]

east el este [ehl 'eh-steh]

easy fácil ['fah-seel]

eat (v) comer [koh-'mehr]

Ecuadorian ecuatoriano [eh-kwah-toh-ree-'ah-noh]

edge orilla, el borde [oh-'ree-yah, ehl 'bohr-deh]

edible comestible [koh-meh-'stee-bleh]

education la educación [lah eh-doo-kah-see-'ohn]

effect efecto [eh-'fehk-toh]

effective eficaz [eh-fee-'kahs]

effort esfuerzo [ehs-'fwehr-soh]

egg huevo ['weh-voh]

either ... or o ... o [oh...oh]

elect (v) elegir [eh-leh-'heer]

election la elección [lah eh-lehk-see-'ohn]

electric eléctrico [eh-'lehk-tree-koh]

elevator el ascensor [ehl ah-sehn-'sohr]

else si no, en caso contrario, más [see noh; ehn 'kah-soh·kohn-'trah-ree·oh; mahs]; **or else** si no, en caso contrario [see noh, ehn 'kah-soh kohn-'trah-ree·oh]; **nothing else** nada más ['nah-dah mahs]

elsewhere en otra parte [ehn 'oh-trah 'pahr-teh]

emancipated emancipado [eh-mahn-see-'pah-doh]

embassy embajada [ehm-bah-'hah-dah]

embrace (v) abrazar [ah-brah-'sahr]

employ (v) emplear, usar [ehm-pleh-'ahr, oo-'sahr]

employed/employee empleado [ehm-pleh-'ah-doh]

employment empleo [ehm-'pleh-oh]

empty vacío [vah-'see-oh]

enclosure (letter) anexo, adjunto [ah-'nehk-soh, ahd-'hoon-toh]

end (v) terminar, acabar [tehr-mee-'nahr, ah-kah-'bahr]

end el fin, el final, término [ehl feen, ehl fee-'nahl, 'tehr-mee-noh]; **at the end** al final [ahl fee-'nahl]

engaged (to) (v) prometerse con, (Am) comprometido [proh-meh-'tehr-seh kohn, kohm-proh-meh-'tee-doh]

England Inglaterra [een-glah-'teh-rrah]

English (lang) inglés [een-'glehs]

English el inglés/la inglesa [ehl een-'glehs, ehl een-'gleh-sah]

enjoy (v) gozar de, disfrutar de [goh-'sahr deh, dees-froo-'tahr deh]

enjoyment gozo, el placer ['goh-soh, ehl plah-'sehr]

enough bastante, suficiente [bah-'stahn-teh, soo-fee-see-'ehn-teh]
enter (v) entrar [ehn-'trahr]; **enter (the country), to** (v) entrar (en el país) [ehn-'trahr (ehn ehl pah-'ees)]
entertainment entretenimiento [ehn-treh-teh-nee-mee-'ehn-toh]; **entertaining** entretenido [ehn-treh-teh-'nee-doh]
enthusiastic (about) entusiasmado (con) [ehn-too-see-ahs-'mah-doh (kohn)]
entitled to autorizado para, con derecho a [ow-toh-ree-'sah-doh 'pah-rah, kohn deh-'reh-choh ah]
entrance entrada, acceso [ehn-'trah-dah, ahk-'seh-soh]
environment el (medio) ambiente [ehl ('meh-dee-oh) ahm-bee-'ehn-teh]
equipment equipo, la dotación [eh-'kee-poh, lah doh-tah-see-'ohn]
equivalent equivalente [ehl eh-kee-vah-'lehn-teh]
estate finca rústica, (Am) finca rural ['feen-kah 'roo-stee-kah; 'feen-kah roo-'rahl]
estimate (v) calcular, tasar [kahl-koo-'lahr, tah-'sahr]
estimate cálculo, tasación ['kahl-koo-'loh, tah-sah-see-'ohn]
Europe Europa [eh-oo-'roh-pah]
European europeo/europea [eh-oo-roh-'peh-oh/eh-oo-roh-'peh-ah]
evening la tarde [lah 'tahr-deh]
event acontecimiento, espectáculo, suceso [ah-kohn-teh-see-mee-'ehn-toh, eh-spehk-'tah-koo-loh, soo-'seh-soh]
every cada, todos ['kah-dah, 'toh-dohs]; **everyone** todos, cada, cada uno ['toh-dohs, 'kah-dah, 'kah-dah oo-noh]; **everybody** todo el mundo ['toh-doh ehl 'moon-doh]; **everything** todo ['toh-doh]; **every day** todos los días ['toh-dohs lohs 'dee-ahs]; **every two hours** cada dos horas ['kah-dah dohs 'oh-rahs]
everywhere por/en todas partes [pohr/ehn 'toh-dahs 'pahr-tehs]
evil malévolo [mah-'leh-voh-loh]
exact(ly) exacto, preciso [ehk-'sahk-toh, preh-'see-soh]; (adv) exactamente [ehk-sahk-tah-'mehn-teh]
exaggerated exagerado [ehk-sah-heh-'rah-doh]
examination el examen [ehl ehk-'sah-mehn]
examine (v) examinar, controlar [ehk-sah-mee-'nahr, kohn-troh-'lahr]

example ejemplo [eh-'hehm-ploh]; **for example** por ejemplo [pohr eh-'hehm-ploh]
excellent excelente, extraordinario [ehk-seh-'lehn-teh, ehk-strah-ohr-dee-'nah-ree-oh]
except excepto [ehk-'sehp-toh]
exception la excepción [lah ehk-sehp-see-'ohn]
exchange cambio ['kahm-bee-oh]; (currency) cambio ['kahm-bee-oh]
excuse (v) excusar, disculpar [ehk-skoo-'sahr, dees-kool-'pahr]
excuse excusa [ehk-'skoo-sah]
exercise ejercicio [eh-hehr-'see-see-oh]
exhausted, sold out agotado [ah-goh-'tah-doh]
exit (v) aplazar [ah-plah-'sahr]
exit salida [sah-'lee-dah]
expenses los gastos [lohs 'gah-stohs]
expensive caro ['kah-roh]
experience experiencia [ehk-speh-ree-'ehn-see-ah]
experiment experimento, prueba, ensayo [ehk-speh-ree-'mehn-toh, proo-'eh-bah, ehn-'sah-yoh]
expire (v) expirar [ehk-spee-'rahr]
explain (v) explicar, aclarar [ehk-splee-'kahr, ah-klah-'rahr]
explicit(ly) expreso, expresamente [ehk-'spreh-soh, ehk-spreh-sah-'mehn-teh]
expression la expresión [lah ehk-spreh-see-'ohn]
extend (v) alargar; prolongar [ah-lahr-'gahr, proh-lohn-'gahr]
exterior exterior [ehks-teh-ree-'ohr]
extinguish (v) apagar [ah-pah-'gahr]
extra adicional, especial [ah-dee-see-oh-'nahl, eh-speh-see-'ahl]
extraordinary extraordinario [ehks-trah-ohr-dee-'nah-ree-oh]
eye ojo ['oh-hoh]
eyeglasses las gafas, (Am) los lentes [lahs 'gah-fahs, lohs 'lehn-tehs]

F

fabric tejido [teh-'hee-doh]
fact hecho ['eh-choh]; **in fact** de hecho, en efecto, efectivamente [deh 'eh-choh, ehn eh-'fehk-toh, eh-fehk-tee-vah-'mehn-teh]
factory fábrica ['fah-bree-kah]

fair correcto, justo [koh-'rrehk-toh, 'hoo-stoh]; *(sport)* limpio ['leem-pee-oh]

faith la fé [lah feh]

fall *(v)* caer [kah-'ehr]

fall caída [kah-'ee-dah]

fall otoño [oh-'toh-nyoh]

fall asleep *(v)* dormirse [dohr-'meer-seh]

false falso, incorrecto ['fahl-soh, een-koh-'rrehk-toh]

family familia [fah-'mee-lee-ah]

famous famoso, célebre [fah-'moh-soh, 'seh-leh-breh]

fan partidario, aficionado [pahr-tee-'dah-ree-oh, ah-fee-see-oh-'nah-doh]

fantastic fantástico, estupendo [fahn-'tah-stee-koh, eh-stoo-'pehn-doh]

far lejano [leh-'hah-noh]

farm finca, granja, *(Am)* estancia, hacienda ['feen-kah, 'grahn-hah, eh-'stahn-see-ah, ah-see-'ehn-dah]

farmer campesino, el agricultor [kahm-peh-'see-noh, ehl ah-gree-kool-'tohr]

fashion moda ['moh-dah]

fast rápido ['rah-pee-doh]; **the clock is fast** el reloj está adelantado [ehl reh-'loh eh-'stah ah-deh-lahn-'tah-doh]

fat gordo, grueso ['gohr-doh, groo-'eh-soh]

father el padre [ehl 'pah-dreh]; **father-land** patria ['pah-tree-ah]

faucet grifo, llave de agua, pluma ['gree-foh, 'yah-veh deh 'ah-gwah, 'ploo-mah]

fault falta, defecto ['fahl-tah, deh-'fehk-toh]

favor favor [fah-'vohr]; **in favor of** en favor de [ehn fah-'vohr deh]

favorable favorable [fah-voh-'rah-bleh]

fear el temor, miedo [ehl teh-'mohr, mee-'eh-doh]

fear, be afraid of *(v)* temer [teh-'mehr]

feather pluma ['ploo-mah]

fee los honorarios [lohs oh-noh-'rah-ree-ohs]

feed *(n)* comida para animales [koh-'mee-dah 'pah-rah ah-nee-'mah-lehs]

feel *(v)* sentir [sehn-'teer]

feel sentir [sehn-'teer]

feel fit *(v)* sentar bien [sehn-'tahr bee-ehn]; venir/ir bien [veh-'neer/eer bee-ehn]

feeling sentimiento [sehn-tee-mee-'ehn-toh]

feminine femenino [feh-meh-'nee-noh]

festive festivo [feh-'stee-voh]

fiancé, fiancée el prometido, la prometida [ehl proh-meh-'tee-doh, lah proh-meh-'tee-dah]

field campo ['kahm-poh]

fill *(v)* llenar [yeh-'nahr]; **fill up** *(v)* poner gasolina [poh-'nehr gah-soh-'lee-nah]

film *(v)* filmar, hacer/sacar una película [feel-'mahr, ah-'sehr/sah-'kahr 'oo-nah peh-'lee-koo-lah]

film película, el film(e) [peh-'lee-koo-lah, ehl 'feelm(eh)]

filter filtro ['feel-troh]

final(ly) final [fee-'nahl]; *(adv)* finalmente [fee-nahl-'mehn-teh]

finally finalmente, por fin [fee-nahl-'mehn-teh, pohr feen]

find *(v)* encontrar [ehn-kohn-'trahr]

fine *(size)* fino, delgado ['fee-noh, dehl-'gah-doh]; *(quality)* delicado [deh-lee-'kah-doh]; *(style)* distinguido, elegante [dee-steen-'gee-doh, eh-leh-'gahn-teh]

fine multa ['mool-tah]

fingertip punta del dedo ['poon-tah dehl 'deh-doh]

finish *(v)* acabar, terminar [ah-kah-'bahr, tehr-mee-'nahr]

fire incendio, fuego [een-'sehn-dee-oh, 'fweh-goh]

fire alarm el avisador de incendios [ehl ah-vee-sah-'dohr deh een-'sehn-dee-ohs]

fire extinguisher el extintor [ehl ehk-steen-'tohr]

firemen los bomberos [lohs bohm-'beh-rohs]

firewood leña ['leh-nyah]

fireworks los fuegos artificiales [lohs 'fweh-gohs ahr-tee-fee-see-'ah-lehs]

firm firme, fijo, duro, resistente ['feer-meh, 'fee-hoh, 'doo-roh, reh-see-'stehn-teh]

first primer, primero/a, en primer lugar, *(Am)* recién [pree-'mehr, pree-'meh-roh(ah), ehn pree-'mehr loo-'gahr, reh-see-'ehn]; **first-born** recién nacido [reh-see-'ehn nah-'see-doh]

first class de primera clase/categoría [deh pree-'meh-rah 'klah-seh/kah-teh-goh-'ree-ah]

fish *(v)* pescar [peh-'skahr]

fish pez [ehl pehs]; *(after it's caught)* pescado [ehl peh-'skah-doh]

fit saludable, en forma, adecuado [sah-loo-'dah-bleh, ehn 'fohr-mah, ah-deh-'kwah-doh]

fix, set *(v)* fijar, establecer [fee-'hahr, eh-stah-bleh-'sehr]

flame llama ['yah-mah]

flash (camera) el flash [ehl flahsh]

flashlight linterna [leen-'tehr-nah]
flat, level bajo, llano ['bah-hoh, 'yah-noh]
flirt flirteo, coqueteo [fleer-'teh-oh]
floor piso ['pee-soh]
flow (v) correr [koh-'rrehr]
flower la flor [lah flohr]
fly (v) volar, ir en avión [voh-'lahr, eer ehn ah-vee-'ohn]
fly mosca ['moh-skah]
foggy brumoso [broo-'moh-soh]
follow (v) seguir [seh-'geer]
follow up on something (v) ocuparse de algo [oh-koo-'pahr-seh deh 'ahl-goh]
fond (of), to be (v) querer a alguien [keh-'rehr ah 'ahl-gee-ehn]
food comida, los alimentos, los comestibles [koh-'mee-dah, lohs ahl-lee-'mehn-tohs, lohs koh-meh-'stee-blehs, lah koh-'mee-dah, lohs ah-lee-'mehn-tohs]
foot el pie [ehl 'pee-eh]
for para, por ['pah-rah, pohr]
forbid (v) prohibir [proh-ee-'beer]
forbidden prohibido [proh-ee-'bee-doh]
force (v) obligar, forzar [ohb-lee-'gahr, fohr-'sahr]
foreigner/alien el/la extranjero/a [ehl/lah ehk-strahn-'heh-roh/ah]
forest el bosque [ehl 'boh-skeh]
forget (v) olvidar [ohl-vee-'dahr]; **to forget something** (v) dejar algo, olvidar algo [deh-'hahr 'ahl-goh, ohl-vee-'dahr 'ahl-goh]
forgive (v) perdonar, excusar [pehr-doh-'nahr, ehk-skoo-'sahr]
forgiveness el perdón [ehl pehr-'dohn]
form (v) formar [fohr-'mahr]
form, application impreso, formulario [eem-'preh-soh, fohr-moo-'lah-ree-oh]
form, shape forma ['fohr-mah]
format formato [fohr-'mah-toh]
forward adelante [ah-deh-'lahn-teh]
fountain la fuente [lah 'fwehn-teh]
fragile frágil ['frah-heel]
France Francia ['frahn-see-ah]
fraud el fraude [ehl 'frah·oo-deh]
free (freedom) libre ['lee-breh]; (no charge) gratis, gratuitamente ['grah-tees, grah-too-ee-tah-'mehn-teh]
freeze (v) helarse, congelarse [eh-'lahr-seh, kohn-heh-'lahr-seh]
freight el flete, carga [ehl 'fleh-teh, 'kahr-gah]
French el francés/la francesa; (lang) francés [ehl frah-'sehs/lah frahn-'seh-sah; frahn-'sehs]

frequent(ly) frecuente (adv) frecuentemente, a menudo [freh-'kwehn-teh; freh-kwehn-teh-'mehn-teh, ah meh-'noo-doh]
fresh fresco ['freh-skoh]; (new) nuevo, reciente [noo-'eh-voh, reh-see-'ehn-teh]; (clean) limpio ['leem-pee·oh]
friend el amigo/la amiga [ehl ah-'mee-goh/lah ah-'mee-gah]
friendly amable, amistoso [ah-'mah-bleh, ah-mee-'stoh-soh]
friendship la amistad [lah ah-mee-'stahd]
frighten (v) asustar [ah-soo-'stahr]; **to be frightened** (v) estar asustado [eh-'stahr ah-soo-'stah-doh]
from de, desde [deh, 'dehs-deh]
front delante, frente [deh-'lahn-teh, 'frehn-teh]; **in front** delante de [deh-'lahn-teh deh]
front door puerta de la casa ['pwehr-tah deh lah 'kah-sah]
fruit fruta ['froo-tah]
fry (v) freír [freh-'eer]
fuel oil el aceite combustible, el fuel-oil [ehl ah-'seh·ee-teh kohm-boo-'stee-bleh, ehl fee·oo-ohl-'oh·ehl]
fulfill (v) realizar, llevar a cabo, lograr [reh-ah-lee-'sahr, yeh-'vahr ah 'kah-boh, loh-'grahr]
full lleno; completo, total ['yeh-noh, kohm-'pleh-toh, toh-'tahl]; (food) lleno, harto, satisfecho ['yeh-noh, 'ahr-toh, sah-tees-'feh-choh]
fun diversión [dee-vehr-see-'ohn]
function (v) funcionar [foonk-see·oh-'nahr]
funny divertido, gracioso [dee-vehr-'tee-doh, grah-see-'oh-soh]
fur la piel [lah pee-'ehl]
furious rabioso, furioso [rah-bee-'oh-soh, foo-ree-'oh-soh]
furnish (v) amueblar [ah-mweh-'blahr]
furniture el mueble [ehl 'mweh-bleh]
fuse (el) el fusible [ehl foo-'see-bleh]
future futuro, el porvenir [foo-'too-roh, ehl pohr-veh-'neer]

G

gain weight (v) engordar [ehn-gohr-'dahr]
Galicia Galicia [gah-'lee-see-ah]

A/Z

Galician gallego/gallega *(lang)* gallego [gah-'yeh-goh/gah-'yeh-gah; gah-'yeh-goh]

game juego [joo-'eh-goh']; *(hunt)* caza ['kah-sah]; *(meat)* venado [veh-'nah-doh]

garage el garaje [ehl gah-'rah-heh]

garbage basura [bah-'soo-rah]

garbage can, trashcan cubo de la basura ['koo-boh deh lah bah-'soo-rah]

garden el jardín [ehl hahr-'deen]

gas gasolina, *(Arg)* nafta [gah-soh-'lee-nah, 'nahf-tah]

gear *(auto)* marcha ['mahr-chah]

general general, usual [heh-neh-'rahl, oo-soo-'ahl]; **in general** en general [ehn heh-neh-'rahl]

gentle delicado [deh-lee-'kah-doh]

genuine verdadero, auténtico [vehr-dah-'deh-roh, ow-'tehn-tee-koh]

German el alemán, la alemana; *(lang)* el alemán [ehl ah-leh-'mahn, lah ah-leh-'mah-nah; ehl ah-leh-'mahn]

Germany Alemania [ah-leh-'mah-nee-ah]

get *(v)* coger, tomar, recibir, procurar, proporcionar, buscar [koh-'hehr, toh-'mahr, reh-see-'beer, proh-koo-'rahr, proh-pohr-see-oh-'nahr, boo-'skahr]; **get back** *(v)* recobrar, recuperar [reh-koh-'brahr-seh, reh-koo-peh-'rahr]

get along with *(v)* entenderse bien, llevarse bien con [ehn-tehn-'dehr-seh 'bee-ehn, yeh-'vahr-seh 'bee-ehn kohn]

get drunk *(v)* emborracharse [ehm-boh-rrah-'chahr-seh]

get lost *(v)* perderse [pehr-'dehr-seh]

get sick *(v)* ponerse enfermo [poh-'nehr-seh ehn-'fehr-moh]

get up/stand up *(v)* levantarse/ponerse de pie [leh-vahn-'tahr-seh/poh-'nehr-seh deh 'pee-eh]

gift regalo [reh-'gah-loh]

girl muchacha, chica [moo-'chah-chah, 'chee-kah]

give *(v)* dar [dahr]; **give back** devolver [deh-vohl-'vehr]

give an opinion *(v)* opinar [oh-pee-'nahr]

gladly con gusto, de buena gana [kohn 'goo-stoh, deh 'bweh-nah 'gah-nah]

glass *(material)* el cristal, vidrio [ehl kree-'stahl, 'vee-dree-oh]; *(recipient)* vaso, copa ['vah-soh, 'koh-pah]

go *(v)* ir [eer]; **go away** *(v)* irse, marcharse ['eer-seh, mahr-'chahr-seh]; **to**

go straight on/ahead ir todo seguido [eer 'toh-doh seh-'gee-doh]; **to go on** seguir adelante, avanzar [seh-'geer ah-deh-'lahn-teh, ah-vahn-'sahr]

go get *(v)* ir a buscar, ir a recoger [eer a boo-'skahr, eer ah reh-koh-'hehr]

go in *(v)* entrar [ehn-'trahr]

go on a trip *(v)* viajar, irse de viaje [vee-ah-'hahr, 'eer-seh deh vee-'ah-heh]

go out *(v)* salir [sah-'leer]

go to bed *(v)* acostarse, ir(se) a la cama [ah-koh-'stahr-seh, 'eer(seh) ah lah 'kah-mah]

go up *(v)* subir [soo-'beer]

goal meta ['meh-tah]

God Dios ['dee-ohs]; **thank God** ¡gracias a Dios! ['grah-see-ahs ah 'dee-ohs]

good *(adj)* bueno, buen; *(adv)* bien ['bweh-noh, bwehn; 'bee-ehn]

good-bye adiós, hasta luego [ah-dee-'ohs, 'ah-stah loo-'eh-goh] **(to say) good-bye** *(v)* decir adiós, despedirse [deh-'seer ah-dee-'ohs, deh-speh-'deer-seh]

goods mercancía, *(Am)* mercadería [mehr-kahn-'see-ah mehr-kah-deh-'ree-ah]

government gobierno [goh-bee-'ehr-noh]

grab *(v)* tomar, coger, *(Am)* agarrar [toh-'mahr, koh-'hehr, ah-gah-'rrahr]

grandfather abuelo [ah-'bweh-loh]

grandmother abuela [ah-'bweh-lah]

grandson/granddaughter el nieto/la nieta [ehl nee-'eh-toh/lah nee-'eh-tah]

grant conceder [kohn-seh-'dehr]

gratitude agradecimiento [ah-grah-deh-see-mee-'ehn-toh]

great grande ['grahn-deh]; *(height)* alto ['ahl-toh]; *(importance)* importante, considerable [eem-pohr-'tahn-teh, kohn-see-deh-'rah-bleh]; *(good)* excelente, maravilloso [ehk-seh-'lehn-teh, mah-rah-vee-'yoh-soh]

greet *(v)* saludar [sah-loo-'dahr]

grief pena ['peh-nah]

ground terreno [teh-'rreh-noh]

ground floor piso bajo, *(Am)* los bajos ['pee-soh 'bah-hoh, lohs 'bah-hohs]

ground, soil suelo, piso, tierra ['sweh-loh, 'pee-soh tee-'eh-rrah]

group grupo ['groo-poh]

grow *(v)* crecer [kreh-'sehr]

guarantee garantía [gah-rahn-'tee-ah]

guard el guarda, el vigilante [ehl 'gwahr-dah, ehl vee-hee-'lahn-teh]

Guatemalan guatemalteco [gwah-teh-mahl-'teh-koh]

guess (v) adivinar [ah-dee-vee-'nahr]
guess suposición [soo-poh-see-see-'ohn]
guest el huésped [ehl 'weh-spehd]
guide (person) el guía [ehl 'gee-ah]; (book) la guía [lah 'gee-ah]
guilt culpa ['kool-pah]
guitar guitarra [gee-'tah-rrah]
gulf golfo ['gohl-foh]

H

habit la costumbre [lah koh-'stoom-breh]
haggle (v) regatear [reh-gah-teh-'ahr]
half medio, la mitad ['meh-dee·oh, lah mee-'tahd]
hall el hall, el pasillo [ehl jahl, ehl pah-'see-yoh]
hammer martillo [mahr-'tee-yoh]
hand la mano [lah 'mah-noh]
hand over (v) entregar [ehn-treh-'gahr]
handle agarrador, asidero [ah-gah-rrah-'deh-roh, ah-see-'deh-roh]
handmade hecho a mano ['eh-choh ah 'mah-noh]
handsome guapo, bien parecido ['gwah-poh, 'bee·ehn pah-reh-'see-doh]
hang (up) (v) colgar [kohl-'gahr]
hang on/from colgar en/de [kohl-'gahr ehn/deh]
happen (v) suceder, pasar, ocurrir [soo-seh-'dehr, pah-'sahr, oh-koo-'rreer]; **what happened?** ¿qué ha pasado? [keh ah pah-'sah-doh]
happy contento, feliz, alegre, de buen humor [kohn-'tehn-toh, feh-'lees, ah-'leh-greh, deh bwehn oo-'mohr]
harass (sexually) (v) molestar, hostigar (sexualmente), faltar el respeto [moh-leh-'stahr, oh-stee-'gahr (sehk-soo-ahl-'mehn-teh), fahl-'tahr ehl reh-'speh-toh]
hard duro ['doo-roh]
hardly apenas [ah-'peh-nahs]
hardness dureza [doo-'reh-sah]
harm (v) dañar, hacer daño [dah-'nyahr, ah-'sehr 'dah-nyoh]
harmful nocivo, dañino [noh-'see-voh, dah-'nyee-noh]
harvest cosecha [koh-'seh-chah]
haste la rapidez, prisa [lah rah-pee-'dehs, 'pree-sah]
have tener [teh-'nehr]
have a good time, to (v) divertirse [dee-vehr-'teer-seh]

have fun (v) divertirse [dee-vehr-'teer-seh]
he él [ehl]
headscarf pañuelo de cabeza [pah-nyoo-'eh-loh deh kah-'beh-sah]
health la salud [lah sah-'lood]
healthy sano ['sah-noh]
hear (v) oír, saber, enterarse de [oh-'eer, sah-'behr, ehn-teh-'rahr-seh deh]
heart el corazón [ehl koh-rah-'sohn]
heat calor [kah-'lohr]; (v) calentar [kah-lehn-'tahr]
heaven cielo [see-'eh-loh]
heavy pesado [peh-'sah-doh]
hectic inquieto, agitado [een-kee-'eh-toh, ah-hee-'tah-doh]
heel el tacón [ehl tah-'kohn]
height altura [ahl-'too-rah]
hello ¡hola! ['oh-lah]
help ayuda [ah-'yoo-dah]
help ayudar, auxiliar [ah-yoo-'dahr, owk-'see-lee-ahr]; **help (someone)** (v) ayudar a alguien [ah-yoo-'dahr ah 'ahl-gee·ehn]
here acá, aquí [ah-'kah, ah-'kee]; **over here** para acá ['pah-rah ah-'kah]
herring el arenque [ehl ah-'rehn-keh]
hesitate (v) vacilar, dudar, tardar [vah-see-'lahr, doo-'dahr; tahr-'dahr]
hide (v) ocultar, esconder [oh-kool-'tahr, eh-skohn-'dehr]
high alto ['ahl-toh]
highlight (peak, climax) punto culminante ['poon-toh kool-mee-'nahn-teh]
hike (v) hacer excursiones a pie [ah-'sehr ehk-skoor-see-'oh-nehs ah 'pee-eh]
hill colina [koh-'lee-nah]
his, her, it (adj) tu, su [too, soo]; (poss pron), (adj) tuyo, tuya, suyo, suya ['too-yoh, 'too-yah, 'soo-yoh, 'soo-yah]
history historia [ee-'stoh-ree-ah]
hobby la afición, el hobby [lah ah-fee-see-'ohn, ehl 'joh-bee]
hole agujero [ah-goo-'heh-roh]
holiday el día de fiesta [ehl 'dee-ah deh fee-'eh-stah]
holidays, vacation las vacaciones [lahs vah-kah-see-'oh-nehs]; **on vacation** de vacaciones [deh vah-kah-see-'oh-nehs]
holy santo, sagrado ['sahn-toh, sah-'grah-doh]
homeland patria ['pah-tree·ah]
Honduran hondureño [ohn-doo-'reh-nyoh]

honor el honor [ehl oh-'nohr]
hook gancho ['gahn-choh]
hope (v) esperar [eh-speh-'rahr]
hope esperanza [eh-speh-'rahn-sah]
horse caballo [kah-'bah-yoh]
hose manguera [mahn-'geh-rah]
hospitality la hospitalidad [lah oh-spee-tah-lee-'dahd]
host/hostess el anfitrión/la anfitriona [ehl ahn-fee-tree-'ohn/lah ahn-fee-tree-'oh-nah]
hot caliente [kah-lee-'ehn-teh]
hotel el hotel [ehl oh-'tehl]
hour hora ['oh-rah]; **half an hour** media hora ['meh-dee·ah 'oh-rah]; **a quarter of an hour** un cuarto de hora [oon 'kwahr-toh deh 'oh-rah]
house casa ['kah-sah]
how cómo ['koh-moh]
however pero, sin embargo, no obstante ['peh-roh, seen ehm-'bahr-goh, noh ohb-'stahn-teh]
huge enorme, inmenso [eh-'nohr-meh, een-'mehn-soh]
human humano [oo-'mah-noh]; **human being** ser humano [sehr oo-'mah-noh]
humid húmedo ['oo-meh-doh]
hundred ciento, cien [see-'ehn-toh, 'see·ehn]; **a hundred times** cien veces ['see-ehn 'veh-sehs]
hunger el hambre [ehl 'ahm-breh]
hungry hambriento [ahm-bree-'ehn-toh]
hurry (v) darse prisa, (Am) apurarse ['dahr-seh 'pree-sah, ah-poo-'rahr-seh]
hurt (v) doler, hacer daño [doh-'lehr, ah-'sehr 'dah-nyoh]
hurtful doloroso [doh-loh-'roh-soh]
husband esposo, marido [eh-'spoh-soh, mah-'ree-doh]
hut cabaña, (Am) bohío [kah-'bah-nyah, boh-'ee-oh]

I

I yo [yoh]
ice hielo ['yeh-loh]
ice cream helado [eh-'lah-doh]
idea idea [ee-'deh-ah]; **no idea!** ¡ni idea! [nee ee-'deh-ah]
identity card (personal) tarjeta/el carnet de identidad [tahr-'heh-tah/ehl kahr-'neht deh ee-dehn-tee-'dahd]
if si [see]

illustration la ilustración [lah ee-loo-strah-see-'ohn]
immediate(ly) (adj) inmediato [een-meh-dee-'ah-toh]; (adv) inmediatamente [een-meh-dee-ah-tah-'mehn-teh]
immediately immediatamente, en seguida, (Am) ahorita [een-meh-dee-ah-tah-'mehn-teh, ehn seh-'gee-dah, ah-oh-'ree-tah]
impolite descortés, mal educado [dehs-kohr-'tehs, mahl eh-doo-'kah-doh]
important importante [eem-pohr-'tahn-teh]; **importance** importancia [eem-pohr-'tahn-see·ah]
impossible imposible [eem-poh-'see-bleh]
impression la impresión [lah eem-preh-see-'ohn]
improve (v) mejorar [meh-hoh-'rahr]
in en [ehn]
in a hurry de prisa [deh 'pree-sah]
in a hurry, to be (v) tener prisa [teh-'nehr 'pree-sah]
in case that en caso de que [ehn 'kah-soh deh keh]
in favor conforme con/en favor de [kohn-'fohr-meh kohn/ehn fah-'vohr deh]
incapable incapaz [een-kah-'pahs]
incident el incidente, contratiempo [ehl een-see-'dehn-teh, kohn-trah-tee-'ehm-poh]
include (v) incluir [een-kloo-'eer]
included incluido [een-kloo-'ee-doh]
incomplete incompleto [een-kohm-'pleh-toh]
inconsiderate desconsiderado [dehs-kohn-see-deh-'rah-doh]
increase (v) aumentar [ow-mehn-'tahr]
incredible increíble [een-kreh-'ee-bleh]
indefinite indeterminado [een-deh-tehr-mee-'nah-doh]
indemnify (v) indemnizar [een-dehm-nee-'sahr]
indicate (v) indicar, señalar [een-dee-'kahr, seh-nyah-'lahr]
indispensable indispensable [een-dee-spehn-'sah-bleh]
individual individual [een-dee-vee-doo-'ahl]
industrious, hardworking trabajador, diligente, aplicado [trah-bah-hah-'dohr, dee-lee-'hehn-teh, ah-plee-'kah-doh]
inevitable inevitable [een-eh-vee-'tah-bleh]
inexact inexacto, impreciso [een-ehk-'sahk-toh, eem-preh-'see-soh]

inexperienced inexperto, sin experiencia [een-ehk-'spehr-toh, seen ehk-speh-ree-'ehn-see·ah]

inferior inferior [een-feh-ree-'ohr]

inflammable inflamable [een-flah-'mah-bleh]

inform *(v)* avisar, informar [ah-vee-'sahr, een-fohr-'mahr]; **to request information (on)** *(v)* pedir información sobre [peh-'deer een-fohr-mah-see-'ohn 'soh-breh]

information la información [lah een-fohr-mah-see-'ohn]

information office oficina de información [oh-fee-'see-nah deh een-fohr-mah-see-'ohn]

inhabitant el habitante [ehl ah-bee-'tahn-teh]

injury herida [eh-'ree-dah]; **injured person** el herido, la herida [ehl eh-'ree-doh, lah eh-'ree-dah]

injustice injusticia [een-hoo-'stee-see·ah]

inland el interior del país [ehl een-teh-ree-'ohr dehl pah-'ees]

inn fonda, posada ['fohn-dah, poh-'sah-dah]

innocent inocente [ee-noh-'sehn-teh]

inquire *(v)* informarse [een-fohr-'mahr-seh]

insect insecto [een-'sehk-toh]

inside dentro ['dehn-troh]; **the inside** el interior [ehl een-teh-ree-'ohr]

insist *(v)* insistir [een-see-'steer]

insist on *(v)* insistir en [een-see-'steer ehn]

instead (of) en vez de, en lugar de [ehn vehs deh, ehn loo-'gahr deh]

insufficient escaso, insuficiente [eh-'skah-soh, een-soo-fee-see-'ehn-teh]

insult *(v)* insultar [een-sool-'tahr]

insult insulto [een-'sool-toh]

insurance seguro [seh-'goo-roh]

intelligence inteligencia [een-teh-lee-'hehn-see·ah]

intend (to) *(v)* pensar, tener la intención de [pehn-'sahr, teh-'nehr lah een-tehn-see-'ohn deh]

intention la intención [lah een-tehn-see-'ohn]

intentionally intencionadamente, a propósito [een-tehn-see-oh-nah-dah-'mehn-teh, ah proh-'poh-see-toh]

interest el interés [ehl een-teh-'rehs]

interested in, to be *(v)* interesarse en [een-teh-reh-'sahr-seh ehn]

interesting interesante [een-teh-reh-'sahn-teh]

international internacional [een-tehr-nah-see-oh-'nahl]

interrupt *(v)* interrumpir [een-teh-rroom-'peer]

introduce *(v)* presentar [preh-sehn-'tahr]

introduction la presentación [lah preh-sehn-tah-see-'ohn]

invalid inválido [een-'vah-lee-doh]

invent *(v)* inventar [een-vehn-'tahr]

investigate *(v)* investigar [een-veh-stee-'gahr]

invitation la invitación [lah een-vee-tah-see-'ohn]

invite *(v)* invitar [een-vee-'tahr]

iron hierro, plancha ['yeh-rroh, 'plahn-chah]

irregular irregular [ee-reh-goo-'lahr]

island isla ['ee-slah]

issue asunto, el tema, la cuestión [ah-'soon-toh, ehl 'teh-mah, lah kweh-stee-'ohn]

itch *(v)* picar [pee-'kahr]

itch picazón [pee-kah-'sohn]

itinerary itinerario [ee-tee-neh-'rah-ree·oh]

J

jellyfish medusa, *(Am)* el aguamala [meh-'doo-sah, ehl ah-gwah-'mah-lah]

jet *(water)* chorro ['choh-rroh]; *(plane)* el avión a chorro, el jet [ehl ah-vee-'ohn ah 'choh-rroh, ehl yeht]

job empleo [ehm-'pleh-oh]

joke broma, el chiste ['broh-mah, ehl 'chee-steh]

joy alegría [ah-leh-'gree-ah]

judge *(v)* juzgar [hoos-'gahr]

judge juez [hoo-'ehs]

judgment juicio [hoo·ee-see·oh]

jump *(v)* saltar [sahl-'tahr]

jungle selva virgen ['sehl-vah 'veer-hehn]

K

keep *(v)* guardar, cumplir, conservar [gwahr-'dahr, koom-'pleer, kohn-sehr-'vahr]; **to keep an object** guardar un objeto [gwahr-'dahr oon ohb-'heh-toh];

to keep a promise cumplir una promesa [koom-'pleer 'oo-nah proh-'meh-sah]; **to keep a holiday** observar una fecha [ohb-sehr-'vahr 'oo-nah 'feh-chah]
key la llave [lah 'yah-veh]
kind amable, benévolo, tipo [ah-'mah-bleh, beh-'neh-voh-loh, 'tee-poh]
kindness la amabilidad [lah ah-mah-bee-lee-'dahd]
kiss (v) besar [beh-'sahr]
kiss beso ['beh-soh]
kitchen cocina [koh-'see-nah]
knapsack mochila [moh-'chee-lah]
knock (v) llamar, tocar (a la puerta) [yah-'mahr, toh-'kahr (ah lah 'pwehr-tah)]
knock llamada, toque (a la puerta) [yah-'mah-dah, 'toh-keh (ah lah 'pwehr-tah)]
knot nudo ['noo-doh]
know (v) saber, conocer [sah-'behr, koh-noh-'sehr]
knowledge el saber, el conocimiento [ehl sah-'behr, ehl koh-noh-see-mee-'ehn-toh]

L

lack (n) falta, escasez ['fahl-tah, ehs-kah-'sehs]; (moral) defecto [deh-'fehk-toh]
ladder escalera [eh-skah-'leh-rah]
lady señora [seh-'nyoh-rah]
lake lago ['lah-goh]
lamp lámpara ['lahm-pah-rah]
land tierra [tee-'eh-rrah]
landlord dueño, el patrón ['dweh-nyoh, ehl pah-'trohn]; (f) la dueña, la patrona [lah 'dweh-nyah, lah pah-'troh-nah]
landscape el paisaje [ehl pah·ee·'sah-heh]
language el idioma, lengua [ehl ee-dee-'oh-mah, 'lehn-gwah]
last (v) durar, tardar [doo-'rahr, tahr-'dahr]
last última, último ['ool-tee-moh, 'ool-tee-mah]
late tarde ['tahr-deh]
late, to be (v) retrasarse, llegar tarde [reh-trah-'sahr-seh, yeh-'gahr 'tahr-deh]
later (adj) posterior, ulterior [poh-steh-ree-'ohr, ool-teh-ree-'ohr]; (adv) después, más tarde [deh-'spwehs, mahs 'tahr-deh]
later luego, después [loo-'eh-goh, deh-'spwehs]
laugh (v) reír(se) [reh-'eer(seh)]

laundry (place) lavandería [lah-vahn-deh-'ree-ah]; (dirty) ropa sucia ['roh-pah 'soo-see-ah]
lawn el césped, (Arg) pasto [ehl 'sehs-pehd, 'pah-stoh]
lazy perezoso, holgazán [peh-reh-'soh-soh, ohl-gah-'sahn]
lead (v) conducir, guiar [kohn-doo-'seer, gee-'ahr]
leaf hoja ['oh-hah]
lean (meat) magro ['mah-groh]
learn (v) aprender; oír, saber, enterarse de [ah-prehn-'dehr; oh-'eer, sah-'behr, ehn-teh-'rahr-seh deh]
least lo menos [loh 'meh-nohs]; **at least** por lo menos [pohr loh 'meh-nohs, ahl 'meh-nohs]
leather la piel, cuero [lah pee-'ehl; 'kweh-roh]
leave (v) dejar [deh-'hahr]; **leave behind** dejar atrás, abandonar [deh-'hahr ah-'trahs, ah-bahn-doh-'nahr]
leave (a country) (v) salir de un país) [sah-'leer (deh oon pah-'ees)]
leave (for) (v) salir/partir para [sah-'leer/pahr-'teer 'pah-rah]
left (direction) izquierda [ees-kee-'ehr-dah]; **leftover** sobrante, restante [soh-'brahn-teh, reh-'stahn-teh]; **on/to the left** a/hacia la izquierda [ah/'ah-see·ah lah ees-kee-'ehr-dah]
left-handed zurdo ['soor-doh]; **left hand** mano izquierda ['mah-noh ees-kee-'ehr-dah]
leftovers sobras, restos ['soh-brahs, 'reh-stohs]
lend (v) prestar [preh-'stahr]
length la longitud [lah lohn-hee-'tood]
less menos ['meh-nohs]
letter carta ['kahr-tah]
lie (v) mentir [mehn-'teer]
lie mentira [mehn-'tee-rah]
lie down (v) echarse, acostarse [eh-'chahr-seh, ah-koh-'stahr-seh]
life vida ['vee-dah]
lift levantar [leh-vahn-'tahr]
light la luz [lah loos]
lightbulb bombilla, (Arg) ampolleta [bohm-'bee-yah, ahm-poh-'yeh-tah]
lighter el encendedor, mechero [ehl ehn-sehn-deh-'dohr, meh-'cheh-roh]
lighthouse faro ['fah-roh]
lightning relámpago [reh-'lahm-pah-goh]
like como, igual que ['koh-moh, ee-'gwahl keh]

likewise igualmente [ee-gwahl-'mehn-teh]

line línea ['lee-neh-ah]; **phone line** línea telefónica ['lee-neh-ah teh-leh-'foh-nee-kah]

linen *(bed)* ropa de cama ['roh-pah deh 'kah-mah]

lining forro ['foh-rroh]

lip labio ['lah-bee-oh]

liquid líquido ['lee-kee-doh]

list lista ['lee-stah]

listen *(v)* escuchar [eh-skoo-'chahr]

lit up alumbrado *(fest)* iluminado [ah-loom-'brah-doh; ee-loo-mee-'nah-doh]

little poco ['poh-koh]; **a little** un poco [oon 'poh-koh]

live *(v)* vivir, habitar [vee-'vehr, ah-bee-'tahr]

lively vivo, vivaz ['vee-voh, kah-'pahs]

load *(v)* cargar [kahr-'gahr]

lock *(v)* cerrar con llave [seh-'rrahr kohn 'yah-veh]

lock el cierre, cerradura [ehl see-'eh-rreh, seh-rrah-'doo-rah]

logical lógico ['loh-hee-koh]

lonely solitario, solo [soh-lee-'tah-ree-oh, 'soh-loh]

long largo ['lahr-goh]

look *(n)* mirada [mee-'rah-dah]

look *(v)* buscar, mirar, parecer, tener aspecto de [boo-'skahr, mee-'rahr, pah-reh-'sehr, teh-'nehr ah-'spehk-toh deh]

look apariencia, estilo [ah-pah-ree-'ehn-see-ah, eh-'stee-loh]

look (at) *(v)* mirar(a) [mee-'rahr(ah)]

look like parecerse a [pah-reh-'sehr-seh ah]

loose suelto ['swehl-toh]

lose *(v)* perder [pehr-'dehr]

lose weight *(v)* adelgazar [ah-dehl-gah-'sahr]

loss pérdida ['pehr-dee-dah]; **lost** perdido [pehr-'dee-doh]

lost and found office oficina de objetos perdidos [oh-fee-'see-nah deh ohb-'heh-tohs pehr-'dee-dohs]

loud alto ['ahl-toh]

loudspeaker el altavoz, *(Am)* el altoparlante [ehl ahl-tah-'vohs, ehl ahl-toh-pahr-'lahn-teh]

love *(v)* amar, querer [ah-'mahr, keh-'rehr]

love el amor [ehl ah-'mohr]

low bajo ['bah-hoh]

lower *(v)* bajar [bah-'hahr]

loyal fiel [fee-'ehl]

luck suerte ['swehr-teh]; **good luck!** ¡mucha suerte! ¡éxitos! ['moo-chah 'swehr-teh; 'ehk-see-tohs]

lucky dichoso [dee-'choh-soh]

lunch comida, *(Am)* almuerzo [koh-'mee-dah, ahl-moo-'ehr-soh]

lust deseo, gana(s) [deh-'seh-oh, 'gah-nah(s)]

luxurious lujoso [loo-'hoh-soh]

luxury lujo ['loo-hoh]

M

machine máquina ['mah-kee-nah]

mail *(v)* enviar (por correo) [ehn-vee-'ahr (pohr koh-'rreh-oh)]

mail correspondencia, correo [koh-rreh-spohn-'dehn-see-ah, koh-'rreh-oh]

main entrance entrada principal [ehn-'trah-dah preen-see-'pahl]

main(ly) *(adj)* principal [preen-see-'pahl]; *(adv)* principalmente [preen-see-pahl-'mehn-teh]

maintain *(v)* afirmar [ah-feer-'mahr]

make *(v)* hacer [ah-'sehr]; *(manufacture)* fabricar [fah-bree-'kahr]

make an appointment *(v)* citarse, darse una cita [see-'tahr-seh, 'dahr-seh 'oo-nah 'see-tah]

make an effort *(v)* esforzarse [ehs-fohr-'sahr-seh]

make coffee *(v)* hacer/preparar el café [ah-'sehr/preh-pah-'rahr ehl kah-'feh]

make possible *(v)* hacer posible, facilitar [ah-'sehr poh-'see-bleh, fah-see-lee-'tahr]

makeup maquillaje [mah-kee-'yah-heh]

male masculino [mah-skoo-'lee-noh]

man hombre ['ohm-breh]; *(marriage)* marido, esposo [mah-'ree-doh, eh-'spoh-soh]

management la dirección [lah dee-rehk-see-'ohn]

manager el director [ehl dee-rehk-'tohr]

map el mapa [ehl 'mah-pah]

mark marca, la señal ['mahr-kah, lah seh-'nyahl]

marriage matrimonio [mah-tree-'moh-nee·oh]

married (to) *(adj)* casado (con) [kah-'sah-doh (kohn)]

married couple matrimonio, pareja [mah-tree-'moh-nee·oh, pah-'reh-hah]

marry *(v)* casarse [kah-'sahr-seh]

A/Z

mass *(rel)* misa ['mee-sah]; *(volume)* masa ['mah-sah]

match *(sports)* partido [pahr-'tee-doh]; *(box)* pelea [peh-'leh-ah]; *(fire)* cerilla, fósforo [seh-'ree-yah, 'fohs-foh-'roh]; **matchbox** caja de cerillas/de fósforos ['kah-hah deh seh-'ree-yahs/deh 'fohs-foh-rohs]

material el material, tela [ehl mah-teh-ree-'ahl, 'teh-lah]

matter asunto [ah-'soon-toh]; **to settle a matter** arreglar un asunto [ah-rreh-'glahr oon ah-'soon-toh]

maybe quizá(s), tal vez [kee-'sahs, tahl vehs]

me me, mí [meh, mee]; **to me** a mí [ah mee]

meadow prado, pradera ['prah-doh, prah-'deh-rah]

meal comida [koh-'mee-dah]

mean *(v)* significar [seeg-nee-fee-'kahr]

mean malo ['mah-loh]

meaning significado [seeg-nee-fee-'kah-doh]

means medios ['meh-dee-ohs]

meanwhile entretanto [ehn-treh-'tahn-toh]

measure medida [meh-'dee-dah]

measure *(v)* medir [meh-'deer]

meat la carne [lah 'kahr-neh]

mechanical device aparato [ah-pah-'rah-toh]

mediator el mediador [ehl meh-dee-ah-'dohr]

Mediterranean Mediterráneo [meh-dee-teh-'rrah-neh-oh]

meet *(v)* encontrar, conocer [ehn-kohn-'trahr, koh-noh-'sehr]

mend, darn *(v)* remendar, repasar [reh-mehn-'dahr, reh-pah-'sahr]

menu carta, el menú, *(Am)* minuta ['kahr-tah, ehl meh-'noo, mee-'noo-tah]

merit *(v)* ameritar [ah-meh-ree-'tahr]

merit mérito ['meh-ree-toh]

message mensaje, aviso [mehn-'sah-heh, ah-'vee-soh]

Mexican mexicano [meh-hee-'kah-noh]

Mexico México ['meh-hee-koh]

middle medio, centro ['meh-dee-oh, 'sehn-troh]

midnight la medianoche [lah meh-dee-ah-'noh-cheh]; **at midnight** a medianoche [ah meh-dee-ah-'noh-cheh]

mild suave ['swah-veh]

mine mío, mía ['mee-oh, 'mee-ah]

minor menor [meh-'nohr]

minus menos ['meh-nohs]; **-2º** dos grados bajo cero [dohs 'grah-dohs 'bah-hoh 'seh-roh]

minute minuto [mee-'noo-toh]

misfortune desgracia [dehs-'grah-see-ah]

miss *(v)* faltar [fahl-'tahr]; **to be missing** estar desaparecido [eh-'stahr dehs-ah-pah-reh-'see-doh]

(to) miss *(v)* perder [pehr-'dehr]; **to miss the train** perder el tren [pehr-'dehr ehl trehn]; **to miss a deadline** no cumplir con el plazo [noh koom-'pleer kohn ehl 'plah-soh]

Miss señorita [seh-nyoh-'ree-tah]

mistake *(v)* equivocar, errar [eh-kee-voh-'kahr, eh-'rrahr]; **be mistaken** *(v)* equivocarse [eh-kee-voh-'kahr-seh]

mistake el error, la equivocacióm [ehl eh-'rrohr, lah eh-kee-voh-kah-see-'ohn]

mistaken, to be *(v)* equivocarse [eh-kee-voh-'kahr-seh]

mistakenly por equivocación [pohr eh-kee-voh-kah-see-'ohn]

mistrust *(v)* desconfiar [dehs-kohn-fee-'ahr]

mistrust desconfianza [dehs-kohn-fee-'ahn-sah]

misunderstand *(v)* entender/interpretar mal [ehn-tehn-'dehr/een-tehr-preh-'tahr mahl]

misunderstanding el malentendido, la mala interpretación, el error, la equivocación [ehl mahl-ehn-tehn-'dee-doh, lah 'mah-lah een-tehr-preh-tah-see-'ohn, ehl eh-'rrohr, lah eh-kee-voh-kah- see-'ohn]

misuse *(v)* abusar (de) [ah-boo-'sahr (deh)]

misuse abuso [ah-'boo-soh]

mix up confusión [kohn-foo-see-'ohn]

mixed mezclado [meh-'sklah-doh]

mixed up, to be *(v)* estar confundido [eh-'stahr kohn-foon-'dee-doh]

model modelo [moh-'deh-loh]

moderate moderado, sobrio [moh-deh-'rah-doh, 'soh-bree-oh]

modern moderno [moh-'dehr-noh]

moist húmedo ['oo-meh-'doh]

moment momento, el instante [moh-'mehn-toh, ehl een-'stahn-teh]

money dinero [dee-'neh-roh]

month el mes [ehl mehs]

monthly *(adj)* mensual [mehn-soo-'ahl]; *(adv)* al mes [ahl mehs]

mood el humor [ehl oo-'mohr]
moon luna ['loo-nah]
more más [mahs]; **more than** más que [mahs keh]; **more or less** más o menos [mahs oh 'meh-nohs]
morning mañana [mah-'nyah-nah]
mosquito mosquito [moh-'skee-toh]
most la mayoría, casi [lah mah-yoh-'ree-ah, 'kah-see]; **at the most** al máximo, a lo más [ahl 'mahk-see-moh, ah loh mahs]
mother la madre [lah 'mah-dreh]
mountain sierra, montaña [see-'eh-rrah, mohn-'tah-nyah]
mouth boca; *(river)* desembocadura ['boh-kah; dehs-ehm-boh-kah-'doo-rah]
move *(v)* mover(se) [moh-'vehr(seh)];
  move out *(v)* mudarse de casa [moo-'dahr-seh deh 'kah-sah]
moved/touched, to be *(v)* sentirse/ estar conmovido [sehn-'teer-seh/eh-'stahr kohn-moh-'vee-doh]
movement movimiento [moh-vee-mee-'ehn-toh]
Mr. el señor [ehl seh-'nyohr]; *(Spain, before name)* don [dohn]
Mrs. señora [seh-'nyoh-rah']; *(Spain, before name)* doña ['doh-nyah]; *(wife)* esposa, la mujer [eh-'spoh-sah, lah moo-'hehr]
much mucho ['moo-choh]; **too much** demasiado [deh-mah-see-'ah-doh]
mud lodo, fango ['loh-doh, 'fahn-goh]
music música ['moo-see-kah]
must *(v)* tener que, deber [teh-'nehr keh, deh-'behr]
my mi [mee]

N

nail clavo ['klah-voh]
naked desnudo [dehs-'noo-doh]
name *(v)* nombrar, llamar [nohm-'brahr, yah-'mahr]
name nombre ['nohm-breh]; **named** llamado [yah-'mah-doh]; **to be named** llamarse [yah-'mahr-seh]; **what's your name?** ¿cómo se/te llamas? ['koh-moh seh 'yah-mah]
name day el (día del) santo [ehl ('dee-ah dehl) 'sahn-toh]
narrow estrecho [eh-'streh-choh]
nasty desagradable, odioso, *(Am)* pesado [dehs-ah-grah-'dah-bleh, oh-dee-'oh-soh, peh-'sah-doh]

nation la nación [lah nah-see-'ohn]
native nativo, aborigen [nah-'tee-voh, ah-boh-'ree-hehn]
natural(ly) *(adj)* natural [nah-too-'rahl]; *(adv)* naturalmente, *(Am)*¡cómo no! [nah-too-rahl-'mehn-teh, 'koh-moh noh]
nature naturaleza [nah-too-rah-'leh-sah]
near cerca, cercano ['sehr-kah, sehr-'kah-noh]
nearby cerca, en los alrededores, en la proximidad ['sehr-kah, ehn lohs ahl-reh-deh-'doh-rehs, ehl lah prohk-see-mee-'dahd]
nearly casi ['kah-see]
neat ingenioso, bonito, lindo [een-heh-nee-'oh-soh, boh-'nee-toh, 'leen-doh]
necessary necesario [neh-seh-'sah-ree·oh]
necessity la necesidad [lah neh-seh-see-'dahd]
need *(v)* necesitar [neh-seh-see-'tahr]
need necesidad [neh-seh-see-'dahd]; **in case of need** en caso de necesi-dad [ehn 'kah-soh deh neh-seh-see-'dahd]
needle aguja [ah-'goo-hah]
negative negativo [neh-gah-'tee-voh]
neglect *(v)* descuidar [dehs-kwee-'dahr]
negligent negligente, descuidado [nehg-lee-'hehn-teh, dehs-kwee-'dah-doh]
negotiation la negociación [lah neh-goh-see-ah-see-'ohn]
neighbor vecino/-a [veh-'see-noh(ah)]
neighborhood vecindario, barrio [veh-seen-'dah-ree-oh, 'bah-rree-oh]
neither...nor ni ... ni [nee...nee]
nephew sobrino [soh-'bree-noh]
nervous nervioso [nehr-vee-'oh-soh]
net la red [lah rehd]
never jamás, nunca [hah-'mahs, 'noon-kah]
nevertheless sin embargo, a pesar de, no obstante [seen ehm-'bahr-goh, ah-peh-'sahr deh, noh ohb-'stahn-teh]
new nuevo [noo-'eh-voh]
news noticia(s) [noh-'tee-see·ah(s)]
next próximo, junto a, al lado de ['prohk-see-moh, 'hoon-toh ah, ahl 'lah-doh deh]
Nicaraguan nicaragüense [nee-kah-rah-'gwehn-seh]
nice amable, bueno, simpático [ah-'mah-bleh, 'bweh-noh, seem-'pah-tee-koh]
niece sobrina [soh-'bree-nah]
night la noche [lah 'noh-cheh]; **tonight** esta noche ['eh-stah 'noh-cheh]

A/Z

No admittance! ¡Prohibida la entrada!, ¡Se prohibe el paso! [proh-ee-'bee-dah lah ehn-'trah-dah; seh proh-'ee-beh ehl 'pah-soh]

no one nadie ['nah-dee-eh]

no way de ningún modo, de ninguna manera [deh neen-'goon 'moh-doh, deh neen-'goo-nah mah-'neh-rah]

no(t) no [noh]; **not even** ni siquiera [nee see-kee-'eh-rah]; **not yet** todavía no [toh-dah-'vee-ah noh]; **no way** de ningún modo [dehn neen-'goon 'moh-doh]; **is it not/isn't it?** ¿(no es) verdad? [(noh ehs) vehr-'dahd]

no, none ninguno, ningún [neen-'goo-noh, neen-'goon]

nobody nadie ['nah-dee-eh]

noise ruido [roo-'ee-doh]

noon el mediodía [ehl meh-dee-oh-'dee-ah]

nor, neither tampoco [tahm-'poh-koh]

normal normal [nohr-'mahl]

normally normalmente [norh-mahl-'mehn-teh]

north el norte [ehl 'nohr-teh]; **north of** al norte de [ahl 'nohr-teh deh]

northern del norte, septentrional [dehl 'nohr-teh; sehp-tehn-tree-oh-'nahl]

note el apunte, nota [ah-'poon-teh, 'noh-tah]

notebook cuaderno [kwah-'dehr-noh]

nothing nada ['nah-dah]; **nothing else** nada más ['nah-dah mahs]

notice (v) notar, observar [noh-'tahr, ohb-sehr-'vahr]

novelty la novedad [lah noh-veh-'dahd]

now ahora [ah-'oh-rah]

nowhere en ninguna parte [ehn neen-'goo-nah 'pahr-teh]

nuisance molestia, estorbo [moh-'leh-stee·ah, eh-'stohr-boh]

number (v) numerar [noo-meh-'rahr]

number número ['noo-meh-roh]

numerous numeroso [noo-meh-'roh-soh]

nun monja ['mohn-hah]

nurse enfermera [ehn-fehr-'meh-rah]

nutrition la nutrición [lah noo-tree-see-'ohn]

nutritious nutritivo [noo-tree-'tee-voh]

O

object objeto [ohb-'heh-toh]

obligation la obligación [lah ohb-lee-gah-see-'ohn]

obliged (to) (v) estar obligado a [eh-'stahr ohb-lee-'gah-doh ah]

observe (v) observar [ohb-sehr-'vahr]

obtain (v) procurar, obtener [proh-koo-'rahr, ohb-teh-'nehr]

occasion ocasión, motivo [oh-kah-see-'ohn, moh-'tee-voh]

occupied ocupado [oh-koo-'pah-doh]

occurrence suceso [soo-'seh-soh]

ocean océano [oh-'seh-ah-noh]

of de [deh]

offence ofensa [oh-'fehn-sah]

offend (v) ofender [oh-fehn-'dehr]

offer (v) ofrecer [oh-freh-'sehr]

offer oferta [oh-'fehr-tah]

office oficina, despacho [oh-fee-'see-nah, dehs-'pah-choh]

official oficial [of-fee-see-'ahl]

often frecuentemente, con frecuencia, a menudo [freh-kwehn-teh-'mehn-teh, kohn freh-'kwehn-see·ah, ah meh-'noo-doh]

oil el aceite [ehl ah-'seh·ee-teh]

old viejo, antiguo [vee-'eh-hoh, ahn-'tee-gwoh]

old-fashioned pasado de moda [pah-'sah-doh deh 'moh-dah]

on a, en, sobre, por [ah, ehn, 'soh-breh, pohr]; **on the Mississippi** junto al Misssissippi ['hoon-toh ahl mee-see-'see-pee]; **on Sunday** el domingo [ehl doh-'meen-goh]; **on duty** de guardia [deh 'gwahr-dee·ah]

on the way en el (el) camino, en el/de viaje [ehn (ehl) kah-'mee-noh, ehn ehl/deh vee-'ah-heh]

once una vez ['oo-nah vehs]

one un/uno, una [oon/'oo-noh, 'oo-nah]

one and a half uno y medio ['oo-noh ee 'meh-dee·oh]

only sólo, solamente ['soh-loh, soh-lah-'mehn-teh]

only, sole único ['oo-nee-koh]

open (adj) abierto [ah-bee-'ehr-toh]

open (v) abrir [ah-'breer]

open abierto [ah-bee-'ehr-toh]

opening apertura [ah-pehr-'too-rah]; **opening hours** horario de apertura [oh-'rah-ree-oh deh ah-pehr-'too-rah]

operate (v) operar [oh-peh-'rahr]

opinion la opinión [lah oh-pee-nee-'ohn]; **in my opinion** en mi opinión [ehn mee oh-pee-nee-'ohn]

opportunity la oportunidad [lah-oh-pohr-too-nee-'dahd]

opposite lo opuesto, lo contrario [oh-'pweh-stoh, loh kohn-'trah-ree-oh]; **opposite to/from** enfrente de, frente a [ehn-'frehn-teh deh, 'frehn-teh ah]

opposite opuesto, contrario [oh-'pweh-stoh, kohn-'trah-ree-oh]

optional opcional, a discreción, a voluntad [ohp-see-oh-'nahl, ah dee-skreh-see-'ohn, ah voh-loon-'tahd]

or o [oh]

order *(rel)* la orden [lah 'ohr-dehn]

order el orden [ehl 'ohr-dehn]

orderly ordenado [ohr-deh-'nah-doh]

organization organización [ohr-gah-nee-sah-see-'ohn]

organize *(v)* organizar [ohr-gah-nee-'sahr]

other otro ['oh-troh]; **the other one** el otro [ehl 'oh-troh]

otherwise si no, en caso contrario [see noh, ehn 'kah-soh kohn-'trah-ree-oh]

our(s) nuestro(s), nuestra(s) [noo-'eh-stroh(s), noo-'eh-strah(s)]

outdoors al aire libre [ahl 'ah-ee-reh 'lee-breh]

outside *(prp)* fuera de ['fweh-rah deh]; *(adv)* fuera ['fweh-rah]; **on the outside** por fuera [pohr 'fweh-rah]

over sobre ['soh-breh]

over there al otro lado [ahl 'oh-troh 'lah-doh]

overcrowded repleto [reh-'pleh-toh]

overseas (el) ultramar [(ehl) ool-trah-'mahr]

overtake *(v)* adelantar, pasar [ah-deh-lahn-'tahr, pah-'sahr]

owe *(v)* deber [deh-'behr]

own *(v)* poseer [poh-seh-'ehr]

own propio ['proh-pee-oh]

owner propietario [proh-pee-eh-'tah-ree·oh]

P

pack *(v)* empacar, empaquetar [ehm-pah-'kahr, ehm-pah-keh-'tahr]

pack bulto, paquete ['bool-toh, pah-'keh-teh]

package el paquete [ehl pah-'keh-teh]

page *(v)* llamar por el altavoz [yah-'mahr pohr ehl ahl-tah-'vohs]

paint pintura [peén-'too-rah]; *(verb)* pintar [peen-'tahr]

painting cuadro, pintura ['kwah-droh, peen-'too-rah]

pair un par, pareja [oon pahr, pah-'reh-hah]

pale pálido ['pah-lee-doh]

Panamanian panameño [pah-nah-'meh-nyoh]

panorama el panorama [ehl pah-noh-'rah-mah]

Paraguayan paraguayo [pah-rah-'gwah-yoh]

parcel el paquete [ehl pah-'keh-teh]

parents los padres [lohs 'pah-drehs]

park *(v)* aparcar, *(Am)* parquear [ah-pahr-'kahr, pahr-keh-'ahr]

park el parque [ehl 'pahr-keh]

part la parte [lah 'pahr-teh]

particular especial [ehn-speh-see-'ahl]; **in particular** en especial [ehn eh-speh-see-'ahl]

party fiesta, el guateque [fee-'eh-stah, ehl gwah-'teh-keh]

pass *(ticket)* pase ['pah-seh]

pass *(v)* pasar [pah-'sahr]

passage, corridor pasaje, corredor, passillo [pah-'sah-heh, koh-rreh-'dohr, pah-'see-yoh]

passage, gateway paso, pasaje ['pah-soh, pah-'sah-heh]

passenger viajero, pasajero [vee-ah-'heh-roh, pah-sah-'heh-roh]

passing through de paso [deh 'pah-soh]

passport el pasaporte [ehl pah-sah-'pohr-teh]

past pasado [pah-'sah-doh]

path senda, sendero ['sehn-dah, sehn-'deh-roh]

patience paciencia [pah-see-'ehn-see-ah]

patient paciente [pah-see-'ehn-teh]

pay *(v)* pagar [pah-'gahr]

pay attention to *(v)* prestarle atención a [preh-'stahr-leh ah-tehn-see-'ohn ah]

pay with cash *(v)* pagar al contado [pah-'gahr ahl kohn-'tah-doh]

payment pago ['pah-goh]

peace la paz [lah pahs]

pear pera ['peh-rah]

peculiar particular, peculiar [pahr-tee-koo-'lahr, peh-koo-lee-ahr]

pedestrian el peatón [ehl peh-ah-'tohn]

pen pluma ['ploo-mah]

penultimate penúltima/penúltimo [peh-'nool-tee-mah/peh-'nool-tee-moh]

people la gente, pueblo [lah 'hehn-teh, 'pweh-bloh]

per por [pohr]; **per person** por cabeza [pohr kah-'beh-sah]

A/Z

percent por ciento [pohr see-'ehn-toh]; **percentage** el porcentaje [ehl pohr-sehn-'tah-heh]

perfect perfecto [pehr-'fehk-toh]

performance *(theater)* la función, la representación [lah foonk-see-'ohn, lah reh-preh-sehn-tah-see-'ohn]; *(business)* rendimiento [rehn-dee-mee-'ehn-toh]

perhaps quizá(s), tal vez [kee-'sahs, tahl vehs]

period punto ['poon-toh]

periphery periferia [peh-ree-'feh-ree-ah]

permission permiso [pehr-'mee-soh]

person persona [pehr-'soh-nah]

personal *(adj)* personal [pehr-soh-'nahl]; **personal information** los datos personales [lohs 'dah-tohs pehr-soh-'nah-lehs]

personnel el personal [ehl pehr-soh-'nahl]

persuade *(v)* persuadir, convencer [pehr-swah-'deer, kohn-vehn-'sehr]

pertinent oportuno [oh-pohr-'too-noh]

Peruvian peruano [peh-roo-'ah-noh]

phone *(v)* llamar por teléfono, telefonear [yah-'mahr pohr teh-'leh-foh-noh, teh-leh-foh-neh-'ahr]

photo(graph) la foto(grafía) [lah 'foh-toh (grah-'fee-ah)]

photograph *(v)* fotografiar, hacer/sacar una foto [foh-toh-grah-fee-'ahr, ah-'sehr/sah-'kahr 'oo-nah 'foh-toh]

photography, photograph la foto(grafía) [lah 'foh-toh (grah-'fee-ah)]

pick *(v)* coger, *(Am)* agarrar [koh-'hehr, ah-gah-'rrahr]

piece pieza, trozo, pedazo [pee-'eh-sah, 'troh-soh, peh-'dah-soh]

pier el muelle [ehl 'mweh-yeh]

pillow almohada [ahl-moh-'ah-dah]

pin el alfiler [ehl ahl-fee-'lehr]; **safety pin** el imperdible [ehl eem-pehr-'dee-bleh]

pipe pipa, tubo, tubería ['pee-pah, 'too-boh, too-beh-'ree-ah]; **gas/water pipe** tubería de gas/agua cañería [too-beh-'ree-ah deh gahs/ah-'gwah]

pity compasión, pena [kohm-pah-see-'ohn, 'peh-nah]; **it's a/what a pity!** ¡es una pena! ¡qué lástima! [ehs 'oo-nah 'peh-nah, keh 'lah-stee-mah]

place *(v)* poner, colocar [poh-'nehr, koh-loh-'kahr]; **take place in** *(v)* tener lugar en [teh-'nehr loo-'gahr ehn]

place lugar [loo-'gahr]

plain llanura [yah-'noo-rah]

plan el plan, la intención [ehl plahn, lah een-tehn-see-'ohn]; *(arch)* plano ['plah-noh]

plant planta ['plahn-tah]

plaster escayola, *(Am)* yeso [eh-skah-'yoh-lah, 'yeh-soh]

plastic plástico ['plah-stee-koh]

plate plato ['plah-toh]; *(printing, metalwork)* placa, chapa ['plah-kah, 'chah-pah]

play (an instrument) *(v)* tocar [toh-'kahr]

play *(v)* jugar [hoo-'gahr]

play juego [hoo-'eh-goh]

plaza plaza, sitio ['plah-sah, 'see-tee-oh]; *(seat)* asiento [ah-see-'ehn-toh]

pleasant agradable [ah-grah-'dah-bleh]

please *(v)* gustar, agradar [goo-'stahr, ah-grah-'dahr]

please por favor [pohr fah-'vohr]

pleased (with) contento (de), satisfecho (de) [kohn-'tehn-toh (deh), sah-tees-'feh-choh]

pleased/happy with, to be *(v)* alegrarse (de) [ah-leh-'grahr-seh (deh)]

pleasure el placer, gusto [ehl plah-'sehr, goo-stoh]

plus más [mahs]

pocket bolsillo [bohl-'see-yoh]

point *(place, argument)* punto ['poon-toh]; *(sharp object)* punta ['poon-tah]

poison veneno [veh-'neh-noh]

poisonous venenoso [veh-neh-'noh-soh]

polite cortés [kohr-'tehs]

politeness cortesía [kohr-teh-'see-ah]

politics política [poh-'lee-tee-kah]

poor pobre ['poh-breh]

port puerto, paso ['pwehr-toh, 'pah-soh]

porter mozo, portero ['moh-soh, pohr-'teh-roh]

position la posición [lah poh-see-see-'ohn]

positive positivo [poh-see-'tee-voh]

possibility la posibilidad [lah poh-see-bee-lee-'dahd]

possible *(adj)* posible, eventual [poh-'see-bleh, eh-vehn-too-'ahl]

possibly *(adv)* posiblemente, eventualmente [poh-see-bleh-'mehn-teh, eh-vehn-too-ahl-'mehn-teh]

post *(v)* echar al correo [eh-'chahr ahl koh-'rreh-oh]; **post a notice** *(v)* poner un anuncio (en la tablilla) [poh-'nehr oon ah-'noon-see-oh (ehn lah tah-'blee-yah)]

postal postal [poh-'stahl]

poster el cartel, *(Am)* el afiche [ehl kahr-'tehl, ehl ah-'fee-cheh]
pot olla, cazuela, puchero ['oh-yah, kah-soo-'eh-lah, poo-'cheh-roh]
pottery (objetos de) alfarería, loza [(ohb-'heh-tohs deh) ahl-fah-reh-'ree-ah, 'loh-sah]
pound libra ['lee-brah]
powder polvo ['pohl-voh]
power of attorney el poder, la autorización [ehl poh-'dehr, lah ow-toh-ree-sah-see-'ohn]
practical(ly) práctico ['prahk-tee-koh]; *(adv)* prácticamente [prahk-tee-kah-'mehn-teh]
practice *(a profession)* ejercer [eh-hehr-'sehr]
practice *(v)* ejercitar, practicar [eh-hehr-see-'tahr, prahk-tee-'kahr]
practice ejercicio, práctica [eh-hehr-'see-see-oh, 'prahk-tee-kah]
praise *(v)* alabar [ah-lah-'bahr]
pray *(v)* rezar [reh-'sahr]
prayer la oración [lah oh-rah-see-'ohn]
precision la precisión, la exactitud [lah preh-see-see-'ohn, lah ehk-sahk-tee-'tood]
prefer *(v)* preferir [preh-feh-'reer]
preference preferencia [preh-feh-'rehn-see-ah]
pregnant embarazada [ehm-bah-rah-'sah-dah]
prepare *(v)* preparar [preh-pah-'rahr]
present presente [preh-'sehn-teh]
present, to be *(v)* estar presente [eh-'stahr preh-'sehn-teh]
pretext pretexto [preh-'tehks-toh]
prevent *(v)* impedir [eem-peh-'deer]
price precio ['preh-see-oh]
priest el sacerdote, el cura [ehl sah-sehr-'doh-teh, ehl 'koo-rah]
private privado [pree-'vah-doh]
prize premio ['preh-mee-oh]
probability la probabilidad [lah proh-bah-bee-lee-'dahd]
probable probable [proh-'bah-bleh]; **probably** probablemente [proh-bah-bleh-'mehn-teh]
procession la procesión [lah proh-seh-see-'ohn]
produce *(v)* producir [proh-doo-'seer]
product producto [proh-'dook-toh]
profession la profesión [lah proh-feh-see-'ohn]
profit ganancia [lah gah-'nahn-see-ah]

program programa [proh-'grah-mah]; *(radio, TV)* la emisión, el programa de radio/televisión [lah eh-mee-see-'ohn, ehl proh-'grah-mah deh 'rah-dee-oh/teh-leh-ve-see-'ohn]
progress progreso [proh-'greh-soh]
promise *(v)* prometer [proh-meh-'tehr]
promise promesa [proh-'meh-sah]
pronounce *(v)* pronunciar [proh-noon-see-'ahr]
pronunciation la pronunciación [lah proh-noon-see-ah-see-'ohn]
proof prueba [proo-'eh-bah]
property propiedad [proh-pee-eh-'dahd]
proposal propuesta, la proposición [proh-'pweh-stah, lah proh-poh-see-see-'ohn]
propose *(v)* proponer [proh-poh-'nehr]
prospect prospecto, folleto [proh-'spehk-toh, foh-'yeh-toh]
protect *(v)* proteger [proh-teh-'hehr]
protection la protección [roh-tehk-see-'ohn]
protest *(v)* protestar [proh-teh-'stahr]
prove *(v)* probar [proh-'bahr]
provide (with) *(v)* proveer de [proh-veh-'ehr deh]
provision la provisión [lah proh-vee-see-'ohn]
provisional provisional [proh-vee-see-oh-'nahl]
provisional(ly) provisional [proh-vee-see-oh-'nahl]; *(adv)* provisionalmente [proh-vee-see-oh-nahl-'mehn-teh]
provoke an accident *(v)* provocar un accidente [proh-voh-'kahr oon ahk-see-'dehn-teh]
public público ['poo-blee-koh]
Puerto Rican puertorriqueño ['pwehr-toh-rree-'keh-nyoh]
pull *(v)* tirar [tee-'rahr]
pump up/inflate *(v)* hinchar, inflar [een-'chahr, een-'flahr]
punctual *(adj)* puntual [poon-too-'ahl]; *(adv)* puntualmente [poon-too-ahl-'mehn-teh]
puncture pinchazo [peen-'chah-soh]
punishment castigo [kah-'stee-goh]
puppet títere ['tee-teh-reh]
purchase compra ['kohm-prah]
purpose el fin, propósito [ehl feen, proh-'poh-see-toh]
purse bolsa ['bohl-sah]
push *(v)* empujar [ehm-poo-'hahr]
push empujón [ehm-poo-'hohn]

A/Z

put *(v)* poner, colocar [poh-'nehr, koh-loh-'kahr]
put (down) *(v)* poner [poh-'nehr]
put on makeup *(v)* maquillarse [mah-kee-'yahr-seh]
put the blinkers/turn signal on *(v)* poner el intermitente [poh-'nehr ehl een-tehr-mee-'tehn-teh]
Pyrenees (los) Pirineos [(lohs) pee-ree-'neh-ohs]

Q

quality la cualidad, la calidad [lah kwah-lee-'dahd; lah kah-lee-'dahd]
quantity la cantidad [lah kahn-tee-'dahd]
quarrel *(v)* disputar, discutir, pelear, pelearse, regañar [dee-spoo-'tahr, dee-skoo-'teer, peh-leh-'ahr, peh-leh-'ahr-seh, reh-gah-'nyahr]
quarrel disputa, pelea, la discusión [dee-'spoo-tah, peh-'leh-ah, lah dee-skoo-see-'ohn]
quarter un cuarto, la cuarta parte; *(Am)* una moneda de 25 centavos de dólar [ehl 'kwahr-toh, lah 'kwahr-tah 'pahr-teh, 'oo-nah moh-'neh-dah deh veh-een-tee-'seen-koh sehn-'tah-vohs deh 'doh-lahr]
question pregunta [preh-'goon-tah]; (problem) la cuestión, el problema, el asunto [lah kweh-stee-'ohn, ehl proh-'bleh-mah, ehl ah-'soon-toh]
quick rápido ['rah-pee-doh]
quick(ly) *(adj)* rápido, *(Am)* ligero ['rah-pee-doh, lee-'heh-roh]; *(adv)* rápidamente, deprisa ['rah-pee-dah-'mehn-teh, deh 'pree-sah]
quiet la tranquilidad, calma [lah trahn-kee-lee-'dahd, 'kahl-mah]; *(person)* tranquilo [trahn-'kee-loh]
quiet tranquilo [trahn-'kee-loh]; *(sound)* bajo, en voz baja ['bah-hoh, ehn vohs 'bah-hah]; *(adv)* tranquilamente [trahn-kee-lah-'mehn-teh]
quite bastante [bah-'stahn-teh]

R

radio la radio [lah 'rah-dee-oh]
rag trapo ['trah-poh]

rage rabia, furia ['rah-bee-ah, 'foo-ree-ah]; **enraged** ponerse rabioso, furioso [poh-'nehr-seh rah-bee-'oh-soh, foo-ree-'oh-soh]
rain *(v)* llover [yoh-'vehr]
rain lluvia ['yoo-vee-ah]
raise *(v)* subir [soo-'beer]
raise subida [soo-'bee-dah]
rape *(v)* violar [vee-oh-'lahr]
rape violación [vee-oh-lah-see-'ohn]
rate tasa ['tah-sah]; **flat rate** suma global, el importe ['soo-mah gloh-'bahl, ehl eem-'pohr-teh]
rather *(adv)* más bien [mahs 'bee-ehn]
reach *(v)* conseguir, lograr, *(distance)* alcanzar [kohn-seh-'geer, loh-'grahr, ahl-kahn-'sahr]
read *(v)* leer [leh-'ehr]
ready preparado, listo [preh-pah-'rah-doh, 'lee-stoh]
real real [reh-'ahl]; **really** realmente [reh-ahl-'mehn-teh]; **reality** la realidad [lah reh-ah-lee-'dahd]
realize *(v)* darse cuenta ['dahr-seh 'kwehn-tah]
reason *(v)* razonar [rah-soh-'nahr]
reason la razón, causa, motivo [lah rah-'sohn, 'kow-sah, moh-'tee-voh]
reasonable razonable, sensato [rah-soh-'nah-bleh, sehn-'sah-toh]
receipt recibo [reh-'see-boh]
receive *(v)* recibir, conseguir, obtener [reh-see-'beer, kohn-seh-'geer, ohb-teh-'nehr]
recent(ly) reciente [reh-see-'ehn-teh]; *(adv)* recientemente, hace poco, el otro día [reh-see-ehn-teh-'mehn-teh, 'ah-seh 'poh-koh, ehl 'oh-troh 'dee-ah]
reception la recepción [lah reh-sehp-see-'ohn]
recipient el recipiente [ehl reh-see-pee-'ehn-teh]
recognize *(v)* reconocer [reh-koh-noh-'sehr]
recommend *(v)* recomendar [reh-koh-mehn-'dahr]
recommendation la recomendación [lah reh-koh-mehn-dah-see-'ohn]
record (sound) *(v)* grabar (sonido) [grah-'bahr (soh-'nee-doh)]
record player el tocadiscos [ehl toh-kah-'dee-skohs]
recover *(v)* reponerse [reh-poh-'nehr-seh]
rectify *(v)* rectificar [rehk-tee-fee-'kahr]

red rojo ['roh-hoh]; **red wine** vino tinto ['vee-noh 'teen-toh]

reduce (v) rebajar, reducir [reh-bah-'hahr, reh-doo-'seer]

reduction rebaja, (price) descuento [reh-'bah-hah, dehs-'kwehn-toh]

reed caña, junco ['kah-nyah, 'hoon-koh]

refer to (v) referirse a [reh-feh-'reer-seh ah]

refreshment refresco [reh-'freh-skoh]

refund (v) devolver (el dinero) [deh-vohl-'vehr (ehl dee-'neh-roh)]

refuse (v) negar, negarse, rechazar, rehusar [neh-'gahr, neh-'gahr-seh, reh-chah-'sahr, reh-oo-'sahr]

region la región [lah reh-hee-'ohn]

register (v) inscribir [een-skree-'beer]; **register oneself** (v) inscribirse [een-skree-'beer-seh]

regret (v) lamentar [lah-mehn-'tahr]

regular regular [reh-goo-'lahr]

regulate (v) regular [reh-goo-'lahr]

reject (v) rechazar [reh-chah-'sahr]

relative pariente, emparentado [pah-ree-'ehn-teh, ehm-pah-rehn-'tah-doh]

reliable de confianza, seguro [deh kohn-fee-'ahn-sah, seh-'goo-roh]

reluctantly de mala gana [deh 'mah-lah 'gah-nah]

remedy remedio [reh-'meh-dee-oh]

remember (v) recordar, acordarse de [reh-kohr-'dahr, ah-kohr-'dahr-seh deh]

remote remoto, retirado [reh-'moh-toh, reh-tee-'rah-doh]

renew (v) renovar [reh-noh-'vahr]

rent (v) alquilar [ahl-kee-'lahr]

rent el alquiler [ehl ahl-kee-'lehr]; **rental** el alquiler [ehl ahl-kee-'lehr]

repair (v) arreglar, reparar [ah-rreh-'glahr, reh-pah-'rahr]

repair arreglo, la reparación [ah-'rreh-gloh, lah reh-pah-rah-see-'ohn]; **repair shop** el taller de reparaciones [ehl tah-'yehr deh reh-pah-rah-see-'ohns]

repeat (v) repetir [reh-peh-'teer]

replace (v) remplazar, sustituir [reh-ehm-plah-'sahr, soo-stee-too-'eer]

replacement remplazo (product) repuesto [reh-ehm-'plah-soh, reh-'pweh-stoh]

reply (v) replicar, contestar [reh-plee-'kahr, kohn-teh-'stahr]

report informe [een-'fohr-meh]

report on (v) informe sobre/acerca [een-'fohr-meh 'soh-breh/ah-'sehr-kah]

request (v) pedir, encargar [peh-'deer, ehn-kahr-'gahr]

request la solicitud, el favor, ruego, pedido, encargo [lah soh-lee-see-'tood, ehl fah-'vohr, roo-'eh-goh, peh-'dee-doh, ehn-'kahr-goh]

rescue (v) rescatar, salvar [reh-skah-'tahr, sahl-'vahr]

reserve (v) reservar [reh-sehr-'vahr]

reserve a seat (v) reservar un sitio [reh-sehr-'vahr oon 'see-tee-oh]

residence domicilio, residencia [doh-mee-'see-lee-oh, reh-see-'dehn-see-ah]

responsible responsable, competente [reh-spohn-'sah-bleh, kohm-peh-'tehn-teh]

rest (v) descansar [deh-skahn-'sahr]

rest descanso, resto [deh-'skahn-soh, 'reh-stoh]

restaurant el restaurante [ehl reh-stah·oo-'rahn-teh]

restless intranquilo, inquieto [een-trahn-'kee-loh, een-kee-'eh-toh]

result resultado [reh-sool-'tah-doh]

return (v) volver, (give back) devolver, regresar [vohl-'vehr, deh-vohl-'vehr, reh-greh-'sahr]

return vuelta ['vwehl-tah]

return home regreso (a casa) [reh-'greh-soh (ah 'kah-sah)]

reverse (adj) contrario [kohn-'trah-ree-oh]; (adv) al revés, al contrario [ahl reh-'vehs, ahl kohn-'trah-ree-oh]; **in reverse** en sentido inverso/contrario [ehn sehn-'tee-doh een-'vehr-soh/kohn-'trah-ree-oh]

revue revista, espectáculo de variedades [reh-'vee-stah, eh-spehk-'tah-koo-loh deh vah-ree-eh-'dah-dehs]

reward (v) recompensar, gratificar [reh-kohm-pehn-'sahr, grah-tee-fee-'kahr]

reward recompensa, la gratificación [reh-kohm-'pehn-sah, lah grah-tee-fee-kah-see-'ohn]

ribbon cinta ['seen-tah]

rich rico ['ree-koh]

ridiculous ridículo [ree-'dee-koo-loh]

right (n) derecho, exacto, preciso, adecuado [deh-'reh-choh; ehk-'sahk-toh, preh-'see-soh; ah-deh-'kwah-doh]; (direction) derecha, derecho [deh-'reh-chah, deh-'reh-choh]

right of way preferencia (de paso) [preh-feh-'rehn-see·ah (deh 'pah-soh)]

rights los derechos [lohs deh-'reh-chohs]

right, to be *(v)* tener razón [teh-'nehr rah-'sohn]

ring anillo, *(Am)* argolla, aro [ah-'nee-yoh, ahr-'goh-yah, 'ah-roh]

ring the bell *(v)* tocar el timbre [toh-'kahr ehl 'teem-breh]

ripe maduro [mah-'doo-roh]

risk riesgo [ree-'ehs-goh]

river río ['ree-oh]

road carretera [kah-rreh-'teh-rah]

roast *(v)* asar [ah-'sahr]

roast asado [ah-'sah-doh]

rock roca, peña ['roh-kah, 'peh-nyah]

room la habitación, el cuarto, *(Am)* pieza [lah ah-bee-tah-see-'ohn, ehl 'kwahr-toh, pee-'eh-sah]

rope soga ['soh-gah]

rotten podrido, corrompido [poh-'dree-doh, koh-rrohm-'pee-doh]

round redondo [reh-'dohn-doh]; *(drinks)* ronda ['rohn-dah]; *(boxing)* el round [ehl 'rah·oond]

round trip (el viaje de) vuelta [(ehl vee-'ah-heh deh) 'vwehl-tah]

route trayecto, trecho, itinerario [trah-'yehk-toh, 'treh-choh, ee-tee-neh-'rah-ree·oh]; **bus route** línea de autobús ['lee-neh-ah deh ow-toh-'boos]

row fila ['fee-lah]

rude grosero [groh-'seh-roh]

rule regla, la prescripción ['reh-glah, lah preh-skreep-see-'ohn]

run *(v)* correr [koh-'rrehr]; **buses are running** los autobuses están circulando [lohs ow-toh-'boo-sehs eh-'stahn seer-koo-'lahn-doh]

S

sack saco ['sah-koh]

sad triste ['tree-steh]

safe *(adj)* seguro [seh-'goo-roh]

safeguard conservar en lugar seguro [kohn-sehr-'vahr ehn loo-'gahr]

safety la seguridad [lah seh-goo-ree-'dahd]

salary sueldo, salario, paga ['swehl-doh, sah-'lah-ree·oh, 'pah-gah]

sale venta ['vehn-tah]

Salvadorian salvadoreño [sahl-vah-doh-'reh-nyoh]

same igual, mismo [ee-'gwahl, 'mees-moh]

same, the el/lo mismo [ehl/loh 'mees-moh]

sample muestra ['mweh-strah]

satisfied satisfecho, contento [sah-tees-'feh-choh, kohn-'tehn-toh]

save *(v)* *(money)* ahorrar; *(rescue)* salvar, rescatar, guardar [ah-oh-'rrahr; sahl-'vahr, reh-skah-'tahr, gwahr-'dahr]

say *(v)* decir [deh-'seer]

school escuela [eh-'skweh-lah]

scissors las tijeras [lahs tee-'heh-rahs]

scorpio el escorpión [ehl eh-skohr-pee-'ohn]

scream *(v)* gritar [gree-'tahr]

scream grito ['gree-toh]

sea el mar [ehl mahr]

sea urchin erizo de mar [eh-'ree-soh deh mahr]

seagull gaviota [gah-vee-'oh-tah]

seam dobladillo [doh-blah-'dee-yoh]

seaside resort la estación balnearia [lah eh-stah-see-'ohn bahl-neh-'ah-ree-ah]

season temporada, la estación [tehm-poh-'rah-dah, lah eh-stah-see-'ohn]; **high season** temporada principal [tehm-poh-'rah-dah preen-see-'pahl]; **off-season, low season** fuera de la temporada principal ['fweh-rah deh lah tehm-poh-'rah-dah preen-see-'pahl]

seat asiento [ah-see-'ehn-toh]

second segunda, segundo [seh-'goon-dah, seh-'goon-doh]; **in the second place** en segundo lugar [ehn seh-'goon-doh loo-'gahr]

secret secreto [seh-'kreh-toh]

secret(ly) *(adj)* secreto, oculto [seh-'kreh-toh, oh-'kool-toh]; *(adv)* en secreto, a escondidas [ehn seh-'kreh-toh, ah-eh-skohn-'dee-dahs]

security garantía, seguridad [gah-rahn-'tee-ah, seh-goo-ree-'dahd]

see *(v)* ver [vehr]

seem *(v)* parecer [pah-reh-'sehr]

seldom *(adv)* rara vez, raramente ['rah-rah vehs, rah-rah-'mehn-teh]

selection la selección [lah seh-lehk-see-'ohn]; *(products)* surtido [soor-'tee-doh]

self-service autoservicio [ow-toh-sehr-'vee-see·oh]

sell *(v)* vender [vehn-'dehr]

send *(v)* enviar, mandar [ehn-vee-'ahr, mahn-'dahr]

sense sentido [sehn-'tee-doh]

sentence la frase [lah 'frah-seh]

separate *(v)* separar [seh-pah-'rahr]

separate separado [seh-pah-'rah-doh]
serious serio; grave ['seh-ree-oh, 'grah-veh]
sermon el sermón, homilía [ehl sehr-'mohn, oh-mee-'lee-ah]
serve (v) servir [sehr-'veer]
service servicio [sehr-'vee-see-oh]
settle (v) arreglar, terminar [ah-rreh-'glahr, tehr-mee-'nahr]
sex sexo ['sehk-soh]
shadow sombra ['sohm-brah]
share (v) compartir [kohm-pahr-'teer]
sharp cortante, afilado, agudo, punti-agudo [kohr-'tahn-teh, ah-fee-'lah-doh, ah-'goo-doh, poon-tee-ah-'goo-doh]
shave (v) afeitar [ah-feh·ee-'tahr]
she ella ['eh-yah]
sheep oveja [oh-'veh-hah]
shine brillar [bree-'yahr]
shiny brillante [bree-'yahn-teh]
shoe zapato [sah-'pah-toh]
shoot (v) disparar [dee-spah-'rahr]
shop window el escaparate, (Am) vidriera [ehl eh-skah-pah-'rah-teh, vee-dree-'eh-rah]
shopping, to go (v) comprar, ir de compras [kohm-'prahr, eer deh 'kohm-prahs]
shore orilla [oh-'ree-yah]
short bajo, pequeño ['bah-hoh, peh-'keh-nyoh]
short-term a corto plazo [ah 'kohr-toh 'plah-soh]
shortage escasez [eh-skah-'sehs]
shortcut atajo [ah-'tah-hoh]
shot tiro ['tee-roh]
shove (v) empujar [ehm-poo-'hahr]
shove empujón [ehm-poo-'hohn]
show (v) enseñar, mostrar [ehn-seh-'nyahr, moh-'stahr]
show espectáculo, representación, función, muestra [eh-spehk-'tah-koo-loh, reh-preh-sehn-tah-see-'ohn, foonk-see-'ohn, 'mweh-strah]
shut (v) cerrar [seh-'rrahr]
shut cerrado [seh-'rrah-doh]; **shut up!** ¡cállate! ['kah-yah-teh]
shy tímido ['tee-mee-doh]
sick enfermo [ehn-'fehr-moh]
side lado ['lah-doh]
sign (v) firmar [feer-'mahr]
sign letrero, signo, señal [leh-'treh-roh, 'seeg-noh, seh-'nyahl]
signal la señal [lah seh-'nyahl]
signature firma ['feer-mah]
silence silencio [see-'lehn-see-oh]

silent silencioso, callado [see-lehn-see-'oh-soh, kah-'yah-doh]
silly tonto ['tohn-toh]
similar semejante, parecido [seh-meh-'hahn-teh, pah-reh-'see-doh]
simple sencillo [sehn-'see-yoh]
simultaneous(ly) simultáneao, al mismo tiempo [see-mool-'tah-neh-oh, ahl 'mees-moh tee-'ehm-poh]; (adv) simultáneamente [see-mool-tah-neh-ah-'mehn-teh]
since desde, a partir de, porque ['dehs-deh, ah pahr-'teer deh, 'pohr-keh]; **since then** desde entonces ['dehs-deh ehn-'tohn-sehs]; **since when?** ¿desde cuando? ['dehs-deh 'kwahn-doh]
sing (v) cantar [kahn-'tahr]
single soltero [sohl-'teh-roh]
sip trago ['trah-goh]
sister hermana [ehr-'mah-nah]
sister-in-law cuñada [koo-'nyah-dah]
sit (down) (v) sentarse [sehn-'tahr-seh]
situation la situación [lah see-too-ah-see-'ohn]
size tamaño [tah-'mah-nyoh]; (length) la longitud [lah lohn-hee-'tood]; (height) altura [ahl-'too-rah]; (clothes/shoes) talla ['tah-yah]; (shoes/hats) número ['noo-meh-roh]
skill(ful) habilidad; (adj) hábil [ah-bee-lee-'dahd; 'ah-beel]
skin la piel [lah pee-'ehl]
skyscraper el rascacielos [ehl rah-skah-see-'eh-lohs]
sleep (v) dormir [dormir]
sleep sueño ['sweh-nyoh]
slender delgado, esbelto [dehl-'gah-doh, ehs-'behl-toh]
slice rebanada [reh-bah-'nah-dah]
slide diapositiva [dee-ah-poh-see-'tee-vah]
slight ligero, (Am) liviano, leve [lee-'heh-roh, lee-vee-'ah-noh, 'leh-veh]
slim delgado [dehl-'gah-doh]
slippery resbaladizo [rehs-bah-lah-'dee-soh]
slope la pendiente, cuesta [lah pehn-dee-'ehn-teh, 'kweh-stah]
slow(ly) (adj) lento ['lehn-toh]; (adv) despacio, lentamente [deh-'spah-see·oh, lehn-tah-'mehn-teh]
small pequeño, chiquito [peh-'keh-nyoh, chee-'kee-toh]; (stature) bajo ['bah-hoh]
smell (v) oler [oh-'lohr]

A/Z

smell el olor [ehl oh-'lohr]

smoke *(v)* fumar [foo-'mahr]

smoke humo ['oo-moh]

smooth liso ['lee-soh]

smuggle *(v)* pasar de contrabando [pah-'sahr deh-kohn-trah-'bahn-doh]

smuggled goods contrabando [kohn-trah-'bahn-doh]

snack bocado, merienda [boh-'kah-doh; meh-ree-'ehn-dah]

snake la serpiente [lah sehr-pee-'ehn-teh]

sneeze *(v)* estornudar [eh-stohr-noo-'dahr]

sneeze estornudo [eh-stohr-'noo-doh]

snore roncar [rohn-'kahr]

snow *(v)* nevar [neh-'vahr]

snow nieve [nee-'eh-veh]

so así, entonces [ah-'see, ehn-'tohn-sehs]

sober sobrio ['soh-bree-oh]

soft *(consistency)* blando ['blahn-doh]; *(texture)* suave ['swah-veh]

some algunos, unos [ahl-'goo-nohs, 'oo-nohs]

somehow de alguna manera [deh ahl-'goo-nah mah-'neh-rah]

someone alguien, algún, alguno, alguna ['ahl-gee-ehn, ahl-'goon, ahl-'goo-noh, ahl-'goo-nah]

someplace a algún sitio [ah ahl-'goo 'see-tee-oh]

something algo ['ahl-goh]

sometimes *(adv)* en ocasiones, a veces [ehn oh-'kah-see-'oh-nehs, ah 'veh-sehs]

somewhere en algún sitio [ehl ahl-'goon 'see-tee-oh]

son hijo ['ee-hoh]

song canto, la canción ['kahn-toh, lah kahn-see-'ohn]

soon pronto ['prohn-toh]; **as soon as possible** lo más pronto posible [loh mahs 'prohn-toh poh-'see-bleh]

soon pronto, dentro de poco ['prohn-toh, 'dehn-troh deh 'poh-koh]

sort tipo, la clase ['tee-poh, lah 'klah-seh]

sound sonido [soh-'nee-doh]

sour agrio ['ah-gree-oh]

South el sur [ehl soor]

South America Sudamérica [sood-ah-'meh-ree-kah]

South American sudamericano/-a [sood-ah-meh-ree-'kah-noh/-ah]

southern del sur, meridional [dehl soor, meh-ree-dee-oh-'nahl]

souvenir recuerdo [reh-'kwehr-doh]

space espacio [eh-'spah-see-oh]

Spain España [eh-'spah-nyah]

Spanish el español/la española [ehl eh-spah-'nyohl, lah eh-spah-'nyoh-lah]; *(lang)* español [eh-spah-'nyohl]

spark chispa ['chee-spah]

speak *(v)* hablar [ah-'blahr]

special especial [eh-speh-see-'ahl]

special(ly) *(adj)* especial [eh-speh-see-'ahl]; *(adv)* especialmente [eh-speh-see-ahl-'mehn-teh]

spectator el espectador [ehl eh-spehk-tah-'dohr]

speed la velocidad [lah veh-loh-see-'dahd]

speed up *(v)* apurar, acelerar [ah-poo-'rahr, ah-seh-leh-'rahr]

spell *(v)* deletrear [deh-leh-treh-'ahr]

spend *(v)* *(money)* gastar [gah-'stahr]; *(time)* pasar [pah-'sahr]; **spend the night** *(v)* pernoctar [pehr-nohk-'tahr]

spicy picante [pee-'kahn-teh]

spin *(v)* girar [hee-'rahr]; **go for a spin** *(v)* dar una vuelta en coche [dahr 'oo-nah 'vwehl-tah ehn 'koh-cheh]

spin giro, vuelta ['hee-roh, 'vwehl-tah]

spoil *(v)* estropear [eh-stroh-peh-'ahr]; *(reflexive)* estropearse, deteriorarse [eh-stroh-peh-'ahr-seh, deh-teh-ree-oh-'rahr-seh]

sport el deporte [ehl deh-'pohr-teh]; **sports field** campo de deportes ['kahm-poh deh deh-'pohr-tehs]

spot el lugar [ehl loo-'gahr]

spring *(bed)* el muelle [ehl 'mweh-yeh]

square cuadrado [kwah-'drah-doh]

staff el personal [ehl pehr-soh-'nahl]

stain mancha ['mahn-chah]

staircase escalera [eh-skah-'leh-rah]

stamp sello *(Am)* estampilla ['seh-yoh, eh-stahm-'pee-yah]

stand *(v)* pararse [pah-'rahr-seh]; **stand in line** hacer cola [ah-sehr koh-lah]

star estrella [eh-'streh-yah]

start *(v)* partir, salir, empezar [pahr-'teer, sah-'leer, ehm-peh-'sahr]

state estado [eh-'stah-doh]

statement la declaración [lah deh-klah-rah-see-'ohn]; **to make a statement** hacer una declaración [ah-'sehr 'oo-nah deh-klah-rah-see-'ohn]

stay estancia, *(Am)* estadía [eh-'stahn-see-ah, eh-stah-'dee-ah]

stay, remain *(v)* quedarse [keh-'dahr-seh]

steal *(v)* robar [roh-'bahr]

steep escarpado [eh-skahr-'pah-doh]
step paso ['pah-soh]; (stairway) el escalón [eh-skah-'lohn]
stick el bastón, palo, vara, (metal) barra [ehl bah-'stohn, 'pah-loh, 'vah-rah, 'bah-rrah]
still quieto, tranquilo [kee-'eh-toh, trahn-'kee-loh]
still todavía, aún [toh-dah-'vee-ah, ah-'oon]
sting (v) pinchar, picar [peen-'chahr, pee-'kahr]
stink (v) oler mal [oh-'lehr mahl]
stone piedra [pee-'eh-drah]
stony pedregoso [peh-dreh-'goh-soh]
stop (v) detenerse, pararse [deh-teh-'nehr-seh, pah-'rahr-seh]
stop parada [pah-'rah-dah]; **bus/train/taxi stop** parada de autobús/tren/taxi [pah-'rah-dah deh ow-toh-'boos/trehn/'tahk-see]
stop! ¡alto! ['ahl-toh]
store tienda [tee-'ehn-dah]
storm la tempestad, tormenta [lah tehm-peh-'stahd, tohr-'mehn-tah]
story historia, cuento [ee-'stoh-ree·ah, 'kwehn-toh]
stove estufa [eh-'stoo-fah]
straight derecho, recto (sex) hetero, heterosexual [deh-'reh-choh, 'rehk-toh, 'eh-teh-roh, eh-teh-roh-sehk-soo-'ahl]
straight ahead todo seguido/derecho ['toh-doh seh-'gee-doh/deh-'reh-choh]
strange raro ['rah-roh]
strap correa [koh-'rreh-ah]
street la calle [lah 'kah-yeh]
strength fuerza ['fwehr-sah]
strict severo, riguroso, estricto [seh-'veh-roh, ree-goo-'roh-soh, eh-'streek-toh]
strike (v) golpear, pegar, ir a la huelga [gohl-peh-'ahr, peh-'gahr, eer ah lah 'wehl-gah]; (clock) dar la hora [dahr lah 'oh-rah]
strike golpe ['gohl-peh]; (workers') huelga ['wehl-gah]
string cuerda, el bramante, el cordón (Am) piola, el piolín ['kwehr-dah, ehl brah-'mahn-teh, pee-'oh-lah, ehl pee-oh-'leen, ehl kohr-'dohn]
stroke el golpe [ehl 'gohl-peh]; (medical) ataque al corazón [ah-'tah-keh ahl koh-rah-'sohn]
stroll paseo, paseíto [pah-'seh-oh, pah-seh-'ee-toh]
strong fuerte ['fwehr-teh]
study (v) estudiar [eh-stoo-dee-'ahr]
stupid estúpido [eh-'stoo-pee-doh]

suburb suburbio, las afueras [soo-'boor-bee·oh, lahs ah-'fweh-rahs]
success éxito ['ehk-see-toh]
such tal [tahl]
sudden(ly) de repente, repentinamente, de pronto [deh reh-'pehn-teh, reh-pehn-tee-nah-'mehn-teh, deh 'prohn-toh]
suffer an accident (v) sufrir un accidente [soo-'freer oon ahk-see-'dehn-teh]
suitable conveniente [kohn-veh-nee-'ehn-teh]
suitcase maleta [mah-'leh-tah]
summit la cumbre, cima [lah 'koom-breh, 'see-mah]
sun el sol [ehl sohl]
sunglasses las gafas de sol [lahs 'gah-fahs deh sohl]
sunny soleado [soh-leh-'ah-doh]
sunrise el alba, la salida del sol [ehl 'ahl-bah, lah sah-'lee-dah dehl sohl]
sunset el crepúsculo, la puesta del sol [ehl kreh-'poo-skoo-loh, lah 'pweh-stah dehl sohl]
superfluous superfluo [soo-'pehr-floo·oh]
support apoyo [ah-'poh-yoh]
surname el nombre (de pila) [ehl 'nohm-breh (deh 'pee-lah)]
surprised (v) asombrarse (de), extrañarse (de) [ah-sohm-'brahr-seh (deh), ehk-strah-'nyahr-seh (deh)]
surprised sorprendido [sohr-prehn-'dee-doh]
suspicion sospecha [soh-'speh-chah]
swamp pantano [pahn-'tah-noh]
swear (v) regañar, insultar [reh-gah-'nyahr, een-sool-'tahr]
sweat (v) sudar [soo-'dahr]
sweet dulce ['dool-seh]
swim (v) nadar, bañarse [nah-'dahr, bah-'nyahr-seh]
swimming pool piscina [pee-'see-nah]
swindle (v) estafar [eh-stah-'fahr]; **swindler** estafador [eh-stah-fah-'dohr]
swindle estafa [eh-'stah-fah]
Swiss suizo/suiza ['swee-soh/'swee-sah]
Switzerland Suiza ['swee-sah]

T

table mesa ['meh-sah]
take (v) llevar, tomar, coger [yeh-'vahr, toh-'mahr, koh-'hehr]; **take with oneself** (v) llevar(se) consigo [yeh-'vahr(seh)

kohn-'see-goh]; **take away** (v) quitar [kee-'tahr]; **take off** (v) despegar [deh-speh-'gahr]; **take out** (v) sacar [sah-'kahr]

take a bath (v) bañarse [bah-'nyahr-seh]

take care of/to look after (v) cuidar a/ocuparse de [kwee-'dahr ah/oh-koo-'pahr-seh deh]

take into account (v) tener en cuenta [teh-'nehr ehn 'kwehn-tah]

take over (v) encargarse de [ehn-kahr-'gahr-seh deh]

take part in (v) tomar parte en [toh-'mahr 'pahr-teh ehn]

take-out food comida para llevar ['koh-mee-dah 'pah-rah yeh-'vahr]

talk (v) hablar [ah-'blahr]

talk el habla [ehl ah-'blah]

taste (v) gustar [goo-'stahr]; **to taste of** (v) saber a [sah-'behr ah]

taste gusto, el sabor ['goo-stoh, ehl sah-'bohr]

tavern taberna [tah-'behr-nah]

taxi el taxi [ehl 'tahk-see]

teach (v) enseñar [ehn-seh-'nyahr]

team equipo [eh-'kee-poh]

tear (v) destrozar [deh-stroh-'sahr]

television la televisión [lah teh-leh-vee-see-'ohn]

tell (v) contar [kohn-'tahr]

tempest la tempestad [lah tehm-peh-'stahd]

temporary pasajero [pah-sah-'heh-roh]

tender tierno [tee-'ehr-noh]

terrible horrible, terrible, espantoso [oh-'rree-bleh, teh-'rree-bleh, eh-spahn-'toh-soh]

terrific magnífico [mahg-'nee-fee-koh]

testimony testimonio [teh-stee-'moh-nee-oh]

thank (v) dar las gracias, agradecer [dahr lahs 'grah-see·ahs, ah-grah-deh-'sehr]

thank you gracias ['grah-see·ahs]

thankful agradecido [ah-grah-deh-'see-doh]

thanks gracias ['grah-see·ahs]

that aquella, aquel, aquello, ese, esa, eso, que [ah-'keh-yah, ah-'kehl, ah-'keh-yoh, 'eh-seh, 'eh-sah, 'eh-soh, keh]

that way por allí/allá [pohr ah-'yee/ah-'yah]

the el, la, lo [ehl, lah, loh]

then entonces [ehn-'tohn-sehs]; (time) después [deh-'spwehs]; (reason) entonces, en ese caso [ehn-'tohn-sehs, ehn 'eh-seh 'kah-soh]

there allí, allá, ahí; (reason) como, ya que, porque [ah-'yee, ah-'yah, ah-'ee, 'koh-moh, yah keh, 'pohr-keh]; **over/down there** allí arriba/abajo [ah-'yee ah-'rree-bah/ah-'bah-hoh]

there is/are hay ['ah·ee]

therefore por eso/esto/ello, por lo tanto, por consiguiente [pohr-'eh-soh/'eh-stoh/'eh-yoh, pohr loh 'tahn-toh, pohr kohn-see-gee-'ehn-teh]

these estas, estos, esas, esos ['eh-stahs, 'eh-stohs, 'eh-sahs, 'eh-sohs]

they ellos, ellas ['eh-yohs, 'eh-yahs]

thin flaco ['flah-koh]

thing cosa ['koh-sah]

think (of) (v) pensar (en) [pehn-'sahr (ehn)]

third tercera, tercero [tehr-'seh-rah, tehr-'seh-roh]; **a third** un tercio [oon 'tehr-see·oh]; **in the third place** en tercer lugar [ehn tehr-'sehr loo-'gahr]

thirst la sed [lah sehd]

thirsty, to be (v) tener sed [teh-'nehr sehd]

this este, esta, esto ['eh-steh, 'eh-stah, 'eh-stoh]

those aquellas, aquellos [ah-'keh-yohs, ah-'keh-yahs]

thought, idea pensamiento, idea [pehn-sah-mee-'ehn-toh, ee-'deh-ah]

threat hilo ['ee-loh]

through por medio de, mediante, a través de [pohr 'meh-dee·oh deh, meh-dee-'ahn-teh, ah trah-'vehs deh]

throw (v) echar, tirar [eh-'chahr, tee-'rahr]

throw tiro, lanzamiento ['tee-roh, lahn-sah-mee-'ehn-toh]

ticket entrada, (Am) boleto [ehn-'trah-dah, boh-'leh-toh]

ticket office caja, boletería ['kah-ha, boh-leh-teh-'ree-ah]; (theater) taquilla [tah-'kee-yah]

tie (v) atar [ah-'tahr]

tighten up (v) apretar [ah-preh-'tahr]

time tiempo [tee-'ehm-poh]; **every time** cada vez, siempre ['kah-dah vehs, see-'ehm-preh]; **from time to time** de vez en cuando [deh vehs ehn 'kwahn-doh]; **some time ago** hace algún tiempo ['ah-seh ahl-'goon tee-'ehm-poh]

time(ly) tiempo [tee-'ehm-poh]; (adv) a tiempo, oportunamente [ah tee-'ehm-poh, oh-pohr-too-nah-'mehn-teh]

tin, can *(preserve)* el bote/caja de conservas [ehl 'boh-teh/'kah-hah deh kohn-'sehr-vahs]
tip punta, extremo, sugerencia, pista ['poon-tah, eks-'streh-moh, soo-heh-'rehn-see-ah, 'pee-stah]
tired cansado [kahn-'sah-doh]
tiring fatigoso [fah-tee-'goh-soh]
toast tostada [toh-'stah-dah]; *(drink)* el brindis [ehl 'breen-dees]
tobacco tabaco [tah-'bah-koh]
today hoy ['oh-ee]; **this evening** esta tarde ['eh-stah 'tahr-deh]; **tonight** esta noche ['eh-stah 'noh-cheh]
together juntos, juntas ['hoon-tohs, 'hoon-tahs]
toilet el retrete, el servicio [ehl reh-'treh-teh, ehl sehr-'vee-see-oh]
toilet paper el papel higiénico [ehl pah-'pehl ee-hee-'eh-nee-koh]
tolerate *(v)* aguantar, soportar [ah-'gwahn-'tahr, soh-pohr-'tahr]
tomorrow mañana [mah-'nyah-nah]
tone tono ['toh-noh]
tongs las tenazas [lahs teh-'nah-sahs]
top *(mountain)* cima, cumbre ['see-mah, 'koom-breh]
touch *(v)* tocar [toh-'kahr]
touch contacto, toque [kohn-'tahk-toh, 'toh-keh]
tour la excursión [lah ehk-skoor-see-'ohn]
tourist el/la turista [ehl/lah too-'ree-stah]
tourist office oficina de turismo [oh-fee-'see-nah deh too-'rees-moh]
towards hacia ['ah-see-ah]
tower la torre [lah 'toh-rreh]; *(church)* campanario [kahm-pah-'nah-ree-oh]
town la población, pueblo [lah poh-blah-see-'ohn, 'pweh-bloh]
toy el juguete [ehl hoo-'geh-teh]
trace vestigio [veh-'stee-hee-oh]
traffic tráfico ['trah-fee-koh]
training la formación [la trahns-fohr-mah-see-'ohn]
transfer *(v)* transferir [trahns-feh-'reer]
transferable transferible [trahns-feh-'ree-bleh]
transit visa visado de tránsito [vee-'sah-doh deh 'trahn-see-toh]
translate *(v)* traducir [trah-doo-'seer]
transport *(v)* transportar [trahn-spohr-'tahr]
transport transportar [trahn-spohr-'tahr]
trash, garbage basura [bah-'soo-rah]
travel *(v)* viajar [vee-ah-'hahr]

travel agency agencia de viajes [ah-'hehn-see-ah deh vee-'ah-hehs]
travel guide *(person)* el guía (turístico) [ehl 'gee-ah (too-'ree-stee-koh)]; *(book)* la guía (turística) [lah 'gee-ah (too-'ree-stee-kah)]
traveler el viajero, la viajera [ehl vee-ah-'heh-roh, lah vee-ah-'heh-rah]
treat *(v)* tratar [trah-'tahr]
treatment tratamiento [trah-tah-mee-'ehn-toh]
tree el árbol [ehl 'ahr-bohl]
trial (law) juicio, experimento, prueba, ensayo ['hoo-ee-see-oh; ehk-speh-ree-'mehn-toh, proo-'eh-bah, ehn-'sah-yoh]
trip el viaje [ehl vee-'ah-heh]
true verdadero, real, auténtico [vehr-dah-'deh-roh, reh-'ahl]; *(adv)* de verdad, de veras [deh vehr-'dahd, deh veh-'rahs]
trust confianza [kohn-fee-'ahn-sah]
trust (in) *(v)* confiar (en) [kohn-fee-'ahr (ehn)]
truth la verdad [lah vehr-'dahd]
try *(v)* (law) juzgar; experimentar, probar, ensayar [hoos-'gahr, ehk-speh-ree-mehn-'tahr, proh-'bahr, ehn-sah-'yahr]
try (on) *(v)* probar(se) [proh-'bahr(seh)]
try hard *(v)* tomarse la molestia de [toh-'mahr-seh lah moh-'leh-stee-ah deh]
tube tubo ['too-boh]
tunnel el túnel [ehl 'too-nehl]
turn vuelta ['vwehl-tah]
turn *(v)* voltear, torcer, doblar [vohl-teh-'ahr, tohr-'sehr, doh-'blahr]; **to turn right/left** torcer a la derecha/izquierda [tohr-'sehr ah lah deh-'reh-chah/ees-kee-'ehr-dah]; **to turn on** encender [ehn-sehn-'dehr]; **to turn off** apagar [ah-pah-'gahr]; **to turn back** volver (a) [vohl-'vehr]
turn *(v)* volver [vohl-'vehr]
turn back *(v)* volver(se), dar la vuelta [vohl-'vehr(seh), dahr lah 'vwehl-tah]
turn on/off the light *(v)* encender/apagar la luz [ehn-sehn-'dehr/ah-pah-'gahr lah loos]
typical típico ['tee-pee-koh]

U

ugly feo ['feh-oh]
umbrella el paraguas, la sombrilla [ehl pah-'rah-gwahs, lah sohm-'bree-yah]
unbearable insoportable, intolerable [een-soh-pohr-'tah-bleh, een-toh-leh-'rah-bleh]

uncertain incierto [een-see-'ehr-toh]
uncle tío ['tee-oh]
uncomfortable incómodo [een-'koh-moh-doh]
uncommon poco común ['poh-koh koh-'moon]
unconscious desmayado, sin conocimiento [dehs-mah-'yah-doh, seen koh-noh-see-mee-'ehn-toh]
undecided indeciso [een-deh-'see-soh]
under abajo, bajo, debajo de [ah-'bah-hoh, 'bah-hoh, deh-'bah-hoh deh]
underpass paso subterráneo ['pah-soh soob-teh-'rrah-neh-oh]
understand (v) entender [ehn-tehn-'dehr]
underwear ropa interior ['roh-pah een-teh-ree-'ohr]
undress (v) quitar la ropa, desnudar [kee-'tahr lah 'roh-pah, dehs-noo-'dahr]
undress oneself (v) quitarse la ropa, desnudarse [kee-'tahr-seh lah 'roh-pah, dehs-noo-'dahr-seh]
unemployed desempleado, parado [dehs-ehm-pleh-'ah-doh, pah-'rah-doh]
unexpected inesperado, imprevisto [een-eh-speh-'rah-doh, eem-preh-'vee-stoh]
unfair injusto [een-'hoo-stoh]
unfavorable desfavorable [dehs-fah-voh-'rah-bleh]
unfit inadecuado, inepto [een-ah-deh-'kwah-doh, een-'ehp-toh]
unfortunately desgraciadamente [dehs-grah-see-ah-dah-'mehn-teh]
unfriendly antipático [ahn-tee-'pah-tee-koh]
ungrateful desagradecido [dehs-grah-deh-'see-doh]
unhappy descontento [dehs-kohn-'tehn-toh]
unhealthy malsano [mahl-'sah-noh]
unimportant sin importancia, insignificante [seen eem-pohr-'tahn-see-ah, een-seeg-nee-fee-'kahn-teh]
unknown desconocido [dehs-koh-noh-'see-doh]
unlikely improbable [eem-proh-'bah-bleh]
unload (v) descargar [dehs-kahr-'gahr]
unlucky desgraciado [dehs-grah-see-'ah-doh]
unnecessary innecesario, superfluo [ee-neh-seh-'sah-ree-oh, soo-'pehr-floo-oh]
unpack (v) deshacer las maletas, desempacar [dehs-ah-'sehr lahs mah-'leh-tahs, dehs-ehm-pah-'kahr]

unpleasant desagradable [dehs-ah-grah-'dah-bleh]
unpractical poco práctico ['poh-koh 'prahk-tee-koh]
unsafe inseguro [een-seh-'goo-roh]
untie (v) soltar, desatar [sohl-'tahr, dehs-ah-'tahr]
until hasta ['ah-stah]; **until now** hasta ahora ['ah-stah ah-'oh-rah]
unwelcome inoportuno [een-oh-pohr-'too-noh]
unwell indispuesto [een-dee-'spweh-stoh]
up arriba [ah-'rree-bah]; **up there** allí arriba [ah-'yee ah-'rree-bah]
uphill cuesta arriba ['kweh-stah ah-'rree-bah]
upward hacia arriba ['ah-see-ah ah-'rree-bah]
urgent urgente [oor-'hehn-teh]
Uruguayan uruguayo [oo-roo-'gwah-yoh]
us nosotros, nos [noh-'soh-trohs, nohs]
use (v) usar, emplear [oo-'sahr, ehm-pleh-'ahr]
use uso, empleo, la utilización ['oo-soh, ehm-'pleh-oh, lah oo-tee-lee-sah-see-'ohn]
used to acostumbrado [ah-koh-stoom-'brah-doh]; **to be used to** (v) acostumbrarse a [ah-koh-stoom-'brahr-seh ah]
useful útil ['oo-teel]
useless inútil [een-'oo-teel]
usual usual, habitual [oo-soo-'ahl, ah-bee-too-'ahl]
usual(ly) usual, habitual [oo-soo-'ahl, ah-bee-too-'ahl]; (adv) usualmente, habitualmente [oo-soo-ahl-'mehn-teh, ah-bee-too-ahl-'mehn-teh]; **as usual** como siempre, como de costumbre ['koh-moh see-'ehm-preh, 'koh-moh deh koh-'stoom-breh]

V

valid válido ['vah-lee-doh]
validity la validez, (Am) vigencia [lah vah-lee-'dehs, vee-'hehn-see-ah]
valley el valle [ehl 'vah-yeh]
valuables los objetos de valor [lohs ohb-'heh-tohs deh vah-'lohr]
vending machine el distribuidor automático [ehl dee-stree-boo-ee-'dohr ow-toh-'mah-tee-koh]
Venezuelan venezolano [veh-neh-soh-'lah-noh]
very muy ['moo-ee]; **very much** mucho ['moo-choh]

video (v) hacer/sacar/grabar un video [ah-'sehr/sah-'kahr/grah-'bahr oon vee-'deh-oh]

video video [vee-'deh-oh]

view vista ['vee-stah]

village aldea, pueblo [ahl-'deh-ah, 'pweh-bloh]

vineyard viña, viñedo ['vee-nyah, vee-'nyeh-doh]

visibility visibilidad [vee-see-bee-lee-'dahd]

visible visible [vee-'see-bleh]

visit (v) visitar, pasar (por casa de alguien) [vee-see-'tahr, pah-'sahr (pohr 'kah-sah deh 'ahl-gee-ehn)]

visit visita [vee-'see-tah]

visit (someone) (v) visitar a alguien, ir a ver a alguien [vee-see-'tahr ah 'ahl-gee-ehn,eer ah vehr ah 'ahl-gee-ehn]

voice la voz [lah vohs]

volt voltio ['vohl-tee-oh]

volume tomo ['toh-moh]

vote (v) votar [voh-'tahr]

vote voto ['voh-toh]

voucher el vale [ehl 'vah-leh]

vulgar vulgar, ordinario [vool-'gahr, ohr-dee-'nah-ree-oh]

W

wagon (train) el vagón, el coche [ehl vah-'gohn, ehl 'koh-cheh]

wait (v) esperar [eh-speh-'rahr]

wake up (v) despertarse [deh-spehr-'tahr-seh]

walk paseo, caminata [pah-'seh-oh, kah-mee-'nah-tah]

walk (v) caminar, pasear, dar un paso, ir a pie, andar [kah-mee-'nahr, dahr oon pah-'seh-oh, eer ah 'pee-eh, ahn-'dahr]

wall la pared, muro [lah pah-'rehd, 'moo-roh]

wallet billetera, cartera [bee-yeh-'teh-rah]

want (v) querer, desear [keh-'rehr, deh-seh-'ahr]

war guerra ['geh-rah]

warm (v) calentar [kah-lehn-'tahr]

warm caliente [kah-lee-'ehn-teh]

warm cordial, sincero [kohr-dee-'ahl, seen-'seh-roh]

warn (of/about) prevenir (acerca de) [preh-veh-'neer (ah-'sehr-kah deh)]

wash (v) lavar [lah-'vahr]; **washing machine** lavadora [lah-vah-'doh-rah]

wasp avispa [ah-'vee-spah]

watch (v) mirar, vigilar [mee-'rahr, vee-hee-'lahr]

water (el) agua [(ehl) 'ah-gwah]

watt vatio ['vah-tee-oh]

way (path) camino, sendero, senda [kah-'mee-noh, sehn-'deh-roh]; (manner) manera, modo, forma [mah-'neh-rah, 'moh-doh, 'fohr-mah]

we nosotros [noh-'soh-trohs]

weak débil ['deh-beel]

weakness la debilidad [lah deh-bee-lee-'dahd]

wealth riqueza, fortuna [ree-'keh-sah, fohr-'too-nah]; **wealthy** acomodado, adinerado, rico [ah-koh-moh-'dah-doh, ah-dee-neh-'rah-doh, 'ree-koh]

wear (v) llevar puesto, usar [yeh-'vahr 'pweh-stoh, oo-'sahr]

weather (estado del) tiempo [(eh-'stah-doh dehl) tee-'ehm-poh]

wedding boda, matrimonio ['boh-dah, mah-tree-'moh-nee-oh]

week semana [seh-'mah-nah]; **in a week** dentro de una semana ['dehn-troh deh 'oo-nah seh-'mah-nah]

weekdays de lunes a viernes, los días laborales (de la semana) [deh 'loo-nehs ah vee-'ehr-nehs; lohs 'dee-ahs lah-boh-'rah-blehs (deh lah seh-'mah-nah)]

weekly semanal, semanalmente, cada semana [seh-mah-'nahl, seh-mah-nahl-'mehn-teh, 'kah-dah seh-'mah-nah]

weigh (v) pesar [peh-'sahr]

weight peso ['peh-soh]

welcome bienvenido [bee-neh-veh-'nee-doh]

well (adv) bien ['bee·ehn]

well pozo ['poh-soh]; (spring) el manantial, la fuente [ehl mah-nahn-tee-'ahl, lah 'fwehn-teh]

well-being el bienestar, la buena salud [ehl bee-ehn-eh-'stahr, lah 'bweh-nah sah-'lood]

well-known conocido, famoso [koh-noh-'see-doh, fah-'moh-soh]

West el oeste [ehl oh-'eh-steh]

western occidental [ohk-see-dehn-'tahl]

what qué [keh]

wheel rueda [roo-'eh-dah]

when cuando, ¿cuándo? ['kwahn-doh, 'kwahn-doh]

whether si [see]

A/Z

while *(prep)* durante [doo-'rahn-teh]; *(conj)* mientras (que) [mee-'ehn-trahs (keh)]

whole completo, entero, el total, el conjunto [kohm-'pleh-toh, ehn-'teh-roh, ehl toh-'tahl, ehl kohn-'hoon-toh]; *(adv)* completamente, del todo, todo, toda [com-pleh-tah-'mehn-teh, dehl 'toh-doh; 'toh-doh, 'toh-dah]

wide ancho ['ahn-choh]

wife esposa, la mujer [eh-'spoh-sah, lah moo-'hehr]

wild salvaje, silvestre [sahl-'vah-heh; seel-'veh-streh]

win *(v)* ganar, triunfar [gah-'nahr, tree-oon-'fahr]

wind viento [vee-'ehn-toh]; **windy** ventoso [vehn-'toh-soh]

wink *(v)* hacer señas [ah-'sehr 'seh-nyahs]

wire alambre [ehl ah-'lahm-breh]; *(el)* tendido eléctrico [tehn-'dee-doh eh-'lehk-tree-koh]

wish deseo [deh-'seh-oh]

with con [kohn]

withdraw *(v)* retirar, retirarse [reh-tee-'rahr, reh-tee-'rahr-seh]

within dentro de, adentro de, en ['dehn-troh deh, ah-'dehn-troh deh, ehn]

without sin [seen]

without obligation sin compromiso [seen kohm-proh-'mee-soh]

witness testigo [teh-'stee-goh]

wonderful maravilloso [mah-rah-vee-'yoh-soh]

wood madera [mah-'deh-rah]

word palabra [pah-'lah-brah]

work *(v)* trabajar [trah-bah-'hahr]

work trabajo [trah-'bah-hoh]; **worker** trabajador [trah-bah-hah-'dohr]

work on *(v)* elaborar [eh-lah-boh-'rahr]

workday día laborable ['dee-ah lah-boh-'rah-bleh]

workshop el taller [ehl tah-'yehr]

world mundo ['moon-doh]

worm gusano [goo-'sah-noh]

worried preocupado [preh-oh-koo-'pah-doh]

worry *(v)* preocuparse de [preh-oh-koo-'pahr-seh deh]

worry *(v)* preocuparse de, cuidar de, tener cuidado de, intranquilizarse [preh-oh-koo-'pahr-seh deh, kwee-'dahr deh, teh-'nehr kwee-'dah-doh deh, een-trahn-kee-lee-'sahr-seh]; **worry about** *(v)* preocuparse de [preh-oh-koo-'pahr-seh deh]

worry la preocupación [lah preh-oh-koo-pah-see-'ohn]

worse malo, grave ['mah-loh, 'grah-veh]

worst peor [peh-'ohr]

worth el valor [ehl vah-'lohr]

worthless sin valor, sin importancia [seen 'vah-lohr, seen eem-pohr-'tahn-see-ah]

wrap *(v)* embalar, empaquetar, envolver [ehm-bah-'lahr, ehm-pah-keh-'tahr, ehn-vohl-'vehr]

wrap embalaje, *(Am)* empaque [ehm-bah-'lah-heh, ehm-'pah-keh]

wrap up *(v)* envolver [ehn-vohl-'vehr]

wristwatch el reloj de pulsera [ehl reh-'loh deh pool-'seh-rah]

write *(v)* escribir [eh-skree-'beer]

write down *(v)* anotar, apuntar [ah-noh-'tahr, ah-poon-'tahr]

writing *(n)* escritura [eh-skree-'too-rah]; **in writing** por escrito [pohr eh-'skree-toh]

wrong *(person)* equivocado [eh-kee-voh-'kah-doh]

wrong, to be *(v)* estar equivocado, no tener razón [eh-'stahr eh-kee-voh-'kah-doh, noh teh-'nehr rah-'sohn]

Y

yawn *(v)* bostezar [boh-steh-'sahr]

year año ['ah-nyoh]

yesterday aquí [ah-'kee]

you tu, usted [too, oo-'stehd]; *(pl)* vosotros, vosotras, *(Am)* ustedes [voh-'soh-trohs/ahs, oo-'steh-dehs]; *(poss prn sing)* tu, tus, su, sus, vuestro, vuestros, vuestra, vuestras [too, toos, soo, soos, 'vweh-stroh/ah, 'vweh-strohs/ahs]

you're welcome de nada, no hay de qué [deh 'nah-dah, noh 'ah-ee deh keh]

young joven ['hoh-vehn]

youth la juventud [lah hoo-vehn-'tood]

SPANISH-ENGLISH DICTIONARY

A

a [ah] to; **al correo** [ahl koh-'rreh-oh] to the post office; **a la mesa** [ah lah 'meh-sah] to the table

abajo [ah-'bah-hoh] under; **cuesta abajo** ['kweh-stah ah-'bah-hoh] downhill; **hacia abajo** ['ah-see-ah ah-'bah-hoh] downwards

abandonar [ah-bahn-doh-'nahr] to abandon

abarcar [ah-bahr-'kahr] to include, encompass

abeja [ah-'beh-hah] bee

abierto [ah-bee-'ehr-toh] open

aborigen [ah-boh-'ree-hehn] aboriginal, native

abrazar [ah-brah-'sahr] to hug, embrace

abreviatura [ah-breh-vee-ah-'too-rah] abbreviation

abrir [ah-'breer] to open

absolutamente [ahb-soh-loo-tah-'mehn-teh] *(adv)* absolutely

abuela [ah-'bweh-lah] grandmother

abuelo [ah-'bweh-loh] grandfather

abundante [ah-boon-'dahn-teh] abundant

aburrido [ah-boo-'rree-doh] boring

abusar (de) [ah-boo-'sahr (deh)] to take advantage (of), to abuse

abuso [ah-'boo-soh] mistreatment, abuse

acá [ah-'kah] here

acabar [ah-kah-'bahr] to end; **todo se acabó** ['toh-doh seh ah-kah-'boh] it's all over

acceso [ahk-'seh-soh] entrance, access

accidente [ahk-see-'dehn-teh] accident

acción [ahk-see-'ohn] *(f)* action

aceite [ah-'seh-ee-teh] *(m)* oil; **aceite combustible** [ah-'seh-ee-teh kohm-boo-'stee-bleh] *(m)* fuel oil

acelerar [ah-seh-leh-'rahr] to speed up, to accelerate

acento [ah-'sehn-toh] accent, emphasis

aceptación [ah-sehp-tah-see-'ohn] *(f)* acceptance

aceptar [ah-sehp-'tahr] to accept, to receive

acercarse [ah-sehr-'kahr-seh] to get close

aclarar [ah-klah-'rahr] to clarify

aclimatarse [ah-klee-mah-'tahr-seh] to get used to

acomodado [ah-koh-moh-'dah-doh] well-off

acompañamiento [ah-kohm-pah-nyah-mee-'ehn-toh] accompaniment

acompañar [ah-kohm-pah-'nyahr] to accompany

aconsejar [ah-kohn-seh-'hahr] to advise

acontecimiento [ah-kohn-teh-see-mee-'ehn-toh] event

acordar [ah-kohr-'dahr] to agree

acordarse de [ah-kohr-'dahr-seh deh] to remember

acostado, estar [ah-koh-'stah-doh, eh-'stahr] to be in bed, to lie down

acostarse [ah-koh-'stahr-seh] to go to bed, to go lie down

acostumbrado [ah-koh-stoom-'brah-doh] accustomed, used to

acostumbrarse a [ah-koh-stoom-'brahr-seh ah] to get used to

actividad [ahk-tee-vee-'dahd] *(f)* activity

actualmente [ahk-too-ahl-'mehn-teh] now, currently, at present

actuar [ahk-too-'ahr] to act

acuerdo [ah-'kwehr-doh] agreement

estar de acuerdo, ponerse de acuerdo [eh-'stahr deh ah-'kwehr-doh, poh-'nehr-seh deh ah-'kwehr-doh] to agree, to be in agreement; **llegar a un acuerdo** [yeh-'gahr ah oon ah-'kwehr-doh] to reach an agreement

adecuado [ah-deh-'kwah-doh] appropriate

adelantar [ah-deh-lahn-'tahr] to go forward, to make progress; **¡adelante!** [ah-deh-'lahn-teh] come in! **adelantarse** [ah-deh-lahn-'tahr-seh] to pass, to get ahead

adelante [ah-deh-'lahn-teh] in front of, ahead

adelgazar [ah-dehl-gah-'sahr] to lose weight

además [ah-deh-'mahs] also

además (de eso) [ah-deh-'mahs (deh 'eh-soh)] besides

adicional [ah-dee-see-oh-'nahl] additional

A/Z

adinerado [ah-dee-neh-'rah-doh] wealthy

adiós [ah-dee-'ohs] good-bye

adivinar [ah-dee-vee-'nahr] to guess

administración [ahd-mee-nee-strah-see-'ohn] *(f)* management, administration

admirar [ahd-mee-'rahr] to admire

aduana [ah-'dwah-nah] customs office

adulto/-a [ah-'dool-toh/-ah] adult, grown-up

afeitar [ah-feh-ee-'tahr] to shave

afiche [ah-'fee-cheh] *(Am)* poster

afición [ah-fee-see-'ohn] *(f)* hobby

aficionado/-a [ah-fee-see-oh-'nah-doh/-ah] fan

afilado [ah-fee-'lah-doh] sharp

afirmar [ah-feer-'mahr] to affirm, to declare

afuera [ah-'fweh-rah] outside

afueras [ah-'fweh-rahs] *(f pl)* suburb

agarradero [ah-gah-rrah-'deh-roh] handle

agarrar [ah-gah-'rrahr] *(Am)* to grab, to take

agencia [ah-'hehn-see-ah] agency; **agencia de viajes** [ah-'hehn-see-ah deh vee-'ah-hehs] travel agency

agitado [ah-hee-'tah-doh] excited, agitated

agotado [ah-goh-'tah-doh] exhausted

agradable [ah-grah-'dah-bleh] nice, agreeable

agradar [ah-grah-'dahr] to like

agradecer [ah-grah-deh-'sehr] to be grateful

agradecido [ah-grah-deh-'see-doh] thankful, grateful

agradecimiento [ah-grah-deh-see-mee-'ehn-toh] gratitude, thanks

agricultor [ah-gree-kool-'tohr] *(m)* farmer

agrio ['ah-gree-oh] sour

agua ['ah-gwah] water

aguantar [ah-gwahn-'tahr] to hold

agudo [ah-'goo-doh] sharp, acute

aguja [ah-'goo-hah] needle

agujero [ah-goo-'heh-roh] hole

ahí [ah-'ee] there

ahora [ah-'oh-rah] now; **ahora mismo** [ah-'oh-rah 'mees-moh] right now

ahorita [ah-oh-'ree-tah] *(Am)* in a moment

ahorrar [ah-oh-'rrahr] to save

aire ['ah·ee-reh] *(m)* air; **al aire libre** [ahl 'ah·ee-reh 'lee-breh] outdoors

alabar [ah-lah-'bahr] to praise

alambre [ah-'lahm-breh] *(m)* wire

alargar [ah-lahr-'gahr] to lengthen

alcanzar [ahl-kahn-'sahr] to reach

alcohol de quemar [ahl-koh-'ohl deh keh-'mahr] alcohol (for a spirit stove)

aldea [ahl-'deh-ah] village

alegrarse (de) [ah-leh-'grahr-seh (deh)] to be happy (that)

alegre [ah-'leh-greh] happy

alegría [ah-leh-'gree-ah] happiness

alegrón [ah-leh-'grohn] *(Am)* drunk

alejado [ah-leh-'hah-doh] distant

alemán [ah-leh-'mahn] *(m)* German; **alemana** [ah-leh-'mah-nah] *(f)* German

Alemania [ah-leh-'mah-nee-ah] Germany

alfiler [ahl-fee-'lehr] *(m)* pin

algas ['ahl-gahs] *(f pl)* algae

algo ['ahl-goh] something

alguien ['ahl-gee-ehn] someone, somebody, anybody

algún [ahl-'goon] *(adj)* some, any; **a algún sitio** [ah ahl-'goon 'see-tee-oh] some place

alguno, alguna [ahl-'goo-noh, ahl-'goo-nah] *(adj)* no, not ... any; **no tiene talento alguno** [noh tee-'eh-neh tah-'lehn-toh ahl-'goo-noh] he has no talent whatsoever, he hasn't any talent; *(pron)* some, one, someone, somebody; **alguno es importante** [ahl-'goo-noh ehs eem-pohr-'tahn-teh] some are important; **de alguna manera** [deh ahl-'goo-nah mah-'neh-rah] one way or the other; **alguno vendrá** [ahl-'goo-noh vehn-'drah] someone will come; **alguno se lo dirá** [ahl-'goo-noh seh loh dee-'rah] somebody will tell him

algunos [ahl-'goo-nohs] *(pl pron)* some, a few

alianza [ah-lee-'ahn-sah] alliance, partnership

alimentos [ah-lee-'mehn-tohs] *(m pl)* food

almacenes, (grandes) [ahl-mah-'seh-nehs ('grahn-dehs)] *(m pl)* department store

almohada [ahl-moh-'ah-dah] pillow

almuerzo [ahl-moo-'ehr-soh] lunch

alojamiento [ah-loh-hah-mee-'ehn-toh] housing, lodging

alquilar [ahl-kee-'lahr] to rent

alquiler [ahl-kee-'lehr] *(m)* rental fee

alrededor de [ahl-reh-deh-'dohr deh] around, about

alrededores [ahl-reh-deh-'doh-rehs] *(m pl)* suburb, surrounding area

A/Z

altavoz [ahl-tah-'vohs] *(m)* loudspeaker

alto ['ahl-toh] tall; loud; **¡alto!** ['ahl-toh] stop!

altoparlante [ahl-toh-pahr-'lahn-teh] *(m)* *(Am)* loudspeaker

altura [ahl-'too-rah] height

alumbrado [ah-loom-'brah-doh] lights, public lighting

allá [ah-'yah] there; **(hacia) allá** [('ah-see·ah) ah-'yah] that way; **allí** [ah-'yee] there; **(hacia) allí** [('ah-see·ah) ah-'yee] that way; **allí abajo** [ah-'yee ah-'bah-hoh] down there; **allí arriba** [ah-'yee ah-'rree·bah] up there, over there

amabilidad [ah-mah-bee-lee-'dahd] *(f)* kindness, niceness

amable [ah-'mah-bleh] kind, nice, lovable

amar [ah-'mahr] to love

amargo [ah-'mahr-goh] bitter

ambos ['ahm-bohs] both

ambulancia [ahm-boo-'lahn-see·ah] ambulance

amigo/-a [ah-'mee-goh/-'ah] friend; **ser amigo (de)** [sehr ah-'mee-goh (deh)] to be a friend (of), to be friends with

amistad [ah-mee-'stahd] *(f)* friendship

amor [ah-'mohr] *(m)* love

amplio ['ahm-plee·oh] *(adj)* wide, spacious, roomy; broad, extensive

ampolleta [ahm-poh-'yeh-tah] *(Arg)* light bulb

amueblar [ah-mweh-'blahr] to furnish

ancho ['ahn-choh] wide

Andalucía [ahn-dah-loo-'see·ah] Andalusia

andaluz [ahn-dah-'loos] *(m)* Andalusian

andar [ahn-'dahr] to go, walk, travel; *(distance)* cover; **andar por la acera** [ahn-'dahr pohr lah ah-'seh-rah] to walk on the sidewalk; **andar 10 millas** [ahn-'dahr dee·ehs 'mee-yahs] cover 10 miles; *(mech)* to run, to work

anexo [ah-'nehk-soh] annex

anfitrión/anfitriona [ahn-fee-tree-'ohn, ahn-fee-tree-'oh-nah] *(m)* host, hostess

anillo [ah-'nee-yoh] ring

animal [ah-nee-'mahl] *(m)* animal

anotar [ah-noh-'tahr] to take note, to write down

antemano, de [deh ahn-teh-'mah-noh] beforehand

antes ['ahn-tehs] before

anticonceptivo [ahn-tee-kohn-sehp-'tee-voh] contraceptive

antiguo [ahn-'tee-gwoh] old

antipático [ahn-tee-'pah-tee-koh] unpleasant, disagreeable

anual [ah-noo-'ahl] annual

anular [ah-noo-'lahr] to annul, to cancel

anunciar [ah-noon-see-'ahr] to announce, to advertise

anuncio [ah-'noon-see·oh] ad, announcement

añadir [ah-nyah-'deer] to add

año ['ah-nyoh] year; **al año** [ahl 'ah-nyoh] *(adv)* yearly, annually

apagar [ah-pah-'gahr] to turn off; *(fire)* to put out

aparato [ah-pah-'rah-toh] machine, device, piece of equipment

aparcar [ah-pahr-'kahr] to park

aparecer [ah-pah-reh-'sehr] to seem, to appear (to be)

aparentemente [ah-pah-rehn-teh-'mehn-teh] apparently

aparte [ah-'pahr-teh] apart, aside, besides, separately; **aparte de eso** [ah-'pahr-teh deh 'eh-soh] apart from

apenas [ah-'peh-nahs] hardly, scarcely; *(Am)* as soon as

apetito [ah-peh-'tee-toh] appetite

apimpado [ah-peem-'pah-doh] *(Am)* drunk

aplauso [ah-'plah·oo-soh] applause

aplazamiento [ah-plah-sah-mee-'ehn-toh] postponement, delay, rescheduling

aplazar [ah-plah-'sahr] to postpone, to delay, to reschedule

aplicado [ah-plee-'kah-doh] applied, studious, diligent

aplicar [ah-plee-'kahr] to apply, to put into practice

apostar [ah-poh-'stahr] to bet

apoyo [ah-'poh-yoh] support

apreciar [ah-preh-see-'ahr] to appreciate

aprender [ah-prehn-'dehr] to learn

apretar [ah-preh-'tahr] to tighten, to squeeze, to grip, to clench

aprobar [ah-proh-'bahr] to approve

aproximadamente [ah-prohk-see-mah-dah-'mehn-teh] approximately

aproximado [ah-prohk-see-'mah-doh] approximate

apuesta [ah-'pweh-stah] *(n)* bet

apuntar [ah-poon-'tahr] to aim, to point, to hint, to point (at), to note, take a note

apunte [ah-'poon-teh] *(m)* note

apurarse [ah-poo-'rahr-seh] to hurry up, to worry, to fret

aquel [ah-'kehl] *(m)* that; **aquella** [ah-'keh-yah] *(f)* that; **aquello** [ah-'keh-yoh] *(neut)* that

aquí [ah-'kee] here

Aragón [ah-rah-'gohn] region in the northeast of Spain bordering on France

árbol ['ahr-bohl] *(m)* tree

arder [ahr-'dehr] to burn

arenque [ah-'rehn-keh] *(m)* herring

Argentina [ahr-hehn-'tee-nah] Argentina

argentino [ahr-hehn-tee-noh] Argentinian

argolla [ahr-'goh-yah] *(Am)* ring

aro ['ah-roh] *(Am)* ring, hoop, rim

arreglar [ah-rreh-'glahr] to arrange, to settle, to fix, to mend, to repair; **arreglar un asunto** [ah-rreh-'glahr oon ah-'soon-toh] to settle a matter

arreglo [ah-'rreh-gloh] *(n)* arrangement, settlement, repair

arriba [ah-'rree-bah] up, above; **cuesta arriba** ['kweh-stah ah-'rree-bah] uphill; **hacia arriba** ['ah-see·ah ah-'rree-bah] upwards

artículo [ahr-'tee-koo-loh] article

asado [ah-'sah-doh] *(adj)* roast

asaltar [ah-sahl-'tahr] to attack, to assault, to mug, to storm, to assail, afflict

asar [ah-'sahr] to roast

ascender [ah-sehn-'dehr] to promote, to rise, to add up to; **ascender a** [ah-sehn-'dehr ah] to be promoted to

ascensor [ah-sehn-'sohr] *(m)* elevator

asegurar [ah-seh-goo-'rahr] to secure, to assure, to affirm, to safeguard, to guarantee

así [ah-'see] also; so

asidero [ah-see-'deh-roh] *(mn)* hold, grasp, handle, holder

asiento [ah-see-'ehn-toh] seat

asno ['ahs-noh] donkey; *(fig)* ass

asociación [ah-soh-see-ah-see-'ohn] *(f)* association

asombrarse (de) [ah-sohm-'brahr-seh (deh)] to be amazed/astonished (of)

aspecto [ah-'spehk-toh] look, appearance; **tener aspecto de** [teh-'nehr ah-'spehk-toh deh] to look like; *(fig)* aspect, side

Asturias [ah-'stoo-ree·ahs] region in the northwest of Spain located on the Bay of Biscay

astuto [ah-'stoo-toh] astute, clever

asunto [ah-'soon-toh] matter, subject, topic, issue, question

asustar [ah-soo-'stahr] to scare, to frighten

atajo [ah-'tah-hoh] shortcut

atar [ah-'tahr] to tie

atascado [ah-tah-'skah-doh] to be stuck, to be bogged down, to be clogged

atención [ah-tehn-see-'ohn] *(f)* attention; **¡atención!** [ah-tehn-see-'ohn] attention!

atento [ah-'tehn-toh] attentive, observant, watchful, polite

Atlántico [aht-'lahn-tee-koh] Atlantic

atrás, hacia [ah-'trahs, 'ah-see·ah] *(adv)* *(place)* back, behind, rear; *(time)* previously, ...ago, before

atracar [ah-trah-'kahr] to dock, to hold up (a bank, etc.), to stuff oneself (with food)

atravesar [ah-trah-veh-'sahr] to cross (over), to go across, to pass though, to go through, to pierce

atreverse a [ah-treh-'vehr-seh ah] to dare to

aumentar [ow-mehn-'tahr] to increase; *(price)* to raise

aún [ah-'oon] *(adv)* still, yet

aunque ['ah-oon-keh] *(conj)* although

ausente [ow-'sehn-teh] absent (from), missing

Austria ['ow-stree-ah] Austria

austríaco/-a [ow-'stree-ah-koh/-kah] Austrian

auténtico [ow-'tehn-tee-koh] authentic, genuine, real

automático [ow-toh-'mah-tee-koh] automatic

auto(móvil) [ow-toh-'moh-veel] *(m)* automobile

autoridad pública [ow-toh-ree-'dahd 'poo-blee-kah] *(f)* authorities

autorización [ow-toh-ree-sah-see-'ohn] *(f)* authorization, permission

autorizado para [ow-toh-ree-'sah-doh 'pah-rah] authorized to

autorizar [ow-toh-ree-'sahr] to authorize

autoservicio [ow-toh-sehr-'vee-see·oh] self-service

avanzar [ah-vahn-'sahr] to advance, to move forward, to promote

averiado [ah-veh-ree-'ah-doh] *(fruit)* damaged, spoiled; *(mech)* faulty, broken down

avión [ah-vee-'ohn] airplane; **avión a chorro** [ah-vee-'ohn ah 'choh-rroh] jet plane

avisador de incendios [ah-vee-sah-'dohr deh een-'sehn-dee-ohs] *(m)* fire alarm

avisar [ah-vee-'sahr] to inform, to notify, tell, to warn

aviso [ah-'vee-soh] piece of information, notification, warning; *(Am)* advertisement

avispa [ah-'vees-pah] wasp

ayuda [ah-'yoo-dah] help, assistance, aid

ayudar a alguien [ah-yoo-'dahr ah 'ahl-gee-ehn] to help/assist/aid someone

ayunas, en [ehn ah-'yoo-nahs] without any breakfast; *(fig)*; **estar en ayunas** [eh-'stahr ehn ah-'yoo-nahs] to be in the dark

B

bahía [bah-'ee-ah] bay

baile ['bah-ee-leh] *(m)* dance; *(fest)* ball

bajar [bah-'hahr] to go down, to lower

bajo ['bah-hoh] under; *(stature)* short; **dos grados bajo cero** [dohs 'grah-dohs 'bah-hoh 'seh-roh] minus 2 centigrades

bajos ['bah-hohs] *(m pl)* *(Am)* ground floor

balanza [bah-'lahn-sah] scales; *(comm)*; **balanza de pagos** [bah-'lahn-sah deh 'pah-gohs] balance of payment

balde ['bahl-deh] bucket, pail; **en balde** [ehn 'bahl-deh] in vain; **de balde** [deh 'bahl-deh] for free

Baleares [bah-leh-'ah-rehs] Baleares

banco ['bahn-koh] bank

banda ['bahn-dah] *(music)* band

bañarse [bah-'nyahr-seh] to take a bath

baño ['bah-nyoh] bath

bar [bahr] *(m)* *(establishment)* bar

barato [bah-'rah-toh] cheap

barca ['bahr-kah] boat

barra ['bah-rrah] *(object)* bar, railing; *(establishment)* bar, bar counter

barrera [bah-'rreh-rah] barrier

barrio ['bah-rree-oh] neighborhood

barro ['bah-rroh] clay

bastante [bah-'stahn-teh] enough

bastar [bah-'stahr] to be enough; **¡basta ya!** ['bah-stah yah] enough! **bastarse a sí mismo** [bah-'stahr-seh ah see 'mees-moh] to be self-sufficient

bastón [bah-'stohn] *(m)* stick

basura [bah-'soo-rah] garbage, trash; **cubo de la basura** ['koo-boh deh lah bah-'soo-rah] garbage can

batería [bah-teh-'ree-ah] battery; drum set

bebé [beh-'beh] *(m)* baby

beber [beh-'behr] to drink

bebido [beh-'bee-doh] to be drunk

belga ['behl-gah] *(m/f)* Belgian

Bélgica ['behl-hee-kah] Belgium

belleza [beh-'yeh-sah] beauty

bello ['beh-yoh] beautiful

benévolo [beh-'neh-voh-loh] benevolent

besar [beh-'sahr] to kiss

beso [beh-'soh] kiss

bici(cleta) [bee-see-'kleh-tah] *(f)* bicycle, bike

bien ['bee-ehn] *(adv)* well, right, successfully, properly; **más bien** *(adv)* rather; *(nm)* [mahs 'bee-ehn] **el bien y el mal** [ehl 'bee-ehn ee ehl mahl] good and evil

bienestar [bee-ehn-eh-'stahr] *(m)* well-being

bienvenido [bee-ehn-veh-'nee-doh] welcome

billete [bee-'yeh-teh] *(m)* ticket

blando ['blahn-doh] soft

bobo ['boh-boh] dumb

boca ['boh-kah] mouth

bocado [boh-'kah-doh] *(n)* bite

boda ['boh-dah] wedding

bohío [boh-'ee-oh] *(Am)* hut

boletín [boh-leh-'teen] *(m)* bulletin, coupon

boleto [boh-'leh-toh] *(Am)* ticket; coupon

Bolivia [boh-'lee-vee-ah] Bolivia

boliviano [boh-lee-vee-'ah-noh] Bolivian

bolsa ['bohl-sah] bag; stock exchange

bolsillo [bohl-'see-yoh] pocket

bolso ['bohl-soh] bag, purse, handbag

bomberos [bohm-'beh-rohs] *(m pl)* fire-fighters

bombilla [bohm-'bee-yah] light bulb

bonito [boh-'nee-toh] pretty

borde ['bohr-deh] *(m)* edge, border, brim, side

borracho [boh-'rrah-choh] drunk, drunkard

bosque ['boh-skeh] *(m)* forest

bostezar [boh-steh-'sahr] to yawn

bote ['boh-teh] *(m)* boat, can, pot, jar; **bote (de conservas)** ['boh-teh (deh kohn-'sehr-vahs)] *(m)* *(preserves)* jar

botella [boh-'teh-yah] bottle

botón [boh-'tohn] *(m)* button
bramante [brah-'mahn-teh] *(m)* twine,
string
brasa ['brah-sah] live coal, hot coal
breve ['breh-veh] short, brief
brillante [bree-'yahn-teh] brilliant, bright,
glittering, sparkling, scintillating
brillar [bree-'yahr] to shine, to glitter, to
sparkle, to scintillate
brindis ['breen-dees] *(m)* *(drinks)* to
toast
broma ['broh-mah] joke
brújula ['broo-hoo-lah] compass
brumoso [broo-'moh-soh] foggy, misty
buen [bwehn] *(adj)* good, right, sound
bueno ['bweh-noh] *(adj)* good, right,
sound, healthy; *(adv interjec)* **bueno,
pues...** ['bweh-noh, pwehs...] well...
burro ['boo-rroh] donkey
buscar [boo-'skahr] to search, to look for

C

caballo [kah-'bah-yoh] horse
cabaña [kah-'bah-nyah] cabin, shack, hut
cabina [kah-'bee-nah] booth; *(truck,
ship)* cabin; *(airplane)* cockpit;
(gym) locker
cada ['kah-dah] each, every; **cada uno**
['kah-dah 'oo-noh] each one, every one;
cada vez ['kah-dah vehs] each time,
every time; **cada dos horas** ['kah-dah
dohs 'oh-rahs] every two hours
cadena [kah-'deh-nah] chain
caer [kah-'ehr] to fall, to drop
café [kah-'feh] *(m)* coffee, café
cafetería [kah-feh-teh-'ree-ah] cafeteria
caída [kah-'ee-dah] fall, drop
caja ['kah-hah] box, case, crate, cash-
box, *(fin)* fund, bank; **caja de ahor-
ros** ['kah- hah deh ah-'oh-rrohs] savings
bank; **caja de jubilaciones** ['kah-hah
deh hoo-bee-lah-see-'oh-nehs] pension
fund
calcular [kahl-koo-'lahr] to estimate, to
calculate, to add up, to compute
calentar [kah-lehn-'tahr] to heat (up),
to warm up
calidad [kah-lee-'dahd] *(f)* quality
caliente [kah-lee-'ehn-teh] hot; **muy
caliente** ['moo-ee kah-lee-'ehn-teh] very
hot
calma ['kahl-mah] *(weather)* calm;
(person) calmness, composure

calmarse [kahl-'mahr-seh] to calm down
calor [kah-'lohr] *(m)* heat
callado [kah-'yah-doh] quiet, silent
callarse [kah-'yahr-seh] to keep quiet
calle ['kah-yeh] *(f)* street
calleja [kah-'yeh-hah] alley
cama ['kah-mah] bed
cámara ['kah-mah-rah] camera
camarote [kah-mah-'roh-teh] *(m)* *(naut)*
cabin
cambiar [kahm-bee-'ahr] to change, to
switch; **cambiar de casa** [kahm-bee-
'ahr deh 'kah-sah] to move out; **cam-
biarse de ropa** [kahm-bee-'ahr-seh deh
'roh-pah] to change clothes
cambio ['kahm-bee-oh] change; switch;
(money) change, exchange
camino [kah-'mee-noh] road, track, way;
en (el) camino [ehn (ehl) kah-'mee-noh]
on the road
campanario [kahm-pah-'nah-ree-oh]
belfry, bell tower
campesino [kahm-peh-'see-noh] farmer
campo ['kahm-poh] field; **campo de
deportes** ['kahm-poh deh deh-'pohr-tehs]
sports field
caña ['kah-nyah] *(bot)* reed, stem, stalk,
cane, rod; **caña de pescar** ['kah-nyah
deh peh-'skahr] fishing rod
canal [kah-'nahl] *(m)* canal
cañaveral [kah-nyah-veh-'rahl] sugar-
cane field
cancelar [kahn-seh-'lahr] to cancel
canción [kahn-see-'ohn] *(f)* song
cañería [kah-nyeh-'ree-ah] *(gas, water)*
pipe, drain
cansado [kahn-'sah-doh] tired
Cantabria [kahn-'tah-bree-ah] Cantabria
cantar [kahn-'tahr] to sing
cantidad [kahn-tee-'dahd] *(f)* amount,
quantity
canto ['kahn-toh] *(n)* singing, chanting,
edge, rim, border, stone
capaz [kah-'pahs] able, capable; **ser
capaz de** [sehr kah-'pahs deh] to be
able to
capilla [kah-'pee-yah] chapel
capital [kah-pee-'tahl] *(f)* capital
carbón [kahr-'bohn] *(m)* coal
carga ['kahr-gah] freight
cargar [kahr-'gahr] to load
cariño [kah-'ree-nyoh] affection
cariñoso [kah-ree-'nyoh-soh] affectionate
carne ['kahr-neh] *(f)* meat

carnet de identidad [kahr-'neht deh ee-dehn-tee-'dahd] *(m)* identity card

caro ['kah-roh] expensive

carpeta [kahr-'peh-tah] folder, file, briefcase

carretera [kahr-rreh-'teh-rah] highway, (main) road

carta ['kahr-tah] letter, charter, document, deed, playing card, menu

cartel [kahr-'tehl] *(m)* poster

cartera [kahr-'teh-rah] wallet, briefcase; *(Am)* handbag

casa ['kah-sah] house, home; **casa de campo** ['kah-sah deh 'kahm-poh] country house; **en casa** [ehn 'kah-sah] at home

casado (con) [kah-'sah-doh (kohn)] married (to)

casarse [kah-'sahr-seh] to get married

casi ['kah-see] almost, nearly

caso ['kah-soh] *(n)* case, instance; **hacer caso** [ah-'sehr 'kah-soh] to obey, to pay attention; **un caso médico** [oon 'kah-soh 'meh-dee-koh] a medical case; **en caso de que ella llegue tarde** [ehn 'kah-soh deh keh 'eh-yah 'yeh-geh 'tahr-deh] in case she's late; **en caso contrario** [ehn 'kah-soh kohn-'trah-ree-oh] if not; **en caso de necesidad** [ehn 'kah-soh deh neh-seh-see-'dahd] in case of need; **en ese caso** [ehn 'eh-seh 'kah-soh] in that case

castaño [kah-'stah-nyoh] chestnut, brown

castañuelas [kah-stah-nyoo-'eh-lahs] *(f pl)* castanets

castellano [kah-steh-'yah-noh] Castilian, Spanish

castigo [kah-'stee-goh] punishment

Castilla [kah-'stee-yah] Castile, region located in central and northern Spain

castillo [kah-'stee-yoh] castle

casual [kah-soo-'ahl] by chance, accidental

casualidad [kah-soo-ah-lee-'dahd] *(f)* chance, accident, coincidence

catalán [kah-tah-'lahn] *(m)* Catalonian

catalana [kah-tah-'lah-nah] *(f)* Catalonian

catálogo [kah-'tah-loh-goh] catalog

Cataluña [kah-tah-'loo-nyah] Catalonia, region located in northeast Spain, bordering on France and the Mediterranean

caución [kah-oo-see-'ohn] *(f)* caution; *(legal)* security, bond

causa ['kah-oo-sah] cause, reason, motive; **a causa de** [ah 'kah-oo-sah deh] because of, on account of

causar [kah-oo-'sahr] to cause

caza ['kah-sah] hunting, game

cazuela [kah-soo-'eh-lah] pan, cooking pot; **en cazuela** [ehn kah-soo-'eh-lah] stewed

célebre ['seh-leh-breh] famous

cementerio [seh-mehn-'teh-ree-oh] cemetery

central [sehn-'trahl] central

centro ['sehn-troh] center

cepillar [seh-pee-'yahr] to brush

cepillo [seh-'pee-yoh] brush

cerámica [seh-'rah-mee-kah] pottery, ceramics

cerca de ['sehr-kah deh] near, close to; **muy cerca** ['moo-ee 'sehr-kah] very close to

cercano [sehr-'kah-noh] near, close, nearby

cerilla [seh-'ree-yah] *(fire)* match

cerrado [seh-'rrah-doh] closed

cerradura [seh-rrah-'doo-rah] lock, act of closing, locking

cerrar [seh-'rrahr] to close, shut; **cerrar con llave** [seh-'rrahr kohn 'yah-veh] to lock

cerrojo [seh-'rroh-hoh] bolt, latch

certificado [sehr-tee-fee-'kah-doh] *(n)* certificate; *(adj)* certified; *(mail)* registered

certificar [sehr-tee-fee-'kahr] to certify

césped ['sehs-pehd] *(m)* lawn, grass

cesta ['seh-stah] basket

chalet [chah-'leht] *(m)* villa, cottage

charlar [chahr-'lahr] to chat, to talk

chica ['chee-kah] girl, young woman

chicle [chee-kleh] *(m)* chewing gum

chico ['chee-koh] boy, young man

chileno [chee-'leh-noh] Chilean

chiringuito [chee-reen-'gee-toh] *(Am)* small shop, stall *(often on street)*

chispa ['chee-spah] spark

chiste ['chee-steh] *(m)* joke

chofer [choh-'fehr] *(m) (Am)* driver; **chófer** ['choh-fehr] *(m)* driver

choque ['choh-keh] *(m)* collision

ciego [see-'eh-goh] blind

cielo [see-'eh-loh] sky, heaven

cien ['see-ehn] hundred; **cien veces** ['see-ehn 'veh-sehs] a hundred times

ciento [see-'ehn-toh] hundred; **por ciento** [pohr see-'ehn-toh] per cent

A/Z

cierre [see-'eh-rreh] *(m)* closing or locking device, act of closing or locking
ciertamente [see-ehr-tah-'mehn-teh] *(adv)* certainly, surely
cierto [see-'ehr-toh] *(adj)* certain, sure, positive, exact, true; **ser cierto** [sehr see-'ehr-toh] to be true
cigarrillo [see-gah-'rree-yoh] cigarette
cigarro [see-'gah-rroh] cigar
cima ['see-mah] top, peak, summit
cinta ['seen-tah] ribbon, tape
circular [seer-koo-'lahr] circular
circunstancias [seer-koon-'stahn-see·ahs] *(f pl)* circumstances
cita ['see-tah] appointment
citarse [see-'tahr-seh] to make an appointment
ciudad [see-oo-'dahd] *(f)* city
claro ['klah-roh] bright, clear, light, distinct; *(consistency)* thin, obvious
clase ['klah-seh] *(f)* class, sort, type
clavo ['klah-voh] nail
cliente [klee-'ehn-teh] *(m/f)* customer, client
clima ['klee-mah] *(m)* climate
coalición [koh-ah-lee-see-'ohn] *(f)* coalition
cobrador [koh-brah-'dohr] *(m)* *(bus)* conductor
cocer [koh-'sehr] to cook
cocido, bien ['bee-ehn koh-'see-doh] *(cooking)* well done
cocina [koh-'see-nah] kitchen
coche ['koh-cheh] *(m)* car, automobile; *(train)* railroad car
coger [koh-'hehr] to take
cojín [koh-'heen] *(m)* cushion
colección [koh-lehk-see-'ohn] *(f)* collection
coleccionar [koh-lehk-see-oh-'nahr] to collect
colega [koh-'leh-gah] *(m/f)* colleague
colgar [kohl-'gahr] to hang
colina [koh-'lee-nah] hill
colocar [koh-loh-'kahr] to put, to place
Colombia [koh-'lohm-bee-ah] Colombia
colombiano [koh-lohm-bee-'ah-noh] Colombian
color [koh-'lohr] *(m)* color; **de color** [deh koh-'lohr] colored; **de colores** [deh koh-'loh-rehs] multicolored
collar [koh-'yahr] necklace; *(mech)* collar, ring
comenzar [koh-mehn-'sahr] to begin
comer [koh-'mehr] to eat

comestible [koh-meh-'stee-bleh] *(n)* foodstuff; *(adj)* edible
comestibles [koh-meh-'stee-blehs] *(m pl)* food, groceries; *(adj pl)* edible
comida [koh-'mee-dah] food; **hacer la comida** [ah-'sehr lah koh-'mee-dah] to fix a meal
comienzo [koh-mee-'ehn-soh] beginning, start
como ['koh-moh] *(adv)* as, like; *(conj)* since; **cómo** ['koh-moh] *(adv)* how?, why?; **¿cómo dice(s)?** ['koh-moh 'dee-seh(s)] can you repeat that?; **¡cómo no!** ['koh-moh noh] *(Am)* of course; **¿cómo no?** ['koh-moh noh] *(Am)* why not?; **como si** ['koh-moh see] as if
comodidad [koh-moh-dee-'dahd] *(f)* comfort
cómodo ['koh-moh-doh] comfortable
compañía, en de [ehn kohn-pah-'nyee-ah deh] company; in the company of
comparación [kohm-pah-rah-see-'ohn] *(f)* comparison
comparar [kohm-pah-'rahr] to compare
compartir [kohm-pahr-'teer] to share
compasión [kohm-pah-see-'ohn] *(f)* compassion, pity
compatriota [kohm-pah-tree-'oh-tah] *(m)* compatriot
competencia [kohm-peh-'tehn-see·ah] competition, competence, field, domain
competente [kohm-peh-'tehn-teh] competent, proper, appropriate
completamente [kohm-pleh-tah-'mehn-teh] *(adv)* completely
completo [kohm-'pleh-toh] complete; full
comportamiento [kohm-pohr-tah-mee-'ehn-toh] behavior
compra ['kohm-prah] purchase; **ir de compras** [eer deh 'kohm-prahs] go shopping
comprador [kohm-prah-'dohr] *(f)* buyer
comprar [kohm-'prahr] to buy, to purchase
comprender [kohm-prehn-'dehr] to understand
comprobar [kohm-proh-'bahr] to check, to verify, to confirm
común [koh-'moon] *(adj)* common, joint, generalized, ordinary; **en común** [ehn koh-'moon] *(adv)* jointly; **poco común** ['poh-koh koh-'moon] uncommon

A/Z

comunicación [koh-moo-nee-kah-see-'ohn] *(f)* communication(s), message, connection, contact; **ponerme en comunicación con** [poh-'nehr-meh ehn koh-moo-nee-kah-see-'ohn kohn] to get in touch with, to contact (someone)

comunicar [koh-moo-nee-'kahr] to communicate, to tell, to report, to connect, to contact, to get in touch

con [kohn] with; **con este tiempo** [kohn 'eh-steh tee-'ehm-poh] in this weather

conceder [kohn-seh-'dehr] to concede, to grant, to admit

concienzudo [kohn-see-ehn-'soo-doh] conscientious

concurso [kohn-'koor-soh] competition, help, support; **con el concurso de** [kohn ehl kohn-'koor-soh deh] with help from

condición [kohn-dee-see-'ohn] *(f)* condition

condón [kohn-'dohn] *(m)* condom

conducir [kohn-doo-'seer] drive

conducta [kohn-'dook-tah] conduct

conductor [kohn-dook-'tohr] *(m adj)* leading, driving; *(phys)* conductor; *(Am)* bus driver, orchestra conductor

confiado [kohn-fee-'ah-doh] trusting

confianza [kohn-fee-'ahn-sah] trust; **de confianza** [deh kohn-fee-'ahn-sah] trustworthy person, reliable person

confiar [kohn-fee-'ahr] to trust

confirmar [kohn-feer-'mahr] to confirm

conforme [kohn-'fohr-meh] consistent, agreed, in agreement, satisfied, content; **estar conforme** [eh-'stahr kohn-'fohr-meh] *(v)* satisfied with; **no estar conforme con** [noh eh-'stahr kohn-'fohr-meh kohn] *(v)* dissatisfied with

confortable [kohn-fohr-'tah-bleh] comfortable

confundir [kohn-foon-'deer] *(v)* to confuse (with), to mistake (with), to confound

congestionado [kohn-heh-stee-oh-'nah-doh] congested

conjunto [kohn-'hoon-toh] *(n)* whole, entirety; *(adj)* joint, united; ensemble; set

conmovido [kohn-moh-'vee-doh] *(v)* to be moved, stirred, shaken

connacional [kohn-nah-see-oh-'nahl] *(m)* *(Am)* compatriot

conocer [koh-noh-'sehr] *(v)* to know, to meet; **conocer a alguien** [koh-noh-'sehr ah 'ahl-gee-ehn] *(v)* to meet someone

conocido/-a [koh-noh-'see-doh/-ah] acquaintance

conocimiento [koh-noh-see-mee-'ehn-toh] knowledge; *(med)* consciousness; **sin conocimiento** [seen koh-noh- see-mee-'ehn-toh] unconcious

consciente [kohn-see-'ehn-teh] aware, conscious

conseguir [kohn-seh-'geer] *(v)* to get, to secure, to obtain, to bring about, to achieve, to attain

consejo [kohn-'seh-hoh] advice; **pedir consejo a alguien** [peh-'deer kohn-'seh-hoh ah 'ahl-gee-ehn] to ask someone for advice

consentir [kohn-sehn-'teer] *(v)* to consent

conservar [kohn-sehr-'vahr] *(v)* to preserve, to conserve

considerable [kohn-see-deh-'rah-bleh] considerable

consideración [kohn-see-deh-rah-see-'ohn] *(f)* consideration

considerar [kohn-see-deh-'rahr] *(v)* to consider

constar en [kohn-'stahr ehn] to be recorded in

constar de [kohn-'stahr deh] *(v)* to consist of

constitución [kohn-stee-too-see-'ohn] *(f)* constitution

construir [kohn-stroo-'eer] *(v)* to build, to construct

consulado [kohn-soo-'lah-doh] consulate

consultar [kohn-sool-'tahr] *(v)* to consult

consumir [kohn-soo-'meer] *(v)* to consume

consumo [kohn-'soo-moh] consumption

contacto [kohn-'tahk-toh] contact

contar [kohn-'tahr] *(v)* to count, to tell (a story); **contar con** [kohn-'tahr kohn] *(v)* to rely on

contener [kohn-teh-'nehr] *(v)* to hold, to contain, to check, to restrain, to curb

contenido [kohn-teh-'nee-doh] content

contento [kohn-'tehn-toh] happy

contestación [kohn-teh-stah-see-'ohn] *(f)* answer

contestar [kohn-teh-'stahr] *(v)* to answer

contigo [kohn-'tee-goh] with you

continuar [kohn-tee-noo-'ahr] *(v)* to continue, to go on

contra ['kohn-trah] against; **estar en contra de** [eh-'stahr ehn 'kohn-trah deh] to be against

A/Z

contrabando [kohn-trah-'bahn-doh] smuggled goods, smuggling; **pasar de contrabando** [pah-'sahr deh kohn-trah-'bahn-doh] *(v)* to smuggle

contrario [kohn-'trah-ree-oh] *(adj)* contrary, opposite; **al contrario** [ahl kohn-'trah-ree-oh] *(adv)* on the contrary; **de lo contrario** [deh loh kohn-'trah-ree-oh] otherwise

contratiempo [kohn-trah-tee-'ehm-poh] setback, accident

contrato [kohn-'trah-toh] contract

controlar [kohn-troh-'lahr] to control

convencer [kohn-vehn-'sehr] to convince

conveniente [kohn-veh-nee-'ehn-teh] convenient

convenir [kohn-veh-'neer] to agree, to suit, to be convenient, to be desirable

conversación *(f)* [kohn-vehr-sah-see-'ohn] conversation

copa ['koh-pah] glass, drink

copia ['koh-pee-ah] copy

coqueteo [koh-keh-'teh-oh] flirtation

corazón [koh-rah-'sohn] *(m)* heart

cordial [kohr-dee-'ahl] cordial, warm

cordialidad [kohr-dee-ah-lee-'dahd] *(f)* cordiality, warmth

cordón [kohr-'dohn] *(m)* (shoe) lace, cord, string

coro ['koh-roh] choir

correa [koh-'rreh-ah] strap

correcto [koh-'rrehk-toh] correct, accurate, polite, proper

corregir [koh-rreh-'heer] to correct

correo [koh-'rreh-oh] mail, post

correr [koh-'rrehr] to run

correspondencia [kohn-rreh-spohn-'dehn-see-ah] correspondent

corriente [koh-rree-'ehn-teh] *(adj)* running, flowing, fluent, common, ordinary, everyday; *(n)* current; **corriente de aire** [lah koh-rree-'ehn-teh deh 'ah-ee-reh] *(f)* draft; **mes corriente** [ehl mehs koh-rree-'ehn-teh] *(m)* the current month

corrompido [koh-rrohm-'pee-doh] corrupt

cortante [kohr-'tahn-teh] sharp

cortar [kohr-'tahr] to cut

cortés [kohr-'tehs] courteous, polite

cortesía [kohr-teh-'see-ah] courtesy

cortina [kohr-'tee-nah] curtain

corto ['kohr-toh] short; **a corto plazo** [ah 'kohr-toh 'plah-soh] short-term

cosa ['koh-sah] thing

cosecha [koh-'seh-chah] crop, harvest

costa ['koh-stah] coast, coastline, shore, shoreline

costar [koh-'stahr] to cost

costarricense [koh-stah-ree-'sehn-seh] *(m)* Costa Rican

coste ['koh-steh] *(m)* cost, price, expensive

costoso [koh-'stoh-soh] costly, pricey, expensive

costumbre [koh-'stoom-breh] *(f)* custom, habit; **como de costumbre** ['koh-moh deh koh-'stoom-breh] as usual

cotidiano [koh-tee-dee-'ah-noh] *(adj)* daily

crear [kreh-'ahr] to create, to invent, to found, to establish

creativo [kreh-ah-'tee-voh] creative

crecer [kreh-'sehr] to grow

crédito ['kreh-dee-toh] credit

creer [kreh-'ehr] to believe

cristal [kree-'stahl] *(m)* glass

criticar [kree-tee-'kahr] to criticize

cruce ['kroo-seh] *(m) (street)* crossing

cuaderno [kwah-'dehr-noh] notebook

cuadrado [kwah-'drah-doh] square

cuadro ['kwah-droh] painting, square; **a cuadros** [ah 'kwah-drohs] checkered

cual [kwahl] which; **¿cuál?** [kwahl] which (one)?

cualidad [kwah-lee-'dahd] *(f)* quality; characteristic

cualquier, -a [kwahl-kee-'ehr] any

cuando ['kwahn-doh] when; **¿cuándo llegaste?** ['kwahn-doh yeh-'gah-steh] when did you arrive?

cuarto ['kwahr-toh] room, fourth, quarter; **un cuarto de hora** [oon 'kwahr-toh deh 'oh-rah] a quarter of an hour

Cuba ['koo-bah] Cuba

cubano [koo-'bah-noh] Cuban

cubo de la basura ['koo-boh deh lah bah-'soo-rah] garbage can

cubrir [koo-'breer] to cover

cucaracha [koo-kah-'rah-chah] cockroach

cuello ['kweh-yoh] neck

cuenta ['kwehn-tah] account; **tener en cuenta** [teh-'nehr ehn 'kwehn-tah] to take into account

cuento ['kwehn-toh] story, tale

cuerda ['kwehr-dah] rope, string, cord; **cuerda de pescar** ['kwehr-dah deh peh-'skahr] fishing line

cuero ['kweh-roh] leather

cuerpo ['kwehr-poh] body

cuesta ['kweh-stah] slope, hill; **cuesta abajo** ['kweh-stah ah-'bah-hoh] downhill; **cuesta arriba** ['kweh-stah ah-'rree-bah] uphill

cuestión [kweh-stee-'ohn] (f) (problem) issue, matter, question

cuidado [kwee-'dah-doh] (n) care; (adj) elegant; (n) ¡**cuidado!** [kwee-'dah-doh] caution! watch out!; **tener cuidado de/con** [teh-'nehr kwee-'dah-doh deh/kohn] to watch out for, to take care of

cuidadoso [kwee-dah-'doh-soh] careful

cuidar de [kwee-'dahr deh] to take care of

culpa ['kool-pah] guilt

cultura [kool-'too-rah] culture

cumbre ['koom-breh] summit, top

cumpleaños [koom-pleh-'ah-nyohs] (m) birthday

cumplir [koom-'pleer] to carry out, to fulfill, to serve, to attain; **cumplir la condena** [koom-'pleer lah kohn-'deh-nah] to serve a jail sentence

cuñada [koo-'nyah-dah] sister-in-law

cuñado [koo-'nyah-doh] brother-in-law

cura ['koo-rah] (m) priest

curioso [koo-ree-'oh-soh] curious

curso ['koor-soh] course, direction; (school) course

curva ['koor-vah] curve

D

dado ['dah-doh] (n) dice; (ptp) of dar

dañar [dah-'nyahr] to damage, to harm, to hurt, to spoil

dañino [dah-'nyee-noh] damaging, harmful

daño ['dah-nyoh] damage; harm, hurt, injury

dar [dahr] give; **el reloj dio las 11** [ehl reh-'loh dee-'oh lahs 'ohn-seh] the clock struck 11; **dar la vuelta** [dahr lah 'vwehl-tah] to turn around; **dar las gracias** [dahr lahs 'grah-see-ahs] to thank; **dar recibo** [dahr reh-'see-boh] to give a receipt; **dar un golpe a** [dahr oon 'gohl-peh ah] to hit (someone); **dar un paseo** [dahr oon pah-'seh-oh] to take a stroll; **darle vuelta a** ['dahr-leh 'vwehl-tah ah] to check in (on someone); **darse prisa** ['dahr-seh 'pree-sah] to hurry up

dato ['dah-toh] fact; **datos personales** ['dah-tohs pehr-soh-'nah-lehs] (m pl) personal information, details about oneself

de [deh] of; from; in, at, with; by; **de Córdoba** [deh 'kohr-doh-bah] from Córdoba; **pintado de verde** [peen-'tah-doh deh 'vehr-deh] painted in green; **a las 12 del día** [ah lahs 'doh-seh dehl 'dee-ah] at noon; **de día/noche** [deh 'dee-ah/'noh-cheh] by day/night

debajo (de) [deh-'bah-hoh (deh)] under

deber [deh-'behr] (n m) duty, obligation; to owe; to ought to, to have to; ¿**cuánto debo?** ['kwahn-toh 'deh-boh] how much do I owe?; **debo cerrar la puerta** ['deh-boh seh-'rrahr lah 'pwehr-tah] I should shut the door

débil ['deh-beel] weak

debilidad [deh-bee-lee-'dahd] (f) weakness

decidir [deh-see-'deer] to decide; **decidirse** [deh-see-'deer-seh] to make up one's mind; **estar/ser decidido** [eh-'stahr/sehr deh-see-'dee-doh] to be determined

decir [deh-'seer] to say

decisión [deh-see-see-'ohn] (f) decision

declarar [deh-klah-'rahr] to declare

defecto [deh-'fehk-toh] flaw, fault, defect

defender [deh-fehn-'dehr] to defend, to protect

definitivamente [deh-fee-nee-tee-vah-'mehn-teh] (adv) definitively

definitivo [deh-fee-nee-'tee-voh] (adj) definitive

dejar [deh-'hahr] to leave, to put; **dejar aparte** [deh-'hahr ah-'pahr-teh] to put aside; **dejar atrás** [deh-'hahr ah-'trahs] to leave behind

delante [deh-'lahn-teh] in front, ahead, opposite; **delante de** [deh-'lahn-teh deh] in front of, ahead of

deletrear [deh-leh-treh-'ahr] to spell

delgado [dehl-'gah-doh] thin, slim, slender, slight

delicado [deh-lee-'kah-doh] delicate

demás [deh-'mahs] (adj pron) other, remaining, rest; (adv) also; **por demás** [pohr deh-'mahs] moreover

demasiado [deh-mah-see-'ah-doh] too much, too many; a lot

demostrar [deh-moh-'strahr] to demonstrate; to show

A/Z

denominación [deh-nom-eeh-nah-see-'ohn] *(f)* denomination

denso ['dehn-soh] dense

dentro ['dehn-troh] inside, in, within; **dentro del automóvil** ['dehn-troh dehl ow-toh-'moh-veel] inside the car; **dentro de la casa** ['dehn-troh deh lah 'kah-sah] in the house; **dentro de poco** ['dehn-troh deh 'poh-koh] shortly, soon after; **dentro de una semana** ['dehn-troh deh 'oo-nah seh-'mah-nah] within a week

denuncia [deh-'noon-see-ah] *(police)* complaint; report (of a crime)

departamento [deh-pahr-tah-'mehn-toh] *(Am)* apartment

deporte [deh-'pohr-teh] *(m)* sport

depositar [deh-poh-see-'tahr] to deposit

deprisa [deh-'pree-sah] *(adv)* quickly

derecho [deh-'reh-choh] *(n)* right, entitlement, law, justice, claim, *(adj)* right, straight, upright, directly; **con derecho a** [kohn deh-'reh-choh ah] entitled to; **a la derecha** [ah lah deh-'reh-chah] to the right

derechos [deh-'reh-chohs] *(m pl)* rights

desagradable [dehs-ah-grah-'dah-bleh] disagreeable, unpleasant

desagradecido [dehs-ah-grah-deh-'see-doh] ungrateful

desaparecer [dehs-ah-pah-reh-'sehr] to disappear

desarrollar [dehs-ah-rroh-'yahr] to develop

desarrollo [dehs-ah-'rroh-yoh] development

desayunar [deh-sah-yoo-'nahr] to have breakfast

descansar [dehs-kahn-'sahr] to rest

descanso [deh-'skahn-soh] rest

descarado [dehs-kahr-'ah-doh] shameless, insolent

descargar [dehs-kahr-'gahr] to unload; *(computers)* to download

desconfiar [dehs-kohn-fee-'ahr] to be distrustful, to distrust, to mistrust, to suspect

desconocido [dehs-koh-noh-'see-doh] unknown

desconsiderado [dehs-kohn-see-deh-'rah-doh] thoughtless, inconsiderate

descontento [dehs-kohn-'tehn-toh] dissatisfied, disgruntled

descortés [dehs-kohr-'tehs] rude

describir [deh-skree-'beer] to describe

descubrir [deh-skoo-'breer] to discover

descuento [dehs-'kwehn-toh] discount

descuidado [dehs-kwee-'dah-doh] careless, negligent

descuidar [dehs-kwee-'dahr] to neglect

desde ['dehs-deh] from; since; **¿desde cuándo?** ['dehs-deh 'kwahn-doh] since when? **desde entonces** ['dehs-deh ehn-'tohn-sehs] since then; **desde arriba** ['dehs-deh ah-'rree-bah] from above

desear [deh-seh-'ahr] to want, to desire, to wish

desembocadura [dehs-ehm-boh-kah-'doo-rah] *(river)* mouth; *(street/road)* end

desembocar [dehs-ehm-boh-'kahr] *(river, street, road)* to run into; *(fig)* to end in

desempleado [dehs-ehm-pleh-'ah-doh] unemployed

deseo [deh-'seh-oh] wish, desire

desesperado [dehs-eh-speh-'rah-doh] desperate

desfavorable [dehs-fah-voh-'rah-bleh] unfavorable

desgracia [dehs-'grah-see-ah] misfortune

desgraciadamente [dehs-grah-see-ah-dah-'mehn-teh] unfortunately

desgraciado [dehs-grah-see-'ah-doh] unlucky, wretched, unhappy, miserable

deshacer [dehs-ah-'sehr] to undo

desilusionado [dehs-ee-loo-see-oh-'nah-doh] disappointed, disillusioned

desmayado [dehs-mah-'yah-doh] unconscious

desmayarse [dehs-mah-'yahr-seh] to faint

desnudarse [dehs-noo-'dahr-seh] to undress

desnudo [dehs-'noo-doh] naked

desorden [dehs-'ohr-dehn] *(m)* disorder, confusion, disarray, turmoil

despacho [dehs-'pah-choh] *(n)* office, act of dispatching or sending; **el despacho de tropas a las colonias** [ehl dehs-'pah-choh deh 'troh-pahs ah lahs koh-'loh-nee-ahs] the dispatch of troops to the colonies

despacio [deh-'spah-see-oh] *(adv)* slowly

despedirse [dehs-peh-'deer-seh] to say good-bye

despertador [deh-spehr-tah-'dohr] *(m)* alarm clock

A/Z

despertar [deh-spehr-'tahr] to wake up

despierto [deh-spee-'ehr-toh] awake

después [deh-'spwehs] after, since, afterwards, later, next to; **después de entonces** [deh-'spwehs deh ehn-'tohn-sehs] since then

destrozar [deh-stroh-'sahr] to smash, to shatter

destruir [deh-stroo-'eer] to destroy

desventaja [dehs-vehn-'tah-hah] disadvantage

detalladamente [deh-tah-yah-dah-'mehn-teh] *(adv)* in detail

detallado [deh-tah-'yah-doh] *(adj)* detailed

detalle [deh-'tah-yeh] *(m)* detail; retail; **detallista** [deh-tah-'yee-stah] retailer

detener [deh-teh-'nehr] to stop

detenerse [deh-teh-'nehr-seh] to linger, to pause

deteriorar [deh-teh-ree·oh-'rahr] to deteriorate, to damage, to spoil

determinado [deh-tehr-mee-'nah-doh] *(adj)* set, fixed; *(person)* determined, resolute

detrás [deh-'trahs] *(adv)* behind, at the back, in the rear; *(prep)* **detrás de** [deh-'trahs deh] behind

deuda [deh-'oo-dah] debt

devolver [deh-vohl-'vehr] to return

día ['dee-ah] *(m)* day; **día de fiesta** ['dee-ah deh fee-'eh-stah] *(m)* holiday; **(día del) santo** [('dee-ah dehl) 'sahn-toh] *(m)* nameday; **los días laborables** [lohs 'dee-ahs lah-boh-'rah-blehs] *(m pl)* workdays, weekdays

diagnóstico [dee-ahg-'noh-stee-koh] *(n m)* diagnose; *(adj)* diagnostic

diapositiva [dee-ah-poh-see-'tee-vah] slide

diario [dee-'ah-ree·oh] *(adj)* daily; *(adv)* **a diario, diariamente** [ah dee-'ah-ree·oh, dee-ah-ree-ah-'mehn-teh]

dibujar [dee-boo-'hahr] to draw

dichoso [dee-'choh-soh] lucky

diferencia [dee-feh-'rehn-see·ah] difference

diferente [dee-feh-'rehn-teh] *(adj)* different

difícil [dee-'fee-seel] difficult

dificultad [dee-fee-kool-'tahd] *(f)* difficulty

diligente [dee-lee-'hehn-teh] diligent, hard-working

dinero [dee-'neh-roh] money

Dios/dios ['dee-ohs/'dee-ohs] God/god

dirección [dee-rehk-see-'ohn] *(f)* address

directamente [dee-rehk-tah-'mehn-teh] *(adv)* directly

directo [dee-'rehk-toh] *(adj)* direct

director [dee-rehk-'tohr] *(m)* director

dirigirse (a/hacia) [dee-ree-'heer-seh (ah/'ah-see·ah)] to go to; to head for; *(fig)* to speak to

disco ['dee-skoh] disk, disc; record; **disco de larga duración** ['dee-skoh deh 'lahr-gah doo-rah-see-'ohn] long-playing record (LP)

discreción [dee-skreh-see-'ohn] *(f)* discretion; **a discreción** [ah dee-skreh-see-'ohn] at one's discretion

disculpar [dee-skool-'pahr] to excuse, to forgive, to pardon; **disculparse** [dee-skool-'pahr-seh] to excuse oneself

discusión [dee-skoo-see-'ohn] *(f)* discussion, argument

discutir [dee-skoo-'teer] to discuss, to debate, to argue

disfrutar [dees-froo-'tahr] to enjoy

disminuir [dees-mee-noo-'eer] to decrease

disparar [dees-pah-'rahr] to shoot

disputa [dee-'spoo-tah] dispute, argument

disputar [dee-spoo-'tahr] to dispute, to question, to challenge, to fight for

distancia [dee-'stahn-see·ah] distance

distante [dee-'stahn-teh] distant

distinguido [dee-steen-'gee-doh] distinguished, prominent

distinguir [dee-steen-'geer] to distinguish, to discern, to differentiate; **distinguirse de** to differentiate oneself from

distinto [dee-'steen-toh] *(adj)* different

distribución [dee-stree-boo-see-'ohn] *(f)* distribution

distribuidor automático [dee-stree-boo-ee-'dohr ow-toh-'mah-tee-koh] *(m)* vending machine

distribuir [dee-stree-boo-'eer] to distribute

diversión [dee-vehr-see-'ohn] *(f)* entertainment, amusement

divertido [dee-vehr-'tee-doh] entertaining, amusing

divertirse [dee-vehr-'teer-seh] to entertain/amuse oneself

dividir [dee-vee-'deer] to divide, to split (up), to separate

doblar [doh-'blahr] to fold

A/Z

doble ['doh-bleh] double
doctor [dohk-'tohr] (*m*) doctor, physician
documento [doh-koo-'mehn-toh] document
doler [doh-'lehr] to hurt
dolor [doh-'lohr] (*m*) pain
doloroso [doh-loh-'roh-soh] painful
domicilio [doh-mee-'see-lee-oh] home, residence
don [dohn] (*before name*) Mr.
donde ['dohn-deh] where
doña ['doh-nyah] (*before name*) Mrs.
dormir [dohr-'meer] to sleep; **dormirse** [dohr-'meer-seh] to fall asleep
dos [dohs] two; **los dos** both
dotación [doh-tah-see-'ohn] (*f*) staff; (*naut*) crew
duda ['doo-dah] doubt; **sin duda** undoubtedly; **¡sin duda!** [seen-'doo-dah] of course
dudar [doo-'dahr] to doubt; **dudar de algo** [doo-'dahr deh 'ahl-goh] to doubt/question something
dudoso [doo-'doh-soh] doubtful
dueño ['dweh-nyoh] owner
dulce ['dool-seh] sweet
duración [doo-rah-see-'ohn] (*f*) duration
duradero [doo-rah-'deh-roh] durable
durante [doo-'rahn-teh] (*prp*) during; **durante un tiempo** [doo-'rahn-teh oon tee-'ehm-poh] for a while; **durante la comida** [doo-'rahn-teh lah koh-'mee-dah] during dinner
durar [doo-'rahr] to last
dureza [doo-'reh-sah] hardness, toughness
duro ['doo-roh] hard, tough

E

ecuatoriano [eh-kwah-toh-ree-'ah-noh] Ecuadorian
echar [eh-'chahr] to throw, to toss, to put in; **estar echado** [eh-'stahr eh-'chah-doh] to lie down; **echar agua** [eh-'chahr 'ah-gwah] to pour water
edad [eh-'dahd] (*f*) age
edificio [eh-dee-'fee-see-oh] building
educación [eh-doo-kah-see-'ohn] (*f*) education
efectivamente [eh-fehk-tee-vah-'mehn-teh] in fact, really, exactly
efecto [eh-'fehk-toh] effect, result; **en efecto** [ehn eh-'fehk-toh] indeed, in effect

eficaz [eh-fee-'kahs] effective
ejemplo [eh-'hehm-ploh] example; **por ejemplo** [pohr eh-'hehm-ploh] for example
ejercer [eh-hehr-'sehr] to exert
ejercicio [eh-hehr-'see-see-oh] exercise, practice
ejercitar [eh-hehr-see-'tahr] to exercise
el [ehl] (*art def m*) the
él [ehl] (*m*) (*person*) he; (*thing*) it
elaborar [eh-lah-boh-'rahr] to elaborate; to make; to prepare
elección [eh-lehk-see-'ohn] (*f*) election
eléctrico [eh-'lehk-tree-koh] electric
elegante [eh-leh-'gahn-teh] elegant
elegir [eh-leh-'heer] to elect
ella ['eh-yah] (*f*) (*person*) she; (*thing*) it
ellas ['eh-yahs] (*f pl*) they
ellos ['eh-yohs] (*m pl*) they
emancipado [eh-mahn-see-'pah-doh] emancipated
embajada [ehm-bah-'hah-dah] embassy
embalaje [ehm-bah-'lah-heh] (*m*) packing, wrapping, crating
embalar [ehm-bah-'lahr] to pack, to wrap, to crate
embarazada [ehm-bah-rah-'sah-dah] pregnant
embarcarse [ehm-bahr-'kahr-seh] (*boat, train, bus, etc.*) to get on board
emborracharse [ehm-boh-rrah-'chahr-seh] to get drunk
emisión [eh-mee-see-'ohn] (*f*) (*radio, television*) broadcast
empapado [ehm-pah-'pah-doh] soaked, steeped in . . .
empaque [ehm-'pah-keh] appearance, look; (*Am*) nerve
empaquetar [ehm-pah-keh-'tahr] to pack
emparentado [ehm-pah-rehn-'tah-doh] related by marriage to
empezar [ehm-peh-'sahr] to begin
empleado [ehm-pleh-'ah-doh] (*n*) employee
emplear [ehm-pleh-'ahr] (*tool, word, time, etc.*) to use, to employ; (*person*) to employ
empleo [ehm-'pleh-oh] employment; job
empresa [ehm-'preh-sah] company
empujar [ehm-poo-'hahr] to push
en [ehn] (*prep*) in, into, on, at, by; **en español** [ehn eh-spah-'nyohl] in Spanish; **en la calle** [ehn lah 'kah-yeh] on the street

encaje [ehn-'kah-heh] *(m)* lace

encantado [ehn-kahn-'tah-doh] haunted, charmed, delighted

encantador [ehn-kahn-tah-'dohr] charming

encargar [ehn-kahr-'gahr] to entrust, to order; **encargarse de** [ehn-kahr-'gahr-seh deh] to take charge of

encargo [ehn-'kahr-goh] assignment, order

encendedor [ehn-sehn-deh-'dohr] *(m)* cigarette lighter

encender [ehn-sehn-'dehr] to light, to set fire to, to turn on, to switch on

encontrar [ehn-kohn-'trahr] to find; **encontrarse** [ehn-kohn-'trahr-seh] to find oneself, to meet each other

enfadado [ehn-fah-'dah-doh] angry, annoyed

enfadarse (por) [ehn-fah-'dahr-seh (pohr)] to get angry with

enfermera [ehn-fehr-'meh-rah] *(f)* nurse

enfermero [ehn-fehr-'meh-roh] *(m)* nurse

enfermo [ehn-'fehr-moh] *(n)* patient, sick person; *(adj)* ill, sick; **ponerse enfermo** [poh-'nehr-seh ehn-'fehr-moh] to get sick

enfrente de [ehn-'frehn-teh deh] opposite to, in front of

engañar [ehn-gah-'nyahr] to deceive

engaño [ehn-'gah-nyoh] deception

engordar [ehn-gohr-'dahr] to gain weight

enhorabuena [ehn-oh-rah-'bweh-nah] congratulations

enorme [eh-'nohr-meh] huge, enormous

enseñar [ehn-seh-'nyahr] to teach, to show

entender [ehn-tehn-'dehr] to understand; **entender mal** [ehn-tehn-'dehr mahl] to misunderstand; **entenderse bien** [ehn-tehn-'dehr-seh 'bee-ehn] to get along well

enterarse de [ehn-teh-'rahr-seh deh] to find out

entero [ehn-'teh-roh] whole

entonces [ehn-'tohn-sehs] then

entrada [ehn-'trah-dah] entrance

entrada principal [ehn-'trah-dah preen-see-'pahl] main entrance; **precio de (la) entrada** ['preh-see-oh deh (lah) ehn-'trah-dah] admission price

entrar [ehn-'trahr] to go in, to come in, to enter; **entrar en** [ehn-'trahr ehn] to go into; **entrar (en el país)** [ehn-'trahr (ehn ehl pah-'ees)] to enter the country

entre ['ehn-treh] between, among; **entre otras cosas** ['ehn-treh 'oh-trahs 'koh-sahs] among other things

entregar [ehn-treh-'gahr] to deliver, to hand

entretanto [ehn-treh-'tahn-toh] in the meantime

entusiasmado (con) [ehn-too-see-ahs-'mah-doh] *(kohn)* excited/delighted (with)

enviar [ehn-vee-'ahr] to send

envolver [ehn-vohl-'vehr] to wrap

equipo [eh-'kee-poh] equipment; *(sport)* team

equivalente [eh-kee-vah-'lehn-teh] *(m)* equivalent

equivocación [eh-kee-voh-kah-see-'ohn] *(f)* mistake; **por equivocación** [pohr eh-kee-voh-kah-see-'ohn] by mistake

equivocar [eh-kee-voh-'kahr] to mistake, to miss; **equivocarse** [eh-kee-voh-'kahr-seh] to be mistaken

erizo de mar [eh-'ree-soh deh mahr] sea urchin

errar [eh-'rrahr] to miss, to wander

error [eh-'rrohr] *(m)* mistake, error

esbelto [ehs-'behl-toh] slim, slender

escalera [eh-skah-'leh-rah] ladder, stairway

escaparate [eh-skah-pah-'rah-teh] *(m)* shop window; *(Am)* *(furniture)* wardrobe

escarpado [eh-skahr-'pah-doh] steep

escaso [eh-'skah-soh] scarce

escayola [eh-skah-'yoh-lah] plaster

escoger [eh-skoh-'hehr] to choose

esconder [eh-skohn-'dehr] to hide

escondidas, a [ah eh-skohn-'dee-dahs] *(adv)* secretly

escorpión [eh-skohr-pee-'ohn] *(m)* scorpio

escribir [eh-skree-'beer] to write

escrito, por [pohr eh-'skree-toh] in writing

escritura [eh-skree-'too-rah] handwriting

escuchar [eh-skoo-'chahr] to listen

escudo [eh-'skoo-doh] shield

escuela [eh-'skweh-lah] school

escultura [eh-skool-'too-rah] sculpture

ese, esa, esos, esas ['eh-seh, 'eh-sah, 'eh-sohs, 'eh-sahs] *(adj ms fs m pl f pl)* that

ése, ésa, ésos, ésas, eso ['eh-seh, 'eh-sah, 'eh-sohs, 'eh-sahs, 'eh-soh] *(prn ms fs m pl f pl neut)* that

A/Z

esforzarse [ehs-fohr-'sahr-seh] to make an effort

esfuerzo [ehs-'fwehr-soh] effort

esmerado [ehs-meh-'rah-doh] careful, polished

esmero [ehs-'meh-roh] care, carefulness, polish

espacio [eh-'spah-see·oh] space

espantoso [eh-spahn-'toh-soh] frightful, terrifying

España [eh-'spah-nyah] Spain

español [eh-spah-'nyohl] Spanish

español/española [eh-spah-'nyohl/eh-spah-'nyoh-lah] Spaniard, Spanish

especial [eh-speh-see-'ahl] special

especialmente [eh-speh-see·ahl-'mehn-teh] *(adv)* specially, particularly

espectáculo [eh-spehk-'tah-koo-loh] show, performance; **espectáculo de variedades** [eh-spehk-'tah-koo-loh deh vah-ree·eh-'dah-dehs] revue, variety show

espectador [eh-spehk-tah-'dohr] *(m)* spectator; (member of) the audience

esperar; [eh-speh-'rahr] to wait

esposa [eh-'spoh-sah] wife

esposo [eh-'spoh-soh] husband

esquina [eh-'skee-nah] corner

esta noche ['eh-stah 'noh-cheh] tonight; **esta tarde** ['eh-stah 'tahr-deh] this evening

establecer [eh-stah-bleh-'sehr] to establish, to set up

estaca [eh-'stah-kah] stake, *(tent, etc.)* peg

estación [eh-stah-see-'ohn] *(f)* station, resort; **estación balnearia** [eh-stah-see-'ohn bahl-neh-'ah-ree·ah] *(f)* spa

estadía [eh-stah-'dee-ah] *(Am)* stay

estado [eh-'stah-doh] state

estafador [eh-stah-fah-'dohr] *(m)* swindler

estafar [eh-stah-'fahr] swindle

estallar [eh-stah-'yahr] to explode

estampilla [eh-stahm-'pee-yah] *(Am)* postal stamp

estancia [eh-'stahn-see·ah] stay; *(Am)* cattle ranch

estar [eh-'stahr] to be; **estar bien** [eh-'stahr 'bee·ehn] to be well; **estar de pie** [eh-'stahr deh 'pee·eh] to stand up; **estar de acuerdo** [eh-'stahr deh ah-'kwehr-doh] to agree

este ['eh-steh] *(m)* west

este, esta, estos, estas ['eh-steh, 'eh-stah, 'eh-stohs, 'eh-stahs] *(adj ms fs m pl f pl)* this

éste, ésta, éstos, éstas, esto ['eh-steh, 'eh-stah, 'eh-stohs, 'eh-stahs, 'eh-stoh] *(prn ms fs m pl f pl neut)* this

estorbar [eh-stohr-'bahr] to hinder, to interfere

estorbo [eh-'stohr-boh] hindrance, obstacle

estornudar [eh-stohr-noo-'dahr] to sneeze

estrecho [eh-'streh-choh] narrow

estrella [eh-'streh-yah] star

estropeado [eh-stroh-peh-'ah-doh] damaged, messed up

estropear [eh-stroh-peh-'ahr] to damage, to mess up; **estropearse** [eh-stroh-peh-'ahr-seh] to get damaged, to get spoiled

estudiar [eh-stoo-dee-'ahr] to study

estufa [eh-'stoo-fah] stove, heater

estupendo [eh-stoo-'pehn-doh] terrific, great

estúpido [eh-'stoo-pee-doh] stupid, dumb

etcétera [eht-'seh-teh-rah] and so on

Europa [eh-'oo-'roh-pah] Europe

europeo [eh-oo-roh-'peh-oh] European

eventual [eh-vehn-too-'ahl] fortuitous, temporary

evitar [eh-vee-'tahr] to avoid

exactitud [ehk-sahk-tee-'tood] *(f)* accuracy

exacto [ehk-'sahk-toh] accurate

exagerado [ehk-sah-heh-'rah-doh] exaggerated, excessive

examen [ehk-'sah-mehn] *(m)* test, examination, inspection

examinar [ehk-sah-mee-'nahr] to test, to examine

excelente [ehk-seh-'lehn-teh] excellent

excepción [ehk-sehp-see-'ohn] *(f)* exception

excepto [ehk-'sehp-toh] except

excursión [ehk-skoor-see-'ohn] *(f)* excursion; hike; **hacer excursiones a pie** [ah-'sehr ehk-skoor-see-'oh-nehs ah 'pee-eh] to hike, to walk

excusa [ehk-'skoo-sah] excuse

excusar [ehk-skoo-'sahr] to excuse, to exempt

exigencia [ehk-see-'hehn-see·ah] demand

exigir [ehk-see-'heer] to demand

éxito ['ehk-see-toh] success

experiencia [ehk-speh-ree-'ehn-see·ah] experience; **sin experiencia** [seen ehk-speh-ree-'ehn-see·ah] inexperienced

experto [ehk-'spehr-toh] *(adj)* expert

explicar [ehk-splee-'kahr] explain
exportar [ehk-spohr-'tahr] to export
expresamente [ehk-spreh-sah-'mehn-teh] on purpose
expresión [ehk-spreh-see-'ohn] (*f*) expression
exterior [ehk-steh-ree-'ohr] exterior
extintor [ehk-steen-'tohr] (*m*) fire extinguisher
extranjero [ehk-strahn-'heh-roh] foreigner, alien
extrañarse (de) [ehk-strah-'nyahr-seh (deh)] to be amazed (by)
extraordinario [ehk-strah-ohr-dee-'nah-ree-oh] extraordinary
extraviarse [ehk-strah-vee-'ahr-seh] to get lost

F

fábrica ['fah-bree-kah] factory
fabricar [fah-bree-'kahr] to manufacture, to make
fácil ['fah-seel] easy
facilitar [fah-see-lee-'tahr] to facilitate
factura [fahk-'too-rah] invoice, bill
facturar [fahk-too-'rahr] to invoice, to bill; (*train*) to check (baggage); (*plane*) to check in
falso ['fahl-soh] false, counterfeit
falta ['fahl-tah] lack, want, need, short-age, failure, fault, error; **sin falta** [seen 'fahl-tah] (*adv*) absolutely, certainly, for sure
faltar [fahl-'tahr] to be lacking, to be absent, to be missing; **me falta tiem-po para leer** [meh 'fahl-tah tee-'ehm-poh 'pah-rah leh-'ehr] I don't have time to read
familia [fah-'mee-lee-ah] family
famoso [fah-'moh-soh] famous
fango ['fahn-goh] mud
fantástico [fahn-'tah-stee-koh] terrific
faro ['fah-roh] lighthouse
fastidiar [fah-stee-dee-'ahr] to bother, to annoy
fatigoso [fah-tee-'goh-soh] tiring
favor [fah-'vohr] (*m*) favor; **en favor de** [ehn fah-'vohr deh] in favor of; **por favor** [pohr fah-'vohr] please
favorable [fah-voh-'rah-bleh] favorable
fe [feh] (*f*) faith
fecha ['feh-chah] date
felicidad [feh-lee-see-'dahd] (*f*) happiness

felicitación [feh-lee-see-tah-see-'ohn] (*f*) congratulations
felicitar [feh-lee-see-'tahr] to congratulate
feliz [feh-'lees] happy
femenino [feh-meh-'nee-noh] feminine
feo ['feh-oh] ugly
feria ['feh-ree-ah] (*comm*) trade fair, carnival
festivo [feh-'stee-voh] festive
fianza [fee-'ahn-sah] bail, bond, security
fiel [fee-'ehl] faithful
fiesta [fee-'eh-stah] party, celebration, festival, holiday
fijar [fee-'hahr] to set, to fix
fijo ['fee-hoh] fixed, set
fila ['fee-lah] row
film(e) [feelm(eh)] (*m*) film; movie
filtro ['feel-troh] filter
fin [feen] (*m*) end, purpose, objective; **por fin** [pohr feen] finally
final [fee-'nahl] (*m*) end, final, last; **al final** [ahl fee-'nahl] at the end
finalmente [fee-nahl-'mehn-teh] finally
finca ['feen-kah] property, land, real estate; (*Am*) farm, small rural property
firma ['feer-mah] company
firmar [feer-'mahr] to sign
firme ['feer-meh] firm, solid
flaco ['flah-koh] thin
flash [flahsh] (*foto*) flash
flete ['fleh-teh] (*m*) freight
flirteo [fleer-'teh-oh] flirting
flor [flohr] (*f*) flower
florecer [floh-reh-'sehr] to bloom
folleto [foh-'yeh-toh] brochure
fonda ['fohn-dah] small restaurant, guest house, boarding house
forastero/-a [foh-rah-'steh-roh/-ah] stranger, outsider, visitor, alien
forma ['fohr-mah] form, shape, manner, way, fitness; **de todas formas** [deh 'toh-dahs 'fohr-mahs] in any case; **en (buena) forma** [ehn ('bweh-nah) 'fohr-mah] fit
formación [fohr-mah-see-'ohn] (*f*) edu-cation, training; formation
formar [fohr-'mahr] to educate, to train, to shape, to create, to form
formato [fohr-'mah-toh] format
formulario [fohr-moo-'lah-ree-oh] (*sheet*) form, application
forro ['foh-rroh] lining
forzar [fohr-'sahr] to force, to compel, to break down; (*eyes*) to strain
fósforo ['fohs-foh-roh] (*fire*) match

foto(grafía) ['foh-toh(grah-'fee·ah)] photography, a photo
fotografiar [foh-toh-grah-fee-'ahr] (*photo*) to photograph, to shoot
frágil ['frah-heel] fragile
francés, francesa [frahn-'sehs, frahn-'seh-sah] (*m*) French
Francia ['frahn-see·ah] France
frase ['frah-seh] (*f*) phrase, sentence
fraude ['frah·oo-deh] (*m*) fraud
frecuentemente [freh-kwehn-teh-'mehn-teh] often, frequently
freír [freh-'eer] to fry
frente ['frehn-teh] (*f*) front, brow, facade, in front of, facing, opposite to; **frente a** [frehn-teh ah] facing the
fresco ['freh-skoh] fresh, new, cool, bad mannered; (*art*) fresco
frío ['free-oh] cold; **tener/pasar frío** [teh-'nehr/pah-'sahr 'free·oh] to be cold
frontera [frohn-'teh-rah] border, frontier
fruta ['froo-tah] fruit
fuego ['fweh-goh] fire; (*cul*) flame; **fuegos artificiales** ['fweh-gohs ahr-tee-fee-see-'ah-lehs] (*m pl*) fireworks
fuel-oil [ehl fee·oo-ehl-'oh·ehl] (*m*) kerosene
fuente ['fwehn-teh] (*f*) fountain, source, spring
fuera ['fweh-rah] outside, out, away, besides, in addition to, other than; **por fuera** [pohr 'fweh-rah] on the outside; **fuera de eso** ['fweh-rah deh 'eh-soh] (*prp*) other than that
fuerte ['fwehr-teh] strong, powerful
fuerza ['fwehr-sah] strength, power; force
fumar [foo-'mahr] to smoke
función [foonk-see-'ohn] (*f*) (*theater*) performance
funcionar [foonk-see-oh-'nahr] to function; (*mech*) to work, to run
furia ['foo-ree·ah] rage, violence, fury
furioso [foo-ree-'oh-soh] enraged, furious, violent
fusible [foo-'see-bleh] (*m*) (*el*) fuse
futuro [foo-'too-roh] future

G

gafas ['gah-fahs] (*f pl*) eyeglasses; **gafas de sol** ['gah-fahs deh sohl] (*f pl*) sunglasses
Galicia [gah-'lee-see·ah] Galicia
gallego [gah-'yeh-goh] (*lang*) Galician

gallego/gallega [gah-'yeh-goh/gah-'yeh-gah] Galician
gallo ['gah-yoh] rooster
gana(s) ['gah-nah(s)] desire, appetite, longing, **de buena gana** [deh 'bweh-nah 'gah-nah] gladly; **de mala gana** [deh 'mah-lah 'gah-nah] unwillingly, grudgingly
ganancia [gah-'nahn-see·ah] profit
ganar [gah-'nahr] to win, to earn, to profit
gancho ['gahn-choh] hook
garaje [gah-'rah-heh] (*m*) garage
garantía [gah-rahn-'tee·ah] guarantee, pledge, warranty
garganta [gahr-'gahn-tah] throat
gasolina [gah-soh-'lee-nah] gas; **poner gasolina** [poh-'nehr gah-soh-'lee-nah] to put gas (in)
gastar [gah-'stahr] spend
gastos ['gah-stohs] (*m pl*) expenses, costs, charges
gato ['gah-toh] cat
gaviota [gah-vee-'oh-tah] seagull
gemelos [heh-'meh-lohs] (*m pl*) binoculars, twins, cufflinks
general [heh-neh-'rahl] general, wide, prevailing, common, usual; **en general** [ehn heh-neh-'rahl] in general
gente ['hehn-teh] (*f*) people
gobierno [goh-bee-'ehr-noh] government
gol [gohl] goal
golfo ['gohl-foh] gulf
golpe ['gohl-peh] (*m*) blow, punch, hit, knock, strike, smack, bump; (*rowing*) stroke; **dar un golpe a** [dahr oon 'gohl-peh ah] to hit (someone); **golpe de estado** ['gohl-peh deh eh-'stah-doh] coup d'état
golpear [gohl-peh-'ahr] to hit, to punch, to knock, to smack, to strike
gordo ['gohr-doh] fat
gota ['goh-tah] drop, bead, drip, dribble, trickle; (*med*) gout
gotear [goh-teh-'ahr] to drip, to dribble, to trickle
gozar de [goh-'sahr deh] to enjoy
gozo ['goh-soh] enjoyment, pleasure, delight, joy
gracias ['grah-see·ahs] (*f pl*) thanks; **¡gracias a Dios!** [grah-see·ahs ah 'dee-ohs] thank God!; **dar las gracias** [dahr lahs 'grah-see·ahs] to thank
gracioso [grah-see-'oh-soh] funny, witty, graceful

grado ['grah-doh] grade, degree
grande ['grahn-deh] big, large, tall, high, great, grand, impressive
granja ['grahn-hah] farm
gratificación [grah-tee-fee-kah-see-'ohn] (f) reward, tip, bonus, gratification, satisfaction
gratificar [grah-tee-fee-'kahr] to reward, to tip, to give a bonus, to gratify, to satisfy
gratis ['grah-tees] free, for nothing, gratis
gratuitamente [grah-too-ee-tah-'mehn-teh] (adv) free, for nothing, gratis, gratuitously
gratuito [grah-too-'ee-toh] free of charge, gratuitous, unfounded
grave ['grah-veh] grave, serious, critical, important, severe
grifo ['gree-foh] faucet
gritar [gree-'tahr] to shout, to yell, to scream
grueso [groo-'eh-soh] stout, heavyset, thick, bulky, big, heavy
grupo ['groo-poh] group, party; **grupo avanzado** ['groo-poh ah-vahn-'sah-doh] advance party
guapo ['gwah-poh] good-looking; (m) handsome, (f) **guapa** ['gwah-pah] pretty; (Am) brave
guarda ['gwahr-dah] (m) guard; custodian; **guarda nocturno** ['gwahr-dah nohk-'toor-noh] night watchman
guardar [gwahr-'dahr] to guard, to watch, to tend, to keep, to save
guatemalteco [gwah-teh-mahl-'teh-koh] Guatemalan
guateque [gwah-'teh-keh] (m) party
guerra ['geh-rrah] war
guía ['gee-ah] (m) (person) guide; (f) (book) guide; **guía (turístico)** ['gee-ah (too-'ree-stee-koh)] m (person) tourist guide
guiar [gee-'ahr] to drive, to guide, to conduct
guitarra [gee-'tah-rrah] guitar
gusano [goo-'sah-noh] worm
gustar [goo-'stahr] to taste, to like, to enjoy
gusto ['goo-stoh] taste, pleasure, liking; **con gusto** [kohn 'goo-stoh] with pleasure, gladly

H

haber [ah-'behr] to have, to possess
hábil ['ah-beel] skillful, capable, clever
habitación [ah-bee-tah-see-'ohn] (f) room; lodging
habitante [ah-bee-'tahn-teh] (m) inhabitant, resident
habitar [ah-bee-'tahr] to inhabit, to live in, to reside in
habitual [ah-bee-too-'ahl] usual, customary, habitual
hablar [ah-'blahr] to speak, to talk
hacer [ah-'sehr] done, to make, to do; (time) ago; to pretend; **hacer cola** [ah-'sehr 'koh-lah] to go on a line; **hacer daño** [ah-'sehr 'dah-nyoh] to make (someone) sick; **hacer una foto** [ah-'sehr 'oo-nah 'foh-toh] (photo) to take a picture; **hacer señas** [ah-'sehr 'seh-nyahs] to wink; **hacer un viaje** [ah-'sehr oon vee-'ah-heh] to make a trip; **hace un momento** ['ah-seh oon moh-'mehn-toh] a moment ago; **hace poco** ['ah-seh 'poh-koh] a short while ago; **hacerse el bobo** [ah-'sehr-seh ehl 'boh-boh] to play the fool
hacia ['ah-see-ah] toward, in the direction of, near, about; **hacia abajo** ['ah-see-ah ah-'bah-hoh] down, downwards; **hacia arriba** ['ah-see-ah ah-'rree-bah] up, upwards; **hacia atrás** ['ah-see-ah ah-'trahs] to go back, backwards; **hacia medianoche** ['ah-see-ah meh-dee-ah-'noh-cheh] about midnight
hacienda [ah-see-'ehn-dah] (Am) cattle ranch
hall [hahl] (m) hall; (in hotel) foyer, lounge
hambre ['ahm-breh] (f) (el) hunger
hambriento [ahm-bree-'ehn-toh] (f) (el) hungry
harto ['ahr-toh] satiated, full
hasta ['ah-stah] (adv) even; (prep) as far as, up to; (prep) until; **hasta ahora** ['ah-stah ah-'oh-rah] until now; **hasta luego** ['ah-stah loo-'eh-goh] see you later
hay ['ah-ee] there is, there are
hecho ['eh-choh] fact; (ptp)
hecho a mano ['eh-choh ah 'mah-noh] handmade
helado [eh-'lah-doh] ice cream
herido/-a [eh-'ree-doh/-ah] injured, hurt, wounded

hermana [ehr-'mah-nah] sister
hermano [ehr-'mah-noh] brother
hermoso [ehr-'moh-soh] beautiful, lovely; *Am (person)* robust, stout, large
hermosura [ehr-moh-'soo-rah] beauty, loveliness
hervir [ehr-'veer] to boil
hielo ['yeh-loh] ice
hierro ['yeh-rroh] iron
hija ['ee-hah] daughter
hijo ['ee-hoh] son
hilo ['ee-loh] thread
hinchado [een-'chah-doh] swollen
hinchar [een-'chahr] to swell, to blow up, to pump up, to inflate
historia [ee-'stoh-ree-ah] history, story, tale
hobby ['jah-bee] *(m)* hobby
hoja ['oh-hah] sheet, leaf, blade (of grass)
hola ['oh-lah] hello
holgazán [ohl-gah-'sahn] lazy
hombre ['ohm-breh] *(m)* man
homilía [oh-mee-'lee-ah] homily
hondo ['ohn-doh] deep, profound
hondureño [ohn-doo-'reh-nyoh] Honduran
honor [oh-'nohr] *(m)* honor, good name, *(fig)* glory
honorarios [oh-noh-'rah-ree-ohs] *(m pl)* professional fees
hora ['oh-rah] hour; time; **media hora** ['meh-dee-ah 'oh-rah] half hour
horario de apertura [oh-'rah-ree-oh deh ah-pehr-'too-rah] opening hours
horrible [oh-'rree-bleh] horrible, dreadful, ghastly, terrible
hospitalidad [oh-spee-tah-lee-'dahd] *(f)* hospitality
hotel [oh-'tehl] *(m)* hotel
hoy ['oh-ee] today
huésped ['weh-spehd] *(m)* guest
huevo ['weh-voh] guest
humano [oo-'mah-noh] human
húmedo ['oo-meh-doh] humid, moist, wet, damp
humo ['oo-moh] smoke
humor [oo-'mohr] *(m)* humor, mood, temper; **de buen humor** [deh bwehn oo-'mohr] good mood, good humor

I

idea [ee-'deh-ah] idea, notion, estimate
¡ni idea! [nee ee-'deh-ah] I haven't a clue
idioma [ee-dee-'oh-mah] *(m)* language
igual [ee-'gwahl] same, equal (to); **igual que** [ee-'gwahl keh] same as
igualmente [ee-gwahl-'mehn-teh] equally, also, likewise; *(response to greeting, etc.)* the same to you
iluminado [ee-loo-mee-'nah-doh] lighted, lit
ilustración [ee-loo-strah-see-'ohn] *(f)* illustration, picture, enlightenment
inmediatamente [een-meh-dee-ah-tah-'mehn-teh] immediately
impedir [eem-peh-'deer] to prevent
imperdible [eem-pehr-'dee-bleh] *(m)* safety pin
importancia [eem-pohr-'tahn-see-ah] importance, significance, magnitude; **sin importancia** [seem eem-pohr-'tahn-see-ah] unimportant
importante [eem-pohr-'tahn-teh] important, significant, considerable, magnificent
importar [eem-pohr-'tahr] to import
importe [eem-'pohr-teh] *(m)* amount, total, cost, value; **importe de la factura** [eem-'pohr-teh deh lah fahk-'too-rah] the (total) amount of the bill
imposible [eem-poh-'see-bleh] impossible
impreciso [eem-preh-'see-soh] vague, imprecise
impresión [eem-preh-see-'ohn] *(f)* impression, printing
impreso [eem-'preh-soh] printed
imprevisto [eem-preh-'vee-stoh] unexpected
improbable [eem-proh-'bah-bleh] improbable, unlikely
inadecuado [een-ah-deh-'kwah-doh] inadequate, inappropriate, unsuitable
incapaz [een-kah-'pahs] incapable, unfit, incompetent
incendio [een-'sehn-dee-oh] fire; **incendio forestal** [een-'sehn-dee-oh foh-reh-'stahl] forest fire
incidente [een-see-'dehn-teh] incident, incidental
incierto [een-see-'ehr-toh] uncertain
incluido [een-kloo-'ee-doh] included
incluir [een-kloo-'eer] to include

A/Z

incómodo [een-'koh-moh-doh] uncomfortable, inconvenient, annoying

incompleto [een-kohm-'pleh-toh] incomplete, unfinished

inconstante [een-kohn-'stahn-teh] inconstant, changeable, fickle

inconveniente [een-kohn-veh-nee-'ehn-teh] *(adj)* inconvenient, inappropriate, unsuitable; *(n m)* obstacle, drawback, difficulty

incorrecto [een-koh-'rrehk-toh] incorrect, inaccurate, wrong

increíble [een-kreh-'ee-bleh] incredible

indecente [een-deh-'sehn-teh] indecent

indeciso [een-deh-'see-soh] undecided, hesitant, indecisive

indemnización [een-dehm-nee-sah-see-'ohn] *(f)* indemnity, reparation, compensation

indemnizar [een-dehm-nee-'sahr] to indemnify, to compensate (for)

indeterminado [een-deh-tehr-mee-'nah-doh] indetermined, inconclusive

indicacion [een-dee-kah-see-'ohn] *(f)* indication, sign, hint; **indicaciones concretas** [een-dee-kah-see-'oh-nehs kohn-'kreh-tahs] concrete instructions; **dar indicaciones** [dahr een-dee-kah-see-'oh-nehs] to give instructions (to)

indicar [een-dee-'kahr] to indicate, to show, to record, to register, to suggest, to hint

indicio [een-'dee-see-oh] indication, sign, clue, trace, vestige

indispensable [een-dee-spehn-'sah-bleh] indispensable

indispuesto [een-dee-'spweh-stoh] indisposed, slightly ill

individual [een-dee-vee-doo-'ahl] *(adj)* individual

individuo [een-dee-'vee-doo-oh] *(n,m)* person, individual

indudable(mente) [een-doo-'dah-bleh ('men-teh)] undoubtedly

inepto [een-'ehp-toh] inept, incompetent

inesperado [een-eh-speh-'rah-doh] unexpected

inestable [een-eh-'stah-bleh] unstable, unsteady

inevitable [een-eh-vee-'tah-bleh] inevitable

inexacto [een-ehk-'sahk-toh] inaccurate, incorrect

inexperto [een-ehk-'spehr-toh] inexperienced

inferior [een-feh-ree-'ohr] inferior

inflamable [een-flah-'mah-bleh] flammable

inflar [een-'flahr] to inflate, to blow up; *(fig)* to exaggerate

información [een-fohr-mah-see-'ohn] *(f)* information

informar [een-fohr-'mahr] to inform, to announce, to report on; **informar a alguien** [een-fohr-'mahr ah 'ahl-gee-ehn] to inform someone; **informarse de** [een-fohr-'mahr-seh deh] to find out about, to inquire about; **informarse acerca** [een-fohr-'mahr-seh ah-'sehr-kah] to gather information about

informe [een-'fohr-meh] *(m)* report

Inglaterra [een-glah-'teh-rrah] England

inglés/inglesa [een-'glehs/een-'gleh-sah] English

injusticia [een-hoo-'stee-see-ah] injustice, unfairness

injusto [een-'hoo-stoh] unjust, unfair

inmediatamente [een-meh-dee-ah-tah-'mehn-teh] *(adv)* immediately

inmediato [een-meh-dee-'ah-toh] *(adj)* immediate, prompt, adjoining

inmenso [een-'mehn-soh] immense, huge, vast

innecesario [een-neh-seh-'sah-ree-oh] unnecessary

inocente [ee-noh-'sehn-teh] innocent

inoportuno [een-oh-pohr-'too-noh] ill-timed; inconvenient

inquieto [een-kee-'eh-toh] anxious, uneasy, worried, restless

inscribirse [een-skree-'beer-seh] to register

insecto [een-'sehk-toh] insect

inseguro [een-seh-'goo-roh] insecure

insignificante [een-seeg-nee-fee-'kahn-teh] insignificant

insistir en [een-see-'steer ehn] to insist on

insoportable [een-soh-pohr-'tah-bleh] unbearable

instalación [een-stah-lah-see-'ohn] *(f)* installation

instante [een-'stahn-teh] *(m)* instant

insuficiente [een-soo-fee-see-'ehn-teh] insufficient, inadequate

insultar [een-sool-'tahr] to insult

inteligencia [een-teh-lee-'hehn-see-ah] intelligence

inteligente [een-teh-lee-'hehn-teh] intelligent

A/Z

intención [een-tehn-see-'ohn] (f) intention, purpose, plan; **tener la intención de** [teh-'nehr lah een-tehn-see-'ohn deh] to intend to

intencionadamente [een-tehn-see-oh-nah-dah-'mehn-teh] deliberately

intentar [een-tehn-'tahr] to attempt, to try, to mean, to intend

intento [een-'tehn-toh] attempt

interés [een-teh-'rehs] (m) interest

interesante [een-teh-reh-'sahn-teh] interesting

interesarse (en/por) [een-teh-reh-'sahr-seh (ehn/pohr)] to be interested in; **interesarse por su salud** [een-teh-reh-'sahr-seh pohr soo sah-'lood] to ask after his (or her) health; **interesarse en la transacción** [een-teh-reh-'sahr-seh ehn lah trahn-sahk-see-'ohn] to be involved in the transaction

interior [een-teh-ree-'ohr] (m) interior, inside, inner, internal, domestic; **interior del país** [een-teh-ree-'ohr dehl pah-'ees] inland, hinterland

internacional [een-tehr-nah-see-oh-'nahl] international

interpretar mal [een-tehr-preh-tahr mahl] misinterpret

interrumpir [een-teh-rroom-'peer] interrupt

interrupción [een-teh-rroop-see-'ohn] (f) interruption

interruptor [een-teh-rroop-'tohr] (m) (el) switch

intolerable [een-toh-leh-'rah-bleh] intolerable

intranquilizarse [een-trahn-kee-lee-'sahr-seh] to get worried, to be uneasy, to be anxious

intranquilo [een-trahn-'kee-loh] worried, uneasy, anxious

inútil [een-'oo-teel] useless

inválido [een-'vah-lee-doh] disabled, invalid

inventar [een-vehn-'tahr] to invent

investigar [een-veh-stee-'gahr] to investigate, to research

invitación [een-vee-tah-see-'ohn] (f) invitation

invitar [een-vee-'tahr] to invite

ir [eer] to go, to move, to travel; **ir a pie** [eer ah 'pee-eh] to walk; **ir a ver a alguien** [eer ah vehr ah 'ahl-gee-ehn] to go see someone; **ir todo seguido** [eer 'toh-doh seh-'gee-doh] to go straight ahead; **ir en avión** [eer ehn ah-vee-'ohn] to fly; **ir a buscar** [eer ah boo-'skahr] to go get, to get **ir bien** [eer 'bee-ehn] to do well; **irse** ['eer-seh] to leave; **ir(se) a la cama** [eer(seh) ah lah 'kah-mah] to go to bed

irregular [ee-rreh-goo-'lahr] irregular

isla ['ee-slah] island

Islas Canarias ['ee-slahs kah-'nah-ree-ahs] Canary Islands

itinerario [ee-tee-neh-'rah-ree-oh] route, itinerary

izquierdo/-a [ees-kee-'ehr-doh/-ah] left; **a la izquierda** [ah lah ees-kee-'ehr-dah] to the left

J

jamás [hah-'mahs] never

jardín [hahr-'deen] (m) garden

jefa ['heh-fah] (f) chief, boss

jefe ['heh-feh] (m) chief, boss

joven ['hoh-vehn] youth, young man

juego ['hoo-eh-goh] game, gambling

jugar [hoo-'gahr] to play, to gamble

juguete [hoo-'geh-teh] (m) toy

juicio ['hoo-ee-see-oh] trial, judgment, opinion

junco ['hoon-koh] reed

junto ['hoon-toh] (adj sing) joined, united, together; (adv) near, close, together; (prep) **junto al Amazonas** ['hoon-toh ahl ah-mah-'soh-nahs] close to the Amazon; (pl) **juntos** ['hoon-tohs] together

justo ['hoo-stoh] just, right, fair, exact, tight

juventud [hoo-vehn-'tood] (f) young people, youth

juzgar [hoos-'gahr] to judge

L

la [lah] (art def f) the; (pron pers) her; you; it; (pron dem) **mi madre y la tuya** [mee 'mah-dreh ee lah 'too-yah] my mother and yours; **esta bolsa y la roja** ['eh-stah 'bohl-sah ee lah 'roh-hah] this bag and the red one; (pron rel) **la que gane** [lah keh 'gah-neh] the one who wins

labio ['lah-bee-oh] lip

lado ['lah-doh] side; **al lado de** [ahl 'lah-doh deh] beside; **al otro lado de la carretera** [ahl 'oh-troh 'lah-doh deh lah kah-rreh-'teh-rah] on the other side of the road; **al otro lado** [ahl 'oh-troh 'lah-doh] across

lago ['lah-goh] lake

lamentar [lah-mehn-'tahr] to regret, to be sorry about, to lament

lámpara ['lahm-pah-rah] lamp

lancha ['lahn-chah] boat

lanzamiento [lahn-sah-mee-'ehn-toh] *(nm)* *(act)* throw, cast, throwing, casting, launch, launching

largo ['lahr-goh] long, length, lengthy; **a lo largo** [ah loh 'lahr-goh] lengthwise, throughout, along

lástima ['lah-stee-mah] pity, compassion; **¡qué lástima!** [keh 'lah-stee-mah] what a pity! too bad!

lata ['lah-tah] can

lavar [lah-'vahr] to wash

leer [leh-'ehr] to read

lejano [leh-'hah-noh] far, distant

lengua ['lehn-gwah] tongue, language

lentamente [lehn-tah-'mehn-teh] *(adv)* slowly

lentes ['lehn-tehs] *(m pl) (Am)* eyeglasses

lento ['lehn-toh] *(adj)* slow

leña ['leh-nyah] firewood

letrero [leh-'treh-roh] notice, sign, poster, label

levantar [leh-vahn-'tahr] to lift, to raise (up); **levantarse** [leh-vahn-'tahr-seh] to rise, to get up, to stand up, to get out of bed

leve ['leh-veh] slight

libre ['lee-breh] free

libro ['lee-broh] book

lícito ['lee-see-toh] lawful, legal, fair, permissible

ligero [lee-'heh-roh] light; *(Am)* quick

límite ['lee-mee-teh] *(m)* limit, end, boundary

limpiar [leem-pee-'ahr] to clean

limpio ['leem-pee-oh] clean; *(sport)* fair

lindo ['leen-doh] pretty

línea ['lee-neh-ah] line, cable; **línea telefónica** ['lee-neh-ah teh-leh-'foh-nee-kah] phone line

linterna [leen-'tehr-nah] flashlight

liquidación [lee-kee-dah-see-'ohn] *(f) (comm)* liquidation, clearance sale

líquido ['lee-kee-doh] liquid

liso ['lee-soh] smooth

lista ['lee-stah] list; *(adj f)* smart; ready

listo ['lee-stoh] *(adj m)* smart; ready

liviano [lee-vee-'ah-noh] *(Am)* light

llama ['yah-mah] flame

llamar [yah-'mahr] to call, to name, to attract; **llamar la atención** [yah-'mahr lah ah-tehn-see-'ohn] to attract attention; **llamar a la puerta** [yah-'mahr ah lah 'pwehr-tah] to knock on the door; **llamar por teléfono** [yah-'mahr pohr teh-'leh-foh- noh] to phone

llano ['yah-noh] *(surface)* flat, level; *(fig)* plain, simple

llanura [yah-'noo-rah] plain, prairie

llave ['yah-veh] *(f)* key

llegar [yeh-'gahr] to arrive, to reach, to attain; **llegar a...** [yeh-'gahr ah] *(followed by inf v)* to manage to... : **llegar a cantar** [yeh-'gahr ah kahn-'tahr] to manage to sing; **llegar a ser** [yeh-'gahr ah sehr] to manage to be/become; **llegar tarde** [yeh-'gahr 'tahr-deh] to be late

llenar [yeh-'nahr] to fill, to cover

lleno ['yeh-noh] full

llevar [yeh-'vahr] to carry, to take, to transport, to convey, to wear; **llevar (puesto)** [yeh-'vahr ('pweh-stoh)] to wear; **llevar consigo** [yeh-'vahr kohn-'see-goh] to have (something) on you; **llevarse** [yeh-'vahr-seh] to carry off

llorar [yoh-'rahr] to cry

llover [yoh-'vehr] to rain

lo [loh] *(art def neut)* the; *(prn)* him, it

loco ['loh-koh] crazy, insane

lodo ['loh-doh] mud

lógico ['loh-hee-koh] logical

lograr [loh-'grahr] to get, to obtain, to attain, to achieve

longitud [lohn-hee-'tood] *(f)* length; *(geog)* longitude

loza ['loh-sah] earthenware, crockery; **loza fina** ['loh-sah 'fee-nah] china

luego ['loo-eh-goh] then, next, later, afterwards

lugar [loo-'gahr] *(m)* place, spot, position; **en lugar de** [ehn loo-'gahr deh] in place of, instead of; **tener lugar** [teh-'nehr loo-'gahr] to take place

lujo ['loo-hoh] luxury, lavishness

lujoso [loo-'hoh-soh] luxurious, lavish

luminoso [loo-mee-'noh-soh] bright, luminous, shining

luna ['loo-nah] moon
luz [loos] (f) light

M

madera [mah-'deh-rah] wood
madre ['mah-dreh] (f) mother
maduro [mah-'doo-roh] ripe
magnífico [mahg-'nee-fee-koh] splendid, wonderful, superb, magnificent
magro ['mah-groh] (meat) lean
mal [mahl] (adv) badly, poorly; (n m) evil, harm, disease, illness; **me siento/estoy mal** [meh see-'ehn-toh/eh-'stoh·ee mahl] I feel bad; **mal educado** [mahl eh-doo-'kah-doh] bad mannered, rude; **el bien y el mal** [ehl 'bee·ehn ee ehl mahl] good and evil; **el mal de Parkinson** [ehl mahl deh pahr-keen-'sohn] Parkinson's disease
maleta [mah-'leh-tah] suitcase
malintencionado [mahl-een-tehn-see·oh-'nah-doh] hostile, malicious
malo ['mah-loh] (adj); **mal** [mahl] (before n m sing) bad, poor, nasty, ill; hard, difficult; **un olor malo/un mal olor** [oon oh-'lohr 'mah-loh/oon mahl oh-'lohr] an unpleasant smell; **mal tiempo** [mahl tee-'ehm-poh] stormy weather; **estar malo** [eh-'stahr 'mah-loh] to be ill
malsano [mahl-'sah-noh] (climate, environment) unhealthy, bad; (mind) morbid
mancha ['mahn-chah] stain
mandar [mahn-'dahr] to send, to order, to command; **mandar a buscar** [mahn-'dahr ah boo-'skahr] to send for; **mandar hacer** [mahn-'dahr ah-'sehr] to have (something) made
manejar [mah-neh-'hahr] (Am) to drive
manera [mah-'neh-rah] way, manner, conduct; **de ninguna manera** [deh neen-'goo-nah mah-'neh-rah] no way
manguera [mahn-'geh-rah] (garden, etc.) hose
manifestación [mah-nee-feh-stah-see-'ohn] (f) demonstration
mano ['mah-noh] (f) hand; **hecho a mano** ['eh-choh ah 'mah-noh] handmade
manta ['mahn-tah] blanket, shawl
mañana [mah-'nyah-nah] morning; tomorrow

mapa ['mah-pah] (m) map
maquillarse [mah-kee-'yahr-seh] to put on makeup
máquina ['mah-kee-nah] machine, engine, camera; (Am) car; **máquina copiadora** ['mah-kee-nah koh-pee·ah-'doh-rah] copying machine
mar [mahr] (m) sea
maravilloso [mah-rah-vee-'yoh-soh] wonderful, marvelous
marca ['mahr-kah] mark, stamp; (product) brand; (sports) record
marcar [mahr-'kahr] to mark, to stamp; (tel) to dial
marcha ['mahr-chah] march, walk, hike; (auto) gear, speed
marchante [mahr-'chan-teh] (m) (Am) customer
marcharse [mahr-'chahr-seh] to leave, to go away
mareado: [mah-reh-'ah-doh] (adj) to feel dizzy, to feel sick; **estar mareado, sentirse mareado** [eh-'stahr mah-reh-'ah-doh, sehn-'teer-seh mah-reh-'ah-doh] **enfermo de catarro** [ehn-'fehr-moh deh kah-'tah-rroh] sick with a cold
marido [mah-'ree-doh] husband
marrón [mah-'rrohn] brown, chestnut (color)
martillo [mahr-'tee-yoh] hammer
más [mahs] more, most; **más que** [mahs keh] more than; **a lo más** [ah loh mahs] at the most; **más bien** [mahs 'bee·ehn] rather; **más tarde** [mahs 'tahr-deh] (adv) later; **más o menos** [mahs oh 'meh-nohs] more or less
masculino [mah-skoo-'lee-noh] masculine, male
mata ['mah-tah] bush, shrub; (Am) plant
material [mah-teh-ree-'ahl] (m) material
matorral [mah-toh-'rrahl] (m) thicket, scrub, brushwood
matrimonio [mah-tree-'moh-nee·oh] marriage, married couple
máximo, al [ahl 'mahk-see-moh] to the maximum, to the utmost
me [meh] me, to me, to myself
mechero [meh-'cheh-roh] lighter, burner
mediador [meh-dee·ah-'dohr] (m) mediator
mediano [meh-dee-'ah-noh] (adj) average, medium-size, middling

medianoche [meh-dee-ah-'noh-cheh] (f) midnight; **a medianoche** [ah meh-dee-ah-'noh-cheh] at midnight

mediante [meh-dee-'ahn-teh] (prep) through, by means of, by, with the help of

médico ['meh-dee-koh] doctor, physician

medida [meh-'dee-dah] measure

medio ['meh-dee-oh] (n m, adj) half, middle, center, mean, average, means, way, method; (Am) rather; quite; **el medio ambiente** [ehl 'meh-dee-oh ahm-bee-'ehn-teh] the environment; **medio kilo** ['meh-dee-oh 'kee-loh] half a kilo

mediodía [meh-dee-oh-'dee-ah] (m) noon, midday; **a(l) mediodía** [ah(l) meh-dee-oh-'dee-ah] at noon

medir [meh-'deer] to measure

Mediterráneo [meh-dee-teh-'rrah-neh-oh] Mediterranean

medusa [meh-'doo-sah] jellyfish

mejor [meh-'hohr] better, best; **el/la/lo mejor** [ehl/lah/loh meh-'hohr] the best; **mejor que te vayas** [meh-'hohr keh teh 'vah-yahs] you better go

mejorar [meh-hoh-'rahr] to improve

menor [meh-'nohr] minor, smaller, lesser, younger

menos ['meh-nohs] minus, less, least, fewer, fewest, except, but; **lo menos posible** [loh 'meh-nohs poh-'see-bleh] the least possible; **al/por lo/a lo menos** [ahl/pohr loh/ah loh 'meh-nohs] at least

mensual [mehn-soo-'ahl] (adj) monthly

mentir [mehn-'teer] to lie

mentira [mehn-'tee-rah] lie

menú [meh-'noo] (m) menu

menudo [meh-'noo-doh] (adj) small, tiny, slight; (adv) **a menudo** [ah-meh-'noo-doh] often, frequently; (n m) small change

mercadería [mehr-kah-deh-'ree-ah] (Am) goods, merchandise

mercancía [mehr-kahn-'see-ah] goods, merchandise

merecer [meh-reh-'sehr] to deserve

meridional [meh-ree-dee-oh-'nahl] southern; (n m) southerner

merienda [meh-ree-'ehn-dah] afternoon snack

mérito ['meh-ree-toh] merit; value, worth

mes [mehs] (m) month; **al mes** [ahl mehs] (adv) monthly

mesa ['meh-sah] table

meta ['meh-tah] goal, aim

mexicano [meh-hee-'kah-non] Mexican

México ['meh-hee-koh] Mexico

mezclado [meh-'sklah-doh] mixed

mi [mee] me, myself; **¡a mí!** [ah mee] (Spain) help!

miedo [mee-'eh-doh] fear; **tener miedo de** [teh-'nehr mee-'eh-doh deh] to be afraid of

mientras [mee-'ehn-trahs] (conj) while

minuta [mee-'noo-tah] (Am) menu

minuto [mee-'noo-toh] minute

mirada [mee-'rah-dah] look, glance; gaze

mirar [mee-'rahr] to look at, to glance at, to gaze at, to watch; **mirar por encima** [mee-'rahr pohr ehn-'see-mah] to give a cursory glance; **mirándolo bien** [mee-'rahn-doh-loh 'bee-ehn] all in all

misa ['mee-sah] (rel) mass

mismo ['mees-moh] same; **el mismo** [ehl 'mees-moh] the same; **lo mismo... que** [loh 'mees-moh...keh] the same thing...as

mitad [mee-'tahd] (f) half

mochila [moh-'chee-lah] knapsack

moda ['moh-dah] fashion

modelo [moh-'deh-loh] model

moderado [moh-deh-'rah-doh] moderate

moderno [moh-'dehr-noh] modern

modo ['moh-doh] way, manner, fashion, mode, method

mojado [moh-'hah-doh] wet, damp, moist

molestar [moh-leh-'stahr] to bother, to annoy, to inconvenience, to upset

molestia [moh-'leh-stee-ah] nuisance, trouble; **tomarse la molestia de** [toh-'mahr-seh lah moh-'leh-stee-ah deh] to take the trouble to

molesto [moh-'leh-stoh] (adj) annoying, troublesome, upset, ill at ease, uncomfortable, embarrassed

momento [moh-'mehn-toh] moment; **en este momento** [ehn 'eh-steh moh-'mehn-toh] right now; **hace un momento** ['ah-seh oon moh-'mehn-toh] a moment ago

moneda [moh-'neh-dah] currency, coin

monja ['mohn-hah] nun

montaña [mohn-'tah-nyah] mountain

morder [mohr-'dehr] to bite

moreno [moh-'reh-noh] brown, dark, tanned; swarthy

morir [moh-'reer] to die
mosca ['moh-skah] fly
mosquito [moh-'skee-toh] mosquito
mostrar [moh-'strahr] to show, to display, to exhibit, to point out, to explain
motivo [moh-'tee-voh] motive, cause, reason
mover [moh-'vehr] to move
movimiento [moh-vee-mee-'ehn-toh] movement
mozo ['moh-soh] *(n, m)* waiter, porter; *(adj, m)* young
muchacha [moo-'chah-chah] girl, young woman
muchacho [moo-'chah-choh] boy, young man
muchedumbre [moo-cheh-'doom-breh] *(f)* crowd
mucho ['moo-choh] *(m, sing)* much, great; a lot of; **muchos** ['moo-chohs] *(m pl)* many, lots of; **¡mucha suerte!** ['moo-chah 'swehr-teh] good luck!
mudar [moo-'dahr] to change, to move; **mudarse de ropa** [moo-'dahr-seh deh 'roh-pah] to change clothes; **mudarse de empleo** [moo-'dahr-seh deh ehm-'pleh-oh] to change jobs; **mudarse (de casa)** [moo-'dahr-seh (deh 'kah-sah)] to move out
mueble ['mweh-bleh] *(m)* piece of furniture
muelle ['mweh-yeh] *(m)* soft, springy; *(naut)* pier; *(fig)* **vida muelle** ['vee-dah 'mweh-yeh] an easy life
muerte ['mwehr-teh] *(f)* death
muerto ['mwehr-toh] dead
muestra ['mweh-strah] indication, sign; *(comm)* sample, trade fair
mujer [moo-'hehr] *(f)* woman
multa ['mool-tah] fine
multicolor [mool-tee-koh-'lohr] multicolored
multitud [mool-tee-'tood] *(f)* crowd
mundo ['moon-doh] world
muñeca [moo-'nyeh-kah] doll
muro ['moo-roh] wall
música ['moo-see-kah] music
mutuamente [moo-too-ah-'mehn-teh] mutually
muy ['moo-ee] very

N

nacido [nah-'see-doh] born
nacimiento [nah-see-mee-'ehn-toh] birth
nación [nah-see-'ohn] *(f)* nation
nada ['nah-dah] nothing, not at all, nothingness, the void, nowhere; **de nada** [deh 'nah-dah] you're welcome; **nada más** ['nah-dah mahs] nothing more; **no es nada extraño** [noh ehs 'nah-dah eh-'strah-nyoh] it's not at all strange
nadar [nah-'dahr] to swim
nadie ['nah-dee-eh] nobody, no one
nafta ['nahf-tah] *(Arg)* gas
nativo [nah-'tee-voh] native
natural [nah-too-'rahl] *(adj)* natural
natural de [nah-too-'rahl deh] a native of
naturalmente [nah-too-rahl-'mehn-teh] *(adv)* of course, you bet, naturally
necesario [neh-seh-'sah-ree-oh] necessary
necesidad [neh-seh-see-'dahd] *(f)* necessity, need; **en caso de necesidad** [ehn 'kah-soh deh neh-seh-see-'dahd] in case of need
necesitar [neh-seh-see-'tahr] to need
negar [neh-'gahr] to deny, to refuse
negarse [neh-'gahr-seh] to refuse (oneself to)
negativo [neh-gah-'tee-voh] negative
negligente [nehg-lee-'hehn-teh] negligent
negociación [neh-goh-see-ah-see-'ohn] *(f)* negotiation
negocio [neh-'goh-see-oh] affair; business
nervioso [nehr-vee-'oh-soh] nervous
nevar [neh-'vahr] to snow
ni … ni [nee … nee] neither … nor; **ni siquiera** [nee see-kee-'eh-rah] not even
nicaragüense [nee-kah-rah-'gwehn-seh] *(m)* Nicaraguan
nieto/nieta [nee-'eh-toh/nee-'eh-tah] grandson/granddaughter
ninguno *(adj)* **ningún** [neen-'goo-noh, neen-'goon] *(before n m sing)* no; **de ningún modo** [den neen-'goon 'moh-doh] in no way; **en ninguna parte** [ehn neen-'goo-nah 'pahr-teh] nowhere; *(pron)* nobody, no one; none; neither; **ninguna de las dos** [neen-'goo-nah deh lahs dohs] neither of them
niño ['nee-nyoh] child
no [noh] no; not

no obstante [noh ohb-'stahn-teh] nevertheless, however, in spite of

noche ['noh-cheh] (f) night; nighttime, late evening; (fig) dark, darkness

nocivo [noh-'see-voh] harmful

no hay de que [noh 'ah-ee deh keh] You're welcome

nombrar [nohm-'brahr] to name, to designate, to mention

nombre ['nohm-breh] (m) name; **nombre (de pila)** ['nohm-breh (deh 'pee-lah)] first name; **nombre y apellidos** ['nohm-breh eh ah-peh-'yee-dohs] full name (first name and surname)

normal [norh-'mahl] normal, regular, usual, natural

normalmente [nohr-mahl-'mehn-teh] normally, usually

norte ['nohr-teh] (m) north; **al norte de** [ahl 'nohr-teh deh] north of; **del norte** [dehl 'nohr-teh] from the north

nos [nohs] (pron pers pl) us, to us, to ourselves, to each other; **nos pertenece** [nohs pehr-teh-'neh-seh] it belongs to us

nosotros [noh-'soh-trohs] we, us, ourselves; **únete a nosotros** ['oo-neh-teh ah noh-'soh-trohs] join us; (f) **nosotras leemos** [noh-'soh-trahs leh-'eh-mohs] we read; **lo queremos para nosotros** [loh keh-'reh-mohs 'pah-rah noh-'soh-trohs] we want it for ourselves

nota ['noh-tah] note, memo; **tomar nota (de)** [toh-'mahr 'noh-tah (deh)] to take note (of)

notar [noh-'tahr] to notice

noticia [noh-'tee-see-ah] news

novedad [noh-veh-'dahd] (f) novelty

nublado [noo-'blah-doh] cloudy

nudo ['noo-doh] knot

nuestro/-a ['nweh-stroh/-ah] our, ours

nuevo ['nweh-voh] new, additional; **de nuevo** [deh 'nweh-voh] again

numerar [noo-meh-'rahr] to number

número ['noo-meh-roh] number; (shoe) size; (newspaper, etc.) issue; (theater) many

numeroso [noo-meh-'roh-soh] numerous

nunca ['noon-kah] never; ever

nutrición [noo-tree-see-'ohn] (f) nutrition

nutritivo [noo-tree-'tee-voh] nutritious

O

o [oh] or; **o ... o** [oh ... oh] either ... or

objeto [ohb-'heh-toh] object, thing, aim, objective; **objetos de alfarería** [ohb-'heh-tohs deh ahl-fah-reh-'ree-ah] pottery (items); **objetos de valor** [ohb-'heh-tohs deh vah-'lohr] valuables

obligación [ohb-lee-gah-see-'ohn] (f) obligation, duty, responsibility

obligado, estar [ohb-lee-'gah-doh, eh-'stahr] to be forced to, to be compelled to

obligar [ohb-lee-'gahr] to force, to compel, to oblige

obrar [oh-'brahr] to act, to behave, to proceed, to work

observar [ohb-sehr-'vahr] to observe, to watch, to notice, to respect

obstruido [ohb-stroo-'ee-doh] blocked, obstructed

obtener [ohb-teh-'nehr] to get, to obtain, to secure

obtenible [ohb-teh-'nee-bleh] achievable, accessible

ocasión [oh-kah-see-'ohn] (f) occasion, time, opportunity, chance, cause, motive; (Am) **de ocasión** [deh oh-kah-see-'ohn] secondhand; bargain; **en algunas ocasiones** [ehn ahl-'goo-nahs oh-kah-see-'oh-nehs] some times

occidental [ohk-see-dehn-'tahl] western

océano [oh-'seh-ah-noh] ocean

ocultar [oh-kool-'tahr] to hide, to conceal

oculto [oh-'kool-toh] (adj) hidden, concealed

ocupado [oh-koo-'pah-doh] occupied, taken, busy

ocupar [oh-koo-'pahr] to occupy, to fill, to take up; **ocupar un puesto** [oh-koo-'pahr oon 'pweh-stoh] to fill a slot; **ocuparse de algo** [oh-koo-'pahr-seh deh 'ahl-goh] to take care of something

ocurrir [oh-koo-'rrehr] to happen

oeste [oh-'eh-steh] (m) western

ofender [oh-fehn-'dehr] to offend, to insult

ofensa [oh-'fehn-sah] offense, slight

oficial [oh-fee-see-'ahl] official

oficina [oh-fee-'see-nah] office; **oficina de información** [oh-fee-'see-nah deh een-fohr-mah-see-'ohn] information office; **oficina de objetos perdidos** [oh-fee-'see-nah deh ohb-'heh-tohs pehr-

'dee-dohs] lost and found office; **oficina de turismo** [oh-fee-'see-nah deh too-'rees-moh] tourism office

ofrecer [oh-freh-'sehr] to offer, to give

oír [oh-'eer] to hear

ojo ['oh-hoh] eye

oler [oh-'lehr] to smell;

oler mal [oh-'lehr mahl] to smell bad, to stink

olor [oh-'lohr] (m) smell

olvidar [ohl-vee-'dahr] to forget

olla ['oh-yah] pot, pan, stew

operar [oh-peh-'rahr] to effect, to produce; (med) to operate on; (Am) to operate machinery, to manage a business

opinar [oh-pee-'nahr] to think, to give one's opinion

opinión [oh-pee-nee-'ohn] (f) opinion; **según/en mi opinión** [seh-'goon/ehn mee oh-pee-nee-'ohn] in my opinion

oportunamente [oh-pohr-too-nah-'mehn-teh] (adv) opportunely, in a timely way, at the right time

oportunidad [oh-pohr-too-nee-'dahd] (f) opportunity

oportuno [oh-pohr-'too-noh] opportune

opuesto [oh-'pweh-stoh] opposite

oración [oh-rah-see-'ohn] (f) sentence, prayer, speech

orden ['ohr-dehn] (m) order

ordenado [ohr-deh-'nah-doh] orderly, tidy, methodical person

ordinario [ohr-dee-'nah-ree-oh] ordinary, usual, common, coarse, vulgar

organizar [ohr-gah-nee-'sahr] to organize

orilla [oh-'ree-yah] edge, border; (river) bank; (lake, sea) shore

orquesta [ohr-'keh-stah] orchestra

os [ohs] (pron pers pl) you, to you, to yourselves

oscuro [oh-'skoo-roh] dark, gloomy, dim, obscure

otro ['oh-troh] (adj sing) another, (pl) other, last, previous, next, following; (pron sing) another one, (pl) others; **al otro día** [ahl 'oh-troh 'dee-ah] next day; **la otra semana** [lah 'oh-trah seh-'mah-nah] the other week; **de otra manera/ forma** [deh 'oh-trah mah-'neh-rah/'fohr-mah] another way/manner; **en otra parte** [ehn 'oh-trah 'pahr-teh] another place; **otra vez** ['oh-trah vehs] another time

oveja [oh-'veh-hah] sheep

P

paciencia [pah-see-'ehn-see-ah] patience

paciente [pah-see-'ehn-teh] patient

padre ['pah-dreh] (m) father; **padres** ['pah-drehs] (m pl) parents

paga ['pah-gah] (n f) pay, salary

pagar [pah-'gahr] to pay; **pagar al contado** [pah-'gahr ahl kohn-tah-doh] to pay cash

página ['pah-hee-nah] page

pago ['pah-goh] payment

país [pah-'ees] (m) country

paisaje [pah-ee-'sah-heh] (m) landscape

pájaro ['pah-hah-roh] bird

palabra [pah-'lah-brah] word

palacio [pah-'lah-see-oh] palace

pálido ['pah-lee-doh] pale

panameño [pah-nah-'meh-nyoh] Panamanian

panorama [pah-noh-'rah-mah] panorama

pantano [pahn-'tah-noh] swamp

paño ['pah-nyoh] cloth, material, cleaning rag

pañuelo [pah-nyoo-'eh-loh] handkerchief, scarf; **pañuelo de cabeza** [pah-nyoo-'eh-loh deh kah-'beh-sah] headscarf

papel [pah-'pehl] (m) paper

papel higiénico [pah-'pehl ee-hee-'eh-nee-koh] toilet paper

paquete [pah-'keh-teh] (m) package, parcel, packet

paquetito [pah-keh-'tee-toh] small package

par [pahr] (m) pair; **un par** [oon pahr] one pair

para ['pah-rah] for; **para acá** ['pah-rah ah-'kah] over here; **para eso** ['pah-rah 'eh-soh] for that (reason)

parada [pah-'rah-dah] (n m) (act of) stopping, stop; **parada de autobús** [pah-'rah-dah deh ow-toh-'boos] bus stop

parado [pah-'rah-doh] standing still, to be unemployed; **salir bien parado** [sah-'leer 'bee-ehn pah-'rah-doh] to come off well

paraguas [pah-'rah-gwahs] (m) umbrella

paraguayo [pah-rah-'gwah-yoh] Paraguayan

parar [pah-'rahr] to stop, to stand up

parecer [pah-reh-'sehr] (n m) opinion, to seem, to look; **parecerse a** [pah-reh-'sehr-seh ah] to look like

parecido [pah-reh-'see-doh] resemblance, similarity; similar (to)

pared [pah-'rehd] (f) wall

pareja [pah-'reh-hah] couple

pariente [pah-ree-'ehn-teh] relative

parque ['pahr-keh] (m) park

párrafo ['pah-rrah-foh] paragraph

parte ['pahr-teh] (f) part, portion, section

particular [pahr-tee-koo-'lahr] (adj) particular, special, personal, private; (n m) matter, individual

partida [pahr-'tee-dah] (n f) departure, certificate; (business) item, entry, shipment; match; party

partidario/-a [pahr-tee-'dah-ree-oh/-ah] partisan, follower

partir [pahr-'teer] to depart, to start, to divide, to split; **a partir de** [ah pahr-'teer deh] starting from

party ['pahr-tee] (m) fiesta

pasado [pah-'sah-doh] (n m adj) past; (food) stale; (fruit) overripe; **pasado de moda** [pah-'sah-doh deh 'moh-dah] old-fashioned

pasaje [pah-'sah-heh] (n m) passage, passing, fare, passengers; passageway

pasajero [pah-sah-'heh-roh] passenger; (adj) passing, fleeting

pasaporte [pah-sah-'pohr-teh] (m) passport

pasar [pah-'sahr] to pass, to give, to cross, to go through, to suffer, to come in, to go in; **pasar (por casa de alguien)** [pah-'sahr (pohr 'kah-sah deh 'ahl-gee-ehn)] to stop by (someone's house); **¡pase!** ['pah-seh] come in!; **pasar frío** [pah-'sahr 'free-oh] to be cold; **pasar de contrabando** [pah-'sahr deh kohn-trah-'bahn-doh] to smuggle

pasarela [pah-sah-'reh-lah] footbridge; gangway

pasear [pah-seh-'ahr] to take a walk, to stroll

paseíto [pah-seh-'ee-toh] short walk

paseo [pah-'seh-oh] walk, stroll; **dar un paseo** [dahr oon pah-'seh-oh] to take a walk

pasillo [pah-'see-yoh] corridor, passage

paso ['pah-soh] (n m) step, pace, passage, (act of) passing, overtaking; **paso subterráneo** ['pah-soh soob-teh-'rrah-neh- oh] underground passage; **de paso** [deh 'pah-soh] incidentally; **estar de paso** [eh-'stahr deh 'pah-soh] passing through

pasto ['pah-stoh] lawn, grass

patio ['pah-tee-oh] courtyard, patio

patria ['pah-tree-ah] fatherland

patrón [pah-'trohn] (m) landlord, employer, boss

paz [pahs] (f) peace; tranquility

peatón [peh-ah-'tohn] (m) pedestrian

peculiar [peh-koo-lee-'ahr] pedestrian

pedido [peh-'dee-doh] order; request

pedir [peh-'deer] to ask for, to request; (business) to order; **pedir algo a alguien** [peh-'deer 'ahl-goh ah 'ahl-gee-ehn] to ask for something from someone; **pedir consejo a alguien** [peh-'deer kohn-'seh-hoh ah 'ahl-gee-ehn] to ask someone for advice; **pedir huevos fritos** [peh-'deer 'weh-vohs 'free-tohs] to order fried eggs; **pedir perdón** [peh-'deer pehr-'dohn] to ask for forgiveness

pedregoso [peh-dreh-'goh-soh] stony

pegar [peh-'gahr] to hit, to stick (to)

pelearse [peh-leh-'ahr-seh] to fight, to quarrel

película [peh-'lee-koo-lah] film

peligro [peh-'lee-groh] danger

peligroso [peh-lee-'groh-soh] dangerous

pelota [peh-'loh-tah] ball

pena ['peh-nah] sadness, grief, regret; **es una pena** [ehs 'oo-nah 'peh-nah] it's a shame

pendiente [pehn-dee-'ehn-teh] (n f) slope; (adj) hanging; (fig) pending

pensamiento [pehn-sah-mee-'ehn-toh] thought; mind

pensar [pehn-'sahr] to think; **pensar en** [pehn-'sahr ehn] to think about

penúltimo/-a [peh-'nool-tee-moh/-mah] penultimate

peña ['peh-nyah] cliff, group, circle of people

peor [peh-'ohr] worse, worst; **el, la, lo peor** [ehl, lah, loh peh-'ohr] the worse/ worst

pequeño [peh-'keh-nyoh] (adj) little, small; (height) short

pequeño [peh-'keh-nyoh] (n) child

pera ['peh-rah] pear

percha ['pehr-chah] clothes hanger

perder [pehr-'dehr] to lose, to waste; (food) **echarse a perder** [eh-'chahr-seh ah pehr-'dehr] to get spoiled

pérdida ['pehr-dee-dah] loss, waste

perdón [pehr-'dohn] (m) forgiveness; **pedir perdón** [peh-'deer pehr-'dohn] to ask for forgiveness

perdonar [pehr-doh-'nahr] to forgive, to pardon

perezoso [peh-reh-'soh-soh] lazy

perfecto [pehr-'fehk-toh] perfect

periferia [peh-ree-'feh-ree-ah] periphery, suburbs

permiso [pehr-'mee-soh] permission, authorization

permitido [pehr-mee-'tee-doh] allowed

permitir [pehr-mee-'teer] to allow

pernoctar [pehr-nohk-'tahr] to spend the night

pero [peh-roh] but, yet

perro ['peh-rroh] dog

persona [pehr-'soh-nah] person

personal [pehr-soh-'nahl] personal, personnel

persuadir [pehr-swah-'deer] to persuade

pertenecer a [pehr-teh-neh-'sehr ah] to belong to

peruano [peh-roo-'ah-noh] Peruvian

pesado [peh-'sah-doh] heavy; *(work, etc.)* heavy, boring; *(person)* a bore

pésame ['peh-sah-meh] *(m)* condolences

pesar [peh-'sahr] *(n m)* grief, sadness, regret; *(v)* to weigh; **a pesar de** [ah peh-'sahr deh] in spite of

pescado [peh-'skah-doh] *(after it's caught)* fish

pescar [peh-'skahr] to fish; **pescar (con caña)** [peh-'skahr (kohn kah-nyah)] angling

peso [peh-soh] weight; *(Am)* currency in some countries

pez [pehs] *(m)* fish

picante [pee-'kahn-teh] spicy

picar [pee-'kahr] to prick, to puncture, to itch, to peck, to nibble; *(insect)* to sting, to bite; *(fish)* to bite; *(sun)* to burn

pie ['pee-eh] *(m)* foot; **estar de pie** [eh-'stahr deh 'pee-eh] to stand

piedra [pee-'eh-drah] stone

piel [pee-'ehl] *(f)* skin; leather

pieza [pee-'eh-sah] piece; *(mech)* part; **pieza de recambio** [pee-'eh-sah deh reh-'kahm-bee-oh] spare part

pinchar [peen-'chahr] to prick, to puncture, to pierce

pinchazo [peen-'chah-soh] prick, puncture

pintar [peen-'tahr] to paint

pintura [peen-'too-rah] painting

piola [pee-'oh-lah] *(Am)* rope, cord, string

piolín [pee-oh-'leen] *(Am)* cord, string

pipa ['pee-pah] pipe

Pirineos [pee-ree-'neh-ohs] *(m pl)* Pyrenees

piscina [pee-'see-nah] swimming pool

piso ['pee-soh] floor, store, apartment

pista ['pee-stah] track, trail, clue; *(sports)* track, court, slope, run

placer [plah-'sehr] *(m)* pleasure

plan [plahn] *(m)* plan

plancha ['plahn-chah] iron, plate, sheet, grill; **bisté a la plancha** [bee-'steh ah lah 'plahn-chah] grilled steak

planchar [plahn-'chahr] to iron *(clothes)*

plano ['plah-noh] map; **plano de la ciudad** ['plah-noh deh lah see-oo-'dahd] map of the city

planta ['plahn-tah] plant, sole *(of the foot)*

plástico ['plah-stee-koh] plastic

plato ['plah-toh] dish, plate

playa ['plah-yah] beach

plaza ['plah-sah] plaza

plazo ['plah-soh] term, deadline, installment; **a corto plazo** [ah 'kohr-toh 'plah-soh] short-term

pluma ['ploo-mah] feather

población [poh-blah-see-'ohn] *(f)* population, city, town, village

pobre ['poh-breh] poor

poco ['poh-koh] little; **un poco** [oon 'poh-koh] a little; **un poco de queso** [oon 'poh-koh deh 'keh-soh] a little cheese; **hace poco** ['ah-seh 'poh-koh] a short time ago

poder [poh-'dehr] *(n m)* power, authority; *(v)* to be able to, may, can

podrido [poh-'dree-doh] rotten

política [poh-'lee-tee-kah] politics

polvo ['pohl-voh] dust

poner [poh-'nehr] to put, to place, to set, to switch on; **poner en comunicación** [poh-'nehr ehn koh-moo-nee-kah-see-'ohn] *(tel)* to connect; **poner gasolina** [poh-'nehr gah-soh-'lee-nah] to put in gas; **poner el intermitente** [poh-'nehr ehl een-tehr-mee-'tehn-teh] to put on the blinkers/turn on the signal; **¿qué ponen en el cine?** [keh 'poh-nehn ehn ehl 'see-neh] what's playing at the movies?; **ponerse de acuerdo** [poh-'nehr-seh deh ah-'kwehr-doh] to make arrangements, to agree; **ponerse enfermo** [poh-'nehr-seh ehn-'fehr-moh] to get sick

por [pohr] for, in order to, because of, from, by, in

por ejemplo [pohr eh-'hehm-ploh] for example; **por escrito** [pohr eh-'skree-toh] in writing; **por eso/esto/ello** [pohr-'eh-soh/'eh-stoh/'eh-yoh] because of that/ this/it; **por esta razón** [pohr 'eh-stah rah-'sohn] for this reason; **por fin** [pohr feen] at last; **por lo visto** [pohr loh 'vee-stoh] evidently

porcentaje [pohr-sehn-'tah-heh] *(m)* percentage

porque ['pohr-keh] *(conj)* because, for, since

porvenir [pohr-veh-'neer] *(m)* future

posada [poh-'sah-dah] inn, guest house, lodging

poseer [poh-seh-'ehr] to have, to own, to possess

posesión [poh-seh-see-'ohn] *(f)* possession, mastery, property

posibilidad [poh-see-bee-lee-'dahd] *(f)* possibility

posible [poh-'see-bleh] possible

posición [poh-see-see-'ohn] *(f)* position

positivo [poh-see-'tee-voh] positive

posterior [pohs-teh-ree-'ohr] *(adj)* back, rear, following

potable [poh-'tah-bleh] drinkable; **agua potable** ['ah-gwah poh-'tah-bleh] clean water, drinking water

pozo ['poh-soh] well

práctico ['prahk-tee-koh] practical, covenient; **poco práctico** ['poh-koh 'prahk-tee-koh] unpractical

pradera [prah-'deh-rah] prairie, meadow

prado ['prah-doh] meadow, field, pasture

precaución [preh-kow-see-'ohn] *(f)* precaution

precio ['preh-see·oh] price; **precio de (la) entrada** ['preh-see·oh deh (lah) ehn-'trah-dah] admission price

precisión [preh-see-see-'ohn] *(f)* precision; accuracy

preciso [preh-'see-soh] precise; accurate

preferencia [preh-feh-'rehn-see·ah] preference; **preferencia (de paso)** [preh-feh-'rehn-see·ah (deh 'pah-soh)] right of way

preferir [preh-feh-'reer] to prefer

pregunta [preh-'goon-tah] question

preguntar [preh-goon-'tahr] to ask, to question; **preguntar por** [preh-goon-'tahr pohr] to ask for

premio ['preh-mee·oh] prize

prenda ['prehn-dah] deposit, security; *(Am)* jewel

preocupación [preh-oh-koo-pah-see-'ohn] *(f)* worry

preocupado [preh-oh-koo-'pah-doh] worried

preocuparse de/por [preh-oh-koo-'pahr-seh deh/pohr] to worry about

preparado [preh-pah-'rah-doh] prepared, ready, qualified

preparar [preh-pah-'rahr] to prepare, to get ready, to teach

prescripción [preh-skreep-see-'ohn] *(f)* prescription; **receta** [reh-'seh-tah] *(Am)*

presentación [preh-sehn-tah-see-'ohn] *(f)* presentation; *(people)* introduction

presentar [preh-sehn-'tahr] to present, to introduce (people)

presente [preh-'sehn-teh] present; **estar presente** [eh-'stahr preh-'sehn-teh] to be present

preservativo [preh-sehr-vah-'tee-voh] condom

prestar [preh-'stahr] to lend, to loan; *(attention, respects, etc.)* to pay; **tomar prestado** [toh-'mahr preh-'stah-doh] to borrow

pretexto [preh-'tehk-stoh] pretext, excuse

prevenir (contra) [preh-veh-'neer] to warn *(against)*

primero [pree-'meh-roh] *(adj)* (**primer** before *n m sing*) first; *(adv)* first; **de primera clase/categoría** [deh pree-'meh-rah 'klah-seh/kah-teh-goh-'ree-ah] first class; **primeros auxilios** [pree-'meh-rohs owhk-'see-lee-ohs] *(m pl)* first aid

primo/prima ['pree-moh/'pree-mah] cousin

principal [preen-see-'pahl] *(adj)* principal, main; **principalmente** [preen-see-pahl-'mehn-teh] *(adv)* mainly

principio [preen-'see-pee·oh] beginning, start

prisa ['pree-sah] hurry, haste; **de prisa** [deh 'pree-sah] quickly; **darse prisa** ['dahr-seh 'pree-sah] to hurry up; **tener prisa** [teh-'nehr 'pree-sah] to be in a hurry

prismáticos [prees-'mah-tee-kohs] *(m pl)* binoculars

privado [pree-'vah-doh] private

probabilidad [proh-bah-bee-lee-'dahd] *(f)* probability

A/Z

probable [proh-'bah-bleh] *(adj)* probable;
probablemente [proh-bah-bleh-'mehn-teh] *(adv)* probably

probar [proh-'bahr] to prove, to try;
(food) to try, to taste

probarse [proh-'bahr-seh] to try on

problema [proh-'bleh-mah] *(m)* problem

proceder [proh-seh-'dehr] *(n m)* conduct;
(v) to proceed, to behave, to come from

procesión [proh-seh-see-'ohn] *(f)* procession

procurar [proh-koo-'rahr] to try, to get, to procure, to manage to

producir [proh-doo-'seer] to produce

producto [proh-'dook-toh] product

profesión [proh-feh-see-'ohn] *(f)* profession

profundo [proh-'foon-doh] deep

programa [proh-'grah-mah] *(m)* program

progreso [proh-'greh-soh] progress

prohibición [proh-ee-bee-see-'ohn] *(f)* ban

prohibir [proh-ee-'beer] to ban, to forbid;
prohibido fumar [proh-ee-'bee-doh foo-'mahr] smoking forbidden;
¡Prohibida la entrada!/¡Se prohibe el paso! [proh-ee-'bee-dah lah ehn-'trah-dah/seh proh-'ee-beh ehl 'pah-soh] No entry!/Do not trespass!

prolongar [proh-lohn-'gahr] to prolong, to extend, to go on

promesa [proh-'meh-sah] promise

prometer [proh-meh-'tehr] to promise, to engage; **prometerse con** *(Am)* **comprometerse** [proh-meh-'tehr-seh kohn, kohm-proh-meh-'tehr-seh] to be engaged to

prometido/-a [proh-meh-'tee-doh/-ah] fiancé, fiancée

pronto ['prohn-toh] soon; **lo más pronto posible** [loh mahs 'prohn-toh poh-'see-bleh] as soon as possible

pronunciación [proh-noon-see-ah-see-'ohn] *(f)* pronunciation

pronunciar [proh-noon-see-'ahr] to pronounce

propaganda [proh-pah-'gahn-dah] propaganda

propiedad [proh-pee-eh-'dahd] *(f)* property, ownership

propietario [proh-pee-eh-'tah-ree-oh] owner

propio ['proh-pee-oh] *(adj)* own, characteristic of

proponer [proh-poh-'nehr] to propose

proporcionar [proh-pohr-see-oh-'nahr] to provide

proposición [proh-poh-see-see-'ohn] *(f)* proposition, proposal

propósito [proh-'poh-see-toh] purpose;
a propósito [ah proh-'poh-see-toh] on purpose

propuesta [proh-'pweh-stah] proposal

prórroga ['proh-rroh-gah] deferment, extension, adjournment

prospecto [proh-'spehk-toh] prospectus, leaflet, brochure

protección [proh-tehk-see-'ohn] *(f)* protection

proteger [proh-teh-'hehr] to protect

protestar [proh-teh-'stahr] to protest

provecho [proh-'veh-choh] advantage, benefit, profit

proveer (de) [proh-veh-'ehr (deh)] to supply (with)

provisión [proh-vee-see-'ohn] *(f)* provision, supply; **provisiones** [proh-vee-see-'oh-nehs] supplies

provisional [proh-vee-see-oh-'nahl] provisional

provisionalmente [proh-vee-see-oh-'nahl-'mehn-teh] *(adv)* provisionally

proximidad [prohk-see-mee-'dahd] *(f)* nearness, proximity

próximo ['prohk-see-moh] near

prudente [proo-'dehn-teh] prudent

prueba [proo-'eh-bah] proof, evidence, test, trial, testing, sampling, trying on

público ['poo-blee-koh] *(n m)* public, audience; *(adj)* public

puchero [poo-'cheh-roh] pot, stew

pueblo ['pweh-bloh] people, nation, village, small town

puente ['pwehn-teh] *(m)* bridge

puerta ['pwehr-tah] door; **puerta de la casa** ['pwehr-tah deh lah 'kah-sah] front door

puerto ['pwehr-toh] port, harbor

puertorriqueño [pwehr-toh-rree-'keh-nyoh] Puerto Rican

pues [pwehs] *(adv)* then, well, well then, so

puesta, a la ... del sol ['pweh-stah, ah lah dehl sohl] at sunset

punta ['poon-tah] tip, point, sharp end

punto ['poon-toh] dot; *(writing)* period, point, item; **punto culminante** ['poon-toh kool-mee-'nahn-teh] highlight

puntual(mente) [poon-too-'ahl('mehn-teh)] punctual(ly)

puro ['poo-roh] *(adj)* pure, unadulterated; *(n m)* cigar; *(Am)* **tabaco** [(tah-'bah-koh]

Q

que [keh] that, who, whom; which

qué [keh] *(pron interrog.)* ¿~? **¿qué pasa?** [keh 'pah-sah] what's going on?

quedar [keh-'dahr] to stay, to remain; **quedarse** [(keh-'dahr-seh)] to remain

queja ['keh-hah] complaint, protest

quejarse (de) [keh-'hahr-seh (deh)] to complain (about)

quemar [keh-'mahr] to burn

querer [keh-'rehr] to want, to like, to love; **querer a alguien** [keh-'rehr ah 'ahl-gee·ehn] to love someone; **querido** [keh-'ree-doh] dear, darling, beloved; **¡querido Jorge!** [keh-'ree-doh 'hohr-heh] dear George!

quieto [kee-'eh-toh] still

quince ['keen-seh] fifteen; **quince días** ['keen-seh 'dee-ahs] fifteen days

quitar [kee-'tahr] to take away, to remove; **quitar la ropa** [kee-'tahr lah 'roh-pah] to get undressed

quizá(s) [kee-'sahs] *(adv)* perhaps, maybe

R

rabia ['rah-bee·ah] rabies, rage

rabioso [rah-bee-'oh-soh] rabid, enraged

radio ['rah-dee·oh] *(f)* radio

ramo ['rah-moh] *(flowers)* bunch; *(tree)* branch; *(business) (fig)* branch

rápidamente ['rah-pee-dah-mehn-teh] *(adv)* quickly

rapidez [rah-pee-'dehs] *(f)* speed

rápido ['rah-pee-doh] *(adj)* quick, fast

raramente [rah-rah-'mehn-teh] *(adv)* seldom

raro ['rah-roh] *(adj)* rare, uncommon, odd, peculiar

rascacielos [rah-skah-see-'eh-lohs] *(m)* skyscraper

rayo [rah-yoh] ray, beam, lightning

razón [rah-'sohn] *(f)* reason; right; **(no) tener razón** [(noh) teh-'nehr rah-'sohn] (not) to be right

razonable [rah-soh-'nah-bleh] reasonable

real [reh-'ahl] real

realidad [reh-ah-lee-'dahd] *(f)* reality; **en realidad** [ehn reh-ah-lee-'dahd] in fact, really

realizar [reh-ah-lee-'sahr] to attain, to achieve, to carry out, to make

rebaja [reh-'bah-hah] lowering, reduction, discount, rebate, price reduction

rebajar [reh-bah-'hahr] *(price)* to lower; *(weight)* to lose

rebanada [reh-bah-'nah-dah] *(bread)* slice

recepción [reh-sehp-see-'ohn] *(f)* reception

recibir [reh-see-'beer] to receive

recibo [reh-'see-boh] receipt

recién [reh-see-'ehn] *(Am)* just, only just

reciente [reh-see-'ehn-teh] recent, fresh, freshly made

recipiente [reh-see-pee-'ehn-teh] *(m)* recipient

reclamación [reh-klah-mah-see-'ohn] *(f)* claim, demand, objection, complaint, protest

reclamar [reh-klah-'mahr] to reclaim

recobrar [reh-koh-'brahr] to recover, to get back, to retrieve

recoger [reh-koh-'hehr] to pick up, to gather; *(money, currency)* to collect, to call in

recomendación [reh-koh-mehn-dah-see-'ohn] *(f)* recommendation

recomendar [reh-koh-mehn-'dahr] to recommend

recompensa [reh-kohm-'pehn-sah] reward

recompensar [reh-kohm-pehn-'sahr] to reward

reconocer [reh-koh-noh-'sehr] to recognize

recordar [reh-kohr-'dahr] to remember, to remind; **recordar algo a alguien** [reh-kohr-'dahr 'ahl-goh ah 'ahl-gee·ehn] to remind someone of something

rectificar [rehk-tee-fee-'kahr] to rectify, to correct

recuerdo [reh-'kwehr-doh] *(n m)* remembrance, memory, recollection, souvenir

recuperar [reh-koo-peh-'rahr] to recover, to retrieve, to recuperate

rechazar [reh-chah-'sahr] to reject, to turn down

red [rehd] *(f)* net

redondo [reh-'dohn-doh] round

reducir [reh-doo-'seer] to reduce, to diminish, to cut down

referirse (a) [reh-feh-'reer-seh (ah)] to refer (to)

refresco [reh-'freh-skoh] cool drink, soft drink; **refrescos** [reh-'freh-skohs] refreshments

regalar [reh-gah-'lahr] to give a present

regalo [reh-'gah-loh] present

regatear [reh-gah-teh-'ahr] to haggle, to give sparingly; **regatear el contrato** [reh-gah-teh-'ahr ehl kohn-'trah-toh] to haggle over the contract;

regañar [reh-gah-'nyahr] to scold

región [reh-hee-'ohn] (f) region

regresar [reh-greh-'sahr] to return, to come back, to go back

regreso [reh-'greh-soh] return; **viaje de regreso** [vee-'ah-heh deh reh-'greh-soh] return trip; **estar de regreso** [eh-'stahr deh reh-'greh-soh] to be back (home)

regular [reh-goo-'lahr] (n m) regular, usual, ordinary, medium, average

rehusar [reh-oo-'sahr] to refuse

reír(se) [reh-'eer(seh)] to laugh

reja ['reh-hah] (window, prison) bars, grating

relación [reh-lah-see-'ohn] (f) relation

relámpago [reh-'lahm-pah-goh] lightning

reloj [reh-'loh] (m) clock, watch; **reloj de pie** [reh-'loh deh 'pee-eh] grandfather clock; **reloj de pulsera** [reh-'loh deh pool-'seh-rah] wristwatch

remedio [reh-'meh-dee-oh] remedy, cure, help, relief

remendar [reh-mehn-'dahr] (sewing) to mend, to patch; (fig) to fix

remitir [reh-mee-'teer] to send, to remit

renovar [reh-noh-'vahr] to renew; (architecture) to renovate, to restore

reparación [reh-pah-rah-see-'ohn] (f) repair; reparation, redress

reparar [reh-pah-'rahr] to repair, to mend, to notice

repasar [reh-pah-'sahr] (sewing) to darn, to mend; (accounts) to check; (texts) to revise, to review quickly; **repasar la lección** [reh-pah-'sahr lah lehk-see-'ohn] to go over the lesson

repente, de [deh reh-'pehn-teh] suddenly

repetir [reh-peh-'teer] to repeat

repleto [reh-'pleh-toh] filled, gorged

replicar [reh-plee-'kahr] to answer, to talk back

reponerse [reh-poh-'nehr-seh] to recover

representación [reh-preh-sehn-tah-see-'ohn] (f) (theater) performance

repuesto [reh-'pweh-stoh] (product) replacement, spare part

resbaladizo [rehs-bah-lah-'dee-soh] slippery

reservar [reh-sehr-'vahr] to reserve, to keep, to conceal

residencia [reh-see-'dehn-see-ah] residence; **residencia universitaria** [reh-see-'dehn-see-ah oo-nee-vehr-see-'tah-ree-ah] college dormitory

resistente [reh-see-'stehn-teh] resistant, strong, tough, hardy

resolución [reh-soh-loo-see-'ohn] (f) decision; (problem) solving; resolve, determination, settlement

resolver [reh-sohl-'vehr] to solve, to decide, to settle

respectivo [reh-spehk-'tee-voh] respective; **respectivo a** [reh-spehk-'tee-voh ah] with regard to

respiración [reh-spee-rah-see-'ohn] (f) breathing, respiration

responder [reh-spohn-'dehr] to answer, to reply, to respond

responsable [reh-spohn-'sah-bleh] (adj) responsible (n m) person in charge

respuesta [reh-'spweh-stah] answer; response, reply

restante [reh-'stahn-teh] remaining

restaurante [reh-stah-oo-'rahn-teh] (m) restaurant

resto ['reh-stoh] rest, remainder

resultado [reh-sool-'tah-doh] result, outcome, effect

retardar [reh-tahr-'dahr] to slow down, to hold up, to delay

retirado [reh-tee-'rah-doh] remote, isolated, quiet; **vida retirada** ['vee-dah reh-tee-'rah-dah] quiet life

retirarse [reh-tee-'rahr-seh] to retire, to withdraw, to move away

retrasarse [reh-trah-'sahr-seh] to be late, to lag behind; (clock) to be slow

retrete [reh-'treh-teh] (m) toilet

revelado [reh-veh-'lah-doh] (photo) developing; revealed

revelar [reh-veh-'lahr] (photo) to develop, to reveal

reventar [reh-vehn-'tahr] to burst

revés [reh-'vehs] (n m) back; (fig) setback; **al revés** [ahl reh-'vehs] the other way around, upside down, inside out

revisar [reh-vee-'sahr] to revise, to review, to go through

revisor [reh-vee-'sohr] *(m)* conductor

revista [reh-vee-'stah] magazine; *(theater)* revue

rezar [reh-'sahr] to pray

rico ['ree-koh] rich

ridículo [ree-'dee-koo-loh] ridiculous

riesgo [ree-'ehs-goh] risk

riguroso [ree-goo-'roh-soh] rigorous

rincón [reen-'kohn] *(m)* corner

río ['ree-oh] river

riqueza [ree-'keh-sah] wealth, richness

robar [roh-'bahr] to steal

roca ['roh-kah] rock

rodeo [roh-'deh-oh] detour

romper, romperse [rohm-'pehr, rohm-'pehr-seh] to break

roncar [rohn-'kahr] to snore

ropa ['roh-pah] clothes, clothing; **ropa de cama** ['roh-pah deh 'kah-mah] bed linen; **ropa interior** ['roh-pah een-teh-ree-'ohr] underwear; **ropa sucia** ['roh-pah 'soo-see-ah] dirty linen

roto ['roh-toh] broken

rueda [roo-'eh-dah] wheel

ruego [roo-'eh-goh] request

ruido [roo-'ee-doh] noise

S

saber [sah-'behr] *(n m)* knowledge; *(v)* to know; *(v)* **saber a** [sah-'behr ah] to taste like

sabor [sah-'bohr] *(n m)* taste

sacar [sah-'kahr] to take out, to get out, to pull out; **sacar fotos** [sah-'kahr 'foh-tohs] to take pictures; **sacar un diente** [sah-'kahr oon dee-'ehn-teh] to pull a tooth

sacerdote [sah-sehr-'doh-teh] *(n m)* priest

saco ['sah-koh] bag, sack; *(Am)* jacket

sagrado [sah-'grah-doh] sacred

sala ['sah-lah] *(house)* living room; *(public building)* hall, courtroom, ward; **sala de baile** ['sah-lah deh 'bah-ee-leh] dance hall; **sala de lo civil** ['sah-lah deh loh see-'veel] civil court; **sala de maternidad** ['sah-lah deh mah-tehr-nee-'dahd] maternity ward

salario [sah-'lah-ree-oh] wages, pay; *(Am)* salary

saldo ['sahl-doh] settlement, payment, balance, remainder; **saldo negativo** ['sahl-doh neh-gah-tee-voh] debit balance

salida [sah-'lee-dah] exit, departure, way out; **a la salida del sol** [ah lah sah-'lee-dah dehl sohl] at the crack of dawn

salir [sah-'leer] to go out, to leave, to appear, to emerge, to turn out to be; **salir de** [sah-'leer deh] to get rid of

saltar [sahl-'tahr] to jump

salud [sah-'lood] *(f)* health

saludar [sah-loo-'dahr] to greet

salvadoreño [sahl-vah-doh-'reh-nyoh] Salvadoran

salvaje [sahl-'vah-heh] wild

salvar [sahl-'vahr] to save

sano ['sah-noh] healthy

santo ['sahn-toh] *(n m)* holy, sacred, saint; *(adj) (person)* saintly

satisfecho [sah-tees-'feh-choh] satisfied, content

se [seh] *(prn)* himself, herself, itself, themselves, yourselves

secar [seh-'kahr] to dry

seco ['seh-koh] dry

secreto [seh-'kreh-toh] secret; **en secreto** [ehn seh-'kreh-toh] *(adv)* secretly

sed [sehd] *(f)* thirst; **tener sed** [teh-'nehr sehd] to be thirsty

seguida, en [ehn seh-'gee-dah] right away, at once

seguir [seh-'geer] to follow, to continue, to go on; **seguir adelante** [seh-'geer ah-deh-'lahn-teh] to keep going

segundo [seh-'goon-doh] second

seguridad [seh-goo-ree-'dahd] *(f)* security, safety, certainty, confidence, **seguridad en sí mismo** [seh-goo-ree-'dahd ehn see 'mees-moh] self-confidence

seguro [seh-'goo-roh] *(adj)* safe, secure, certain, sure, confident

selección [seh-lehk-see-'ohn] *(f)* selection

selva ['sehl-vah] forest; **selva virgen** ['sehl-vah 'veer-hehn] jungle

sello ['seh-yoh] stamp, seal

semana [seh-'mah-nah] week

semanal(mente) [seh-mah-'nahl('mehn-teh)] weekly

semejante [seh-meh-'hahn-teh] *(adj)* similar, alike, such

sencillo [sehn-'see-yoh] simple

senda ['sehn-dah] path, track; *(fig)* path; *(auto)* lane

sendero [sehn-'deh-roh] path, track

sensato [sehn-'sah-toh] sensible

sentar [sehn-'tahr] to seat, to sit; **sentar bien** [sehn-'tahr 'bee·ehn] to go down well; **estar sentado** [eh-'stahr sehn-'tah-doh] to be seated; **sentarse** [sehn-'tahr-seh] to seat oneself

sentido [sehn-'tee-doh] *(n m) (body, judgment, direction)* sense; meaning; *(adj)* regrettable; **en sentido inverso/contrario** [ehn sehn-'tee-doh een-'vehr-soh/kohn-'trah-ree-oh] in the opposite direction

sentimiento [sehn-tee-mee-'ehn-toh] feeling

sentir [sehn-'teer] to feel; **me siento mal** [meh see-'ehn-toh mahl] I feel bad/ill

señal [seh-'nyahl] *(f)* sign, symptom, indication, signal

señalar [seh-nyah-'lahr] to mark, to point to/out, to indicate; *(price)* to fix

señas ['seh-nyahs] *(f pl)* address; **poner las señas** [poh-'nehr lahs 'seh-nyahs] to address (a letter)

señor [seh-'nyohr] *(n m)* man; Mr.

señora [seh-'nyoh-rah] woman, Mrs.

señorita [seh-nyoh-'ree-tah] *(generally)* young woman, Miss

separado [seh-pah-'rah-doh] separate(d), detached

separar [seh-pah-'rahr] to separate, to detach

septentrional [sehp-tehn-tree-oh-'nahl] northern

ser [sehr] *(n m)* being; *(v)* to be; **ser de Los Angeles** [sehr deh lohs 'ahn-heh-lehs] to be from L.A.

sereno [seh-'reh-noh] night watchman; serene

serio [seh-ree-oh] serious, earnest, responsible

sermón [sehr-'mohn] *(n m)* sermon

serpiente [sehr-pee-'ehn-teh] *(f)* snake

servicio [sehr-'vee-see-oh] service, toilet

servir [sehr-'veer] to serve; **servirse** [sehr-'veer-seh] *(at table)* to help oneself

severo [seh-'veh-roh] severe, harsh, strict

sexo ['sehk-soh] sex

si [see] if, whether

sí [see] yes

siempre [see-'ehm-preh] always, ever, all the time; **como siempre** ['koh-moh see-'ehm-preh] as usual

sierra [see-'eh-rrah] saw, mountain range

significado [seeg-nee-fee-'kah-doh] meaning

significar [seeg-nee-fee-'kahr] to mean, to signify

signo ['seeg-noh] sign

silencio [see-'lehn-see-oh] silence

silencioso [see-lehn-see-'oh-soh] silent

silvestre [seel-'veh-streh] wild

silla ['see-yah] seat, chair

simpático [seem-'pah-tee-koh] nice, likeable, charming

sin [seen] without, with no...; **sin compromiso** [seen kohm-proh-'mee-soh] without obligation; **sin embargo** [seen ehm-'bahr-goh] however

sino ['see-noh] but, except, save

sinvergüenza [seen-vehr-'gwehn-sah] scoundrel, creep

sitio ['see-tee-oh] place

situación [see-too-ah-see-'ohn] *(f)* situation

sobrante [soh-'brahn-teh] remaining, surplus

sobrar [soh-'brahr] to exceed, to surpass, to remain, to be left over

sobras ['soh-brahs] *(f pl)* leftovers, scraps

sobre ['soh-breh] *(n m)* envelope; *(prep)* on, upon, on top of, over, above; **sobre todo** ['soh-breh 'toh-doh] above all; **dos grados sobre cero** [dohs 'grah-dohs 'soh-breh 'seh-roh] 2 degrees Celsius

sobrina [soh-'bree-nah] niece

sobrino [soh-'bree-noh] nephew

sobrio ['soh-bree-oh] sober, restrained, cool

sociedad [soh-see-eh-'dahd] *(f)* society, company

soga ['soh-gah] rope

sol [sohl] *(m)* sun

solamente [soh-lah-'mehn-teh] only

soleado [soh-leh-'ah-doh] sunny

sólido ['soh-lee-doh] solid

solitario [soh-lee-'tah-ree-oh] solitary

solo ['soh-loh] *(adj)* sole, single, alone, lonely

sólo ['soh-loh] *(adv)* just, only

soltar [sohl-'tahr] to release, to let go of, to drop

soltero [sohl-'teh-roh] single, unmarried

sombra ['sohm-brah] shadow
sonar [soh-'nahr] (v) to ring, to blow, to sound, to make a noise
sonido [soh-'nee-doh] sound
soñar [soh-'nyahr] to dream
soportar [soh-pohr-'tahr] to bear, to support, to hold up, to carry; (fig) to endure
sorprendido [sohr-prehn-'dee-doh] surprised
sospecha [soh-'speh-chah] suspicion
su [soo] (adj poss) his, her, its, one's; (with usted) your; (pl) **sus** their; (with ustedes) your
suave ['swah-veh] soft, mild, delicate
subir [soo-'beer] to raise, to go up, to get on/in; **subir al automóvil** [soo-'beer ahl ow-toh-'moh-veel] to get in the car
suceder [soo-seh-'dehr] to happen, to follow
suceso [soo-'seh-soh] happening, event, incident
suciedad [soo-see-eh-'dahd] (f) dirt, filth
sucio ['soo-see·oh] dirty, filthy
sucursal [soo-koor-'sahl] (f) branch; subsidiary
Sudamérica [sood-ah-'meh-ree-kah] South America
sudamericano/-a [sood-ah-meh-ree-'kah-noh/-ah] South American
sudar [soo-'dahr] to sweat
suerte ['swehr-teh] (f) luck; **¡buena suerte!** ['bweh-nah 'swehr-teh] good luck!
sueldo ['swehl-doh] salary, pay
suelo ['sweh-loh] floor
suelto ['swehl-toh] loose, free, detached
sueño ['sweh-nyoh] sleep, dream
suficiente [soo-fee-see-'ehn-teh] enough, sufficient
sufrir [soo-'freer] to suffer, to experience; **sufrir un accidente** [soo-'freer oon ahk-see-'dehn-teh] to suffer an accident
sugerencia [soo-heh-'rehn-see·ah] suggestion
Suiza ['swee-sah] Switzerland
suizo/suiza ['swee-soh/'swee-sah] Swiss
sujetar [soo-heh-'tahr] to hold, to hold down/tight, to seize, to clutch, to fasten
suma ['soo-mah] addition, sum, total; **suma global** ['soo-mah gloh-'bahl] lump sum
sumar [soo-'mahr] to add, to add up
superfluo [soo-'pehr-floo·oh] superfluous

suplementario [soo-pleh-mehn-'tah-ree·oh] supplementary, additional
suponer [soo-poh-'nehr] to assume, to suppose, to guess
suposición [soo-poh-see-see-'ohn] (f) assumption, supposition, guess
sur [soor] (m) south; **al sur de** [ahl soor deh] south of; **del sur** [dehl soor] southerner
surtido [soor-'tee-doh] (n m) assortment, selection; stock; (adj) mixed, assorted
sustituir [soo-stee-too-'eer] to replace

T

tabaco [tah-'bah-koh] tobacco; (Am) cigar
taberna [tah-'behr-nah] bar, pub
tal [tahl] such; **tal cosa** [tahl 'koh-sah] such a thing; **tal como** [tahl 'koh-moh] such as/just as; **con tal** [kohn tahl] provided that; **tal vez** [tahl vehs] perhaps
talón [tah-'lohn] (n m) heel, stub
talla ['tah-yah] height, size, carving
taller [tah-'yehr] (n m) workshop
tamaño [tah-'mah-nyoh] size
también [tahm-bee-'ehn] also
tampoco [tahm-'poh-koh] neither, no ... either; nor
tanto ['tahn-toh] so much, as much, so many, as many, **con tanto que...** [kohn 'tahn-toh keh] provided that; **en tanto (que)...** [ehn 'tahn-toh (keh)] while...; until...; **hasta tanto que...** ['ah-stah 'tahn-toh keh] until...
tapar [tah-'pahr] to cover; to conceal, to cover up
taquilla [tah-'kee-yah] (theater) box office
tardar [tahr-'dahr] to take a long time, to be late, to delay; **tardar en irse** [tahr-'dahr ehn 'eer-seh] to take a long time to leave
tarde ['tahr-deh] (adj) late; (n f) afternoon; early evening, evening; **por la tarde** [pohr lah 'tahr-deh] in the afternoon, in the evening; **¡buenas tardes!** ['bweh-nahs 'tahr-dehs] good afternoon
tarjeta [tahr-'heh-tah] card; **tarjeta postal** [tahr-'heh-tah poh-'stahl] post-card; **tarjeta de identidad** [tahr-'heh-tah deh ee-dehn-tee-'dahd] identity card

A/Z

tasar [tah-'sahr] to appraise; **tasar en** [tah-'sahr ehn] to value, to price

taxi ['tahk-see] *(m)* taxi

te [teh] you; (to) you; (to) yourself; **te di un abrazo** [teh dee oon ah-'brah-soh] I hugged you; **te lo di** [teh loh dee] I gave it to you; **¡contrólate!** [kohn-'troh-lah-teh] control yourself!

techo ['teh-choh] roof

tejido [teh-'hee-doh] fabric; *(anat)* tissue

tela ['teh-lah] cloth, material, fabric

telefonear [teh-leh-foh-neh-'ahr] to phone

televisión [teh-leh-vee-see-'ohn] *(f)* television

tema ['teh-mah] subject, topic; theme

temer [teh-'mehr] to be afraid, to fear

temor [teh-'mohr] *(n m)* fear

tempestad [tehm-peh-'stahd] *(f)* storm

temporada [tehm-poh-'rah-dah] season; **temporada principal** [tehm-poh-'rah-dah preen-see-'pahl] high season

temprano [tehm-'prah-noh] early

tenazas [teh-'nah-sahs] *(f pl)* pliers, tongs, pincers

tendido [tehn-'dee-doh] *(el)* cables

tener [teh-'nehr] to have; **tener que** [teh-'nehr keh] to have to; **tener lugar** [teh-'nehr loo-'gahr] to take place

tercero/-a [tehr-'seh-roh/-ah] third; **en tercer lugar** [ehn tehr-'sehr loo-'gahr] in third place

tercio ['tehr-see·oh] (one) third

terminar [tehr-mee-'nahr] to finish, to end, to conclude

término ['tehr-mee-noh] finish, end, conclusion; **por término medio** [pohr 'tehr-mee-noh 'meh-dee·oh] *(adv)* on the average

terreno [teh-'rreh-noh] terrain, a piece of land, field, area

terrible [teh-'rree-bleh] terrible, awful, dreadful

testigo [teh-'stee-goh] witness

testimonio [teh-'stee-moh-nee-oh] testimony

ti [tee] you, yourself; **a ti** [ah tee] to you; **para ti** ['pah-rah tee] for you, for yourself

tía ['tee-ah] aunt

tiempo [tee-'ehm-poh] time, weather; **a tiempo** [ah tee-'ehm-poh] on time; **al mismo tiempo** [ahl 'mees-moh tee-'ehm-poh] at the same time; **con este tiempo** [kohn 'eh-steh tee-'ehm-poh] with this weather

tienda [tee-'ehn-dah] store, shop, tent

tierno [tee-'ehr-noh] tender

tierra [tee-'eh-rrah] earth, land, soil, ground

tijeras [tee-'heh-rahs] *(n f pl)* scissors

timbre ['teem-breh] *(n m)* bell, fiscal stamp; **tocar el timbre** [toh-'kahr ehl 'teem-breh] to ring the bell

tímido ['tee-mee-doh] shy

tinte ['teen-teh] *(n m)* dye

tintorería [teen-toh-reh-'ree-ah] dry cleaner

tío ['tee-oh] uncle

típico ['tee-pee-koh] typical

tirar [tee-'rahr] to throw, to shoot, to fling, to hurl

tiro [tee-roh] throw, shot

tocadiscos [toh-kah-'dee-skohs] *(m)* record player

tocar [toh-'kahr] to touch, to feel; **tocar el timbre** [toh-'kahr ehl 'teem-breh] to ring the bell

todavía [toh-dah-'vee-ah] still, yet; **todavía no** [toh-dah-'vee-ah noh] not yet

todo ['toh-doh] *(n m pron sing)* all, everything; *(pl)* **todos/todas** ['toh-dohs/ 'toh-dahs] everybody; every one of them; *(adj)* all; entire, whole; every; *(adv)* all, entirely, completely; **todo el mundo** ['toh-doh ehl 'moon-doh] everybody; **todos los días** ['toh-dohs lohs 'dee-ahs] every day; **de todas formas** [deh 'toh-dahs 'fohr-mahs] anyway; **por/en todas partes** [pohr/ehn 'toh-dahs 'pahr-tehs] every-where; **no es del todo cierto** [noh ehs dehl 'toh-doh see-'ehr-toh] it's not entirely true; **todo seguido/derecho** ['toh-doh seh-'gee-doh/ deh-'reh-choh] straight ahead

tomar [toh-'mahr] to take, to drink; **tomar nota de algo** [toh-'mahr 'noh-tah deh 'ahl-goh] to take note of some-thing; **tomar parte en** [toh-'mahr 'pahr-teh ehn] to take part in; **tomar el tren** [toh-'mahr ehl trehn] to take the train; **tomar agua** [toh-'mahr 'ah-gwah] to drink water

tomo ['toh-moh] volume

tono ['toh-noh] tone; **subir el tono** [soo-'beer ehl toh-'noh] to raise one's voice; **fuera de tono** ['fweh-rah deh 'toh-noh] inappropriate; **darse tono** ['dahr-seh 'toh-noh] to put on airs; **estar a tono con** [eh-'stahr ah 'toh-noh kohn] to be in tune with

tonto ['tohn-toh] fool, idiot

torcer [tohr-'sehr] to turn, to twist; **torcer a la derecha/izquierda** [tohr-'sehr ah la deh-'reh-chah/ees-kee-'ehr-dah] to turn right/left

tormenta [tohr-'mehn-tah] storm

torno ['tohr-noh] (*m*) turn; **en torno a** [ehn 'tohr-noh ah] around, about

toro ['toh-roh] bull

torre ['toh-rreh] (*n f*) tower

toser [toh-'sehr] to cough

tostada [toh-'stah-dah] (*bread*) toast

tostado [toh-'stah-doh] toasted, tanned; (*color*) dark brown

total [toh-'tahl] total, complete, whole

trabajador [trah-bah-hah-'dohr] (*n m*) worker; (*adj*) hard-working

trabajar [trah-bah-'hahr] to work

trabajo [trah-'bah-hoh] work

traducir [trah-doo-'seer] translate

traer [trah-'ehr] to bring, to carry, to get

tráfico [trah-fee-koh] traffic

trago ['trah-goh] (*n m*) drink

traje ['trah-heh] (*n m*) dress, suit; **traje regional** ['trah-heh reh-hee-oh-'nahl] regional costume

tranquilidad [trahn-kee-lee-'dahd] (*n f*) calm; tranquillity, peacefulness, stillness

tranquilizarse [trahn-kee-lee-'sahr-seh] to calm down

tranquilo [trahn-'kee-loh] calm, peaceful, quiet

transcurrir [trahns-koo-'rreer] (*time*) to go by, to pass, to elapse

transferible [trahns-feh-'ree-bleh] transferable

transferir [trahns-feh-'reer] to transfer, to postpone

transportar [trahns-pohr-'tahr] to transport, to carry, to take

trapo ['trah-poh] rag

trasladar [trahs-lah-'dahr] to move, to transfer

tratamiento [trah-tah-mee-'ehn-toh] treatment

tratar [trah-'tahr] to try, to treat

través, a de [ah trah-'vehs deh] through, across, over

trayecto [trah-'yehk-toh] route, stretch, journey

trecho ['treh-choh] stretch, distance

tribunal [tree-boo-'nahl] (*n m*) (*justice*) court

tripulación [tree-poo-lah-see-'ohn] (*n f*) crew

triste ['tree-steh] sad

trozo ['troh-soh] piece, chunk, fragment

tu [too] (*adj poss*) your

tú [too] (*pron pers*) you

tubería [too-beh-'ree-ah] (*gas, water*) pipes

tubo [too-boh] pipe; (*anat, TV*) tube

túnel ['too-nehl] (*n m*) tunnel

turbio ['toor-bee-oh] (*water*) cloudy, muddy; (*sight*) blurred; (*business*) shady, dubious; **negocios turbios** [neh-'goh-see-ohs 'toor-bee-ohs] shady business

turista [too-'ree-stah] (*m/f*) tourist

U

ulterior [ool-teh-ree-'ohr] (*adj*) subsequent, eventual

último/-a ['ool-tee-moh/-ah] last, latest, latter, furthest, most remote, utmost; **en último lugar** [ehn 'ool-tee-moh loo-'gahr] in the last place

ultramar [ool-trah-'mahr] (*m*) overseas

un, una [oon, 'oo-nah] (*art indef*) a, an; (*adj nm*) one

único ['oo-nee-koh] only, single, sole, unique

unir [oo-'neer] to join, to unite, to fasten, to mix

uno ['oo-noh] (*adj sing*) one, **unos/unas** ['oo-nohs/'oo-nahs] (*pl*) some, a few; about; (*pron*) one; somebody

urgente [oor-'hehn-teh] urgent

uruguayo [oo-roo-'gwah-yoh] Uruguayan

usar [oo-'sahr] to use, to wear

uso ['oo-soh] (*n m*) use; wear

usted [oo-'stehd] (*sing*) you; **ustedes** [oo-'steh-dehs] (*pl*) you (*polite address*)

usual [oo-soo-'ahl] usual, ordinary; regular

útil ['oo-teel] useful

utilización [oo-tee-lee-sah-see-'ohn] (*n f*) use

V

vaca ['vah-kah] cow

vacaciones [vah-kah-see-'oh-nehs] (n f pl) holidays; vacations; **de vacaciones** [deh vah-kah-see-'oh-nehs] to be away on vacation

vacío [vah-'see-oh] empty

vagón [vah-'gohn] (n m) wagon

vale ['vah-leh] (n m) voucher, coupon, promissory note; (Am) bill

valer [vah-'lehr] (comm) to be worth; **valer mucho** [vah-'lehr 'moo-choh] to be worth a lot

validez [vah-lee-'dehs] (nf) validity

válido ['vah-lee-doh] valid; **ser válido** [sehr 'vah-lee-doh] to be valid

valor [vah-'lohr] (n m) value; worth; **sin valor** [seen vah-'lohr] worthless

valle ['vah-yeh] (n m) valle

vara ['vah-rah] road

variado [vah-ree-'ah-doh] assorted, varied, mixed

variar [vah-ree-'ahr] to vary, to change, to alter

vasco ['vah-skoh] Basque; (lang) Basque

Vascongadas [vah-skohn-'gah-dahs] (n f pl) Basque Provinces

vascuence [vah-'skwehn-seh] (n m) (lang) Basque

vasija [vah-'see-hah] container, receptacle

vaso ['vah-soh] glass, vase

vatio ['vah-tee-oh] watt

vecino/-a [veh-'see-noh/-ah] neighbor

vela ['veh-lah] candle

velocidad [veh-loh-see-'dahd] (n f) speed

venado [veh-'nah-doh] deer; (meat) venison

venda ['vehn-dah] (n f) bandage; (n m) **vendaje** [vehn-'dah-heh] bandaging; (v) **vendar** [vehn-'dahr] to bandage

vender [vehn-'dehr] to sell

veneno [veh-'neh-noh] poison

venenoso [veh-neh-'noh-soh] poisonous

venezolano [veh-neh-soh-'lah-noh] Venezuelan

venir [veh-'neer] to come; **venir de** [veh-'neer deh] to come from; **venir bien** [veh-'neer 'bee-ehn] to be convenient, to fit

venta ['vehn-tah] sale; **en venta** [ehn 'vehn-tah] for sale

ventaja [vehn-'tah-hah] advantage

ventajoso [vehn-tah-'hoh-soh] advantageous

ventanilla [vehn-tah-'nee-yah] (car, train, bank, ticket office, etc.) window

ventilar [vehn-tee-'lahr] to air

ver [vehr] to see

veras, de [deh 'veh-rahs] truly, really; **¿de veras?** [deh 'veh-rahs] is that so?

verdad [vehr-'dahd] (n f) truth; **de verdad** [deh vehr-'dahd] (adv) really, truly; **¿(no es) verdad?** [(noh ehs) vehr-'dahd] is/isn't that true?

verdadero [vehr-dah-'dehr-oh] (adj) true, truthful; real, veritable

vestido [veh-'stee-doh] dress, clothing; **vestido regional** [veh-'stee-doh reh-hee-oh-'nahl] regional costume

vestigio [veh-'stee-hee-oh] trace

vestir [veh-'steer] to dress; **vestirse** [veh-'steer-seh] to get dressed

vez [vehs] (n f pl); **veces** ['veh-sehs] time, occasion; instance; **a veces** [ah 'veh-sehs] at times; **cada vez** ['kah-dah vehs] each time; **una vez** ['oo-nah vehs] once; **dos veces** [dohs-'veh-sehs] twice; **de vez en cuando** [deh vehs ehn 'kwahn-doh] from time to time; **en vez de** [ehn vehs deh] instead of

viajar [vee-ah-'hahr] to travel; **viajar en tren** [vee-ah-'hahr ehn trehn] to travel by train

viaje [vee-'ah-heh] (m) trip; **en el viaje** [ehn ehl vee-'ah-heh] during the trip; **hacer un viaje** [ah-'sehr oon vee-'ah-heh] to make a trip

viajero/-a [vee-ah-'heh-roh/-ah] traveler

vida ['vee-dah] life

vidriera [vee-dree-'eh-rah] (Am) shop window

vidrio ['vee-dree-oh] (material) glass

viejo [vee-'eh-hoh] old

viento [vee-'ehn-toh] wind; **hace/hay viento** ['ah-seh/'ah-ee vee-'ehn-toh] it's windy

vigencia [vee-'hehn-see-ah] validity

vigilante [vee-hee-'lahn-teh] (n m) vigilant, watchful; watchman

vigilar [vee-hee-'lahr] to watch, to watch over

vino ['vee-noh] wine; **vino blanco** ['vee-noh 'blahn-koh] white wine; **vino tinto** ['vee-noh 'teen-toh] red wine

viña ['vee-nyah] vine; **viñedo** [vee-'nyeh-doh] vineyard

violar [vee-oh-'lahr] to rape, to violate, to break

violentar [vee-oh-lehn-'tahr] to force, to break into, to assault

visible [vee-'see-bleh] visible

visita [vee-'see-tah] visit

visitar [vee-see-'tahr] to visit; **visitar a alguien** [vee-see-'tahr ah 'ahl-gee-ehn] to visit someone

vista ['vee-stah] eyesight, to look, to glance, to gaze

vivaz [vee-'vahs] lively

vivienda [vee-vee-'ehn-dah] housing, dwelling (house, apartment); **vivienda amueblada** [vee-vee-'ehn-dah ah-mweh-'blah-dah] furnished house/apartment

vivir [vee-'veer] to live

vivo ['vee-voh] alive, living, lively, vivid, sharp, clever, *(Am)* sly, unscrupulous

volar [voh-'lahr] to fly

voltear [vohl-teh-'ahr] *(Am)* to turn

voltio ['vohl-tee-oh] volt

voluntad [vohl-loon-'tahd] *(n f)* will; **a voluntad** [ah voh-loon-'tahd] at will

volver [vohl-'vehr] to turn, to return, to go; **volver a...** [vohl-'vehr ah] to do something again: **volver a leer** [vohl-'vehr ah leh-'ehr] to read again, **volver a buscar** [vohl-'vehr ah boo-'skahr] to look again, **volver a nadar** [vohl-'vehr ah nah-'dahr] to swim again; **volver a ver** [vohl-'vehr ah vehr] to see (someone) again; **volverse...** [vohl-'vehr-seh] to become, to get, to go: **volverse ciego** [vohl-'vehr-seh see-'eh-goh] to go blind; **volverse rico** [vohl-'vehr-seh 'ree-koh] to get rich

vosotros/-as [voh-'soh-trohs/-ahs] *(pers pron)* we

votar [voh-'tahr] to vote

voz [vohs] *(n f)* voice; **en voz baja** [ehn vohs 'bah-hah] softly

vuelta ['vwehl-tah] *(n f)* turn, round, return, walk, stroll, short drive/spin; **vuelta en coche** ['vwehl-tah ehn 'koh-cheh] short drive/spin; **el viaje de vuelta** [ehl vee-'ah-heh deh 'vwehl-tah] return trip; **estar de vuelta** [eh-'stahr deh 'vwehl-tah] to be back; **dar una vuelta** [dahr 'oo-nah 'vwehl-tah] to take a walk

vuelto ['vwehl-toh] *(Am)* change

vuestro ['vweh-stroh] your, yours

vulgar [vool-'gahr] vulgar, ordinary, common

Y

y [ee] and

ya [yah] already, now, at once, right away; **ya que** [yah keh] as...; since...

yeso ['yeh-soh] chalk; plaster

yo [yoh] I

Z

zapato [sah-'pah-toh] shoe

zona ['soh-nah] area, zone

zonzo ['sohn-soh] *(Am)* dumb

Notes

Notes